THE NATURAL REMEDY BOOK FOR DOGS & CATS

by

DIANE STEIN

The Crossing Press
Freedom, CA 95019

For Kali and Copper
and
for Sue

The alternative healing methods of this book are not meant
to take the place of expert veterinary care.
When your pet is ill, consult a holistic veterinarian.

For information on bulk purchases or group discounts for this and other Crossing Press titles, please contact our Special Sales Manager at 800-777-1048.

Visit our Website on the Internet at: www.crossingpress.com

Library of Congress Cataloging-in-Publication Data

Stein, Diane, 1948-
   The natural remedy book for dogs and cats / Diane Stein
      p.   cm.
   ISBN 0-89594-686-6
   1. Alternative veterinary medicine. 2. Dogs—Diseases—Alternative treatment. 3. Cats—Diseases—Alternative treatment. I. Title.
SF745.5.S745 1994
636.7'08958—dc20   94-22084
                                                             CIP

Acknowledgments

I gratefully thank Dr. Wendy Thacher, DVM for her thoughtful critique, preface, and check of veterinary accuracy of this book; and Marion Webb-DeSisto for her Appendix material on using gemstone healing with dogs and cats, as well as her chakra and aura information. Thanks also to Leslie Kaslow of Ellon USA, for support and flower remedy information; Susan Griffin, Diane Deubler and Cheryl Lenard of the Clip Joint and Naturals for Animals for flea and skin, nutritional, and behavioral information; and Jill Turner and Jane Brown for general healing and support both for my dogs and myself.

Thanks also and always to Elaine and John Gill and the wonderful folks of The Crossing Press, who have made this book both beautiful and possible. Thanks to Amy Sibiga for her artwork, and Davida Johns for her photo of Kali and Copper.

Preface

Diane Stein's book provides extensive and detailed guidelines for healing our animal companions in ways that work above, beyond, and sometimes in spite of the realm of traditional medicine.

While traditional Western medicine has many badges of success, such as the healing of wounds and broken bones, the treatment of shock, the prevention of infectious diseases, and the control and treatment of chronic diseases like hypothyroidism and diabetes, it still has a long, long way to go. Allopaths, or traditional practitioners, are taught to spend too much time focusing on the disease and its symptoms. They consider remission of symptoms a sign that health has returned.

Diane's words awaken us to the needs of the entire animal, which may actually be harmed by successful symptom remission (suppression). Astute practitioners and guardians are beginning to realize that health is more than a lack of symptoms—true well-being resonates beyond the physical, measurable bodily functions.

For example, in the veterinary hospital, there are still many mysteries. Why do animals with the same disease, the exact same blood test values, and identical treatments experience completely different levels of recovery? Why does the same virus cause different symptoms in each animal, barely causing a sneeze in one, nearly killing another? What causes a patient to get better and thrive "against all odds"? What is that certain something that makes the difference?

Natural Remedies for Dogs and Cats guides us to that immeasurable space where help can be found. Through proper nutrition, herbs, homeopathy, acupuncture, and other remedies, we can heal our companions in the places traditional medicine cannot touch. As we begin communicating on this deeper level, we will be able to detect and prevent imbalances before physical symptoms appear.

The practice of true healing is very humbling, because we must constantly listen to the voice of our patients, and learn from the inherent wisdom contained in their bodies. We begin to realize that true talent lies not in matching the medicine to the disease, but rather in matching the therapy precisely to the needs of the individual animal. Discovering that match takes a good bit of careful listening. Diane helps us begin this long journey of understanding, which will benefit not only our animals, but also ourselves, and ultimately, our world.

Wendy Thacher, DVM

Women are mistresses of the beasts and guardians of the animals. When we attune to the powers of the beasts, we are fearless. We are also concerned about male control of the animals, since the beasts first trusted women when they agreed to live with humans . . . .

Attuning to the animals rather than controlling them is the pathway to the stars.

—Barbara Hand Clow,
Signet of Atlantis

Grandmother Earth, hear me! The two-leggeds, the four-leggeds, the winged, and all that move upon You are Your children. With all beings and all things we shall be as relatives; just as we are related to You, O Mother.

—Black Elk

Contents

Appendix

Introduction
Healing the Animals,
the Earth, and Ourselves

This is a book of natural remedies for dogs and cats, listed by methods and dis-eases. It briefly describes eight methods of pet healing, then applies these methods for use with fifty dis-eases common to companion animals. The healing methods are: nutrition, naturopathy, vitamins and minerals, herbs, homeopathy, acupuncture/acupressure, flower essences, and gemstones. The methods and directions on how to use them comprise the first part of this book, and the dis-eases are in alphabetical order in the second section. Though the methods are summarized, this book is meant as a companion and continuation to my previous book, *Natural Healing for Dogs and Cats* (The Crossing Press, 1993). The remedies and methods are also applicable to other small animals and to horses by adjusting them to body weight; they are safe for humans, as well. Some of the methods, *i.e.*, homeopathy, flower essences, gemstones, and acupressure, require no adjustment at all for use with larger or smaller bodies. For human holistic healing, refer to my previous books, *All Women Are Healers* and *The Natural Remedy Book for Women*, both published by The Crossing Press.

Natural remedies are not meant to replace qualified veterinary care for a seriously ill pet. Their primary purpose is to prevent dis-eases at their onset—nutrition and vitamins and minerals are the key—and to keep small dis-eases from becoming serious ones. They are also a support to veterinary care and greatly increase the pet's comfort and rate of recovery. In many cases veterinary attention is made unnecessary by natural healing started soon after the symptoms are noted. Moreover, it is a first defense in any situation. In incidents that are not life-threatening, try natural methods first, and then go to chemicals and the veterinary/medical system, if the pet does not respond. I have found that natural healing works with my own two dogs often when veterinary methods and drugs fail.

When a professional is needed, I highly recommend contacting a holistically oriented veterinarian. She will often do phone consultations if she is too far away, and she will frequently work with the diagnosis of a standard veterinarian if she cannot examine the dog or cat personally. To locate a holistic vet in your area, contact

The American Holistic Veterinary Medical Association
2214 Old Emmorton Road
Bel Air, MD 21014
(410) 569-0795

The phone hours are 8:30 AM - 4 PM Monday and Wednesday, and 8:30 AM - 2 PM on Thursdays. Know the holistic practitioner in your area before your pet needs care and use that veterinarian routinely so that she is familiar with your pet.

To locate referrals for veterinary homeopathy and veterinary acupuncture (they may be the same veterinarians as above) contact

> International Veterinary Acupuncture Society
> c/o Meredith Snader, VMD
> 2140 Conestoga Road
> Chester Springs, PA 19425
> (215) 827-7245
>
> National Center for Homeopathy
> 801 N. Fairfax Street
> Alexandria, VA 22314
> (703) 548-7790

Many or most holistic veterinarians are also homeopaths and an increasing number are becoming veterinary acupuncturists. See the Referrals section at the end of this book for further listings, and for veterinary chiropractors as well.

The horrors and abuses of technological medicine are increasing for both people and animals. Veterinary/medical philosophy wages a so-called "war" against dis-ease and too often uses warrior methods on the fragile bodies and psyches of its patients. If a body part is dis-eased or not used, or its use is unknown, the standard impulse of technological medicine is to cut it out. If there is nothing that can be cut out, burn it out with chemicals whose side effects may be harsher than the original dis-ease. To make a synthetic drug tolerable to the human or animal patient, or to heal the damage of the side effects, other pharmaceutical drugs are added that may also have side effects. If our pets do not heal by the current rigid protocol of prescribed drugs and surgeries, the advice is euthanasia. Far too many dogs and cats (and people) die unnecessarily because the technological medical model cannot heal them or because their symptoms do not fit within the model.

The cost of this kind of care is astronomical. The price of technology —the gadgets themselves and the testing and review processes of the drugs—is passed on to the consumer. Increasingly, medical system abuses of humans are being extended to animals. Overtesting, unneeded machines and monitors, the high cost of fad medications, the overuse of medications with questionable effectiveness, the overuse of surgeries, and expensive and repeated office visits and hospitalizations all add to both the misery of health care and the cost. Much of what is done to our pets and to ourselves in the name of medical care is unnecessary and much of it causes more harm than good. Because of these abuses, the cost of pet health care is getting out of reach for many.

Holistic methods are the primary alternatives to this situation. They are low cost and low technology (many can be made at home), do not require prescriptions because they are totally safe when used with common sense, and are often as effective or more effective than chemical pharmaceutical drugs. There are no side effects beyond an occasional cleansing reaction, and the materials needed are readily available. They support the body's own healing process and natural bent for wellness without trauma or increase of pain and discomfort. No fear is engendered in the pet or human using natural methods. Many cats and dogs that veterinarians have written off and for whom euthanasia was advised have regained full health by using natural methods. In every way, they are a better buy, and they can be used in virtually all healing situations.

Needless to say, the standard veterinary/medical system has no use for alternative healing methods; it does its best to discredit them, because these alternative healing methods take money away from hospitals, medics, technology manufacturers and drug corporations.

Taking our own and our pets' health and wellness into our hands is a radical act because it works and because it is empowering. The same patriarchal forces that are destroying the planet are destroying human and animal health in the name of greed and corporate profits. Natural healing for people and pets is a way to say *no*, and to regain our heritage and freedom. Do not let establishment voices frighten you. Most people who try natural healing for themselves, their children, and their animals recognize the effectiveness and value. Few return to standard veterinary/ medicine except as a last resort.

This book, like my other books, discusses both holistic natural remedies and metaphysical healing. The term "holistic," which includes both of these, comes from the word "whole" or "wholeness." It means that the full animal or person is treated, rather than just the dis-ease or dis-eased part. Where standard medicine works only with the injured leg or skin rash or feline leukemia, holistic healing looks at the animal or person as a whole individual. Natural remedies work at healing these conditions but go beyond the dis-ease to the pet herself.

Metaphysical/holistic healing is based on the concept of the four bodies—the physical, emotional, mental, and spiritual. Veterinary/medical treatment, in contrast, recognizes only the first and most dense of the bodies, the physical body level. The physical body involves an animal's or person's physiology and anatomy, the organs and systems (skin, bones, muscles, respiration, elimination, etc.). This is the level defined and analyzed by scientific method and direct observation. It is the same for all individuals of a given species—all dogs have the same anatomy that functions in the same ways, as do all cats or all humans.

The medical/veterinary system works entirely from the physical level and from the premise that all individuals of a species (all cats or all dogs) are identical and will react in standardized, predictable ways. One dog's heart dis-ease (or diabetes, or birthing situation) is treated the same as another dog with the same pathology. Other-than-physical causes of dis-ease are not recognized, nor is it recognized that three cats with the same illness will have three different, more than physical causes for it. Levels of Be-ing that are not visible or quantifiable—the emotional, mental, and spiritual components that make every Be-ing unique—cannot be proven by science and therefore are not believed by the veterinary/medical system to exist.

Holistic healing treats the physical body but continues beyond that level. In metaphysical theory, all dis-ease has an emotional component, and until the causative emotions are resolved, full healing cannot take place. This concept is gaining increased recognition in human healing and in medicine; it is also a factor in healing for dogs and cats. A cat or dog with an illness, especially a chronic or recurring illness, may have an emotional reason for the dis-ease. In a simple example, the cat's skin rash or the dog's sore paw may be happening because the pet needs more love and attention. If being sick is the means to fill the pet's need for love, she will continue to be sick. The rash or sore may heal, but will come back again despite physical level treatment. This is not in any way to say that the animal is faking.

Companion animals also absorb the emotions of the homes they live in and often suffer for this. In a house where the people are upset or in discord the pets will reflect the discord and sometimes become physically sick. Dogs and cats cannot release their frustrations and worries by talking about them. They are often frightened by a situation they cannot understand. They feel the emotional climate in their bodies, and the stress, fear, frustration, confusion, and turmoil can manifest as physical dis-ease. A house where there has been a death or divorce is likely to contain both people and pets that need healing.

Pets also sacrifice themselves for the well-being of the humans they have bonded to. Animals take negative energy or situations into themselves and thereby protect their people. Both cats and dogs act as buffers between their people and the dangers and negativities of the world. Humans are aware of this on a conscious level when a dog runs back into a burning house to save a child or puts herself between her person and an attacker and dies. The same scenario happens on an energy level daily although the humans involved may never be aware of it. The cat in a troubled family may manifest her guardian's cancer, clearing the human's aura and taking the dis-ease into her own body. Emotional level healing includes helping the pet to release the negative energy and emotions she has absorbed from her household, and having her own needs met in that household.

This clearing is done by first attempting to understand what's going on and then resolving it. If the dog or cat needs more attention, ways must be found to give it to her on an ongoing basis—not only when she is sick. If the household is in crisis, efforts must be made to calm and reassure the animal that she is loved, is in no danger, can feel secure, etc. Often all the members of the family—all the humans and all the animals —need healing, even when it is only the pet that appears to be sick.

A number of holistic methods work to release dis-ease from the causative emotional body. Homeopathy is one of the most important methods. Others include gemstones, flower essences, and psychic communication. Psychic healing, massage, and acupuncture/acupressure are deep relaxants that release negative energies and emotions from the seen and unseen bodies.

Animals feel (have emotion) more than they rely on thought (mental reasoning), but cats and dogs do think and reason. Pet behavior is a reflection of the mental body. Like people, pets have memories, and what has happened to them in the past affects their behavior and wellness in the present. Misunderstanding, miscommunication, and previous abuse or traumatic experiences can manifest in physical dis-ease. Negative behavior coincident with physical illness is a clue to a mental body disease source.

A dog or cat adopted from a shelter is the most frequent example of dis-ease originating in the mental body. Pound rescue pets, except newborns kept with their mothers until adoption, almost always require physical healing and virtually always require mental healing. They arrive with runny noses, diarrhea, or infected ears (physical symptoms). They also develop a series of testing, traumatized, or aberrant behaviors that clear up over time. It generally takes six months to a year to heal these behaviors in a young animal, longer if ever in an older one. This is not a reason to avoid shelter cats and dogs, but be aware of their healing process.

Some cats may hide from humans, refuse to be touched, and scratch or bite. Some dogs may show aggressiveness or cringing, urinate from nervousness, soil indoors, rip things up, or show great jealousy of other pets or people in the family. By acting gently and consistently and not forcing the situation too soon (or letting the animal become a canine-feline terrorist), the cat or dog becomes more secure. The behaviors and physical illnesses gradually lessen and finally cease.

Physical dis-eases that manifest in a traumatized dog or cat require more than healing the pet's body. Relaxation techniques like massage, Tellington TTouch, and acupuncture/acupressure help immensely here. So do psychic communication and psychic healing that reassure the cat or dog that she is safe, loved, and has come home. By using psychic communication to understand what the pet is reacting to, many traumas can be eased and solved. These methods can be used to let the animal know that "things are okay now." Flower essences, crystals and gemstones, and homeopathy also address the mental body. Once the dog or cat feels relaxed and safe, both the negative behaviors and the physical dis-eases are released and disappear.

Animals are also spiritual Be-ings, at least as much as people are. In their bonding with humans they have a purpose for being here. Each pet's purpose is her own, and it is the driving force of her existence. It is no coincidence that a particular dog or cat is with a particular person or family. They have a job to do together, and the animals are infinitely patient with their people or that job. One cat's job may be to clear her home and environment of negative energy and calm her human. Another's may be to be a clown and make her guardian laugh. One dog may be a protection for her person and home, while another's job is to baby-sit the kids. Some cats catch mice for a living and a few dogs still herd sheep or otherwise work. Animals need a purpose in life to be healthy and happy —just like people.

Dogs and cats are highly psychic creatures; they are aware of stresses and energy flows that their people cannot define. They see auras. They have auras, chakras, and energy flows in their more-than-physical bodies. They also have sensory systems (sight, scent, hearing, touch) that are far superior to humans. Cats and dogs have had past lives and may reincarnate again and again to be with their chosen guardian. The deep and intense bond that develops between human and pet is a source of the pet's existence—it's her job.

An animal who feels that her job is done may choose to die, and pets have been known to commit suicide. This can happen when a dog's or cat's person dies, when the pet is separated from her person and she believes the separation to be permanent, when she feels that she cannot do her job or no one wants her to do her job. An abused pet or street animal may choose to die, as well. In such cases, a pet can deliberately leave the abuser and will manifest a dis-ease (or run in front of a car) to put her decision into effect. A willing pet that feels unwanted and un-loved may choose to die if she cannot find a more appreciative human to bond with. A loved house pet suddenly left in a shelter or lost and traumatized on the street may also choose to manifest her own death.

A pet ill on the spiritual level is ill indeed; she will probably be very ill in body, as well. Love is the best healing, along with a new job or purpose or person in her life. Animals grieve deeply when their person/ job is gone and it may take much persuading to turn the situation around. Cats are far more independent in this situation than dogs, but they still can manifest dis-ease from the spiritual level. All Be-ings, animal and human, need a purpose for being here.

Psychic healing probably goes the furthest in reaching a pet or person at the spiritual level. *Reiki* is wonderful for this work, and other forms of laying on of hands and touch healing. Flower essences and gemstones reach the spiritual level, and sometimes homeopathy. Transmitting love and loving touch on a continual basis is the key. Dogs or cats determined by vets to be dying have healed completely with such care, whatever their medical disease label.

How does this apply to healing a cat or dog that is sick from a physical dis-ease? Physical level healing is the first step, of course, whether holistic or veterinary. Stabilize the physical body first. In holistic healing this is done with optimal nutrition and healing foods (naturopathy), homeopathy, vitamins and minerals, and medicinal herbs. In case of accidents or injuries, it means first aid and sometimes veterinary intervention and surgeries. Always make sure a surgery is actually necessary before allowing it. Holistic methods and good nutrition can prevent or heal many dis-eases before they become serious enough to need medical intervention. When the veterinarian is needed, holistic methods support and speed the healing.

Healing the other three bodies—the emotional, mental, and spiritual—becomes holistic healing. The person living with the dog or cat usually has the best insight as to what other factors are involved. I cannot overemphasize the value of psychic communication and a knowledge of animal behavior. Ask the pet what's wrong! And be prepared to make some changes to honor her answer. Does she need more time with you? More attention? More reassurance? Does she think she's been "bad" and you don't love her anymore? Is she missing someone who has gone away (including another animal)? Is there something she is afraid of? Thought, observation, and psychic contact will offer answers.

Whenever possible, resolve the problem. Spend more time with the cat or dog that needs you. Offer love, reassurance, and patience. Massage and Tellington TTouch work wonders here, as does touch healing. Often long walks or trips in the car are what is needed for dogs. When my puppy Kali becomes hyperactive or disobedient she usually wants a trip to the beach, whereas Copper asks for walks. Homeopathic remedies work with the emotional components of dis-ease, as do flower essences. (Test the animal individually rather than reading the uses from a chart and picking the remedies intellectually.) Gemstones and crystals resonate emotionally. Do stress-reducing methods, too.

These are as important for the person as for the pet. Often the remedy needed by the dog or cat is also needed by her guardian. Remember that our companion animals absorb our feelings, and when the people of a house are upset, the pet is also upset. Unable to release fear or frustration in other ways, the cat or dog may develop a physical dis-ease. Finding out what is upsetting the animal and clearing it heals everyone emotionally and physically.

Mental healing is similar to emotional healing. When a pet is ill, consider her background. If turmoil in her previous family led to a breakup or death that resulted in losing her home, turmoil in her new home may warn the dog or cat that it's going to happen again. The pet may totally misunderstand the situation, and even may think she is the cause. Again, reassurance, love, and psychic communication are necessary. By helping her to understand that she is secure and safe, the acting out (negative behavior) stops and the physical dis-ease heals. A pet that has been abused may expect the abuse to happen again.

Stress is the direct cause of eighty-five percent (or more) of human dis-ease, and dogs and cats share and mirror human lives. Stress is the direct cause of much or most of the dis-ease in companion animals, and a lot of that stress is absorbed directly from humans. Mental healing uses the same holistic methods as emotional healing and is individual—no two pets react the same way or need the same things. Healing animal and human stress together leads to happier homes for everyone.

To heal a pet on the spiritual level means that she must have a person or family to bond with and a job to do. An animal with one or either of these factors missing is likely to die, particularly the pet with no person. Some animal rightists insist that pet guardianship is slavery. They have no understanding of the human-animal bond or the pets' choice in spending their lives with particular humans. The bond fills a deep need in both person and pet; in the case of dogs, this bond is their reason for Be-ing. People and animals living together form a partnership. More humans need to be aware of this fact and to respect and treat their pets accordingly. We do not own our pets; but we are their guardians with the responsibility of protecting them. All healing methods help in spiritual level pet healing, but the most crucial methods are showing understanding, caring, and love constantly and daily. Our cats and dogs deserve no less.

To be a healer means working with all the bodies, not only the physical body. (This applies to animals, people, and our planet.) There are four bodies, not just one. The physical body is what may be seen and touched in physical ways. It is the only body that is open to technology or scientific analysis at this time. Veterinary/medical "cures" reach only this level, and do so by drugs and surgeries. Yet healing that stops with this level is incomplete.

A veterinarian or doctor pays little attention to the emotional, mental, and spiritual levels. A healer takes these into full account. If the non-physical bodies are left untreated the dis-ease may clear only partially if at all, may recur, or may reappear in another place. Healing that works with and clears dis-ease from all four bodies is complete healing. The animal or person is made well and the dis-ease does not return.

Non-physical body healing is known today as *vibrational healing*. The methods reach beyond the scientifically acceptable physical level to release dis-ease from the unseen/non-physical layers. Emotional healing, mental healing, and spiritual healing result, thereby removing the dis-ease from the aura template, i.e. the computer DNA/RNA coding of the animal or person. That this form of healing is not presently measurable and is ignored by science makes it no less real.

Holistic physical level healing differs from veterinary/medical "cures." Where a veterinarian or doctor uses synthetic drugs to treat a dis-ease or removes the affected body part, holistic physical healing uses natural, non-invasive methods that support the body's own process of self-healing. Nutrition, herbs, food supplements, vitamins and minerals are holistic healing methods on the physical level. They help the pet's own body to resolve the dis-ease by supporting the animal's life force (ch'i or Vital Force).

Only holistic healing goes beyond the physical body; the veterinary/medical system ignores the non-physical levels. This is partly because holistic methods are individual rather than standardized and predictable in response. What is not machine-measurable and doesn't create an always-repeatable test result is considered nonexistent. No two pets or people will have identical responses on the unseen levels, though their physical dis-eases are the same.

On the emotional level, one dog with chronic hip dysplasia may be panicky and stressed, while another with the same dis-ease may be lethargic and indifferent. On the mental level, one cat that has been injured may react by aggressiveness and biting, whereas another injured in the same way may want attention and large amounts of cuddling. On the spiritual level, one pet may feel her purpose in life is with her person, while another cat or dog may feel her "job" is with the animal pack or her mate. Healing for each individual is different, even for two individuals with the same dis-ease. In time of illness each animal has her own beyond-the-physical needs, and if she is to heal completely these needs and differences must be met.

Holistic healing includes all four bodies and uses various methods to address the pet's or person's situation on all these levels. While medically oriented readers may resonate more to physical level "provable by science" holistic methods, all levels are equally important. To heal a dog's or cat's physical symptoms is not enough; the symptoms will return. To heal the physical symptoms plus release the dis-ease from the non-physical bodies provides the only real "cure." For those who may be more comfortable with herbs or vitamins as "respectable" and provable holistic methods, but may question psychic communication, crystals, homeopathy, or other vibrational methods I can only suggest trying all methods. If done properly and observed closely, the results will speak for themselves.

This book focuses on recipes for specific dis-eases. It is meant to accompany *Natural Healing for Dogs and Cats*, and to be used with both physical and non-physical level methods. Suggestions for treating a dis-ease may be taken from more than one category, and I encourage doing so. It is perfectly safe to use a homeopathic remedy along with an herb, gemstone, flower essence, and dietary changes, although acupuncture and homeopathy may interfere with each other's actions. All are valid, as each method addresses a different vibrational level and a different aspect of the dog's or cat's dis-ease.

It is possible to work with all of the methods, or only one or some of them, or some at different times. Some may be more important or more effective for a particular pet at a particular time than others. There may be highly individualized responses to any method. Though psychic work and Reiki are less emphasized in this book than in the previous one, remember to include them. One method or another among the choices may be the key to a specific pet's needs and healing. There may be highly individualized responses to any method.

Americans and Europeans need to be aware of the government's threats to holistic healing and our freedom to have holistic remedies and nutrients available to us. This is a crisis issue in the United States today (1993), and since FDA rulings often become the basis for government policies in Canada and Europe, it affects them as well. Big business, the medical system, and the pharmaceutical drug industry want to take herbs, homeopathic remedies, and low-cost vitamins and supplements off the open market. Once that happens, these same corporations will return them to us as "drugs" by prescription only and at very high prices. Since the same holistic products that are used for people are the ones that heal our dogs and cats, this is a political issue of enormous consequence and a clear and present danger to both humans and pets.

Natural substances, plants, and elements intrinsically found in the human or animal body are not patentable. These items include vitamins and minerals, enzymes, coenzymes, and amino acids which are found in the physiology of the mammal body, and herbs which are free-growing plants. A patent can only be obtained if a substance is not available over the counter or in food stores. Most holistic remedy items are classed as foods and therefore cannot be patented. Obtaining a patent gives the corporation that holds the patent exclusive rights to a substance and its profits.

Since business cannot control or profit from holistic remedies that are natural substances sold on the open market as foods and since health food products are becoming increasingly competitive to the medical/veterinary system and pharmaceutical drug industry, these interests want them taken from free use. The media has consistently supported the industries at pushing for this and the American government has an interest in supporting the corporations. The FDA (Federal Food and Drug Administration) is the harassing agency. Why?

> Perhaps one reason the FDA attacks the supplement industry is because the FDA grows in size and power when large pharmaceutical companies spend hundreds of millions of dollars to substantiate safety and efficacy for new synthetic patented drugs—all of which must be approved by the FDA. For natural products, however, you rarely find companies willing to spend even a fraction of this amount to gain new drug approval for a substance that is unpatentable. Without a patent, they don't get market exclusivity and cannot recoup their investment.[1]

With its extreme bias against natural remedies and vitamins, the FDA has waged an ongoing vendetta against the health food industry and imposed increasing regulations and restrictions against herbs, vitamins, homeopathic remedies, and other supplements. They have recently gone so far as to perform illegal raids at gunpoint on health food stores and the offices of practitioners (doctors, naturopaths, chiropractors, etc.), and they want legislation to sanction this behavior.

The medical and corporate systems are becoming increasingly hostile to natural remedies—because the remedies work and cause the systems to lose money. Holistics provide a self-empowering alternative to the invasiveness, technology, poor results, high costs, and noxious side effects of chemical drugs and medical/veterinary surgeries and treatments. Both people and pets live longer and with a better quality of life on natural methods. A *Time Magazine* poll (November 4, 1991) revealed that eighty-four percent of people who have tried natural remedies will continue to use them and would also choose an alternative practitioner over a standard medical doctor.[2]

Herbs, vitamins, and natural remedies are totally safe and effective. Some herbs have been used traditionally for thousands of years—their effectiveness is long proven. Vitamins, minerals, and other supplements occur in nature and are constituents of the human and animal anatomy. Extensive use has proved their effectiveness. Reports of toxicities in herbs and supplements have been greatly exaggerated by the government and the media. If common sense is used, harmful side effects do not occur. Yet access to these simple, safe products is being restricted and denied. Human and pet well-being is being seriously compromised in the name of corporate greed.

In April, 1993, the FDA removed from the market two highly effective and totally safe herbs, claiming them to be toxic. These are comfrey and chaparral. Comfrey has been used for thousands of years as an aid to healing bone fractures and tissue damage, as well as infected wounds. It heals even gangrenous sores, prevents bone non-unions, and soothes and heals internal tissues of the lungs and intestines. Chaparral is a plant first used by Native Americans of the American West. It is a detoxifying herb used for cancer, tumors, leukemia, both osteo- and rheumatoid arthritis, and is an anti-bacterial and anti-viral. Other herbs have been removed from the shelves as well—lobelia and St. John's wort were removed a few years ago but have since been returned to health food store shelves. Sassafras is another herb that has been banned from sale on the open market; it is a safe hormone balancer for women in menopause. FDA officials made their gunpoint raids nationally on Asian groceries (May 20, 1993) to remove and ban Cow's Head, a Chinese herbal effective for arthritis. Only the most effective natural remedies and herbs come under FDA notice; the drug companies remove their competition.

For each of these cases, the FDA has claimed toxicity. In each case, the evidence (when there was any at all) was based on one or two sensationalized examples of gross misuse. Any over-the-counter product including aspirin would be toxic under similar circumstances, but no over-the-counter product is harassed or banned. They are patented and protected by corporate interests that the government supports. Rumors and predictions suggest that other herbs and vitamins/supplements will be removed from the shelves in the near future, including goldenseal, echinacea, ephedra, lobelia, all amino acids, biofavinoids, selenium, germanium, chromium, CO Q10, some of the B-vitamins, and vitamin A.[3] People and pets will suffer greatly if this happens.

Alpha-tryptophan, an amino acid useful for insomnia, anxiety, depression, body pain, and hyperactivity has also been banned (1989) based on a single Japanese company's contaminated manufacturing process. (Yet Tylenol was not banned after the tampering of the bottles and subsequent deaths.) In addition, increasing restrictions are placed on homeopathic remedies, requiring higher potencies and nosodes to have a prescription and forcing single-use labeling that is meaningless.

All of these items are safe, having been used for far longer periods of time than most of the pharmaceutical drugs. Some have been used for centuries and all of them are proven effective. All are life-saving for people and pets, are naturally occurring substances, and are drug-free means of easing animal and human suffering. How many of these banned items will now be released in synthesized, ingredient-isolated form complete with drug side effects sold at high prices and by prescription only, under veterinary/medical corporate control? Chemical drug alternatives are often dramatically less effective, with frequent noxious side effects (chemotherapy vs. chaparral). The herbs grow wild and can be cultivated (still legally, I believe) and therefore are still available.

In 1962 and with AMA (American Medical Association) collusion, the FDA established its intent to halt open marketing of vitamins and minerals by declaring them drugs available only by prescription. The ensuing public outcry resulted in the 1976 Proxmire Act that prevented the FDA from classifying and then regulating vitamins or minerals as drugs. The FDA moved again in 1991 with Bill H.R. 2597, which gave the FDA ludicrously harsh enforcement authority over health food products. This bill met the same public outcry and was withdrawn, but was later reintroduced as H.R. 3642 and S. 2135. The bills were not voted on and are expected to be reintroduced at the beginning of 1994. Raids on health food stores and alternative practitioners are sanctioned in these bills, with ludicrously excessive fines for possession of banned vitamins, herbs, amino acids, etc. (The FDA has been conducting these raids and fines anyway, without legal sanction.) Up to fifty percent of all nutritional supplements could be banned if these bills are passed.[4]

On June 11, 1992, the Health Freedom Act was introduced in both houses of Congress (S. 2385 and H.R. 5703; the 1993 House Bill number is H.R. 509). This act protects access to vitamins, minerals, and natural supplements and contains the following provisions:

1. Defines "dietary supplement" to include herbs and other natural remedies.

2. States unequivocally that "dietary supplements" are not drugs or food additives (and therefore cannot come under drug and additive regulations or restrictions).

3. Allows the FDA to restrict "dietary supplements" only on the basis of safety. (There are cautions here, see below.)

4. Permits information on the uses and benefits of supplements, if truthful and scientific. (No claims or information whatsoever are allowed now, though much scientific evidence is available.)

5. Prior FDA approval of claimants (see #4 above) will not be required.

6. FDA warnings and decrees may be challenged in court. (There is now no appeal to any FDA action.)[5]

It is obviously vital that the Health Freedom Act be passed, for the sake of civil freedom and our lives and our well-being and that of our pets. Activism is required here; write your Senators and Congresspeople. Be watchful that new restrictions are not introduced in any form. Do not expect that passage of this good bill is the end of the battle—remember that the Proxmire Act of 1976 should have ended it. Be aware that the FDA has claimed toxicity (with no scientific proof) as an excuse for the removal and banning of safe herbs, amino acids, vitamins, and other supplements, and will continue to do so if not stopped.

The veterinary/medical system does not want people to take charge of their own health or that of their pets. Human and pet care is a multibillion-dollar industry based upon the multibillion-dollar pharmaceutical drug industry. Why should we be permitted to heal our pets with licorice root extract at six dollars a bottle instead of cortisone shots at seventy-five dollars a veterinary visit? Why should we be allowed to keep our pets and ourselves healthy with optimal nutrition and vitamins instead of paying the vets, medics, and drug companies? If the world is to be free, such restrictions cannot be allowed.

The methods and remedies presented in this book are all totally safe and they have been proven effective. I have used them on myself and my dogs for almost thirty years without toxic effects of any kind. I have witnessed their use on hundreds of cats and dogs and thousands of people, again without any harm whatsoever and a great deal of good. For best results, begin holistic remedies as soon as possible in the course of a disease and do not hesitate to use them along with veterinary care. Remember that healing is more than physical. Realize too that dogs or cats receiving quality nutrition (preservative-free foods plus vitamins and minerals or a home-cooked diet) will need remedies far less often, because they will be less often sick. A description of how to use each of eight holistic methods follows, then specific suggestions for a variety of possible dog and cat dis-eases. I offer this book with love for all the cats, dogs, and other animals that share our lives.

> April 30, 1993
> May Eve
> Second Quarter Moon in Virgo

---

[1]James L. Beck, "The Nutritional Labeling and Education Act (NLEA)," in *Stop the FDA: Save Your Health Freedom*, ed. John Morganthaler and Steven Wm. Fowkes (Menlo Park, CA: Health Freedom Publications, 1992, p. 116).

[2]*Ibid.*, p. 117.

[3]Michael Onstott, "In the Name of Consumer Protection," in *Stop the FDA*, p. 81.

[4]Nutritional Health Alliance, "Fight for Your Family's Rights," in *Natural Health Magazine*, July-August, 1992, pp. 104-105.

[5]James Beck, "The Nutritional Labeling and Education Act (NLEA)," in *Stop the FDA*, pp. 121-122.

The Methods

I - Healing Nutrition

The old saying goes, "You are what you eat," and this is just as true for dogs and cats as it is for people. What cats and dogs ate in the pre-human wild (or what people ate a hundred years ago) was far cleaner, safer, and better in nutritional quality than it is today. It is the lack of safe, fresh, and uncontaminated food, water, and air that is seriously decreasing our companion animals' lifespans—and our own. It is the same lack that is destroying our planet. This situation must be changed quickly if animals, people, and the Earth are to survive.

The supermarket does not provide safe food for pets or people, despite all the television commercials that insist their brand is so complete that only love is missing. Nor does the pet store or vet's office, despite their claims of better quality food or special needs diets. America is the richest nation in the world but its people are malnourished, and despite all the media hype about good health in a bag or can, so are our pets. The reason goes back to the same old story—patriarchal corporate greed and excessive profit.

The bagged or canned cat and dog foods billed as "complete and balanced diets" by their manufacturers are primarily made of garbage (or what should have become garbage). They consist mainly of beef or poultry by-products which translates to mean ground-up hooves, hides, horn, hair, bones, feathers, beaks, feet, organs, entrails, and waste. By-products in pet foods also contain dis-eased or cancerous animal tissue from cattle or poultry that have been condemned for human use, usually because it is dis-eased or cancerous. Or the meat is spoiled or the animals have died on the way to the slaughterhouse for various reasons, including feed-chemical (mostly carcinogens) overdose. Blood-soaked sawdust from the slaughterhouse floor is also considered a meat or poultry by-product. These by-products comprise forty percent of pet food. Beef, by the way, is the highest allergenic agent for both dogs and cats.

The other percentage of commercial pet food consists primarily of vegetable fiber, grain, and chemicals. Vegetable fiber is the euphemism for ground-up corn cobs, corn husks, peanut hulls, or other such nutritionless waste. Or it may be grain or soy meal condemned for human consumption because of rancidity, mold, debris, odors, or bacterial contamination.[1] Corn and wheat are also highly allergenic for some pets.

Pet foods are steamed to kill bacteria, destroying both bacteria and food value. The enzymes essential for digestion are heat-sensitive as are many vitamins. Some synthetic vitamins may be reintroduced to make up a portion (however small) of what the food never contained or what was lost to processing. Only a few of the many necessary nutrients are replaced. Salmonella and other dis-ease causing bacteria have still been found in finished products.

Then there are the chemical contaminants. Beef, poultry, and other food and farm animals in this country are fed a heavy mix of chemicals. Some of these are hormones and growth inducers to bring the animals to slaughter weight as early as possible. Some are pesticides used on feed grains in the field and afterwards, and on the animals themselves. Other chemicals include high amounts of antibiotics needed because stressed factory-farmed animals have little dis-ease resistance and succumb easily. The antibiotics are not only given to sick animals but are placed routinely in the feeds. Animals raised for slaughter are also heavily vaccinated, again because the stress and overcrowding make them easily liable to epidemics. These are also immune system reducers that affect the meat, eggs, and milk. (See the section on Vaccination/Vaccinosis in the second part of this book or in *Natural Healing for Dogs and Cats*, p. 89-90.)

All of these chemicals remain in the flesh of the slaughtered meat animal, and are passed on to the pet or person that eats the meat. In the process of manufacturing pet food from this not-so-healthy flesh, many more chemicals are added. These include artificial flavorings and colorings, sugar and salt, preservatives to prevent the fat in the foods from going rancid, and chemicals known to cause animals (especially cats) to become addicted to the foods. ("She won't eat any other brand.") Lead and aluminum contamination, both of which are dangerous, are also common.

Most of the ingredients in a can or bag of dog or cat food cannot easily be pronounced. Most of these should not be eaten; they are dangerous and contain no nutrition. This food which no normal pet would touch becomes her daily dinner for all of her life. While the FDA harasses health foods, neither that department nor any other government agency polices the pet food industry. Manufacturers can use anything they choose in their products. Any chemical or contamination is legal. There have been a number of pet food recalls over the years and an unknown number of cat and dog deaths.

One of the most prevalent of the preservatives is ethoxyquin. This is used in the premium veterinary lines of dog and cat foods as a preservative. People buy these more expensive foods thinking that they are giving their animals a better deal. In fact, ethoxyquin was developed by Monsanto as a rubber hardener and insecticide. It is believed to cause liver and kidney dis-ease, cancer, immune dis-eases, skin problems and hair loss, gross birth deformities, and thyroid problems. Watch for it and for BHA and BHT as particularly prevalent pet food hazards and avoid foods containing these chemicals.

Sugar and salt are also added to dog and cat foods as preservatives. The salt may be present in dangerous amounts. This may prompt heart dis-ease and kidney failure which are routine pet killers today. As recently as forty years ago these dis-eases were unknown in pets. Sugar can comprise as much as twenty-five percent of the semi-moist dog food packets, and a high proportion of dog biscuits. Its cat equivalent, propylene glycol, comprises as much as ten percent of cat food. These two chemicals are addictive—pet food companies foster such addictions—and they are killers. They result in diabetes, hypoglycemia, arthritis, cataracts, allergies, overweight, tooth decay, and nervousness—all "human" dis-eases caused by the sugar, salt, and preservatives in processed foods that people eat too. The connection between poor diets, early death and high rates of chronic dis-ease cannot be ignored.

Animals and people lived longer a hundred years ago, or even thirty to forty years ago, than they do today. Most of the infectious dis-eases that brought quick death to many in the past have been eliminated by simple sanitation. Today's dis-eases are chronic and long term, usually involving the slow and painful degeneration of the body by breaking down the immune system or the organs. Cancer, kidney dis-ease, and heart dis-ease were rare in people a hundred years ago; they were rare in pets forty years ago. Today they are the top killers of both. Human AIDS and feline leukemia/feline AIDS were unknown twenty years ago. Our animals are manifesting "human" dis-eases and dying of them in numbers never before seen or imagined. People and pets are both being fed nutritionless foods loaded with toxic chemicals.

Holistic healing means bringing optimal health to ourselves and our dogs and cats. A Be-ing in full good health rarely gets sick. Healing begins with a basis for prevention—foods that offer wellness and support the quality of life instead of non-foods without nutrition and filled with toxins and chemicals. Feeding quality nutrition means feeding our pets (and ourselves) good health, long life, and a lack of dis-ease. Obviously the corporations and big business won't give us that; we have to seek it elsewhere or create it for ourselves.

The easiest place to start is with preservative-free pet foods for both cats and dogs. These were started by veterinarian Alfred Plechner in his studies of allergies in pets. Some of the primary dog and cat allergens are the main ingredients in commercial pet foods: beef, yeast, milk products, corn, wheat, and tuna.[2]

Chemical preservatives and dyes, he found, create the same behavior and hyperactivity problems in pets as they do in children. He became very aware of the low level of health available to companion animals fed on commercial diets. He began Nature's Recipe pet foods based on his research. Other companies, small but growing, have followed Plechner's lead. These preservative-free foods are not found in supermarkets, but are usually available at pet stores. The companies remain small; they are not like the commercial pet food companies which are mega-conglomerate corporations.

There are major differences in these pet foods. Beef, corn, and wheat are usually not included, but lamb or poultry, rice, and grains such as millet are primary ingredients. The meat is not *by-products*, which contain contamination and inedible waste, but *meal*, which is clean and of a far higher quality. The grains are whole grains of types not implicated in allergies, and do not include the wastes and hulls.

There are no chemical preservatives, dyes, or additives in these foods, no sugar, and little salt. The fat content (fat is necessary for both dog and cat health) is kept from spoiling by vitamins A, C, or E instead of ethoxyquin, BHA, or BHT. Balanced amounts of vitamins and minerals, amino acids, and other essential nutrients are added. Although they do not contain enough for total health, they are far closer to it than commercial brands. The food is clean and wholesome, and is based on pet needs rather than corporate profits.

The price of these foods is only slightly higher than supermarket brands and equivalent to the cost of the veterinary pet food lines. Preservative-free pet foods are becoming quite easy to find in most areas. Try pet shops or feed stores. Some quality brand names include Natural Life, Nature's Recipe, Lick Your Chops, Solid Gold, Precise, PetGuard, Cornucopia, Wysong, and Natural Balance. Unlike these, Iams, Eukanuba, Hills, Science Diet, Pro-Plan, and Purina are *not* preservative-free, all of which contain ethoxyquin.

A chemical-free pet food is often enough by itself to make profound changes in a dog's or cat's health. With a few additions it can result in total health and observable changes in a pet's condition and well-being. Some possible additions include a little *raw* meat daily (human grade, cheaper cuts are fine; limit liver and kidney meat to once a week and avoid pork); a few *raw* veggies (whatever you are steaming for your own dinner; my dogs love cucumber, snap peas, asparagus ends); and some additional vitamins and minerals. Use a general pet multiple vitamin and mineral supplement daily plus extra vitamins C and E for both cats and dogs.[3] See below.

Here is veterinarian Wendell Belfield's daily protocol for supplementing cats on a commercial or preservative-free diet. The information is also for the cat that is eating a whole foods diet made at home.

1. Weaned and adult cats receive a multivitamin and mineral. Follow the dosage instructions on the label of the product. These cats also receive extra vitamin C (500-750 mg).

2. Pregnant and lactating cats and aged cats receive a multivitamin and mineral plus extra C and E. (Pregnant and lactating cats: 1000 mg vitamin C and 100 IU vitamin E. Aged cats: 500-750 mg vitamin C and 50 IU vitamin E.)

3. Preweaned kittens receive vitamin C pediatric drops. (1-5 days use 20 mg; 5-10 days, 35 mg; and to weaning, 65 mg. For weaned kittens, the vitamin C starts at about 250 mg and increases by six months to 500 mg.)[4]

To administer, most cats (or dogs) will take the multi-tablet from your hand as a treat, or it can be crushed and sprinkled on food. Do not give small kittens or puppies whole tablets; crush them instead. Vitamin C can be sprinkled on food—sodium ascorbate C is almost without taste. If refused, the C tablets or powder can be dipped in corn oil or butter and pets will usually accept them. For vitamin E, puncture the capsule and squirt it onto food—50 IU is half a 100 IU capsule, the rest will keep till the next day. Avoid trying to force pills down the animal's throat. To prevent diarrhea with vitamin C, start with a very low amount and increase it gradually, dividing it into two daily doses with each meal. If the pet develops diarrhea, cut the dose very slightly and stay at the level that doesn't cause problems. This is called going to bowel tolerance. A sick animal will take much more vitamin C than a well one.

The daily protocol for dogs is much the same, but dogs vary widely in size.

1. Preweaned puppies: Vitamin C pediatric drops (from a pharmacy). Use the following amounts. Small breeds: 1-5 days old, 20 mg; 5-10 days, 35 mg; to weaning, 65 mg. Medium breeds: 1-5 days, 35 mg; 5-10 days, 65 mg; to weaning, 100 mg. Large or giant breeds: 1-5 days, 65 mg; 5-10 days, 100 mg; to weaning, 135 mg.

2. Weaned puppies: Multiple vitamin and mineral tablet, follow directions on the bottle. Begin vitamin E at six months old. For vitamin C use the following. First 6 months: small breeds 250 mg, medium breeds 500 mg. Six months to a year, gradually increase to adult levels: small breeds 250 to 500 mg, medium breeds 500 to 1500 mg.

   For larger breeds: First four months gradually increase from 500 to 1000 mg; for giant breeds 750 to 2000 mg. From four to eighteen months, gradually increase to adult levels: large breeds 2000 to 3000 mg, giant breeds 2000 to 6000 mg. (1000 mg = 1 gram).

3. Adult dogs: Multiple vitamin and mineral tablet, follow directions on the bottle. Vitamin C and E:

	Small	Medium	Large	Giant
Vitamin C	500 mg -	1500 mg -	3000 mg -	6000 mg -
	1500 mg	3000 mg	6000 mg	7500 mg
Vitamin E	100 IU	200 IU	200 IU	400 IU

4. Pregnant and lactating females and dogs under high stress: Multiple vitamin and mineral supplement, follow directions on the bottle, and

	Small	Medium	Large	Giant
Vitamin C	1500 mg	3000 mg	6000 mg	7500 mg
Vitamin E	100 IU	200 IU	400 IU	600 IU[5]

Two other supplement protocol choices are notable: one for cats from Anitra Frazier; and for dogs and cats from holistic veterinarian Richard Pitcairn. These also are added to the pet's daily diet, whether the animal is on a commercial, preservative-free, or homemade diet. The additions result in optimal health and full nutrition available in no other way. Anitra Frazier adds the following Vita-Mineral Mix to each cat's meal at the amount of one teaspoonful per meal (two meals per day). This is an alternative to the Wendell Belfield protocol, not used along with it. Vita-Mineral Mix in already prepared form is now available in some health food stores and natural pet catalogs.

Vita-Mineral Mix
1-1/2 cups yeast powder (any food yeast: brewer's, tarula, or
   nutritional)
1/4 cup kelp powder (*or* 1/4 cup mixed trace mineral powder)
1 cup lecithin granules
2 cups wheat bran
2 cups bone meal, calcium lactate, or calcium gluconate

In addition to the above, give each cat once a week:

400 IU vitamin E (alpha-tocopherol, not mixed tocopherols)
10,000 IU vitamin A with 400 IU vitamin D (one capsule)[6]

Stir the Vita-Mineral Mix into food. Puncture the vitamin capsules and squirt the contents on the cat's meal. Most cats like the fishy taste of vitamin A. If the cat refuses the oil, squirt the contents of the punctured capsule into the cheek pouch at the side of the mouth or across the cat's tongue. Do not squirt it down her throat as she may choke.

Richard Pitcairn offers the following Cat Powder and Oil Mix and Dog Powder and Oil Mix. Like Wendell Belfield's vitamins and Anitra Frazier's Vita-Mineral Mix plus vitamins, these mixes turn an okay diet into an optimal one. Even though you use these supplements, the preservative-free diet or the natural homemade diet (see below) is a must. In the supplements below for cats, feed a teaspoon of the Cat Powder Mix and a teaspoon of the Cat Oil Mix daily along with thirty to fifty IU of vitamin E.

Cat Powder Mix

1/2 cup nutritional yeast
1/4 cup bone meal
1/4 cup kelp powder (can use part alfalfa powder)

Cat Oil Mix

3/4 cup vegetable oil
1/4 cup cod liver oil
20-40 IU vitamin E (to prevent spoilage of above)

The Dog Powder and Dog Oil Mixes are given below. Since dogs vary so much in size, a feeding chart by weight is also given.

Dog Powder Mix

2 cups nutritional yeast
1-1/2 cups bone meal
1/2 cup kelp powder (can use part alfalfa powder)

Dog Oil Mix

1-3/4 cups vegetable oil (safflower oil is best)
1/4 cup cod liver oil
50-100 IU vitamin E (to prevent spoilage)

Daily Quantities for Dogs

Weight	Powder	Oil	Vitamin E
5-15 pounds	2 tsp.	1 tsp.	50 IU
15-30	4 tsp.	2 tsp.	100 IU
30-50	2 T.	1 T.	150 IU
50-80	3 T.	1-1/2 T.	200 IU
80-110	1/4 cup	2 T.	300 IU
110 +	1/3+ cup	2-1/2+ T.	400 IU[7]

Oils and powders are mixed separately in quantity and kept in closed jars, the oils in the refrigerator. Ingredients are easily available from health food stores. Avoid making large amounts of these in advance. If feeding supermarket pet foods, reduce the bone meal for larger dogs and omit it entirely for small ones; also use a little less cod liver oil.

Using one of the above supplement protocols with a preservative-free diet offers full nutrition and complete pet health. Using these supplements with a homemade natural diet, if it is carefully put together, is probably an even better way to create optimal dog or cat nutrition, and it is not difficult to do. A natural pet food diet made at home is based on raw meat, cooked whole grains, raw vegetables and fruits, with the same vitamins added as above. Most sources recommend that cats need sixty percent of the diet to be meat and fat (protein) while dogs require about forty percent of the diet to be meat. Pioneer holistic veterinarian Gloria Dodd, DVM, recommends about a sixty percent meat/protein diet for both dogs and cats. Pat McKay in *Reigning Cats and Dogs* (Oscar Publications, 1992) uses the following percentages of meat, veggies, and whole grains, plus the added supplements:

	Meat	Veggies	Grains
Kittens	70%	15%	15%
Cats	60%	20%	20%
Puppies	50%	25%	25%
Dogs	30%	35%	35%[8]

I feel that thirty percent protein is far too low for adult dogs, and prefer Gloria Dodd's recommendations of sixty percent.

Tiger Tribe, the holistic cat magazine, recommends for adult cats Pat McKay's percentages (60% meat, 20% veggies, 20% grain) but for older/aging cats recommends less meat. Their amounts for older felines are forty percent protein, thirty percent vegetables, and thirty percent grains.[9] High protein is considered a cause of kidney dis-ease in older dogs and cats, but this does not happen on a preservative-free or natural home-made diet. You will know that your cat or dog is receiving enough protein when her flesh feels firm to the touch, rather than soft and mushy under the skin.

Cat expert Anitra Frazier suggests the following as a model diet for cats; it can be a dietary model also for healthy dogs. She calls it "The Superfinicky Owner's I'll-Do-Anything-For-My-Cat Diet." If using this for dogs, use vitamin supplement protocols designated for dogs, rather than her cat formula.

60 percent protein: Use raw ground chuck, raw organic chicken, raw organic egg yolk; cooked egg white; tofu (only in small amounts); cooked chicken, turkey, lamb, or beef (no cooked poultry bones).

20 percent vegetable: Use finely grated raw zucchini or carrot; finely chopped alfalfa sprouts; lightly steamed broccoli, carrot, or corn; baked winter squash, Chinese broccoli in garlic sauce; a little yam or sweet potato.

20 percent grain: Use soaked oat bran, cooked barley, millet, oat flakes, brown rice, teff, quinoa, amaranth, sweet corn, or mashed potato.

Into each portion add: 1 teaspoon Vita-Mineral Mix, 1/4 teaspoon feline enzymes (for the first month only, then they're optional). Once a week give each cat: 1 capsule 400 units vitamin E . . . and 1 capsule vitamin A and D (10,000 units A and 400 units D).[10]

Raw meat is the central ingredient in optimal diets for both dogs and cats. Both animals are carnivores and require flesh-derived protein to live and thrive. Dogs can possibly survive on a careful (very careful) vegetarian diet plus supplements, but cats cannot. Without the amino acid taurine, found only in flesh-based protein, a cat will die in less than a year. Synthetic taurine supplements that claim to make cats vegans are available, but the jury is still out on their long-term safety and effectiveness. Dogs and cats need their natural diets of meat, grain, and vegetables, and a responsible pet guardian provides it. Even though that guardian herself may be a happy vegetarian, her pets require meat.

The meat used for animal food protein should be of human-consumption quality but the cheaper cuts are fine. Organic meat, from food animals that have not been fed hormones, steroids, pesticides, and antibiotics is best (for people, too), but it is more expensive and not so easy to find. The meat is generally fed raw because cooking inactivates the enzymes in it needed for digestion, as well as many vitamins. Besides, animals in the wild state ate their food this way. Use beef (but remember that many dogs and cats are allergic to it), lamb, chicken or turkey, but not pork. Egg yolks but not whites can be fed raw, but because of recent salmonella outbreaks, it is best to soft-cook all eggs. Feed some fish, cottage cheese, yogurt, and tofu. Do not feed other cow's milk products or tuna. Organ meats such as heart, liver, kidneys, or gizzards can be fed, but only once or twice a week.

Never feed dogs or cats pork; it is high in preservatives and carries a risk of trichinosis. When feeding chicken parts or eggs, cook them slightly to antidote the incidence of salmonella, which seems to be nationally on the increase. My dogs developed salmonella poisoning from raw egg yolks and were very sick for a week. For raw poultry, Pat McKay suggests marinating it for one hour in a tablespoon of three percent food-grade hydrogen peroxide, or four drops of grapefruit seed extract liquid concentrate, to six ounces of pure water. Pour this over the meat and mix it in well, or let chunks of meat soak in the refrigerator. This kills salmonella bacteria.[11] She also suggests that lazy, lethargic pets not be fed turkey, but that hyperactive animals could benefit from it because of turkey's natural amounts of the amino acid tryptophan.

Remember that beef, tuna, and milk products are high on Alfred Plechner's list of pet allergens—some animals will develop skin problems, hyperactivity, allergies, and even epilepsy or asthma from them. Cats get easily addicted to tuna, the oil of which robs their bodies of vitamin E and can result in a muscular dystrophy type of deficiency disease called steatitis. If you feed your cat tuna, limit it as much as possible, and supplement with vitamin E.

Chopped or grated raw vegetables are the second ingredient in a homemade pet food diet. Most animals will eat them chopped into small pieces, but my dogs take them from my hand faster than I can slice them. It may take a few days or a week of offering these before a pet will accept them—chop them small and mix them with the meat at least at first. Beans may cause pets gas, lettuce has little food value for people or pets, and the nightshade family (tomato, potato, peppers, eggplant) should probably be avoided. Otherwise use some of whatever you are steaming for your own dinner: broccoli, sprouts, carrots, cabbage, squash, sauerkraut, zucchini, asparagus, peas, etc. Never use canned veggies, and use frozen ones only when necessary. Use fresh, raw vegetables (and non-citrus fruits).

Whole cooked grains are the third basic pet food ingredient. These include barley, millet, oat bran or flakes, brown rice, teff, quinoa, cornmeal, amaranth, or spelt. Many pets and people are allergic to wheat. All grains must be cooked, as they would be for human consumption. White rice, which is not a whole grain, is almost valueless as a food. Wheat, if used, must be whole wheat. Breakfast cereals from supermarkets usually contain high amounts of sugar and chemical preservatives—avoid them. Cereals and cereal mixes from health food stores can be used, but dry flakes need to be soaked in water. Whole grain breads can be used occasionally. Brown rice is probably the best known of whole grains and is good to use, but avoid the five-minute varieties. Before the flour-refining process was perfected in 1910, heart dis-ease, high blood pressure, and cancer were rarities in people, and dogs' and cats' lifespans were doubled. Therefore, use whole, unrefined grains.

Meals can be made up in quantity and stored in portions in the refrigerator or freezer. Serve them at room temperature, neither hot nor cold. Again with the homemade diet, add one of the vitamin and mineral protocols suggested earlier in this chapter.

When a dog or cat that has been on supermarket glop all her life is suddenly faced with a new healthy diet, she may balk at the change. Cats particularly are creatures of habit, and dogs, too, may not recognize veggies as food. Try putting them on *your* plate first and let them watch! Remember that the pet food companies add lots of good tasting sugar and chemicals to get animals addicted to their brand. Such animals may have never seen real food. Start by introducing the new diet, finely chopped or grated, slowly. Make it a quarter of the meal first, mixed with the same old stuff. If the pet picks out all the meat pieces (my dogs did this at first) and puts them on the floor, still repeat the meal the next day.

Gradually increase the amounts of the new food and decrease the old until the dog or cat is fully on the preservative-free or homemade diet with supplements. Crush vitamin tablets and mix the powder with the food, and pierce capsules squirting the vitamins E and A on top. Some sources suggest a day or two fast for a healthy adult pet before introducing the new diet. Anitra Frazier insists that cats should not have food available to them between meals. This applies to dogs as well. Give them half an hour to eat and then take the bowls and remaining food away. My Siberian Huskies made me nuts with their fussy eating until I learned this years ago. If the food is available only for a short time, they are more likely to eat it rather than playing with it. If a pet refuses to eat but seems to be acting normally otherwise, allow her to fast if she chooses, but within a reasonable period of time. On a rich preservative-free diet, my dogs skip meals occasionally.

Delphia changed Penny's diet to a preservative-free one for the first time and wrote me of the results. Penny is an elderly poodle with heart dis-ease. She had been on the H/D special diet. Delphia was concerned about salt content in the new food.

> I changed her (and my other, younger dog's) food to Lick Your Chops Senior; the salt content difference between that and Science Diet H/D was negligible. What surprised me was how those two dogs pigged out for the first couple of days . . . they would even get up and eat in the middle of the night! They tapered off after the initial novelty of eating REAL food wore off. And like you said, they did detox a bit. But they're doing really well on it. I'm also feeding them bits of fresh vegetables and fruit, which they are beginning to like.[12]

A dog or cat that is receiving a diet high enough in protein for optimal health feels solid in flesh to the touch. Her body and muscles are hard rather than mushy-feeling, and the change becomes noticeable within a couple of months after beginning the new diet. After the first few days (it may take longer), the cat or dog may go through a cleansing process—usually some diarrhea and excess urination. Occasionally there may be mucus, runny eyes, body odor or bad breath, itching or even vomiting. This usually lasts only a few days; do not try to stop the process or prevent it; it will clear. After a month or so, the pet may shed her coat more heavily than usual. Once the new coat comes in, you will begin to see wonderful changes in the animal's health.

Pets on a full nutrition diet are lively, calm, and glowing. Skin diseases, dandruff, and digestive problems clear up, and chronic organ diseases lessen or can clear fully. Mucous, ear infections, body odors and gas, bad breath, tumors, asthma, and rashes may all disappear. Animals that have been hyperactive become calmer, behavior problems lessen or stop, and lethargic pets grow more active. Overweight animals lose weight; they are no longer seeking nutrition from empty food that does not provide it. Old animals act young again and age more gently. Arthritis eases with the detoxification process, and feline urinary tract infections (FUS) disappear. The cats and dogs on preservative-free and homemade diets plus supplements have full, shiny coats, firm flesh, experience less shedding and have better dispositions than before. They gradually grow healthy and they stay healthy.

Most of the information in the chapters that follow becomes unnecessary for cats and dogs fed a full-health natural foods diet. These animals seldom get sick or need healing because their bodies have the ability and wellness needed to be resistant to dis-ease. By increasing quality nutrition and eliminating sugar, starch, chemicals, allergy causing foods, and nutritionally inadequate and unclean foods, pets live a longer and happier time. Preservative-free feeding lessens or eliminates such chronic and debilitating dis-eases as kidney and liver dis-ease, arthritis, asthma, skin rashes and dandruff, diabetes, heart dis-ease, and even cancer. A cat or dog with any preexisting dis-ease benefits greatly from the dietary change.

I once met a cat that was thirty-four years old and had an offspring in the same house of thirty-two. As a child I knew a dog that had died at twenty-one and another that lived twenty-four years. Today's dogs die at nine or ten and cats at ten to fourteen years old. We have commercialized pet foods to thank for the cancer and other degenerative dis-eases killing our beloved animals. Preservative-free and homemade feeding with supplements are a large part of the answer for giving our dogs and cats longer, healthier, and more pain-free lives.

All of the remedy processes of this book are dependent upon a natural foods/preservative-free diet for the pet. Without it, healing in full is less likely to happen; with it the animal gains a quality of life she may never have had even before her illness. All healing begins with optimal nutrition—the place where the healing of dis-ease in pets and people always starts.

For more information on pet nutrition and homemade diets read: *Reigning Cats and Dogs* by Pat McKay (Oscar Publications, 1992); *The New Natural Cat* by Anitra Frazier (Plume Books, 1990); *Dr. Pitcairn's Complete Guide to Natural Health for Dogs and Cats* (Rodale Press, 1982; and *The Healthy Cat and Dog Cook Book* by Joan Harper (Pet Press, 1988).

[1]Pat Lazarus, *Keep Your Pet Healthy the Natural Way* (New Canaan, CT: Keats Publishing, 1983), p. 3; and Alfred J. Plechner, DVM, and Martin Zucker, *Pet Allergies: Remedies for an Epidemic* (Inglewood, CA: Very Healthy Enterprises, 1986), pp. 12-13.

[2]Alfred J. Plechner, DVM, and Martin Zucker, *Pet Allergies: Remedies for an Epidemic*, p. 20.

[3]Wendell O. Belfield, DVM, and Martin Zucker, *The Very Healthy Cat Book* (New York: McGraw-Hill and Co., 1983), p. 152; and *How to Have a Healthier Dog*, (New York: New American Library, 1981), pp. 156-160.

[4]Wendell O. Belfield, DVM, and Martin Zucker, *The Very Healthy Cat Book*, pp. 152-155. Figures are combined.

[5]Wendell O. Belfield, DVM, and Martin Zucker, *How to Have a Healthier Dog*, pp. 156-160.

[6]Anitra Frazier with Norma Eckroate, *The New Natural Cat: A Guide for Finicky Owners* (New York: Plume Books, 1990), p. 55.

[7]Richard H. Pitcairn, DVM, and Susan Hubble Pitcairn, *Dr. Pitcairn's Complete Guide to Natural Health for Dogs and Cats* (Emmaus, PA: Rodale Press, 1982), pp. 23-26.

[8]Pat McKay, *Reigning Cats and Dogs: Good Nutrition, Healthy Happy Animals* (S. Pasadena, CA: Oscar Publications, 1992), p. 126.

[9]Luke Granfield, "Cafe Feline," in *Tiger Tribe Magazine*, March-April, 1993, p. 30.

[10]Anitra Frazier with Norma Eckroate, *The New Natural Cat*, pp. 61-62.

[11]Pat McKay, *Reigning Cats and Dogs*, pp. 16-18.

[12]Delphia (Patty Keller), Personal Communication, May 13, 1993.

II - Naturopathy and Pets

Naturopathy includes all of the healing methods in both this book and *Natural Healing for Dogs and Cats*. Its philosophy is based on using natural means to support the pet or human body in gaining and maintaining the balance that is good health. "Natural" refers to remedies and processes found in nature; they are non-chemical and non-invasive, and therefore cause no side effects or toxicities. When you use a vitamin, herb, or food for healing, what happens is called the effects of that vitamin, herb or food, both welcome and unwelcome. In contrast, the veterinary/medical system calls the positive results of its methods effects and the negative results side effects; it often tries to deny that the side effects (which can be severe) are an effect of their drugs. Naturopathic methods use non-toxic foods and remedies found in nature that cause no side effects but have healing effects.

Healing happens in the dog's or cat's own body. No matter what remedies and methods the pet's guardian may use, veterinary or holistic, unless the animal chooses to heal and her body is strong enough to do so, no healing can take place. Often, offering remedies alone is not enough. Psychic communication is extremely helpful in convincing the cat or dog to heal something that's amiss, and also helpful in finding out why she has manifested the dis-ease to begin with. The role of naturopathy, and of all holistic healing, is to support the animal's self-healing. Naturopathic methods, unlike chemical/veterinary ones, do not interfere with the process. Standard medicine *attacks* dis-ease, but naturopathy instead *supports* the body in its return to wellness.

In naturopathic theory, dis-ease is the result of a negative living environment. A healthy life requires good nutrition, uninterrupted rest, enough exercise, fresh air and water, a clean place to live, and an emotionally safe and calm home with people who give the pet enough love and attention for her needs. A stressed or worried cat or dog will not be healthy, nor will an animal on an improper diet be healthy. Dis-ease and wellness both come from within, and a pet living in a healthy environment will not get sick.

Naturopathy sees dis-ease as the body's process of healing itself by releasing toxins to return the pet or person to balance. Its methods are both catabolic and anabolic, Catabolic means the breaking down of toxins in the pet's body with fasting, enemas, detoxifying herbs, and cleansing foods.

Anabolic methods boost the immune system and build vitality with good nutrition, vitamins, and specific strength-building herbs and foods.

Since most of the anabolic methods are treated in their own chapters—nutrition, vitamins and minerals, herbs, etc.—it is primarily catabolic methods that are discussed in this section. These include fasting and detoxification methods, and some healing foods. In all naturopathic/holistic healing, the preservative-free diet discussed in the last chapter is essential and is the place to start. This makes the pet or human healthy and keeps them healthy. The rest of the methods of this chapter and book are designed to support the healing of an animal that is ill and return her body to balance/wellness.

Fasting is considered primary in healing dis-ease, particularly viral and bacterial illness, fever, skin problems, and digestive disorders in cats and dogs. The theory is that when an animal or human is ill, the energy spent on the digestion process robs her of her healing ability and can worsen the dis-ease. A pet fighting an acute illness needs detoxifying to support her process (catabolic); anabolic healing is used to build her up once the crisis has passed. Without food for a few days, the pet's body detoxifies rapidly and releases the dis-ease quickly.

For healthy animals, pet herbal authority Juliette de Bairacli Levy recommends a twenty-four-hour full-day fast once a week for adult dogs and cats, and a half-day fast (last evening meal till the following noon) once a week for kittens and puppies over four months of age. She recommends a full-day fast once a month, in addition to the half-days weekly, for young animals, as well. Clean fresh water should be available at all times, and the animal encouraged to eat grass outdoors for further cleansing.[1]

When changing pets to a preservative-free diet for the first time, a couple of days fasting (one to three) may help overcome finicky eaters' distaste for something new in their diet. It also starts the detoxifying process from the chemicals and impurities of supermarket diets.

In using the weekly fast with healthy animals, follow these tips from Pat McKay's *Reigning Cats and Dogs*:

1. Fast only healthy mature (for full day) cats and dogs that are on the preservative-free or natural homemade diet.

2. Provide fresh air and exercise during the fast.

3. Discontinue vitamins and food supplements while the pet is not eating. (Liquid supplements may be continued.)

4. Give small amounts of fruit or vegetable juices (one or the other, not both) during the fast.

5. Other liquids that can be given are chicken, barley, or vegetable broths.

6. Aloe vera juice can be given to aid detoxification (see below, under foods).

7. A raw beef knucklebone helps to keep the dog or cat occupied.

8. Bathing during a fast helps the body to release toxins.

9. Expect loose stools and frequent, strong-smelling urine—they are releasing toxins from the animal's body.

10. Give lots of affection, especially at mealtimes.

11. Do not fast very young or old animals; pets with cancer, diabetes, or heart dis-ease; or pets on veterinary medications without expert supervision.

12. Be positive—your pet accepts your attitude about fasting and everything else.[2]

For animals that are ill, rapid detoxification can make the difference between survival and death. Juliette de Bairacli Levy makes fasting with laxatives or enemas the center of her treatment program for any fever-bearing dis-ease:

> Treatment must begin with a fast of at least two days on water or honey-water only. Two to three days is usually sufficient to cure a straightforward fever case. During fasting all the body powers released from food digestion are concentrated on elimination of internal toxins, and therefore chances of curing the ailments are made more favorable. Urgency of toxin elimination supplies the important reason for use of a daily laxative when fasting or on the fluid diet of goat milk and honey. During long fasts if there is no natural bowel action, a warm-water enema is given. Until the temperature is normal and steady at normal, fasting *must* be continued. To feed solid food during a fever means complication of the ailment and often also fatal results.[3]

Differentiate between cow's milk and goat's milk. Most pets are allergic to cow's milk and it should not be used. Raw unfiltered honey can be given straight or mixed with water during a fast, or the juice of fresh grapes, apples, or pomegranates. Use two teaspoonsful at mealtimes for a medium-sized dog, adjusting the amount for cats or larger dogs accordingly. Bairacli Levy also suggests a level teaspoonful of garlic juice (made by crushing the peeled cloves) and a teaspoonful of strong rosemary herb tea twice daily. Again, these amounts are for a medium-sized dog, adjust them for your dog's size.[4] This is the regimen she uses for all infectious dis-eases (fever dis-eases), including distemper. With this regimen she claims the complete cure of many dogs and cats that otherwise would have died. The animals heal without the nervous system damage that so often accompanies a veterinary/medical "cure" of infectious dis-eases.

To give an enema to a dog or cat, use an enema bag with a small bulb syringe or a Fleet enema bottle that is sized for a baby or child, depending on the size of the pet. Do not use the Fleet enema fluid itself, but empty the bottle and use your own fluid combination. For a large dog,

Juliette de Bairacli Levy suggests using a pint to a pint-and-a-half of warm water with a teaspoon of liquid witch hazel (or lemon juice or strong black tea liquid). For a cat, Anitra Frazier uses a half cup of spring water plus an eighth cup each of liquid chlorophyll and liquid acidophilus. She also suggests using lots of psychic communication during the entire process.[5]

Coat the syringe/applicator with vaseline and, placing the pet on her side, insert the applicator into her rectum. An extra person to help is invaluable here. Inject all of the fluid into the animal's lower bowel gently and slowly, stroking and scratching the pet's lower back and praising her all the way. When the bottle is empty, slowly slide the syringe from the rectum, but encourage the pet to remain still for as long as possible (one to three minutes). Then place the cat near her litter box or send the dog quickly outdoors. If there is no bowel evacuation, wait an hour or so and repeat the enema. The animal may be dehydrated. If in inserting the syringe you meet a hard mass of stool, try to angle the syringe into the rectum but do not force it. If the liquid will not pass into the rectum, take your pet to a veterinarian to remove the blockage.

The dog or cat must remain on the fast with enemas or natural laxatives (not mineral oil laxatives) until her fever is completely gone. A temperature of 101.5°F is about normal for both cats and dogs (puppies and kittens run a bit higher, about 102°). Dr. Wendy Thacher, DMV, notes that many cats and dogs, when they are truly healthy, have lower body temperatures, closer to 100°F. This is also why healthy animals repel fleas better. Most animals with a fever will normally refuse food during this time, even if it takes several days for the temperature to return to normal. A greedy appetite, however, is not an indication that the animal is ready for food. A fast that lasts for several days is healing rather than harmful. If the fever returns after ending the fast, begin it again. Juliette Levy suggests waiting four days at normal temperature before beginning to end the fast.

A fast must be ended gradually and slowly. Handing your dog or cat a full meal after a few days of fasting will make her very sick indeed. This is much less of an issue after a healthy animal has fasted for one day or half a day. Make sure that all foods fed at this time are natural and chemical-free, and work back to a normal daily diet very slowly, over several days. Richard Pitcairn, DMV, suggests that the transition period last two or three days for every seven days that the pet is fasted on liquids. (Most fasts will not last this long; seek expert advice for one that does.) Start with a day of clear soup, vegetable broth, or goat's milk with a small amount of yogurt or steamed vegetables.

After a day or so of that, add some cooked grain, oatmeal or barley, with honey and a small amount of chopped figs or prunes (laxative). The next day add cottage cheese, tofu, or some raw meat, and gradually for the next few days go back to the daily diet and vitamins.[6] Keep the meals small and frequent, and gradually increase the amounts. Fresh water, preferably distilled or spring water (non carbonated) should be available to the animal at all times during and after a fast, and every day thereafter.

Along with detoxification by fasting and enemas, naturopathy utilizes a number of foods and food supplements (plus vitamins and minerals) that have healing properties to draw upon in dis-ease or dis-ease prevention states. Many of these are known because of their benefit to humans. A few are discussed briefly below. Some of these are other people's favorites, and some of them are my own.

Aloe Vera is Pat McKay's favorite healing food, used externally as a gel and internally as aloe vera juice. Make sure that the product (from health food stores) is *pure* aloe vera (ninety-nine percent or more) preserved with citric acid or ascorbic acid/vitamin C. Watch for and avoid aloe preserved with sodium benzoate or benzoic acid, as this is poisonous to cats. She adds the juice or gel to every pet meal every day in the following amounts:

Kittens and small cats	1 tsp.
Cats, puppies, tiny dogs	2 tsp.
Large puppies and small dogs	1 T.
Dogs 20-40 pounds	2 T.
Dogs 40-60 pounds	3 T.
Dogs 60-80 pounds	4 T.
Dogs 80-100 pounds	6 T.
Dogs over 100 pounds	6 T.[7]

Aloe vera juice used internally is a bowel cleanser and detoxifier. It is the safest pet laxative for constipation, diarrhea, and internal cleansing during illness, fasts, or as a general preventive. It is also a detoxifier and healer for such dis-eases as arthritis, allergies, colitis and digestive disorders, hairballs, liver and kidney dis-ease, overweight or underweight, yeast infections, dental gum dis-ease, and any infectious dis-ease. She uses it for any skin or coat problems both internally and externally, including hot spots, lick granulomas, and ringworm. Pets with unhealthy coats of fur respond to internal aloe vera as well—change the diet to preservative-free or natural homemade with vitamins and minerals. Internally, use aloe vera juice with liquid chlorophyll (see more on chlorophyll below) for even better results.

For ear mites or infections, McKay mixes one teaspoonful of three percent food-grade hydrogen peroxide to two ounces of aloe vera juice in a spray bottle. She fills each ear full of the solution, massages the ear bases for a minute or two, then lets the cat or dog shake it off. This solution can also be used as an external antiseptic for wounds or bites, hot spots, and lick granulomas. For these dis-eases, also try two ounces of aloe vera juice or gel mixed with a teaspoonful of calendula tincture. Use externally. Note: Do not use aloe internally during the first month of a cat or dog pregnancy.[8]

Garlic is another miracle herb and one of my favorite healing foods. It is an herbal antibiotic that is anti-viral, anti-fungal, and anti-bacterial in the same ways that penicillin is. It lowers high blood pressure and blood sugar, reduces blood cholesterol levels, builds the immune system's ability to resist or throw off dis-ease, and heals infections and infectious dis-eases of all types. Garlic clears yeast overruns from the body; pets get these as well as humans, especially after courses of antibiotics. It is highly effective in healing and preventing urinary tract infections—feline urologic syndrome. Lung and respiratory dis-eases respond to garlic and it is useful as an internal flea repellent, in deworming, and as an intestinal cleaner and worm preventive.

Richard Pitcairn recommends garlic for overweight animals that have been on high protein diets and are arthritic or dysplastic. Use one-half to three cloves grated into food per day, depending on body weight.[9] To give raw garlic to cats that refuse it, Anitra Frazier suggests putting a few chips of the garlic clove into a small size gelatin capsule and giving it that way.[10] Many dogs and cats accept garlic readily from your hand.

Odorless garlic, Kyolic or other brands, may be used where garlic is needed as an antibiotic or for deworming, but it will not repel fleas, which seem to be repelled by the garlic odor. When using odorless garlic tablets or capsules, plan the dose by body weight, using a quarter of the human dose for cats, half the human adult dose for small dogs, three-quarters dose for medium-sized dogs, and the full adult dose for large dogs. This is a food, and actual overdose is unlikely. Look for a brand with as few extra ingredients as possible, and avoid using kitchen garlic salt or other cooking seasonings.[11] Crush the tablets or open the capsules and mix with food.

Apple Cider Vinegar is another of my favorites for both pets and people. A high-potassium electrolyte balancer, cider vinegar remineralizes the body and normalizes the blood's acid alkaline balance. It is anti-bacterial and anti-fungal and boosts the immune system. Cider vinegar, because it breaks down calcium deposits in the joints while remineralizing the bones, is helpful in arthritis and hip dysplasia. It is a remedy for food poisoning and digestive upsets, a digestive enzyme balancer (hydrochloric acid), a remedy for urinary tract and kidney infections, and it lowers high blood pressure. Use it after exhaustion or heatstroke (electrolyte balance) rather than salt. Apple cider vinegar is a detoxifier for obesity, excess mucous, allergies, skin and coat problems, and a remedy for infertility when litters are wanted but the female does not conceive after breedings. For a dog or cat on diuretics or heart medication, cider vinegar can often replace potassium supplements. Where digestive enzymes are needed, it may be enough for an enzyme-deficient dog or cat.

To use this wonder remedy, put a teaspoonful per pint of water in the cat's or dog's water bowl. It can be used every day as a mild tonic and detoxifier. A pet drinking it daily is less likely to have fleas or intestinal worms. A teaspoonful can be mixed with the animal's food daily, instead. It can also be used with a teaspoonful of raw honey. My dogs resisted the taste of it in their water at first, then grew to like it. Use it only in non-metal bowls.

Cider vinegar is cheap, easy to use and it really works. Make sure to use the golden apple cider vinegar rather than the white distilled vinegar. The unpasteurized type from health food stores is considered to be best. The research on this was done in the 1950s by a Vermont doctor, D.C. Jarvis, M.D., who observed its results first on cows, goats, chickens, and other farm animals. He began using it on people with great success, and its applications for cats and dogs are solidly positive. Read his book *Folk Medicine* (Fawcett Crest Books, 1958) for interesting information on this highly useful daily supplement that increases a pet's resistance to dis-ease and her ability to repair injuries. It also speeds her recovery from any illness.

Liquid Chlorophyll is another detoxifier and tonic at the same time, both catabolic and anabolic in action. It is an intestinal, internal and local antiseptic, and it inhibits bacterial growth. It is a blood cleanser/detoxifier and red blood cell builder, and a general energy tonic without hyperactive results. The chemical composition of chlorophyll is one molecule away from that of hemoglobin, the oxygen-carrying portion of the red blood cell. Instead of an iron molecule, chlorophyll's composition contains calcium. This is highly useful for animals and people with arthritis, hip dysplasia, bone dis-eases, or muscle cramping. Chlorophyll removes toxins from the bones, blood, tissues, and intestines, particularly heavy metals and lead. (Lead accumulation is a hazard of feeding a pet some commercial pet foods.) Chlorophyll is useful used internally and externally for a pet with body odor, abscesses, or skin sores. Use it internally for any digestive problems, constipation, or diarrhea, and any situation where detoxification is indicated.

One of liquid chlorophyll's most useful applications is in balancing blood sugar for hypoglycemic or diabetic dogs or cats. When using it with a pet on insulin, monitor blood sugar levels frequently. For *some* pets on controlled diets that do not require injection insulin, adding liquid chlorophyll *may* make other medications unnecessary. Again, monitor blood sugar levels carefully. The preservative-free or natural homemade diet with supplements is required here.

Use liquid chlorophyll or Green Magma rather than the powders. The liquid is more easily assimilated and unlike the hard-to-dissolve powders or spirulina, it has very little taste. Avoid spilling it, it stains. Chlorophyll is especially good to add to aloe vera juice. Taken together, they may be used daily as a general tonic for a weak, ill, or recovering dog or cat. Anitra Frazier adds it to her enema mix, and uses an eighth teaspoon three times daily for cats with diarrhea, irritable bowel syndrome, oily coat, skin problems, and FIP (feline infectious peritonitis). For general use, add it to food; for pets on a fast add it to liquids (herbal teas, broth, or water). For dogs use one to three teaspoonsful per day—more will do no harm. This is a whole food rather than a medication.

Honey and Bee Products, among the oldest of healing agents, are used frequently by Juliette de Bairacli Levy:

> A diet of goat's milk and honey only can sustain life for months in humans and animals. It has been well and long time proven that honey is also highly medicinal and will inhibit growth of harmful bacteria in the entire digestive tract and destroy those of a toxic nature.[12]

Raw unpasteurized honey from health food stores is high in potassium, copper, iron, calcium, magnesium, and other minerals, enzymes, protein, carbohydrates, and vitamin C. It is a strong anti-bacterial, a natural sedative, a laxative, immune builder, and energy-enhancing, predigested food. Bee pollen, royal jelly, honeycomb, and propolis contain the same properties but are more concentrated. Feed honey by the teaspoonful for sick cats or dogs on a fast; it may be fed alone or mixed with water, pure natural fruit juice, broth, or herb tea. For weak animals it can be used every day. For orphaned puppies or kittens use it in replacement milk formulas with goat's (not cow's) milk, and use it in the weaning process. For older pets, use it with apple cider vinegar—a teaspoonful of raw honey and a teaspoonful of cider vinegar to a pint of pure drinking water.

Honey used externally on burns prevents blistering and reduces tissue damage. Externally and internally, honey and bee products are pain relievers. Internally, honey and other bee products are a tonic for the nervous system and heart, and a healer of the lung and respiratory system. They are useful for infectious dis-eases, allergies, sinusitis, pleurisy, and pneumonia. Use them for abscesses and arthritis, constipation and digestive disorders, coughs, muscle cramp and twitching, fatigue, and recovery after illness, birthing, surgery, or hard exercise.

Bee pollen aids digestion and circulation, and boosts the immune system. It speeds healing, reduces allergy symptoms, slows aging, and increases resistance to dis-ease and stress. It helps in anemia, artery dis-ease, constipation, diarrhea, pregnancy and milk production. It reduces breast tumors and is a cancer preventive and a brain stimulant.

When using bee pollen, use the tablets or granules, feeding a quarter teaspoonful for cats and small dogs daily, a half teaspoonful for medium dogs, and a teaspoonful per day for large dogs. For tablets use a quarter the adult human dosage listed on the bottle for cats, half for medium dogs, and a full adult dose for large dogs.[13] Pollen powder can be sprinkled on food or dissolved in aloe vera juice; the tablets are soft and crumble easily. My dogs consider bee pollen tablets a treat and take them readily from my hand. All bee products taste wonderfully sweet. Start with small amounts and increase the dosage slowly. Keep bee products in the refrigerator for best potency.

Propolis is especially useful for dogs or cats with infections, inflammations, bruises, or abscesses. It is an immune builder. Raw honeycomb, which pets chew, is anti-allergic and useful for asthma, respiratory allergies, sinusitis, and allergic nasal discharge. It may be a preventive for respiratory infectious dis-eases. Royal jelly is high in anti-allergic vitamins B-5 and B-6 and helpful for pets with flea problems, liver and kidney dis-ease (this is a *digestible* sugar), pancreatitis, broken bones, and skin problems. Like other bee products, it is also an immune strengthener.

Kelp, a seaweed, is a natural iodine and mineral supplement in Anitra Frazier's Vita-Mineral Mix and Richard Pitcairn's daily Dog and Cat Powders. (See the previous chapter.) It is a way of returning what is depleted from the Earth (and Earth-grown plants and animals) back to pet and human bodies for more optimal health. The iodine in kelp is necessary for a properly functioning thyroid, good metabolism, and for a strong glandular system. It may be the answer for many pets now on synthetic thyroid medication, with bone problems, anemia, obesity, dry skin and hair loss, bad teeth or nails, or digestive problems. Iodine and minerals are required for the growth and development of healthy kittens and puppies, and for reproductive growth. Iodine deficiency may be a factor in breast cancer, which affects dogs and cats as well as women. Kelp is an aid to any detoxifying program.

D.C. Jarvis uses kelp to balance hypertension and relieve angina and heart pain, to aid bone healing after fractures, and to heal and prevent mineral deficiencies of all sorts.[14] It is the best possible trace mineral supplement; alfalfa is its nearest alternative but is not as good. Daniel B. Mowrey, in his index to *The Scientific Validation of Herbal Medicine* (Keats Publishing, 1986), gives a half page to the various uses of kelp. A few include healing of arthritis, pain, high blood pressure and heart disease, high cholesterol, constipation, kidney and bladder infections, reproductive organ dis-eases, cancer, heavy metal accumulation in the body and impure blood, infections, infertility, mastitis, skin dis-eases, senility, and respiratory dis-orders. Kelp is an anti-bacterial agent (but do not use liquid *iodine* externally as it burns tissues). It is an anti-cancer, antiarthritic, antibiotic, and antioxidant.[15]

Kelp supplies minerals to the body, minerals that are important in every aspect of dog and cat health and healing. Alfred Plechner's dietary research found the following benefits of feeding pets a daily trace mineral powder, which kelp is, over a six-month period:

1. Darker, thicker, shinier coats.

2. Less scratching.

3. Less skin flakiness.

4. Better maintenance of body weight with reduced caloric intake.

5. In aged cats and dogs, increased activity, weight gain, and better coat condition.

6. Animals with heavy flea and fly infestations appear less attractive to insect pests after three weeks of supplementation.

7. Better general health.[16]

He also lists benefits in controlling flea dermatitis and food allergies, pancreatic deficiencies, glandular-immune imbalances, and chronic hepatitis in dogs. In cats the same as above applies, plus improvements in animals with feline leukemia and FIP (feline infectious peritonitis).

Kelp is available in powder and in concentrated liquids: the tablets are not recommended for pets. Use the powder in the Vita-Mineral Mix or Dog/Cat Powder Mix. Use the liquid about one drop per day for a cat or small dog, two drops for medium to large dogs, and three drops for extra large dogs. (As a guideline, for my own thyroid deficiency I use six drops per day in water with chlorophyll and/or aloe vera juice.) Use the powder or liquid added to food in the daily diet. Kelp is very inexpensive and is available from any health food store or food co-op. Avoid kelp which is harvested from polluted U.S. coastal waters; Norwegian kelp is considered to be clean and safe.

Digestive Enzymes are important for the health of many dogs and cats. Some animals are genetically deficient in these enzymes. Also commercial pet food which is processed by high heat destroys the enzymes in the food. If changing a pet from a commercial diet to a preservative-free or natural homemade diet with supplements does not result in full health, enzyme supplements can be the answer. Sometimes short-term use is all that is needed. Anitra Frazier recommends that enzymes be added to a cat's food for a month while you switch over to a natural diet. Alfred Plechner in his dietary research for pets found that an inability to digest food properly was the source of allergy symptoms in about half the animals he treated.

Suspect enzyme deficiency in a dog or cat on a natural diet if there is weight loss despite a large appetite and the animal is passing a large amount of stool. Stool eating is considered to be a clear and classic deficiency symptom; the cat or dog is not digesting the food and the nutrients remain in the waste. So many pets are enzyme-deficient as to make this an important supplement for many companion animals.[17]

Dis-eases that may be an indication of digestive enzyme deficiency include any chronic allergy condition that does not resolve with a quality diet. Indications are coat and skin disorders, inability to gain weight, and even lameness from the pet's inability to assimilate minerals. Older pets may develop an enzyme deficiency as a result of aging.

Anitra Frazier in *The New Natural Cat* supplements cat diets with digestive enzyme supplements in the following additional dis-eases: when a cat (or dog) is stressed or ill; in cases of allergies, arthritis, feline infectious peritonitis (FIP), hyper- or hypothyroidism, hypoglycemia, liver or kidney dis-ease, coat or skin problems, anorexia, or malabsorption. Lameness and bone problems, constipation or diarrhea, urinary tract infections, scratching, and asthma are other indications.

You can purchase digestive enzymes for dogs and cats from the natural pet health catalogs, or you can use human-designed digestive enzyme tablets from health food stores. Dosage is a quarter to half teaspoonful of powdered enzymes per cup of food. Anitra Frazier recommends a quarter teaspoonful of feline enzyme powder per meal or half a health food store tablet for cats. Alfred Plechner recommends up to a teaspoonful of enzyme powder per cup of food in cases of malnutrition, poor appetite, aging pets, stool eating, and for animals with loss of condition due to antibiotic treatment. For very sensitive cats or dogs look for an enzyme supplement that is vegetarian (not based on beef or pork), and has no chemical preservatives. Such supplements are available from Very Healthy Enterprises, POB 4728, Inglewood, CA 90309, (310) 672-3269, and other sources. Results can appear within a week of use.

Shark Cartilage is something new and at this time still quite expensive on the market. For animals with cancer, tumors, psoriasis, or severe arthritis, however, it may be a virtual lifesaver. Research on this supplement has been based upon the fact that sharks do not develop cancer, despite polluted waters and the increasing incidence of tumors and cancer in other sea creatures that swim in the same areas. The supplement is useful for dogs and cats, as well as people, and is usually available in better-stocked health food stores.

Dosage is one capsule of Cartilade™ per eleven pounds of body weight, divided into two doses daily. It can be mixed with food, given as a pill, or mixed with water and squirted into the animal's mouth. Cats and dogs find it attractive because of its fishy taste. Results are usually seen in about six weeks but may take longer, and *Tiger Tribe Magazine* describes several cat cancer cures. Make sure the product is pure shark cartilage and not half something else. Cartilade™ may be ordered through Ocean Products at (800) 437-4148. Recommendations are beginning to appear about this supplement.[18]

Naturopathy as a healing system includes every method of holistic healing for dogs, cats, and people, and this chapter has presented only a brief overview. The dis-ease information listed under "naturopathy" in this book is limited primarily to diet, detoxification, and healing foods.

---

[1]Juliette de Bairacli Levy, *The Complete Herbal Book for the Dog and Cat* (London and Boston: Faber and Faber Co., 1991, original 1955), p. 46.

[2]Pat McKay, *Reigning Cats and Dogs*, pp. 158-159.

[3]Juliette de Bairacli Levy, *The Complete Herbal Handbook for the Dog and Cat*, pp. 139-140.

[4]*Ibid.*, p. 144.

[5]*Ibid*, pp. 138-139; and Anitra Frazier with Norma Eckroate, *The New Natural Cat*, pp. 231-234.

[6]Richard Pitcairn, DVM, and Susan Hubble Pitcairn, *Dr. Pitcairn's Complete Guide to Natural Health for Dogs and Cats*, p. 160.

[7]Pat McKay, *Reigning Cats and Dogs*, pp. 105-107.

[8]*Ibid*, pp. 103-108.

[9]Richard Pitcairn, DVM, and Susan Hubble Pitcairn, *Dr. Pitcairn's Complete Guide to Natural Healing for Dogs and Cats*, p. 65.

[10]Anitra Frazier with Norma Eckroate, *The New Natural Cat*, p. 255.

[11]Pat McKay, *Reigning Cats and Dogs*, pp. 109-110.

[12]Juliette de Bairacli Levy, *The Complete Herbal Handbook for the Dog and Cat*, p. 36.

[13]Pat McKay, *Reigning Cats and Dogs*, p. 111.

[14]D.C. Jarvis, *Folk Medicine: A New England Almanac of Natural Health Care from a Noted Vermont Country Doctor* (New York: Fawcett Crest Books, 1958), pp. 125-137.

[15]Daniel B. Mowrey, Ph.D., *The Scientific Validation of Herbal Medicine* (New Canaan, CT: Keats Publishing Co., 1986), p. 308.

[16]Alfred J. Plechner, DVM, and Martin Zucker, *Pet Allergies: Remedies for an Epidemic*, p. 44.

[17]*Ibid.*, pp. 6, 49, and 104.

[18]Luke Granfield, "Jaws, The Cure," in *Tiger Tribe Magazine*, March-April, 1993, pp. 11-12. This publication is highly recommended for all holistic pet guardians.

III - Vitamins, Minerals, and Pet Healing

The Earth is not as abundant now as it was a hundred years ago. Humans have abused, drained, and overpopulated the planet, drowned Her in chemicals and toxins, destroyed her forests and rangelands, and farmed Her eroded soils until there is almost nothing left. Today's food, grown on these soils, is less nutritious, more polluted, and far less tasty than food was in the past when it was grown on healthy land with organic, non-chemicalized methods. A drained or toxic soil makes devitalized and polluted food plants. These plants are eaten in turn by animals and people as their basic nutrients, and by the grazing animals that become the milk and meat foods for meat-eating people and animals. Devitalized soil = devitalized plants = devitalized animals and people. The poor health of the Earth is the poor health of us all.

Chemical fertilizers do not replace what is lost to bad soil management practices. Soil that is depleted of minerals and chemically fertilized produces plants that are unable to resist insects, fungi, weeds, and other pests. This results in agribusiness turning to chemical pesticides, herbicides, and antibiotics which are toxins. These become part of already deficient plant tissue and make the crops even more susceptible to dis-ease. The plants are eaten (often too long after harvesting) by meat and dairy animals and poultry, as well as people and pets. On this deficient and chemicalized diet, the meat animals' immune systems break down, resulting in the use of still more antibiotics and pesticides. Factory farmers want meat for the market quickly so more chemicals are added—hormones for growth and steroids to combat the overcrowded, unnaturally raised animals' stress reactions, plus vaccinations to prevent epidemics of dis-ease. At the slaughterhouse, the fear hormones produced by terrified creatures dying also becomes part of the meat. And then the additional chemicals of food processing begin—dyes, preservatives, flavorings, additives, bactericides, and high heat that destroys vitamins and enzymes.

Is it any wonder that people and pets in the richest country in the world are malnourished? Even on a natural diet, there is no escaping the losses to pollution, toxins, and planetary depletion. Plants are the basis of the mammal food chain and they require healthy soil, fresh air, and clean water to grow. These things are not available to us anymore, even with organic farming. Linus Pauling, two-time Nobel Prize winner and champion researcher of vitamin C, calls our condition "ordinary poor health." A preservative-free natural diet is essential and a key factor in upgrading the health of pets and people. But people and companion animals still get sick—because we are all subject to the depletions and toxins of the planet and because the best nutrition we can obtain is still no longer good enough.

Little research has been done on the subject of human nutrition; even less is known of what our dogs and cats (especially cats) really need. The amount of each vitamin and mineral required to prevent a deficiency dis-ease like scurvy or pellagra is known for both people and pets, but not how much of each is needed for optimal good health. For dogs and cats, much of the knowledge is only rudimentary despite the claims on pet food packages. The amount of each vitamin and mineral present or bio-available (usable by the animal) in pet food varies from product to product and almost from bag to bag or can. The containers for commercial pet foods may state the percentage of protein or fat or fiber in the product, but that percentage may not be usable to the dog or cat. Each cat, dog, or human is an individual, and individual needs for specific nutrients can also vary widely. Storage time destroys what may be in the bag or can when it leaves the factory as well.

Nutritional research, the stepchild of science in the modern western world, has defined a number of vitamins and minerals, enzymes, coenzymes, and vitamin-like factors found in food and in the mammal body. It is possible and likely that science, which gives little funding for such research, has not discovered them all. Most nutritional research today is done by the manufacturers of foods, pet foods, and food products (including chemical non-food additives). The research is directed at making products profitable, and testing can be made to show anything that corporate self-interest wants to show. The end result is megabusiness wealth and pets and people that are malnourished, living less than optimal lives, suffering "ordinary poor health," and dying early deaths from unnecessary dis-eases.

The FDA (Federal Food and Drug Administration) is the government agency responsible for guarding the safety and nutritional value of human food products. Instead of doing so, this agency has become the tool of big business and guards corporate interests. It accepts self-serving nutritional testing and claims of additive safety though the "science" is conducted by the corporations themselves. In the case of vitamin and mineral supplements, the FDA stance is that a "balanced diet" is all that is needed and supplements are "quackery" and a waste of money. This is the food industry's stance on the subject, and it is clearly untrue.

The FDA has established a list of vitamin, mineral, and nutrient guidelines called the RDAs (Recommended Dietary Allowances) that give amounts of each nutrient required to prevent deficiency dis-eases. They are not amounts that offer full health. The FDA insists that no more is needed. It wants to class supplements containing higher amounts as drugs, along with many nutrients not listed in the RDA. Yet sometimes optimal health requires hundreds of times the RDA of any given vitamin or mineral. Despite volumes of independent study, the FDA continues to disparage vitamins and persecute the health food industry, despite the growing epidemics of dis-ease and the declining lifespans.

In the case of vitamins, minerals, and nutritional supplements for pets, the situation is infinitely worse. Virtually no government-accepted study of cat or dog nutritional requirements has been done in the past thirty years. Most studies are made by the pet food companies, and while some of the findings are valid, most are not. The corporations want to produce dog and cat food as cheaply as possible and sell it for as much as it can get. A large portion of the cost of supermarket foods goes into advertising and packaging, not into the ingredients or even into research.

The Department of Agriculture is the governmental agency setting pet food standards. These standards are based on little real research or knowledge of pets' needs. No government agency polices the pet food industry on its advertising claims or on what nutrients (or lack of them) go into the foods. Unsupervised, the companies can do anything they please. The advertising claims that a dog or cat food is a "complete and balanced diet" are all too often untrue. The corporations tell us that table scraps (real food, if the family eats real food) are bad for our pets so they can sell more low quality, denutritionalized, overchemicalized products. We're told that "All you need to add is love," and few pet guardians think of looking further. Yet our dogs and cats are sick and dying of diseases that were unheard of when we fed them unprocessed table scraps made at home in the days before refined flour and white sugar.

By feeding a preservative-free or natural homemade diet, pet guardians do far better for our animals, but we still have the depleted state of the Earth Herself to deal with. No one diet for pets or people can overcome this obstacle. The suggested vitamins are sufficient only to prevent deficiency dis-eases. They will not work for every individual. For full wellness and optimal nutrition, supplementation is definitely necessary. For pets that are not in full good health, a vitamin or mineral deficiency is frequently the reason, and supplementation is the answer. Many of the modern epidemic dis-eases are simply vitamin or mineral deficiencies. When a cat or dog is sick or simply not doing well, vitamins and minerals can be the first step towards healing.

Vitamin C is a good place to begin. Because both cats' and dogs' bodies produce about forty milligrams of vitamin C per kilogram (2.2 pounds) of weight per day, pet food companies do not add it to the foods. Humans do not produce vitamin C in their bodies at all. Even the preservative-free pet foods and pet multivitamin supplements add very little.

Yet this small amount is only a fraction of the vitamin C needed for good health, and the amount an animal's body produces may not be enough to prevent even deficiency dis-eases. Pet vitamin researcher, Wendell Belfield, DVM, believes a number of pet dis-eases to be forms of sub-clinical scurvy, the vitamin C deficiency dis-ease. Some of these in dogs include hip dysplasia, lameness, arthritis, spinal myelopathy, ruptured discs, viral dis-eases, and skin problems. In cats, he attributes killer viral dis-eases including feline leukemia, FUS (feline urologic syndrome), fading kitten deaths, poor coats, and general ill health to sub-clinical scurvy due to lack of vitamin C.[1] I add cancer to the list. Too many of our pets are dying of these dis-eases or suffering because of them.

This vitamin is basic to all life processes and necessary for sound immune systems. It is the basis of collagen production, the substance that binds connective tissue together—muscles, ligaments, tendons, cartilage, and blood vessels—and holds minerals into the bones. "Without collagen, the body would become unglued and collapse. Scurvy."[2] Vitamin C regulates the pet (or human) body's biochemical balance and is the body's major detoxifier and repairer of the damages of stress. Toxins and stress are major reasons why we and our animals need more vitamin C than our bodies can produce, and why this was less true fifty or a hundred years ago.

We come back to the issue of a polluted, depleted, and high stress Earth. Stress drains vitamin C. Our pets, who are not living natural lives and who take on our emotions, are under stress constantly. The animal and human immune systems are continually under attack from unclean air, impure food and water, from chemical toxins everywhere, from vaccinations, lack of exercise and freedom, depleted food, and the fast pace of "civilized" living. Stress of any sort reduces the levels of vitamin C in the body, and with more and more stress, more of this vitamin is needed. Vitamin C is the primary detoxifier of heavy metal pollutants such as lead, cadmium, aluminum, mercury, and PCBs—all of which are present on the planet and are devastating to animal and human health.

What this all means is that we and our pets cannot produce enough vitamin C to combat the onslaught. Since foods don't contain it either, supplements are necessary. Vitamin C is available inexpensively in powdered form at health food stores. Use the sodium ascorbate form for pets, as it is less acidic and has almost no taste. Follow the guidelines of the nutrition chapter for using vitamin C daily as a health builder and dis-ease preventive. For animals that are sick and on a fast, put 500 mg powdered vitamin C with bioflavinoids (about an eighth teaspoonful of powdered C or crush a tablet) into honey water, herb tea, or broth and feed three times a day for cats or small dogs. Use higher amounts proportionately for larger dogs (as much as from three to eight grams). The secret here seems to be to use enough—to the point where the dog or cat develops diarrhea—then cut back slightly. This means going to bowel tolerance. The sicker the animal, the more C she will take before reaching this bowel tolerance level.

For acute viral infectious dis-eases, which can lead to life or death crises for dogs and cats, Belfield uses vitamin C intravenously in high amounts. He uses a half gram weight twice a day for several days. He feels that the high doses are essential.[3] Injectable C is available for horses at feed stores. There is no threat of overdose or toxicity with this vitamin, other than simple diarrhea at bowel tolerance. Contrary to rumor, vitamin C does not cause kidney stones. It dissolves them. For a dog with parvovirus, or a cat with feline leukemia or FUS, vitamin C can mean life instead of death.

For chronic dis-eases feed powdered vitamin C daily mixed with the pet's food, and go to bowel tolerance. This is highly useful for animals with arthritis, asthma, cancer, feline leukemia/feline AIDS, bone problems, anemia, gum or tooth dis-ease, digestive problems, skin dis-eases, recurring urinary infections, etc. For feline leukemia, supplementing with vitamin C to bowel tolerance can revert the dis-ease to test-negative status; feline leukemia may actually be a vitamin C deficiency dis-ease. Supplementation with vitamin C from weaning (or even earlier) totally prevents hip dysplasia in large breed puppies, and C greatly reduces debility and discomfort in dysplastic older dogs. Pediatric vitamin C drops (from a pharmacy) given to newborns prevents fading puppy or kitten deaths, and human crib deaths (SIDS). An animal supplemented from birth with vitamin C is less likely to develop either chronic dis-eases or acute ones. See the nutrition chapter for amounts to supplement with infant pets.

Vitamin E is the next miracle vitamin that dogs and cats need. Vitamin E is essential for healing dis-eases of the circulatory system and preventing them, including heart tachycardia and arteriosclerosis. It promotes fertility, slows aging, prevents cataracts, boosts the immune system, protects the body against pollutants and cancer, prevents or heals scarring, and heals the skin. Vitamin E prevents steatitis in cats and boosts muscle power and endurance in working dogs. It helps in dissolving tumors, especially in breasts, and in relieving posterior paralysis and disc problems in dogs. (See a chiropractor and acupuncturist for this.) Vitamin E oxygenates the blood and improves the function of all internal organs; its antioxidant abilities protect the lungs. In humans, vitamin E deficiency disorders include heart dis-ease, muscular dystrophy, brain and neurological problems, and reproductive failures.

Doses range from 100 IU per day for cats to 400 IU or more for larger dogs in healing dis-ease. I have used up to 800 IU per day on a forty-five-pound puppy for a period of three months with good results and no side effects; higher doses in this individual animal resulted in vomiting. Wendell Belfield used amounts of 1200 IU per day to cure cats of steatitis, a vitamin E deficiency dis-ease usually caused by deficient food or too much tuna (the oils in tuna drain vitamin E from the cat's body).[4] Because the liver stores this vitamin for only a short time, overdoses are unlikely; with pets that have heart dis-ease, however, start with a very low dosage and increase it slowly. Vitamin E is one of the vitamins to use that should be used daily as part of the optimal diet. For cats that eat fish or dogs with skin problems, it is a necessity.

Pat McKay warns that vitamin E alone is not enough for either full nutrition or healing, and that E alone (or any vitamin alone) is useless. Instead there needs to be a balance of all the vitamins, minerals, and nutrients as each is dependent upon the next in order to function. A deficiency of vitamin E, for example, may not be a deficiency of E itself but of the nutrients needed for its absorption in the pet's body. Full nutrition is the key here, with additional single vitamins added if the animal's state of health indicates it. She lists among vitamin E deficiency diseases the following: adrenal gland, pancreas, kidney, heart or liver disease; abnormal fatty deposits; and loss of collagen. The taking of synthetic hormones like cortisone or prednisone interferes with vitamin E absorption, as does chlorine and iron.[5] Dogs with mange may respond favorably to high amounts of vitamin E, plus zinc.

Vitamin A deficiency can be the cause of a number of skin, coat, and mucous membrane problems in cats and dogs. These include lung and respiratory tract, eye membrane, bladder lining, teeth and gums, digestive tract, the layers that comprise the skin and the glandular system. Like vitamins C and E, vitamin A is an antioxidant, a protector against pollutants and toxins from the environment including automobile exhaust, PCBs and nitrite food additives. It is also necessary for development and growth of puppies and kittens, and immune system protection from infections (bacteria, viruses, fungi).

Dry, itching skin is the first indication of vitamin A deficiency. Consider it for any skin or hair problem in dogs or cats. Other indications for cats include cataracts, retinal degeneration, pneumonia, convulsions, watery diarrhea, and hind limb weakness. In dogs, deficiency symptoms include nerve degeneration, reproductive failure, night blindness, incoordination, seizures, failure to gain weight, and deafness. Other symptoms for both dogs and cats are arthritis, diabetes, appetite loss, allergies, asthma, and respiratory infections. Like vitamins C and E, supermarket pet foods largely overlook this vitamin and even the preservative-free brands contain too little.

Wendell Belfield supplements a healthy twenty-five-pound dog with about 3,000 IU daily, and gives a dog this size with bad skin 10,000-20,000 IU per day. He gives cats 10,000 IU daily short-term to clear up skin and mucous membrane problems. Anitra Frazier recommends for healthy cats 10,000 IU vitamin A with 400 IU vitamin D once a week. Despite FDA insistence of toxicity, puppies have been given 10,000 IU of vitamin A *per kilogram (2.2 pounds) of body weight* daily for ten months without toxicity, and Wendell Belfield reports toxicity only after levels of 100,000 IU per kilogram. Cats can develop toxicities by feeding too much cod liver oil or fish oil in the daily diet, appearing as neck and forelimb involvement with pain.[6] The symptoms disappear after stopping the vitamin. Human vitamin expert Adele Davis reports using 200,000 units of vitamin A daily in adult people over a period of six months with no signs of toxicity. Toxicity in adults begins to appear only when 100,000-500,000 IU of vitamin A are taken daily for fifteen months or longer.[7]

Vitamin A capsules often come with **Vitamin D**, usually 10,000 IU of A to 400 IU of D. Pet requirements for this vitamin which is needed for strong bones and teeth are not known. Since vitamin D is produced by sunlight on the skin, the indoor cat or couch potato dog probably needs some supplementing. Lack of calcium and phosphorus are also indications of a need for vitamin D. This vitamin regulates the thyroid and nervous system, heart, skin respiration, and blood clotting. Rickets is the vitamin D deficiency dis-ease. Pat McKay indicates the following as deficiency symptoms in cats and dogs: allergies; kidney and urinary disorders; diarrhea; arthritis; poor metabolism; poorly developed bones, muscles, or teeth; and irritability.[8] Supplement your pets primarily with fish liver oils or with vitamin A, but use cautiously. Toxicities are possible, much more so than for vitamin A, and dosages for pets are not delineated by any dog or cat source.

Vitamin A capsules come with or without vitamin D, and when using high amounts of vitamin A, it is usually A alone. Anitra Frazier recommends 400 IU of vitamin D per week for healthy cats, contained in the 10,000 IU vitamin A capsule. For dogs with larger body weights and a higher incidence of bone dis-eases try 25,000 IU of vitamin A with 400-800 IU of vitamin D once or twice a week. The Dr. Pitcairn Dog/Cat Oil and Powder mixes provide enough of these vitamins for most animals. Give your pet the benefit of sunshine for at least fifteen minutes a day; the daily sunbath makes vitamin D on the animal's own body naturally.

The **B-Complex** vitamins, listed here as a group, are necessary for proper functioning of pet and human brain and nervous systems. B-vitamins are usually taken in the complex or group as each needs the others to work, and pet multivitamin supplements contain a balance of them.

The B-vitamins are particularly sensitive to depletion by heat, pet food processing, and storage deterioration. Thiamine (vitamin B-1) in particular loses fifty to sixty percent of potency during heat processing and can lose another half of the remainder in six months of storage—not an unusually long shelf life for commercial pet foods. Vitamin B-1, thiamine, and vitamin C are major deficiencies for pets on supermarket diets. Seizures, unsteadiness, uncoordinated movement, hyperactivity, vomiting, appetite loss, reduced learning ability, and flea or parasite overruns are symptoms of thiamine deficiency.[9] Cats need twice as much thiamine as dogs.

B-vitamins in general reduce pain and protect the body from stress. They are required for emotional and mental health (behavior problems can be B-complex deficiencies); energy; immune system and infection fighting ability; nervous system health; and the proper functioning of skin, hair, eyes, liver, muscles, and digestion. The B-vitamins are water soluble and cannot be overdosed, since excess is released through the urine. A cat or dog with cataracts, adrenal problems, allergies, skin disorders, blood vessel dis-ease, learning difficulties, anemia, runny eyes, slow weight gain or growth, erratic appetite, stool eating, or reproductive problems needs B-complex supplementation. Meat is fed raw in the natural diet primarily because when meat is cooked, B-vitamins and digestive enzymes are lost. These vitamins are supplemented in the pet multiple vitamin-mineral tablet and also in brewer's yeast. Be aware, however, that many pets are allergic to yeast. Alfred Plechner's theory is that the natural diet (raw meat, cooked *whole* grains, veggies, and fruits) or the preservative-free hypo-allergic diet will provide enough of these vitamins, and so he does not recommend yeast supplements. Remember, however, that not every dog or cat is yeast sensitive.

Even with a quality diet, pets still showing B-complex deficiency dis-eases heal nicely when they are provided with B-vitamins. Use a *low potency* human B-complex supplement and/or the individual B-vitamin in small amounts. If using niacin (B-3) use the flush-free niacinamide form or give only in the full B-complex. Many or most health food store B-vitamins are yeast, corn, sugar, and salt free. Do not give brewer's yeast to cats during FUS attacks; do give vitamins B-6 and B-9 (pyridoxine and folic acid) before breeding and during pregnancy to prevent birth defects. Use pantothenic acid (B-5) with vitamin C for animals with asthma or allergies.

Many pet daily vitamin supplements do not contain **minerals** and the level of minerals in commercial pet foods is dangerously low. Yet mineral deficiencies are probably the source of most pet allergy problems. They may also be the source of the "ordinary poor health" supermarket-fed animals and people suffer. The kelp and bone meal components of Dog and Cat Powder or Anitra Frazier's Vita-Mineral Mix address this need, and Alfred Plechner's choice of supplement here is trace mineral powder. All of these are available in health food stores. See the Nutrition chapter for the powder recipes and amount and Chapter II for information on kelp. Mix these with the animal's food on a daily basis. When a dog's or cat's health does not improve on preservative-free foods alone, trace mineral supplements can make the difference. Plechner prefers the "shotgun approach" of an all-mineral supplement to trying to find which of the many items an individual pet may need. Make sure multivitamin supplements contain minerals and consider adding a trace mineral compound like kelp to the daily diet.

Plants take minerals directly from the soil. Since our soil today is seriously depleted, the entire food chain is affected. Minerals are required for all growth and body function in cats, dogs, and people. The Earth can no longer provide them adequately in food alone. Bone is primarily composed of minerals, as are teeth. Tissue, skin, hair, and nails require adequate minerals, as does oxygen transport in the blood. The enzymes required for digestion and other biochemical functions in the body are formed by minerals' actions on vitamins.

Alfred Plechner's research puts heavy emphasis on mineral supplementation for dogs or cats in poor health or with allergy symptoms.

> In dogs I have found it helpful in controlling food allergies, flea allergy dermatitis, exocrine pancreatic deficiency, endocrine-immune imbalances, chronic active hepatitis and inhalant allergies.

> In cats it has helped for miliary dermatitis, food allergy, flea allergy dermatitis, chronic active hepatitis, leukemia and infectious peritonitis.

> I have had quite a few cases where vitamin supplements, special diets and standard medication weren't working satisfactorily until I added the trace minerals.[10]

There is more discussion on individual minerals and vitamins in my book, *Natural Healing for Dogs and Cats*. Like vitamins only an overview is given here. I strongly recommend reading Alfred Plechner's *Pet Allergies: Remedies for an Epidemic*, and Wendell Belfield's books, *How to Have a Healthier Dog* and *The Very Healthy Cat Book*.

One primary mineral, however, needs individual discussion. It is **zinc**. Zinc is necessary for all the functions of tissue repair and healing in the pet or human body, for the proper functioning of the immune system, and for the skin and coat. Vitamin absorption, especially of the B-vitamins, is dependent upon zinc. Zinc is needed in the production of enzymes and white blood cells and also helps to detoxify lead from the body. The mineral is a cancer preventive, as well, and many pets' skin "allergies" are actually zinc deficiencies. The mineral is a bactericide and is highly important for healing burns or after surgery or injury. Aging pets need additional amounts and Siberian Huskies and other northern breeds are more likely to be deficient than other breeds.

Signs of zinc deficiency in cats include emaciation, vomiting, conjunctivitis or corneal inflammation, debility, poor health, and retarded growth. Look for dry skin, poor coat and allergies, abscesses and sores, slow healing and dis-ease recovery, and prostate problems in older unneutered males. Dogs with skin parasites like mange mites or ringworm need extra zinc. Animals under stress require more of this mineral as do pets with any immune deficiency.

Zinc is now deficient in the soil on a worldwide basis. It is not supplemented in commercial pet diets. The supermarket generic brands are particularly lacking in zinc. Feed a natural diet with supplements and use additional small amounts of zinc if your pet displays any of the above deficiency indications. For my dogs, I use a human chewable zinc gluconate (10 mg) with vitamin C (30 mg) throat lozenge. They like the taste and take it from my hand. For cats 5 mg per day should do the job.

Many dog and some cat breeders supplement heavily with **calcium**, especially for breeding and lactating females and large breed puppies. They are urged by Wendell Belfield to use caution here, as it is vitamin C that prevents hip dysplasia and bone growth problems, and it is a shortage of vitamin D or excess of phosphorus that causes calcium deficiencies. Too much calcium can cause kidney failure and stones, but lactating females and pets on a high meat diet may still need additional amounts. The natural homemade or preservative-free diet with daily supplements should be enough except in the case of animals that are nursing litters.

Calcium absorption requires vitamin D. Two other minerals, phosphorus and magnesium, must also be in balance. An overbalance of meat in the diet creates an excess of phosphorus and unbalances the other two minerals. Calcium deficiencies in dogs and people result in osteoporosis, usually first seen in the jaw with gum erosion and tooth loss. Other signs are easily broken bones, convulsions, milk fever/eclampsia in nursing females, reproductive failures, and hemorrhages. In cats, calcium deficiency symptoms are nervousness, lameness, thin bones, and cats that lie in dark corners and refuse handling. When supplementing, use 500 mg of a calcium/magnesium balanced supplement to every hundred grams of meat fed.[11] Extra phosphorus is not required.

This is only the briefest overview of vitamins and minerals for pet healing. The basic protocol again is feeding an optimal preservative-free or natural homemade diet with daily multivitamin and mineral supplements. This protocol goes a long way toward bringing a dog or cat to full health and a minimum of dis-eases that need additional treatment. When a cat or dog is ill, however, additional amounts of a key vitamin or mineral can make a great difference. Zinc speeds healing and recovery and vitamin C is virtually a lifesaving, all-round healer.

The use of vitamins as dis-ease healing agents was discovered and promoted by vitamin C expert, Linus Pauling, who named the practice orthomolecular medicine. He and other researchers found vitamin-mineral treatment made the difference between life and death in a great number of chronic and acute dis-eases. Large doses of vitamin C are the key for healing infectious dis-eases in dogs, cats, and people. In pets these are such killers as parvovirus, feline and canine distemper, feline leukemia/feline AIDS, canine infectious hepatitis, and pneumonia. It is also at least part of the answer for such dis-eases as arthritis, FUS, FIP, allergies, heart dis-ease, and cancer. Vitamin E is the heart and artery healing vitamin, and vitamin A is for the lungs, skin, and digestive tract. Trace mineral powders or kelp can make the difference between continual miserable scratching and skin rashes, and full glowing pet wellness.

On a depleted planet no one has full health. It is up to people to replace for our cats and dogs what they can no longer obtain for themselves. This replacement is required for humans, too. The best natural diet is not enough without supplements. Vitamins and minerals for healing begin with the daily diet and continue to orthomolecular healing in times of dis-ease. These are our greatest tools for health on an Earth that needs healing.

---

[1]Wendell O. Belfield, DVM, and Martin Zucker, *How to Have a Healthier Dog*, pp. 48-51; and *The Very Healthy Cat Book*, pp. 38-39.

[2]Wendell O. Belfield, DVM, and Martin Zucker, *How to Have a Healthier Dog*, p. 54

[3]*Ibid.*, pp. 237-238.

[4]Wendell O. Belfield, DVM, and Martin Zucker, *How to Have a Healthier Dog*, pp. 81-88; and *The Very Healthy Cat Book*, pp. 72-76.

[5]Pat McKay, *Reigning Cats and Dogs*, pp. 76-80.

[6]Wendell O. Belfield, DVM, and Martin Zucker, *How To Have a Healthier Dog*, pp. 67-69; and *The Very Healthy Cat Book*, pp. 58-60.

[7]Adele Davis, *Let's Get Well* (New York: New American Library, 1965), pp. 123 and 313.

[8]Pat McKay, *Reigning Cats and Dogs*, pp. 79-80.

[9]Wendell O. Belfield, DVM, and Martin Zucker, *How to Have a Healthier Dog*, pp. 70-72; and *The Very Healthy Cat Book*, p. 63.

[10]Alfred J. Plechner, DVM, and Martin Zucker, *Pet Allergies: Remedies for an Epidemic*, p. 44.

[11]Wendell O. Belfield and Martin Zucker, *The Very Healthy Cat Book*, pp. 77-78; and *How to Have a Healthier Dog*, pp. 88-90.

IV - Healing Pets with Herbs

Plants were the first healing remedies. Dogs and cats in the wild knew what they needed and would travel long distances to find the right growing green. Today's confined pets have far less choice but still seek out plants—crabgrass for digestive cleansing and plaintain for pain, as well as other herbs for their iron and nutrient qualities. Plants contain nutrients that cats and dogs need. Animals making a kill in the wild or domestically go first to the semi-digested plant contents in the stomachs of their prey. Vitamins and minerals that a dog or cat needs more of can be found in the pet's choice of edible greens. The same weeds that humans so vigorously pull up and poison from their lawns contain medicinal properties that can save pet and human lives, or make those lives more free of dis-ease and pain.

Greens have healing properties on the mammal body. Wild animals came to know this by instinct, intelligence, and their vastly superior sense of smell. People watched animals choose these plants and tried them. They began to learn how to use the herbs for healing. People learned to dry and preserve these herbs. In the winter when the plants were gone or when the tribe moved to different territories, the preserved herbs were still available. Over the course of millennia an herbal healing tradition developed. People knew what plants were useful for what dis-ease and how best to take them. They learned to treat themselves, their families, and their farm and domestic animals. Though the range of medicinal plants changed from location to location and country to country, there were plants in every place to treat and heal every dis-ease. Each tribe or family group had at least one midwife/medicine woman who dedicated her lifetime to learning the ways of healing plants. These women were the first doctors and veterinarians.

As time passed, animals were domesticated and confined, and people grew less mobile and less connected to the ways of the Earth. With the beginnings of cities, people moved away from Earth awareness and rejected it as "uncivilized." What was then provided by the new male medical system, however toxic and without merit, was preferred to the old country ways of "witches and dirty midwives." The witches and herb women were put to death in the Inquisition, were prevented from practicing, or were simply degraded and discredited. Many died. The chain of oral teaching was disrupted; much knowledge of healing plants was lost. People and pets suffered greatly from the restriction of knowledge.

Traditional healing herbs became the basis for first the pharmacologic and then the synthetic drug industries. What science determined to be the "active ingredient" of a plant was isolated and concentrated, then made into a synthetic copy. Now a drug, this substance was separated from its full plant properties and may become unnaturally strong. Others developed negative side effects because the "non-active" constituents that prevented these effects were removed. Whole plants used for healing have *effects*. Plants that had negative effects were dropped early from medicinal use. This has not been the case with synthetic copies of active plant compounds, where the side effects can be worse than the dis-ease, causing real harm. Safe plants became less safe drugs. Digitalis and digoxin were derived from the foxglove plant; aspirin and Tylenol from white willow bark; Premarin from natural wild yam estrogen; and cortisone and prednisone from licorice root and yucca.

Modern medicine dropped the use of whole safe plants for a number of reasons. First, the early male medical system refused to learn from "dirty midwives" or use their methods. This was male chauvinism and misogyny, because the women healers and midwives knew a great deal, more than men did, about sanitation and medicine. With the Inquisition the information died out or went underground and was no longer available to male (or women's) medicine. Though herbal healing is still used worldwide and though there has been a great renaissance of herbal knowledge even in the technical West, the corporate profit motive has caused medicine to continue to spurn herbal healing.

In today's over-legalized and over-greedy world, plants are used for healing only by a small number of knowledgeable people; the value of these plants has been denied by the medical/veterinary system. The medical system in the modern West is run by insurance companies and the pharmaceutical drug industry. In patent law, an item found in nature cannot be patented or held exclusive to the sales of one founding company. Herbs are wild or cultivated whole plants and therefore do not come under patent exclusivity rights. A company that owns a patent on a drug can market it for very high prices. A plant cannot be patented and is therefore not sufficiently profitable.

To be able to market a drug in the United States (other countries have similar systems), the drug must be tested by rigorous hard science protocols over a period of years and approved by the FDA—all at great expense. No drug company will submit to this long drawn out and highly expensive process for an item that they cannot patent and hold exclusive rights on. Therefore it is only synthesized products, life-based or not, that go through the testing process and become certified as medicines in the West. These synthesized drugs, even if plant-derived, usually bear little resemblance to the action of the original plants by the time they are marketed. There are side effects and toxicities to these drugs that were never part of the plant or herbal, and only a fraction of the herb's original effectiveness is available.

Despite the pervasiveness and hard-sell tactics of the drug industry and despite medicine's total rejection of herbal healing, plants still contain healing powers that are effective and without negative side effects. Even though few people recognize the useful wild plants and city people have little access to unpolluted herbs growing in the wild, herbal healing is returning to people's awareness and use. The heavy side effects of medical drugs have sent more and more people looking for alternatives for themselves and their pets. The herbal alternative is still viable and safe.

An increasing number of organic sources grow and market healing herbs, and increasing numbers of health food stores and food cooperatives make them easily available and at a cheap price. More books are being written that teach how to use herbs for healing, though the FDA bans any information placed on herb packaging. While the FDA, the AMA, and the pharmaceutical industry would prefer that people know nothing about safe healing with plants, the information is there and herbs are increasingly popular. Plants and herbs are among our most important healing alternatives.

Herbal healing works today for pets and people, just as it always has. Herbs are safe choices that can prevent the need for toxic, expensive chemical drugs and veterinary visits. Why destroy the dog's immune system with cortisone shots when a six dollar bottle of licorice root or yucca extract does the job of adrenal balancing safely? Why use antibiotics that may cause yeast infections or may not work at all when herbs like goldenseal, echinacea, eyebright, or garlic can be used instead? Why let an animal with bruised tissue or broken bones suffer for weeks when comfrey can speed healing by twenty to forty percent and prevent bone non-unions? Why use barbiturates for pain when there are a number of safe herbal alternatives like valerian, scullcap, and St. John's wort?

For almost any medical drug or pet dis-ease (or human dis-ease) there is an effective herbal alternative. There may be times when the speedy action of medical drugs is necessary, but when there is no emergency, herbs may replace these drugs. Early use of herbal healing keeps small dis-eases small and heals them fast. They do not progress to the point where the more potent and rapid acting chemical drug intervention is needed. In many chronic cases herbs can replace daily medications totally. Herbs support the cat's and dog's body in their healing process as drugs do not. They help the pet's own body regain good health rather than just attacking the dis-ease symptoms and often the pet with it.

Herbs are very cheap and are available in several forms. The closest to nature is the fresh plant, which is usually dried and made into a tea. Newly picked fresh plant leaves are used for a number of remedies, mostly external poultices. Fresh crushed plantain or chickweed leaves can be used externally over sores, insect bites, rashes, or wounds for soothing and rapid healing. The gel inside a fresh-picked leaf of aloe vera is nature's best burn ointment. Both herbs can be eaten raw, and pets who need them will do so. Fresh dandelion or parsley leaves are good detoxifiers as well as diuretics and liver cleansers. Dogs and cats like to eat growing wheatgrass and crabgrass; they are nutrients and detoxifiers. When fresh undried plant material is used for a tea, three times the specified dried tea amount must be used because of the high water content of the fresh plant. Fresh herbs must also be used immediately after picking.

Most herbal preparations begin with dried herbs. The fresh plant leaves, stems, flowers, or roots are picked in the morning after the dew evaporates. They are dried in a dark, cool place. They must be turned frequently to allow the air to reach every part of the plant. This prevents mold. The stems can be tied together in bundles and hung with the plant heads or flowers down for drying. Different plants are picked at different times in the growing season. Dandelion leaves are best before the plant has flowered (early spring), while yarrow is picked in full flower (July) before the heads begin to seed. Blue violet is picked in flower also, and the leaves, stems, and flowers are used.

Never strip a plant bare of all its leaves or blooms, but pick only one leaf or flower in five. When pulling up whole plants for their roots take only a few plants from each clump and leave the rest to grow and multiply. Some healing plants like goldenseal are becoming rare from overpicking, so don't be greedy. I like to pick healing herbs during the waxing moon (New to Full phases) for flowers, stems, fruit, bark, or leaves; I pick root herbs in the waning quarters (Full to New Moon). A good herbal field guide can tell you when to harvest a particular plant. Before picking, ask permission of the nature devas of each species and return something in thanks for what you take. A bit of corn meal or chemical-free tobacco makes a good gift. Do not pick plants that grow up to fifty feet from a roadway; they will be polluted by lead and carbon monoxide from auto exhaust and probably are sprayed with pesticides. Pick only healthy-looking plant specimens.

Dried herbs can be crumbled and placed into jars or brown paper bags, labeled, and stored in a dark place. They will keep their potency for healing for about a year this way. The dark-colored glass jars that keep out light are best. Use the herbs directly from the bag or jar to make herb teas, decoctions, and infusions. They can be pulverized very fine with a mortar and pestle and put into gelatin capsules. Kept in an airtight dark jar in a dark place, these will remain potent for about two years. To keep herbs permanently potent they must be made into alcohol tinctures (extracts) and stored in brown glass bottles. For healing purposes, use only herbs that retain a green smell and fresh color. Those contaminated by mold must be thrown away, as well as herbs that are grey and lifeless and have no plant fragrance.

For use with dogs and cats, fresh plants may be cut small and mixed with food. Animals used to veggies in their bowl accept them readily. Herbal teas, decoctions, and infusions are used by the teaspoonful and can be given by placing them in an eyedropper or small squeeze bottle. Place the liquid in the animal's cheek pouch by pulling out the pet's lip and dripping the liquid in. Never squirt liquids down the pet's throat as she could choke on it. Some cats and dogs will lap up herbal teas freely. They can also be placed in food.

For standard tea infusions use an average of two level tablespoons of the liquid for a medium-sized dog (cocker spaniel size, about twenty-five to thirty pounds), twice or three times a day. Increase and decrease amounts by body weight; a cat would receive one to two teaspoonsful per dose. Unless you are mixing herbs with food, do not give pets herbs at meals. The exact dosage is not critical, because herbs are safe when used with common sense. For a strong infusion (described below) use about half the liquid amount of a standard infusion.[1]

When using alcohol tinctures, the dose is much smaller; so in my opinion, the tinctures are the ideal way to use herbs for healing. For cats use only two drops three times daily, and for dogs the dosage is two to six drops according to body weight. (I use five or six drops when dosing my fifty-five and sixty-five pound Siberian Huskies.) Place the drops from the eyedropper into the cheek pouch or directly onto the pet's tongue (don't squirt down the throat). Tinctures can also be diluted in a bit of water to take away the bad taste. Hot water evaporates the alcohol content. Drops can also be placed in food, on a dog biscuit, or in a bit of honey or honey and water. Gelatin capsules are sometimes necessary to get an herb with a nasty taste into the pet (cayenne, goldenseal) or to take herbs into the digestive system (garlic and wormwood deworming preparations). In general, however, capsules are not ideal because dogs and cats are carnivores and their bodies have a harder time dissolving the gelatin (cellulose) of the capsules.

Herbs can be used when the animal is on a fast for any fever, infectious dis-ease, or short-term detox situation. They can also be used when a pet is eating normally. Herbs are used both short term and long term— for acute dis-eases that come suddenly and stop in a few days as well as for long-term chronic situations like diabetes (yarrow) or heart dis-ease (hawthorn). In acute situations, make sure that the pet is completely healed before stopping herbal treatment, as symptoms can disappear before the dis-ease is really gone and can return if treatment stops too soon. This is particularly so for viral infectious and respiratory dis-eases. Continue herbal healing for at least several days after symptoms disappear, then decrease slowly before stopping. If symptoms return, start treating again.

In chronic situations, stopping the herbs can have negative effects on the pet's health. For diabetic animals, for example, monitor blood sugar levels carefully both when starting herbs, and if the herbs are stopped. Also monitor frequently during use. The herbs regulate blood sugar levels and if they are working, they are needed. It is best to continue them as they decrease the animal's need for insulin or may even replace insulin completely. This is also true of pets with heart troubles on hawthorn. If in doubt, let a holistic veterinarian guide you.

To make a **standard infusion** herb tea or tissane, start with dried plant matter, using about two heaping tablespoons of herb to a pint (two cups) of cold water. Use filtered, spring, or distilled water if possible. Bring the water to a boil in a stainless steel, glass, or enameled pot (never aluminum) and pour it over the dried herbs which have been placed in a tea strainer or tea basket in a glass or ceramic container. Let the herbs steep in the hot water for ten to fifteen minutes, then lift the strainer from the liquid. The tea can be steeped in a teapot—put the herbs in the pot and pour the boiling water over them. Strain before using by pouring through the tea strainer.

When using plant roots, bark, or hard woody stems, the process is slightly different and is called a *decoction*. In this case, place both herbs and water in the pot on the stove burner. Bring the mix to a boil and allow to boil for about two minutes. Shut the flame and let the pot sit to cool. Then strain and use. Leftover infusions or decoctions, once strained, can be kept in the refrigerator overnight. If the liquid develops a sour odor or a scum on the top, discard it. Always dose the dog or cat with infusions or decoctions at room temperature.

Juliette de Bairacli Levy, the noted pet herbalist, makes her standard infusions somewhat differently, in the European style. Using the same two heaping tablespoonsful of dried herb to a pint of water, she steeps them longer to make a stronger brew. Place the herbs in the water and simmer them until near the boiling point (do not boil). Then take the pot from the heat and allow to steep in the pot for four hours. Without straining, pour the infusion into a covered jar, where it will keep fresh for two or three days. Use at the dosages given above. This is stronger than the first tea infusion (American) example, and need not be refrigerated.

For the herbs designated as a **strong infusion**, bring the pot containing herbs and water to a boil and allow to boil for no longer than three minutes. Take the pot from the flame and steep overnight or for at least seven hours, keeping a tight cover on the pot at all times. After steeping, transfer without straining to a covered jar, and again the mixture will keep for two or three days before spoiling.[2] This is much stronger than the standard infusion; give half the amount.

Herb tinctures or extracts take six to eight weeks to prepare and must be bought or made in advance. One ounce bottles of herb tincture cost about six to ten dollars and last a very long time. I keep a medicine chest of these—unlike dried herbs or capsules, they never spoil or lose potency—and make some of my own at home. If the FDA threatens to take an herb you use off the market, buy up the health food store supplies and put it up into tinctures. I have done this recently with chaparral and comfrey. This is also a good way to preserve quantities of field-picked plants—dried herbs last for only a year otherwise. The tinctures are simple to make but require some outlay of money for supplies; the expensive ingredient is the alcohol preservative.

Take four ounces of fresh or dried herb and place it in a pint-sized brown glass bottle with a screw-on cap. These bottles are available from pharmacies, but it may take some coaxing to obtain them; they have cost me anywhere from twenty cents to a dollar each. Also try prune juice bottles from the supermarket. Make sure they are glass, not plastic. Use a funnel to get the crushed herb into the bottle. Then fill the bottle to the very top with *food-grade* alcohol sixty proof or higher. Brandy tastes better than vodka for this and is cheaper. Place the cap on the bottle and label the contents, including the date filled and the finish date six to eight weeks away. I like to start my tinctures on New Moons and finish/ decant them on the second Full Moon following. Put the bottles in a dark cupboard and shake them twice a day until finished.

On the finish date, open the bottles and pour the liquid (now the herb tincture) through a fine mesh strainer and into other brown bottles. I use pint bottles for this, filling a one-ounce dropper bottle from them for easy use. Dropper bottles, brown glass only and with glass eyedroppers if possible, are also available from pharmacies for under a dollar each. Dose from the eyedropper bottle. If the animal's mouth touches the dropper in dosing, rinse it in running tap water before replacing it in the bottle. When decanting the tinctures make sure to thoroughly squeeze out the plant matter before discarding it. Then return the used herbs to the Earth.

Tinctures are my preferred way to use herbs for healing. They are easiest to get into the pet, retain potency, require little storage space, and are highly effective. In most places, herb tinctures are easily available and there is no concern about how long they have sat on a store shelf. Tinctures can also be made with cider vinegar but these keep only for a year or two. Some extracts are now being made with vegetable glycerin. Although these taste good, they have a limited potency life. Alcohol tinctures are tried and true, and they work. To remove the alcohol (so small an amount when only dosing two to six drops) put the drops into a tea-spoonful of hot water and the alcohol evaporates, leaving only the herb. Alcohol tinctures may taste bad, but they go down fast. I dare children and pets to "show me the worst face they can make" as the drops go down!

One further way to prepare herbs for pet internal use is to make them into **homeopathic elixirs**. For more on homeopathy and why the following method works, see the next chapter. This method is preferred by holistic veterinarian Richard Pitcairn and by cat expert Anitra Frazier. The following method is from Anitra Frazier's *The New Natural Cat* (Plume Books, 1990).

1. Into a new one-ounce glass dropper bottle put 2/3 bottle full of distilled or spring water and 3 drops of herbal tincture.
2. Cover and shake vigorously 108 times, hitting bottle against a thick rug or padded arm of a chair each time.
3. Shake 12 times before each use.
4. Dosage is 1/4 dropperful 20 minutes before meals.
5. Keeps in refrigerator 7 days.[3]

She suggests that when herbs are used for nutrition (kelp, alfalfa, yarrow, etc.) use the herb tincture; when they are used for healing a disease or condition, use the elixir. Elixirs are used like homeopathic remedies, rather than like herbs. As soon as *any* change in the animal's condition is noted, stop the treatment temporarily. Usually there is an improvement, but occasionally the pet seems to get worse, then improves again. When the improvement seems to stop, give another dose and continue twice a day. If the pet improves, the usual reaction, continue twice a day until a plateau is reached, that is, the pet does not seem to get better or worse. Then make a 1:100 dilution of the first elixir and repeat.[4]

If the elixir is made with half brandy or vodka and half spring water, instead of all spring water, it will keep indefinitely without refrigeration. Keep it in a dark glass bottle in a dark place. If you use hot water to evaporate the alcohol in an elixir, you will also destroy the healing potency of the remedy.

For external use, herbs are made into compresses, poultices, salves, and oils. A compress is a washcloth dipped in warm herb tea and placed on the skin. The compress should be as warm as is comfortable for the cat or dog. A poultice is the herb infusion tea dregs, the warmed plant matter, wrapped into a gauze packet and placed on the skin. Both poultices and compresses are usually bound in place and changed frequently, as soon as they cool. Salves and oils are made with dried herbs in beeswax or vegetable oil. For pets, the oils are usually ear oils. See my books

Natural Healing for Dogs and Cats, All Women Are Healers, or *The Natural Remedy Book for Women* (all from The Crossing Press) for recipes.

Some of the properties of a few key herbs are listed below. These are not the only herbs for pet healing, of course, but they are representative of the scope of herbal healing for people and pets. They are listed in the briefest ways. Note that when using herbs for healing cats, aspirin precursor herbs, white willow and white oak barks, are not to be used.

Commonly Used Herbs[5]

Alfalfa: Many vitamins and minerals, alkalinizing, kidneys, appetite, digestion, arthritis.

Barberry Bark: Tonic, constipation, digestion, antiseptic, liver, general debility.

Bayberry Bark: Tonic, stimulant, astringent, generates body heat, cold feet, hands, etc.

Bee Pollen: Survival food, endurance, strength and stamina, total food, all enzymes.

Black Cohosh: Female estrogen, menstrual cramps, poisonous bites, relieves birth pain.

Black Walnut: Astringent, alternative, tonic, skin diseases, sores, herpes, eczema, worms.

Blessed Thistle: Tonic, diaphoretic, female problems, blood to brain, heart and lungs.

Blue Cohosh: Diuretic, antispasmodic, regulates menstruation, rheumatic affections, spasms.

Buckthorn: Tonic, laxative, cathartic, bowels, skin diseases, rheumatism, gout.

Burdock Root: Alterative, diuretic. One of the finest blood purifiers in the herbal kingdom.

Cactus: Cereus Schotti, Senita, from Mexico. Nutritious, natural sugar and fats, heart problems.

Capsicum: Stimulant, tonic, equalizes circulation throughout body, non-narcotic.

Capsicum/Garlic: Stimulant, antibiotic, infections, fever, iron, yeast infection, blood pressure.

Chamomile: Antispasmodic, nervine, sedative, stomachic, colds, stomach pains, colic, earache.

Cascara Sagrada: Laxative, tonic, constipation, dyspepsia, indigestion and hemorrhoids.

Catnip: Antispasmodic, stimulant, tonic, fever, flatulence and digestive pain, sleep, nerves.

Chaparral: Antiseptic, diuretic, expectorant, tonic. Rheumatism, malignant melanoma, acne.

Chickweed: Refrigerant. Swellings, scabs, boils, burns, eyes, gout, liver, psoriasis.

Comfrey Root: Demulcent, astringent, cell proliferant, calcium, bones, tendons, lungs.

Damiana: Aphrodisiac, tonic, stimulant, sexual rejuvenator, laxative, nervous disorders.

Dandelion: Diuretic, tonic, stomachic, vitamins A, B, and C. Liver, gall, spleen, eczema, blood.

Desert Herb: Diuretic, tonic. Kidney & bladder, fever, blood purifier, mucous discharges.

Eyebright: Slightly tonic, astringent. Diseases of sight, weakness of the eye.

Fennel: Stimulant, stomachic, aromatic, appetite, colic, abdominal cramps, flatulence.

Fenugreek: Emollient, poultice, boils, carbuncles, inflamed stomach and intestines, hair.

Garlic: Antiseptic, diaphoretic, diuretic, coughs, colds, asthma, regulate blood pressure.

Ginger: Stimulant, carminative, tonic, diuretic, stomach and bowel pains, colds, female problems.

Ginseng: Aphrodisiac, stimulant, stomachic, nervine, lymph glands, antispasmodic, aging.

Golden Seal: Antiseptic, astringent, diuretic, laxative, tonic, douche, pyorrhea, skin.

Gotu Kola: Memory improvement, perpetual youth, blood purifier, rheumatism, ulcers.

Hawthorne Berry: Cardiac, antispasmodic, sedative, vasodilator, blood pressure, insomnia.

Horsetail: Sulphur, potassium, magnesium, iron, etc., silicon, calcium, nails, hair, bones.

Kelp: Iodine, silicone, sulphur, numerous minerals and vitamins, pituitary and adrenal glands.

Juniper Berries: Antiseptic, carminative, diuretic, tonic, produces hydrochloric acid.

Hops: Hypnotic, sedative, diuretic, tonic, nerves, diarrhea, insomnia, appetite, flatulence.

Licorice: Diuretic, expectorant, laxative, bronchial problems, cortisone, adrenal glands.

Lobelia: Antispasmodic, emetic, expectorant, nervine, asthma, epilepsy, heart, glands.

Marshmallow: Demulcent, diuretic. Irritated tissue, poultice, burns, vaginal douche, eyes.

Mullein: Anodyne, pectoral. Coughs, spitting blood, chest ailments, colic, hemorrhoids.

Mistletoe: Cardiac, diuretic, stimulant, vasodilator, circulation, low blood pressure.

Myrrh Gum: Antiseptic, astringent, stomachic, mouthwash teeth and gums, coughs, asthma.

Papaya: Digestive, stomachic, papain (a protein-digesting enzyme), allergies, wounds.

Parsley: Antispasmodic, diuretic, dropsy, jaundice, asthma, vitamins C and A, many minerals.

Passion Flower: Sedative, insomnia, restlessness, hysteria, headache, nervine.

Pennyroyal: Carminative, diaphoretic, menstruation, fever, colds. Do not use during pregnancy.

Peach Bark: Sedative, diuretic, expectorant, stimulates urine flow, nerves, chest congestion.

Poke Root: Anodyne, cathartic, laxative, pain, inflammation, rheumatism, skin parasites.

Psyllium: Swells into gelatinous mass, lubricates intestine. Used for dysentery in tropics.

Raspberry: Astringent, cardiac, refrigerant, nausea, vomiting, miscarriage, milk, labor pains.

Red Clover: Alterative, sedative, cancer, ulcers, scrofula, sores, burns, nerves.

Red Beet: Nutritious, contains natural iron, excellent liver cleanser.

Rose Hips: 10-100 times more vitamin C than any known food, A, E, B-1, B-2, B-3, K, P, calcium, iron.

Rosemary: Antispasmodic, stimulant, stomachic, liver, bile, digestion, raises blood pressure.

Safflower: Diaphoretic, diuretic, produces perspiration, colds, hysteria, chlorosis.

Sage: Tonic, astringent, expectorant, diaphoretic, antiseptic, hair, sexual debility.

Sarsaparilla: Alterative, diuretic, stimulant, purifies blood, rheumatism, gout, ringworm.

Sassafras: Stimulant, tonic, diuretic, thins blood, childbirth, skin, hangovers.

Saw Palmetto: Diuretic, expectorant, tonic. Colds, asthma, bronchitis, aphrodisiac.

Scullcap: Tonic, nervine, hysteria, convulsions, hydrophobia, St. Vitus' dance, rickets.

Slippery Elm: Diuretic, emollient, total food, soothing and healing all internal tracts.

Squawvine: Diuretic, astringent, dropsy, diarrhea, releases urine, all uterine problems.

St. John's wort: Expectorant, diuretic, bronchitis, bed wetting, low back pain.

Thyme: Tonic, carminative, hysteria, headache, nightmares, spasms, suppressed menstruation.

Uva Ursi: Astringent, diuretic, specific for urinary organs, gravel, kidney, bladder.

Valerian: Anodyne, antispasmodic, nervine. It allays pain and promotes sleep, non-narcotic.

White Oak Bark: Astringent, tonic, antiseptic, post-nasal drip, hemorrhages, hemorrhoids.

Wild Lettuce: Anodyne, antispasmodic, sedative, induces sleep and nervous disorders.

Wood Betony: Aromatic, astringent, alterative, tonic in dyspepsia and alterative, rheumatism.

Yarrow: Astringent, tonic, indigestion, eyes, lungs, bowels, hemorrhoids, internal bleeding.

Yellow Dock: Alterative, tonic, iron, blood, glands, running ears, ulcerated eyelids, skin.

Yucca: Laxative, diuretic, antiseptic, ulcers, sore, rheumatic joints, arthritis.

Single Herbs[6]

Alfalfa: Nourishes the entire system: good for the pituitary gland. It alkalizes the body rapidly and helps detoxify the liver. Helps rebuild decayed teeth and relieve arthritic and rheumatic pain.

Aloe Vera: Aloe Vera is a potent medicine and healer. An excellent colon cleanser. Healing and soothing to the stomach as well as liver, kidneys, spleen and bladder. Also an excellent remedy for piles and hemorrhoids. Works with your immune system to keep you healthy, strong and vibrant.

Bayberry: Effective in clearing congestion from the nose and sinuses. Made into a tea it is excellent as a gargle for sore throats. Valuable for all kinds of hemorrhages.

Bee Pollen: A miracle food from nature rich in vitamins, minerals and amino acids. Reduces or eliminates the craving for protein.

Black Cohosh: Natural estrogen: helps relieve menopause symptoms. Good for high blood pressure (equalizes circulation) and helps relieve pain in childbirth.

Black Walnut Hulls: Expels internal parasites and tapeworms. Rich in manganese which is important for nerves, brain and cartilage and helps relieve many kinds of skin problems.

Burdock: Cleanses and eliminates impurities from the blood. An excellent diuretic. Soothing to the kidneys.

Cayenne (Capsicum): Used as a catalyst in herbal formulas. Helps equalize the circulation, stimulate the heart, and helps heal ulcers of the stomach and colon. Combined with Lobelia, it is excellent for the nerves.

Cascara Sagrada: Very good remedy for gallstones. Increases secretion of bile, and one of the best remedies for chronic constipation.

Catnip: Excellent for small children with colic. Very good as a sleeping aid, and soothing to the nerves. Useful in allaying pain caused by spasms.

Chaparral: Blood purifier. Very useful in cases of acne, arthritis, chronic backache, tumors, warts, and skin blotches.

Chickweed: Used extensively to help lose weight. One of the best remedies for tumors, piles and swollen testes. Excellent bronchial cleanser. Heals and soothes.

Comfrey Root: Good blood cleanser. Helps heal ulcers and kidney problems. Best remedy for blood in urine. Also a powerful remedy for coughs and catarrh.

Damiana: A great sexual rejuvenator. Gives new energy.

Dandelion: Excellent for anemia because it is high in iron, calcium and other vitamins and minerals. A very good diuretic. Useful in kidney and bladder problems.

Devil's Claw: Very effective for arthritis symptoms as well as liver and kidney problems.

Dong Quai: An ancient Chinese herb commonly referred to as the female equivalent to Ginseng. Used by Oriental women for thousands of years for nourishing female glands, regulating monthly periods, rebuilding the blood and helping conditions in the mother after the birth of a baby. Also, it is taken by men and women for eczema, hypertension and kidney disorders.

Eyebright: It is the main herb for protecting and maintaining the health of the eye. Acts as an internal medicine for the constitutional tendency to eye weakness. Will remove cysts that have been caused by chronic conjunctivitis.

Fennel: Helps suppress the appetite. Aids in digestion when uric acid is the problem. Good for gas, acid stomach, gout and colic in infants.

Fo-ti: Excellent for mental depression. Has been used to help the memory.

Garlic: Stimulates the activity of the digestive organs. It is used to emulsify the cholesterol and loosen it from the arterial walls. Proven useful in asthma and whooping cough. Valuable in intestinal infections and effective in reducing high blood pressure.

Ginger: Modern sickness aid. In a recent university study, ginger root capsules proved to be far more effective at controlling motion-induced nausea than either a drug or placebo. And one of the nicest things they discovered was that it had no sedative effects on the central nervous system, unlike the drugs. It helps absorb toxins, restore gastric activities to normal, and helps control diarrhea and vomiting that often accompanies gastrointestinal flu.

Ginseng, Korean: Promotes mental and physical vigor, metabolism, appetite and digestion. Mildly stimulates the central nervous system.

Ginseng, Siberian: A physical restorative. Regenerates and rebuilds sexual centers. Anciently known as a male hormone, and used for longevity.

Golden Seal Herb: Contains many of the same properties as the root but in milder form. Relieves nausea. The infusion makes a good vaginal douche. Used as an antiseptic mouthwash.

Golden Seal Root: A powerful agent used in treating ulcers, diphtheria, tonsillitis and spinal meningitis. One of the best substitutes for quinine, it acts as an insulin.

Gotu Kola: Contains remarkable rejuvenating properties. It is known as "The Secret of Perpetual Youth." It strengthens the heart, memory and brain.

Horsetail (Shavegrass): Contains a great deal of silica, which helps keep the elasticity in the skin. Also a diuretic. Helps with kidney stones.

Kelp, Norwegian: Excellent for the thyroid gland and goiters. Has a remedial and normalizing action on the sensory nerves. Good for nails, hair, and radiation.

Licorice Root: Natural cortisone. Used for hypoglycemia, adrenal glands and stress. Also for coughs and chest complaints, gastric ulcers and throat conditions.

Lobelia: A powerful relaxant. Reduces palpitation of the heart and strengthens muscle action. Good for fevers, pneumonia, meningitis, pleurisy, hepatitis and peritonitis. Emetic in large amounts.

Parsley: Rich in vitamin B and potassium. An excellent diuretic and one of the most excellent herbs for gall bladder problems. Expels gallstones.

Pau d'Arco: Greatest treasure the Incas left us. Medical literature confirms that this South American herb possesses antibiotic, tumor-inhibiting, virus-killing, antifungal and antimalarial properties. Consumer publications report success for the symptoms of anemia, asthma, psoriasis, colitis and resistance to various infections by building the immune system.

Psyllium: Excellent colon cleanser, cleans out compacted pockets. Creates bulk. Relieves autointoxication.

Red Clover: A good blood purifier. Contains silica and other earthy salts. Relaxing to nerves and entire system.

Red Raspberry: As a tea, excellent for morning sickness in pregnancy. Helps prevent miscarriage, and strengthens uterine walls prior to giving birth.

Saffron: A natural hydrochloric acid (utilizes sugar of fruits and oils), thus helping arthritics get rid of the uric acid which holds the calcium deposited in joints. Also reduces lactic acid buildup.

Sarsaparilla: Eliminates poisons from the blood and helps cleanse the system of infections. Useful for rheumatism, gout, skin eruptions, ringworm, scrofula, internal inflammation, colds and catarrh.

Scullcap: More effective than quinine, and not harmful. Good for neuralgia, aches and pains, and nervous tension. Helps reduce high blood pressure, helps heart conditions and disorders of the central nervous system such as palsy, hydrophobia and epilepsy.

Slippery Elm: Very valuable for inflammation of the lungs, bowels, stomach, kidneys and bladder. Will soothe ulcerated or cancerous stomach when nothing else will.

Uva Ursi: Very useful in diabetes and all kinds of kidney troubles. Excellent remedy for piles, hemorrhoids, spleen, liver, pancreas and gonorrhea. Also good where there are mucus discharges from the bladder with pus and blood.

Valerian Root: A nerve tonic. Used for epileptic fits, nervous tension or irritations. Promotes sleep. Excellent for children with measles and scarlet fever.

White Oak Bark: Good for varicose veins. Used in douches and enemas for internal tumors and swellings. One of the best remedies for piles, hemorrhoids, hemorrhages or any trouble of the rectum. Normalizes the liver, kidneys and spleen.

White Willow Bark: Nature's aspirin. No herb used by man throughout the ages for health purposes has a longer recorded history or a wider use in the world. It is one of nature's greatest gifts to mankind as a pain-relieving, fever-lowering, anti-inflammatory agent without any side effects. Helps relieve symptoms of headache, fever, arthritis, rheumatism, bursitis, dandruff, eye problems (eyewash), influenza, chills, eczema, and nosebleed. Most effective in concentrated extract form.

Yellow Dock: Mineral-rich plant, especially in iron. Excellent as a blood purifier and toning up the entire system.

Yucca: New hope for arthritics. Has been used with surprising success for arthritis and rheumatism symptoms.

Aspirin, Tylenol, Motrin and other aspirin (salicin, salicylic acid) derivatives can be fatal to cats in even the smallest amounts. Dogs may be given these herbs occasionally, but not on a daily basis. Cats should not be given catnip as a stomachic and sedative, as it is an aphrodisiac for them; however, it is fine to use for dogs. These are the only instances where herbal healing for pets differs from human herbal use, other than in dosage adjusted to the animals' smaller body sizes. The information below is from my many years of herbal experience with people and pets, and from the following references: Velma Keith and Montene Gordon, *The How-To Herb Book* (Mayfield Publishing, 1984); Louise Tenney, MH, *Health Handbook: A Guide to Family Health* (Woodland Books, 1987); and Billie Potts, *Witches Heal: Lesbian Herbal Self-Sufficiency* (Hecuba's Daughters Press, 1981).

Alfalfa is an all-nutrient containing every vitamin and mineral. It is a detoxifier and blood cleanser, lowers cholesterol, benefits the endocrine and digestive systems, and increases the effectiveness of any other herb or supplement used with it. Use for allergies, arthritis, diabetes, kidney and urinary tract dis-ease, lactation, and as a tonic.

Blue Violet is used with red clover as a detoxifier and blood cleanser. Use it for cancer, tumors, cysts, boils and abscesses, skin cancer, and chronic skin dis-eases.

Calendula or marigold is used as a skin wash for the fast healing of wounds, burns, insect bites, skin lesions, cuts and abrasions. A favorite of homeopaths, it is used in compresses and salves as a very effective first aid remedy. On wounds and abscesses, make sure the opening is completely cleaned out and all pus removed before applying the salve or compress—calendula closes the skin rapidly and no toxins should remain inside the wound once the skin is closed. Calendula oil is used for ear infections.

Chamomile is a mild sedative, anti-spasmodic, digestive and gentle cleanser for the liver and kidneys. Used in a steamer it soothes the lungs for pets with asthma, bronchitis, respiratory dis-eases, or allergies. Use it for spasms, pain, vomiting, gas, to stimulate appetite, and to calm the cat or dog that has been through a harrowing experience. A gentle tonic and calmative.

Comfrey has been a woman's all-healer for thousands of years. Because it works, the FDA has banned its sale. Find it growing wild or grow your own. Comfrey used internally and externally speeds the healing of bruises, tissue and ligament tears, and broken bones by as much as twenty to forty percent. It prevents and heals bone non-unions. It kills streptococcus and staphylococcus bacteria, heals urinary tract infections with blood in the urine, heals the lungs and respiratory problems, and heals skin wounds, bites and itching (externally). It is a nutrient, detoxifier, blood cleanser, contact healer, and infection/inflammation fighter. Write your Senators and Congresspeople!

Echinacea is an herbal antibiotic on the level of penicillin. It is an infection fighter active against strep bacteria (abscesses and boils), a blood cleanser (blood poisoning, snake bite, poisonous insects), and a glandular and lymphatic system cleanser. Use it particularly for respiratory infections and any dis-ease above the waist. Use it only when really needed, and keep the pet or person on it for a minimum of two weeks to prevent symptoms from returning.

Golden Seal is another major herbal antibiotic, an equivalent to sulfa. It is a liver cleanser and antiseptic, and is used for internal bleeding and bowel dis-eases (colitis, etc.). It lowers blood sugar and is a natural insulin. It heals the mucous membranes and is used externally for skin cancer. Use goldenseal as an elixir for pets with cancer, feline leukemia, feline infectious peritonitis, and tumors. Do not use goldenseal with hypoglycemic animals or add licorice root to goldenseal for them. Monitor diabetic pets closely. Use particularly for any infections below the waist—stomach, bowel, digestive.

Hawthorn is a heart strengthener and may be used daily on a long-term basis on pets with high blood pressure, heart dis-ease or weakness, or heart valve problems. It is a stress reducer and adrenal balancer, calmative, and aids circulation and edema. I have seen miracles when people and animals use this herb.

Horsetail Grass contains silica which is needed for calcium metabolism. Use it for arthritis; broken bones; muscle, ligament and tissue injuries; spinal problems; internal bleeding; urinary tract and kidney infections; circulation and artery dis-ease. Horsetail builds the immune, glandular, and nervous systems, plus skin, coat, teeth, and nails. It helps in expelling parasites/worms and is a diuretic.

Licorice Root is a natural cortisone and estrogen. Use it for adjusting female hormones after spaying (skin problems, etc.), for hypoglycemia and diabetes, adrenal balancing, constipation and intestinal healing, for the heart and circulatory system. Licorice is used in cough formulas and to stimulate digestive enzymes. Dogs love the taste. Do not use on a pet with high blood pressure.

Milk Thistle or silymarin is a liver cleanser, detoxifier, and repairer. Use it for liver or kidney damage, hepatitis, jaundice, leptospirosis, and parvovirus recovery. It may be helpful in chronic skin disorders, tumors, and cancer. This is a major antioxidant. Pets that have been on a lot of veterinary drugs, heartworm prevention or medication, vaccinations, deworming drugs, or chemotherapy need this healing.

Parsley is a nutrient, digestive tract tonic and diuretic. It is high in potassium, minerals, and vitamins. Use it for bladder and kidney infections, incontinence, and for the stomach and liver. Parsley is a blood cleanser, cancer preventive, immune builder, and a tonic for the blood vessels. It helps a mother dog or cat stop lactating and aids in afterbirth pains. Do not use it while the animal is nursing.

Raspberry Leaf is used throughout gestation to strengthen the mother, prevent miscarriage, and aid in easy deliveries and lactation. It is also useful for diarrhea, gas, indigestion, nausea, and vomiting.

St. John's wort or hypericum is a major pain reliever for arthritis, rheumatism, wounds, burns, and body injuries. Use it for nerve pain and nerve damage from trauma, and use it for spinal problems and slipped discs. Most known as a homeopathic, hypericum is an anti-spasmodic, anti-hemorrhagic, and heals the lungs, urinary tract, and reproductive organs. Its primary use is for pain in cases where the skin is unbroken.

Scullcap is a calmative, nerve and nervous system repairer, antispasmodic, and pain reliever. It is used for epilepsy, spinal problems and injuries, neuritis, twitching muscles, rheumatism, high blood pressure, stress, worry, and restlessness. Scullcap may be used in small amounts long-term for hyperactivity and anxiety, or for seizures, without toxicity.

Slippery Elm is Juliette de Bairacli Levy's "tree bark's flour." It is a nutrient and food for very young, old, or very weak cats or dogs. It coats and heals all inflamed tissue internally and externally, and is used for the stomach, ulcers, bowels and kidneys, constipation, diarrhea, dysentery and colitis, and the entire digestive tract. Use it externally for wounds, burns, rashes, abscesses, boils, or insect bites, and internally for the lungs, coughing, vomiting, and for stomach or bowel cancer. Use slippery elm as a food in convalescence, mixed with a bit of honey and water. It tastes sweet and pets take it readily.

Valerian is a sedative and painkiller, stronger than other herbal sedatives. It reduces anxiety, hysteria, and pain; soothes the nervous system; and reduces high blood pressure. Valerian slows and strengthens the heart and calms palpitations. It is useful for muscle spasms, arthritic pain, and spinal injuries. It aids indigestion and gas. Though synthesized to Valium, valerian is safe and non-addictive.

White Willow is the herbal aspirin that is not to be used for cats. Aspirin was synthesized from this herb, but willow has none of aspirin's side effects (internal bleeding, nausea, upset stomach, heartburn, ulcers). The herb is a fever reducer, pain reliever, and anti-inflammatory. Use occasionally for dogs.

Yarrow is for fever and infectious dis-eases; stops internal bleeding; cleanses the liver, kidneys, and bladder; heals the mucous membranes; stops diarrhea; heals the lungs and circulation; and balances the endocrine system. Its chemical makeup is close enough to insulin that yarrow may be a significant remedy for some pets with diabetes. For an animal with this condition, proceed slowly and with expert help, and monitor blood sugar levels frequently. There can be no stopping and starting in treating diabetes; if the remedy works, keep the pet on it, and monitor closely. Externally, yarrow is an antiseptic for wounds, rashes, and deep punctures—use as a poultice or compress.

Yucca is gaining increasing attention among dog guardians for its success in treating arthritis, hip dysplasia, and other bone and joint diseases. It reduces pain and increases mobility by production of natural steroids in the body. Yucca also aids digestion and is a liver, blood, and digestive system detoxifier. It is helpful for allergies, asthma, skin problems, body odor, and stress.

Even from this brief listing, it is evident that herbs have a great deal to offer in dog, cat, and human healing. I have been using herbs for myself and my animals for many, many years with consistent success. For more information and for the major reference sources for herbal remedies in this book, read the books listed above, plus Juliette de Bairacli Levy's *The Complete Herbal Handbook for the Dog and Cat*, and *Cats Naturally* (Faber and Faber, 1955 and 1991). Herbs are a major healing method for the dis-eases listed in this book.

----

[1]Juliette de Bairacli Levy, *The Complete Herbal Handbook for the Dog and Cat*, pp. 136-137.

[2]*Ibid.*, pp. 136-137.

[3]Anitra Frazier with Norma Eckroate, *The New Natural Cat*, p. 260.

[4]Richard Pitcairn, DVM, and Susan Hubble Pitcairn, *Dr. Pitcairn's Complete Guide to Natural Health for Dogs and Cats*, p. 193.

[5]Herb store handout, Goldenseal, Pittsburgh, Pennsylvania.

[6]LaDean Griffin, *Original Herb Formulas*, herb store handout. Note that white willow and white oak barks should not be given to cats.

V - Dogs, Cats, and Homeopathy

Homeopathy is a major movement just waiting to happen. It is a two-hundred-year-old advanced idea whose time has come. It is also an ideal healing system for pets and people. Homeopathic remedies are taken in tiny milk sugar pellets crushed and placed on the animal's tongue or used by the drop in alcohol tinctures. The pellets are sweet tasting, and animals don't fuss, and the dosage literally doesn't matter. One pellet or drop of a 30C remedy or five are still 30C. A cat, horse, human, large or small dog, puppy, kitten, mouse, or infant all take the same remedy in the same potency, and in whatever amount per dose.

The remedies are also very inexpensive—under five dollars for a tube of seventy-five or a hundred pellets and under ten dollars for liquid preparations and combination remedies. More and more health food stores carry homeopathic remedies. They can also be ordered by phone and mail from a variety of toll-free sources. A complete homeopathic pharmacy starts at about sixty dollars and contains fifty or sixty remedies. Smaller kit assortments start at about fifteen dollars. This is an all-round healing system for everyone in the household.

Homeopathy is a complicated system. However, there are a number of good homeopathic guides for home use that make choosing the right remedy relatively easy. There are guidebooks for cats and dogs. Try George Macleod's *Cats: Homeopathic Remedies* and *Dogs: Homeopathic Remedies* (C.W. Daniel Co., 1990 and 1983), and Francis Hunter's *Homeopathic First-Aid Treatment for Pets* (Thorsen's, 1984). Guidebooks for people work just as well for pet dis-eases, as homeopathic treatment is based on symptoms and the symptoms are the same for all. My favorite all-use guide is Steven Cummings and Dana Ullman's *Everybody's Guide to Homeopathic Medicines* (J.P. Tarcher, 1984). These and a few remedies or access to them will give you and your pets a start. The guidebooks above are the major remedy sources for homeopathy in this book, and the sources that I use for my own animals. When this fascinating healing system becomes a major part of your life, one further book, a homeopathic *Materia Medica and Repertory*, will become important to have on hand.

Homeopathy is the first of the healing methods of this book to reach beyond the physical body level for healing. Homeopathy is not used on healthy people and animals, with the exception of low potency cell salts that are sometimes used as nutrients. This is a healing system to use when something is wrong, when energy is disrupted. It quickly and almost miraculously returns the pet's energy vibration to balance and wellness. Physical symptoms disappear but the focus is on the emotional and mental states behind the physical dis-ease and causing it. Where all of the previous methods in this book have been based on either prevention or physical level healing, homeopathy is a form of vibrational medicine that goes further, addressing and healing the mental and emotional level bases of dis-ease.

Most healers involved with holistics and metaphysics believe that dis-ease is only the physical manifestation of illness or imbalance in the non-physical bodies. These bodies include the emotional, mental, and spiritual realms. The pet or human body has a propensity for good health and wellness; it has a template or blueprint at the spiritual body level to create that wellness. It is this spiritual blueprint that determines why a new-grown cell in our and our dogs' and cats' ever-changing and ever-growing bodies develops as a liver cell rather than a hair cell.

Cells are programmed for good health and for a distinct purpose; when a cell designed to become part of a healthy organ instead becomes a cancer cell, something is very wrong. Something has disrupted that cell's normal blueprint-designated growth—usually somewhere between the physical level and the physical body. The disruption occurs in the intervening levels it must pass through; to be complete the healing must occur where the disruption is.

Homeopathic remedies are not physical substances, though they begin that way and are incorporated into a physical medium (milk sugar or tincture) for administration. Beyond a remedy dilution potency of 12C (considered a low potency remedy), no physical molecules remain of the original remedy substance. Yet the further the dilution, the more potent and deeper acting the remedy. Beyond this 12C strength there is no physical level action; the remedies act by vibrational imprint of the substance. This higher-than-physical vibration reaches the non-physical bodies, heals the dis-ease where the blueprint energy vibration is disrupted, and the physical level healing follows from the vibrational change and rebalancing.

Healing with homeopathy can border on the miraculous. A woman I knew had an eleven-year-old tomcat that developed tumors all over his body. She was about to have the cat euthanized when I gave her a tube of homeopathic *Thuja* 30C and urged her to try it. Within two weeks and only a couple of repeats of the first dose, the cat was completely free of tumors. Tumors are one of the symptoms of vaccinosis (negative reactions to the yearly vaccinations) and *Thuja* is the remedy for antidoting the negative effects. The tumors had appeared just after the cat's latest vaccination series, which proved to be one series too many. Note that the 30C potency (my preferred dosage size) is greater than the 12C beyond which no molecule of the original substance (Tree of Life plant) remains.

My red Siberian Husky Copper came to me from the Humane Society with parvovirus and an assortment of other ills, neglect, and abuse. He weighed only thirty-five pounds full-grown. He survived the parvo on IVs and a self-imposed fast, but it left a great deal of digestive system damage. For six months he continued to have periods of bloody vomiting and diarrhea, great anxiety and hyperactivity, and he gained only three pounds. Periods of panic, and then depression preceded the periods of digestive disruption, and any threat, real or imagined, would trigger them. A dozen different vets refused to treat the dog and insisted he be put down.

I began to write *All Women Are Healers* and to do research for a chapter on homeopathy, but I was slow to try it myself. I asked Sidney Spinster to check the chapter's accuracy, and as she did so I asked her if homeopathy could help Copper. She questioned me about his symptoms, background, and personality, then told me to order homeopathic *Phosphorus* in a 12C potency liquid. She said to give the dog "a few drops on his tongue" and I would see a difference within a week. I ordered the remedy, was surprised at how quickly it came, and gave the dog his dose.

Within a few minutes Copper curled up and went to sleep in the kitchen and slept deeply and quietly all day. This in itself was unusual behavior. He had had a severe bout of diarrhea, to the point where I was making him sleep in the yard at night (it was summer). From the time he took those drops on his tongue, the diarrhea and vomiting stopped. Copper developed a ravenous appetite and gained fifteen pounds in three weeks. After about ten days, I noticed diarrhea beginning again and gave the dog a second dose of the *Phosphorus*. The diarrhea stopped immediately and returned once more in slighter form in another three weeks. I dosed him again and it was the last time it was needed. At about six years old now (five years later) he is in beautiful perfect health; he is calm and solid of temperament, and he weighs sixty-five pounds.

Recently Kali, my other red Siberian Husky that had also been a pound rescue, started chewing sores between her footpads and on her skin. Standard veterinary treatment consisted of antiseptic sprays externally and two to three week internal runs of antibiotics. As soon as the medication stopped, new sores appeared; this happened three times. The dog had obviously been abused before I got her at about six months of age, and she was now going through adolescence at just over a year old. She exhibited periods of hyperactive behavior, wildness, roughness and disobedience, and jealous bullying of Copper (who behaved like a gentle dog through it all).

I first tried homeopathic *Arsenicum* 6C and 30C. The dog responded with much calmer behavior and no increase in chewing and sores, but the sores remaining were still inflamed and did not fully heal. I next tried

Silica 30C and the sores healed up overnight. I alternated the remedies, one dose every second day, with the doses a week apart. After a month, she had no more sores but still an occasional period of hyperactive behavior which happened less and less often. A "hyperactivity" combination remedy from Newton Homeopathic Labs has done the rest. I was sold on homeopathy.

Sometimes the first remedy just doesn't work. You think you have the symptom picture matched but nothing happens when you give the dose. After a couple of tries go back to the guidebook or *Materia Medica*. Look for a key symptom of the physical dis-ease, but the determining factor is the remedy's match to the cat's or dog's emotional state or behavior. Careful observation is involved, and sometimes trial and error to find the remedy that works. If there is no result or change within twenty-four hours, it's the wrong remedy.

There is no harm to the animal from a remedy error. There simply is no change. If the pet's emotional or mental state improves but not her physical dis-ease symptoms at first, the remedy is working and the physical changes will follow. Match the pet's or person's symptoms as closely as possible to the remedy's description in the guidebook. The closer the match, the more likely it is to work. Pay careful attention to matching non-physical signs, as these are the key. Give one dose and wait.

There is some controversy among homeopaths as to which potency is the best for home use. While there is probably no one answer here, I prefer the 30C potency, but I tell people that if 30C is not available take whatever they can get. The potencies are designated either as X or C after the number. X means dilution by tens, and C by hundreds. Here is how they are made. To make a 1X remedy, take a single drop of the original alcohol-tinctured substance (it could be an herb tincture, or a tincture made from a mineral, chemical, or animal substance), and add it to nine drops of water or food-grade alcohol and water. The remedy is then shaken and tapped one hundred and eight times.

To make a 2X remedy, take one drop of the 1X solution to nine more drops of water or alcohol and water, and shake and tap (succuss) it again. Each dilution by tens raises the number by one (1X, 2X, 3X, etc.). To make a 1C remedy, do the same thing but this time use one drop of the original (Mother) tincture to ninety-nine drops of water or alcohol and water. The dilution is by one hundred rather than by ten. The herb elixir instructions of the last chapter create a 1C homeopathic remedy from a standard herb tincture.

The difference between an X dilution and a C is in the strength (potency). The more diluted by the succussion (shaking and tapping) process, the stronger the remedy. Instead of relying on the physical substance, homeopathic remedies work by the vibrational imprint of that substance. Remedies today are potentized by machine, and a 30C remedy is a low standard dose. When using X remedies, the dose needs to be repeated much more often and takes longer to show results, though they eventually do work. Remedies are available in far higher potencies, in thousand and ten thousand dilutions, but these should be used only by experts. They often require a prescription.

The argument against higher potencies is that they sometimes cause a temporary worsening before the symptoms clear. This is called an *aggravation*. At a 30C potency an aggravation will last (if it happens) for probably less than an hour. The aggravation may not be noticeable at all, and when it passes, the pet or person shows great improvement. An aggravation is considered a good sign, as it happens only when you have chosen the right remedy to match the symptoms and a healing is taking place.

In a 6X or 12X potency, or even a 6C, 9C, or 12C there will probably be no aggravation, but the remedy, if chosen correctly, works slowly and may also not completely clear the dis-ease. If in using a potency lower than a 30C, the dog or cat improves but does not fully heal, or reaches a plateau, try a higher potency. If the same thing happens when dosage is raised to 30C, after a period of time go to 200C, but only if you are certain that it is the right remedy and the pet is responding to it. A 30C potency does the job for almost all acute dis-eases and most long-term ones; it carries only minor aggravation.

How often to give the dose is another matter. Homeopathics other than the low potency cell salts (6X) are not generally used on a so-many-times-a-day, everyday basis. They require careful observation. I also like to use a pendulum in deciding when to repeat the dose. It can vary: an hour, a few hours, a day, or a week may be the right time. The general rule is to give the dog or cat the first dose and then wait. Place one or two crushed pellets or a few drops of the liquid on the animal's tongue; withhold water for fifteen minutes and food for at least half an hour. Avoid touching the pellets or drops with your hands. Do not use peppermint herb tea at any time during a homeopathic healing, or expose the animal or remedies to strong fragrances (camphor, mothballs, some floor disinfectants). These will antidote (cancel) the remedy's action. For people, coffee or peppermint toothpaste is an antidote also. If the remedy is antidoted in this way, remove the canceling substance and repeat the dose.

After giving the remedy, watch the pet's reactions. I find that if the remedy is the right one my dogs get very relaxed and go to sleep within a few minutes. They may wake up within an hour and the problem appears a little worse. Kali's sores looked redder and she was licking at them again. The tumors on the cat may have seemed a little bigger. This is the aggravation phase, and for my dogs on a 30C potency it seems to last about fifteen minutes to half an hour. Then the pet calms down, the sores seem less red, and the animal goes back to her daily life. If you give the dose at bedtime, you may not notice the aggravation phase at all.

From there, with the right remedy, the pet begins to improve. On one dose of *Silica* 30C, Kali's sores disappeared overnight; on one dose of *Phosphorus* 12C, Copper's six-month diarrhea stopped. As long as the improvement continues or the dis-ease completely clears, there is no need for another dose. If the animal's symptoms return or start to worsen again after improvement, it's time to repeat. (These symptoms will generally be much improved from the way they were originally.) Sometimes one dose will clear a dis-ease situation completely, especially if it is given early in the dis-ease and in high enough potency. Sometimes a number of repeated doses are needed. The changes are subtle but can be quite miraculous; observe carefully. If there is no response at all after perhaps two doses, go back to the guidebooks for a different remedy.

As a further guideline, but not a hard and fast one, veterinary homeopath Francis Hunter suggests giving 30C remedies with the following frequency for dogs and cats. In the case of acute, urgent attacks, give one dose every fifteen minutes up to four doses, then every two hours up to another four doses. For less urgent conditions, give the remedy three or four times a day for a few days. For chronic, long-term dis-eases, give the remedy three times a day for four to seven days, then wait and repeat if needed.[1]

Homeopathy explains its miracles by three primary principles: The Law of Similars, the Law of the Minimal Dose, and Hering's Law of Cure. The **Law of Similars** is the basis of homeopathy: like cures like. Its premise is that any substance that can produce a given set of symptoms in a healthy person or animal will cure those same symptoms in a person or animal that is ill. The homeopathic remedies are such substances, tested or *proved* on humans. There is no animal testing in homeopathy, the remedies are proved on people: they are cruelty-free. Each substance's proving brings to light a *remedy picture*, a set of specific and detailed symptoms. When these symptoms are displayed by a pet or person in need of healing, that substance prepared homeopathically is the healing remedy. Finding the right remedy means matching the remedy picture of the substance that most clearly describes the dis-ease to be healed.

The closer the animal's or human's symptoms are to the remedy picture of a specific substance, the more likely that remedy is to complete a full cure. A *Materia Medica* is a book of remedy pictures and an index (Repertory) for matching symptoms to find the right remedy. Every body part, emotion, mental state, and behavior pattern is described in a remedy picture in great detail. Usually not all of a pet's body parts will be affected, so only pieces of the picture will match. The key again is to look for major physical symptoms and mental-emotional states, as well as behavioral changes in the pet. For example, in arthritis, the animal whose symptoms seem worse for movement and activity matches for *Bryonia*, where a pet that is stiff on getting up but then seems fine responds to *Rhus tox*. An arthritic or dysplastic dog or cat whose key behavior is her restlessness matches the description for *Rhus tox*—if her physical symptoms match that remedy's description, as well.

The homeopathy guidebooks for home use attempt to simplify this method by listing remedies by dis-ease, but the art of homeopathy is healing by symptom pictures rather than labels and thus any given remedy will have effectiveness in a variety of seemingly unrelated cases. *Rhus Tox*, for example, where the key symptom is that motion brings relief, is used for arthritis and muscle pain, but also for some cases of fevers and infectious dis-eases, allergies, skin rashes, and injuries—when the restlessness and better-for-motion picture applies, along with the physical symptoms of this remedy. The symptoms are described in great detail. The first try remedy may not match closely enough, especially with beginners to the method, so that further tries are needed. When the remedy is chosen where the symptom picture correctly fits the pet's or person's dis-ease, the effectiveness and speed of healing are truly amazing.

This concept of like cures like is very different from standard veterinary/medical practice, which uses drugs to suppress symptoms rather than to match them, and calls the symptom the dis-ease. To accept the homeopathic concept is to change the whole medical/veterinary model of what dis-ease is and what heals. *Tiger Tribe Magazine*'s Luke Granfield puts it this way:

> So how does this change our notion of illness? The underlying assumption of this law is that the symptoms of illness are an attempt to cure disease, they are not the disease itself. The belief that symptoms are the disease is so ingrained in our society (see the countless ads on television for symptomatic relief) that it is really difficult for us to understand the opposite.

> Yet this idea presents a fundamentally more positive view of life, a view which sees living creatures as having been endowed with the ability to heal themselves. It is also an empowering idea and one that makes us more responsible and capable of taking care of ourselves and our animal companions.[2]

If the Law of Similars is the central basis for homeopathy, the **Law of the Minimal Dose** (less is more) is what makes it possible. Many homeopathic remedies express the symptom pictures of highly toxic substances. Even if like *does* cure like—and it does—we will not swallow phosphorus, arsenic, or mercury. The homeopathic process of making remedies allows us to use these substances, because the X and C dilutions and succussions leave virtually no physical level trace of the actual substance. The least amount of the beginning substance/tincture that remains (the higher the dilution/potency), the more effective the remedy. It is the energy vibration imprint of the substance that is the remedy match to the pet's or person's dis-ease, rather than the original chemical, mineral, or plant. All toxicity, therefore, is removed at the same time as the effectiveness of the remedy is increased.

This also has implications that contrast with veterinary/medical methods. In the medical system, pharmaceutical drugs that *are* toxic and have dangerous effects are prescribed. Moreover, they are prescribed in the highest amounts the patient's body can withstand. The attitude is one of "killing" or "attacking" the dis-ease in the form of the manifested symptoms. These drugs have noxious side effects, some of which may be more dangerous or uncomfortable than the original dis-ease. There are also frequent cases of overdosing. Drugs are designed to suppress the symptoms, which the medical system says *is* the dis-ease, but which homeopathy says is the body's expression of healing. The symptoms are not the dis-ease *cause*. When symptoms are suppressed rather than released from the energy vibration and healed, the dis-ease is not "cured," it is only driven deeper. Its next expression—and when drugs are used there will be one—can only be more severe.

Homeopathy describes the process of healing as releasing dis-ease from the physical and non-physical bodies by changing disrupted energy patterns to orderly ones in the unseen bodies. **Hering's Law of Cure** describes in detail how that process of healing and movement through the energy bodies takes place. Long observation has established this law which tells the homeopathy user or pet guardian just which way things are going and whether or not healing is happening. It is a useful guideline in any form of holistic healing, although it is here specifically applied to homeopathy.

All this is easy to observe when using homeopathy on dogs and cats or on people. In practical use, Hering's Law can be proven. The three laws of homeopathy make a strong philosophical contrast with the medical/veterinary system. Homeopathy—perhaps because it works, is inexpensive, and is usable by laypeople—is quite unpopular with standard veterinary/medical doctors. The AMA in the United States was founded to drive the homeopaths out of American medicine; unfortunately it has all but succeeded. In the rest of the world, however, homeopaths comprise at least half of the doctors and veterinarians. Homeopathy, despite the AMA, the drug industry, and legislative repression, is regaining its hold.

Many, many laypeople use homeopathic remedies at home for themselves and their pets and farm animals, even in this country. A great many holistic veterinarians use homeopathy extensively in their practices. See the Referrals section at the end of this book for a list of homeopathic veterinarians. Homeopathic vaccinations made with nosodes, remedies potentized from killed dis-ease viruses, are safe and effective and do not cause vaccinosis reactions. Homeopathy in general is a way of healing without causing the greater harm of pharmaceutical drug side effects and suppressions. It is a major way to heal dogs, cats, and people.

Homeopathic veterinarian Francis Hunter suggests the following list of remedies to comprise a basic cat and dog homeopathic medicine chest. The same selection is a good start for using homeopathy with humans.[3]

Aconite	Hepar sulph
Apis mel	Hypericum
Arnica	Merc cor
Arsenicum	Merc sol
Bryonia	Nux vomica
Cantharis	Pulsatilla
Carbo veg	Rhus tox
Chamomilla	Scutellaria
Cocculus	Silica
Colocynthus	Sulphur
Euphrasia	Symphytum
Gelsemium	Urtica

A personal suggestion here is to add *Thuja*, *Phosphorus* and *Hydrastis* to the list, perhaps in place of *Scutellaria* (scullcap), which can be used as the herb tincture or infusion. *Symphytum* is a homeopathic preparation of comfrey, and *Hydrastis* of goldenseal. *Hypericum* is familiar as the herb St. John's wort.

Classical homeopathy works with single remedies and uses only one remedy at a time, seldom or never mixing them. Modern homeopathy often combines remedies and at least two companies make up combination remedies that are specifically for pets and pet dis-eases. These include the Dr. Goodpet Pet Pharmacy Remedies (Very Healthy Enterprises, POB 4728, Inglewood, CA 90309, (310) 672-3269), and Newton Homeopathic Laboratories Pets-A-Care line (612 Upland Trail, Conyers, GA 30207, (800) 448-7256). Health food store combinations for people are also valid for cats and dogs in the same doses. These remedies are listed by dis-ease labels, rather than by symptom descriptions.

The advantage of combinations is that if one of the remedy ingredients is incorrect for the pet's needs, another ingredient in the mix will probably work. The disadvantages are that too many doses of the wrong remedy are not good homeopathic practice, and also that the combinations usually come only in very low potencies (3X, 6X, rarely higher).

Classical homeopaths want to know which remedy was the effective one and this is not possible to discern when using combinations. Classical homeopathy is the traditional way, time-proven over two hundred years. I endorse and recommend it, and I choose it for my own use. Yet, for the inexperienced user of homeopathy who has a pet that needs healing, the combinations remove the guesswork and they are valid.

Combination remedies are usually available in liquid alcohol tinctures at a price under ten dollars. They are labeled by dis-ease, with remedies for pets that include Diarrhea, Flea Relief, Calm Stress, Skin, Nervousness, Kidney Help, Worms, Ear Relief, Feline Leukemia, and Good Breath.

The homeopathy suggestions in this book come from a variety of overlapping sources, guidebooks, the *Materia Medica*, and my own experience. Check the references and guides listed in this chapter, as well as books on homeopathy for people. Many good guides for dogs and cats come from England, where homeopathy is on a par with standard medicine for both animals and humans. Homeopathy for pet and people healing is a system I can't praise highly enough, and I urge you to try it. Once you have tried it, you will keep on using it to your pet's benefit and your own.

---

[1] Francis Hunter, MRCVS, *Homeopathic First-Aid for Pets* (Northamptonshire, England: Thorsen's Publishing Group), p. 16.

[2] Luke Granfield, "Cats and Classical Homeopathy: A Marriage Made in Heaven," in *Tiger Tribe Magazine*, March-April, 1993, p. 24.

[3] Francis Hunter, MRCVS, *Homeopathic First-Aid for Pets*, p. 18.

VI - Animal Acupuncture/Acupressure

Acupuncture for small animals was not developed in China, as you might think, but in Europe, in recent times, primarily in France. Used for thousands of years in Asia, acupuncture may have been developed first for use on horses. Since then, it has been used extensively on other farm animals and on people. There are acupuncture charts for elephants, water buffalo, pigs, chickens, sheep, and camels. The system of Traditional Chinese Medicine (TCM) involves extensive use of both acupuncture and herbal healing. These were primarily for human use, as the attitude in China toward healing animals was and is strictly economic. But horses were useful in war and as work vehicles and had to be kept running; cows, sheep, and pigs were necessary for food and to accumulate wealth, and expensive to replace, so acupuncture was extended to them for practical reasons.

Chinese regarded dogs and cats as useful but not economically important and therefore did not use acupuncture on these animals. Moreover, both are considered food animals in Asia, so the bond between people and pets was not fostered. In China today a special license is required to own a pet and few Chinese are able to obtain one. Acupuncture for dogs and cats is growing more popular in western Europe and the United States among holistic veterinarians. Some acupuncturists who work on people will also accept pets as patients.

In acupuncture theory and Chinese medicine, the pet or human body incarnates with a specific amount of life force energy, called ch'i. This energy is depleted by daily living, but food and water replenish it. Disease is caused by an imbalance of ch'i, either a deficiency, or a backing-up/blockage that causes excess in an organ or energy channel with deficiency in another. The energy channels, called meridians, run in pairs through the body and are associated with major organs. When energy (ch'i) is flowing freely, the pet or human is well. Acupuncture and needleless acupressure relieve the deficiency or excess states in the meridians, rebalancing ch'i in the body and returning it to wellness.[1]

There are fourteen major meridians or energy channels in the human or pet body. Along these channels are about one thousand reflex points. The reflexes are selectively stimulated with hair-fine needles on these reflex points in acupuncture, or with finger pressure on the reflex points in acupressure. The meridians and reflex points have been extensively mapped for people and large animals in China, and these maps are being translated for dogs and cats. There are full meridian and reflex point acupuncture maps for dogs but only one acupressure map available at this time for cats. The points, however, are the same and the Dog Chart (see below) is valid for cats and dogs both. By stimulating blocked or deficient energy points (reflex points along the meridians), ch'i is returned to balance and dis-ease is released from the body. It is the body's electrical system (unseen levels, etheric double primarily), rather than the physical body that is stimulated. Acupuncture/acupressure is another form of vibrational medicine that is highly effective for pets.

Working essentially through the electrical (etheric) and autonomic nervous systems, point stimulation in acupressure/acupuncture causes the following effects:

1. Increase of circulation to an area.
2. Decrease of inflammation.
3. Release of endorphins (the body's natural pain relievers).
4. Relief of muscle spasms.
5. Stimulation of nerves.
6. Stimulation of the body's immune system.
7. Release of hormones.
8. Release of (positive) substances in the brain and spinal cord.[2]

Acupuncture/acupressure is often effective when other medical/veterinary means fail, particularly for cases of spinal problems and disc disease. Here it is the treatment of choice, having prevented the need for many surgeries and euthanasias. It is effective for arthritis, hip dysplasia, nervous system dis-eases, nerve deafness, lameness, balance problems, skin dermatitis, and behavioral disorders. Chronic pain responds to acupuncture and can be completely healed with it in many cases. High success rates have been obtained for a number of other pet disorders including chronic digestive disturbances, nerve injuries, lick granulomas, epilepsy, chronic respiratory dis-eases, allergies, asthma, distemper, and feline leukemia. It has also been used successfully for safe anesthesia during surgery (human and veterinary) and in birthing and caesarean sections. For aging cats and dogs, or those with terminal dis-eases, acupuncture treatments can extend lifespan. These animals at their time of death, says veterinarian Nancy Scanlan, "seem to slip quietly away, without requiring a decision for euthanasia."[3] Acupuncture, however, is usually not recommended for cancer treatment.

The hair-fine acupuncture needles are inserted from one-eighth to three-eighths of an inch into the skin. They are much finer in thickness than injection needles. The needles seem to sedate the animals, who do not fight the treatments but appear to doze through them. The needles are then stimulated in one of a variety of ways. In China moxibustion—heating with mugwort herb—was used. Other ways used today include electrical stimulation, soft laser, or by injecting sterile water, pain relievers, or vitamin B-12 into the reflex points. This injection method is frequently used on pets, particularly on cats. Tiny metal beads or staples can be inserted surgically for ongoing stimulation of a particular meridian point in such dis-eases as epilepsy or chronic pain. This method gives permanent relief. Pet treatments last from five to twenty-five minutes. Often a series of sessions may be required. Even for serious chronic diseases most animals need less than eleven treatments and the animals come to enjoy them.

Acupuncture with needles is a technical skill that is not recommended for home use without specialized training. Acupressure, however, the stimulation of reflex points by finger pressure on the skin, is easy to do and can be done effectively without such training. A specific set of reflex points is used for each dis-ease, and the meridian and reflex points are the same for acupressure and acupuncture.

To use finger acupressure for a dog or cat, locate the points—indicated in each dis-ease section of this book on the maps that follow. Apply gentle pressure with your thumb or index finger for about thirty seconds. A steady, gentle push or a massaging motion may be used. When the point is cleared, you will feel a slight, light pulsing under your finger. Move to the next point in the sequence. Repeat the whole sequence two or three times a day for acute (short-term) dis-eases. For chronic cases, begin the acupressure once a day and increase gradually to two or three times daily. The pet may begin to detoxify from the sessions.

The meridian and their thousand reflex points cover the entire body. There is a full acupuncture/acupressure body map on the skin flaps of cats' and dogs' ears as well, and a gentle but firm ear massage stroking in the direction of hair growth gives a full body healing. Most pets like this and relax to it. Dogs and cats also have the full body map in their front and back paws. These are harder to use, however, as dogs have hard pads on their feet, and though cats' feet are soft they are also very small. Both dogs and cats tend to be foot shy and resist paw handling, making foot reflexology with them difficult. Gentle, repeated foot handling may make some pets less shy and make this form of acupressure more feasible.

There is also a series of reflex points called Diagnostic or Alarm points. These reflex to specific body organs, and if they are tender when palpated (the cat or dog flinches when you massage one) it may be an indication of dis-ease in the corresponding organ. It is good to check these points weekly in a pet body massage to catch a pending problem early—sometimes before it even reaches the physical manifestation level. If a point here is congested, releasing it with gentle pressure now may prevent further dis-ease. Dis-ease manifests first in the unseen bodies; the electrical system of the meridians is also the etheric double aura layer, and disturbance of energy (ch'i) happens there before it reaches the physical body. If a point continues to be sensitive after several daily release sessions, a veterinary check is in order.

The maps that follow include the ear acupressure map and a map of the Diagnostic/Alarm points with a key to corresponding organs. There is also a series of meridian maps with the reflex points of each pet meridian on them. The charts show a dog but are valid for cats as well. The primary charts that follow, however, are the Shin Dog Chart and its key. The reflex points are numbered, as well as named, and their meridian placements are identified. Each point has indications given for use in specific dis-eases for both dogs and cats. The John Ottaviano Cat Chart is an acupressure chart and the most complete acupressure/acupuncture map available specifically for cats. It also locates its points by number and describes specific dis-ease uses for each point. Again, these points are valid for both cats and dogs.

To use acupressure on your pet, look up your pet's dis-ease in the Remedy section of this book. The points from both the Shin Dog Chart and the Cat Acupressure Chart are given for each dis-ease. Locate the points on the maps that follow, then find them on your pet. Work each sequence of points one by one until each releases. Repeat the treatment daily in chronic cases until it is no longer needed. In urgent acute situations, such as shock, the points are repeated every thirty seconds until the animal responds. In short-term non-urgent illness, do the sessions about three times a day. Use acupuncture/acupressure along with other veterinary or holistic healing methods. In any serious or urgent situation do the points on the way to the vet.

The information for acupuncture and the maps that follow are from the following which are available in English. The Shin Dog Chart key and maps are from Sheldon Altman, DVM, *An Introduction to Veterinary Acupuncture* (Chan's Corporation, 1981) and Alan M. Klide, VMD, and Shiu H. Kung, PhD., *Veterinary Acupuncture* (University of Pennsylvania Press, 1979). The John Ottaviano Cat Acupressure Chart is from Judy Fireman's *Cat Catalog* (Workman Press, 1976). The ear acupuncture map is from Linda Tellington-Jones' *The Tellington TTouch* (Viking Press, 1992), and the map of the Diagnostic points is from Dr. Michael Fox, *The Healing Touch* (Newmarket Press, 1981). The charts for shock resuscitation and immune boosting are from Sheldon Altman and Dr. Gloria Dodd, DVM, respectively. Further information on acupuncture/acupressure for dogs and cats may be found in these books and in my own *Natural Healing for Dogs and Cats* (The Crossing Press, 1993).

To locate a veterinary acupuncturist in your area, see the Resources section at the end of this book, or write for referral to International Veterinary Acupuncture Society, c/o Meredith L. Snader, VMD, 2140 Conestoga Rd., Chester Springs, PA 19425, (215) 827-7245.

For many dis-eases that otherwise would end in the euthanasia of a beloved animal, acupuncture can result in complete cures.

Acupuncture Body Map—Shin Dog Chart[4]
(Dog or Cat)

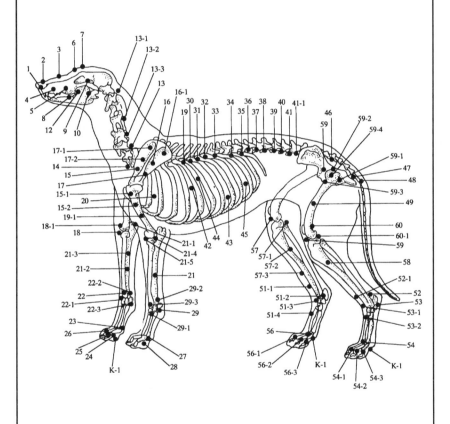

Shin Dog Chart Key[5]

Number	Name	Indications
1. GV-26	Jen chung	shock, sunstroke, resuscitation
2. GV-25	Pi liang	shock, sunstroke, sinusitis, cold, early distemper
3. GV-16	Ta feng men	seizure, distemper, tetany, encephalitis, convulsion
4. CG-3	Shang kuan	facial paralysis, deafness
5. ST-7	Hsia kuan	same as above
6. BL-1	Ching ming	conjunctivitis, keratitis, enlargement of third eye membranes
7. ST-1	Cheng chi	conjunctivitis, optic nerve atrophy, retinitis
8. (not given)	Erh chien	shock, sunstroke, cold, colic and spasm
9. TH-17	Yi feng	facial paralysis, deafness
10. GV-14	Ta chui	fever, neuralgia, rheumatism, bronchitis, epilepsy
11. GV-13	Tao dao	neuralgia and sprain (forelimb and shoulder), epilepsy
12. GV-12	Shen chu	pneumonia, bronchitis, distemper, sprain and neuralgia of shoulder
13. GV-10	Ling tai	hepatitis
14. GV-7	Chung su	gastritis, boosts appetite
15. GV-6	Chi chung	indigestion, diarrhea, enteritis, lack of appetite
16. GV-5	Hsuan shu	rheumatism, sprain of loin, indigestion, enteritis, diarrhea
17. GV-4	Ming men	rheumatism and sprain of loin, chronic enteritis, hormonal imbalance, impotence, nephritis, urinary disorders, lack of appetite
18. GV-3	Yang kuan	hypogonadism, endometritis, metritis, ovaritis, cystic ovary, atrophy of ovary or uterus, prolonged estrus, rheumatism and sprain of loin
19. GV-2.5	Kuan hou	endometritis, cystic ovary, cystitis, paralysis of large intestine, constipation
20. GV-20B	Pai hui	nervous disorders, sciatica, posterior paralysis, prolapse of rectum

Number	Name	Indications
21. BL-31	Erh yen	posterior paralysis, neuralgia
22. GV-2	Wei ken	posterior paralysis, paralysis of tail, anal prolapse, diarrhea, constipation
23. GV-1.2	Wei chieh	same as above
24. GV-1.1	Woei kan	same as above
25. GV-T	Woei chien	shock, sunstroke, gastroenteritis
26. CV-1	Chiao cho	diarrhea, prolapse of rectum, paralysis of sphincter muscles
27. LU-1	Fei yu	pneumonia, bronchitis, cough
28. P-1	Shin yu	mental stress, heart dis-ease
29. LIV-14	Kan yu	hepatitis, jaundice, eyes
30. GB-24	Wei yu	gastritis, stomach distension, indigestion, enteritis, lack of appetite
31. LIV-13	Shiao chung yu	enteritis, intestinal spasm, diarrhea
32. GB-25	Pi yu	indigestion, chronic diarrhea, lack of appetite
33. BL-23	Shen yu	urinary disorders, nephritis, sex hormone imbalances, sterility, impotence, sprain of lumbar region, rheumatism
34. BL-46	Yi yu	pancreatitis, indigestion, chronic diarrhea, diabetes
35. BL-25	Nuan cho	hormonal insufficiency disorders, cystic ovary
36. BL-26	Tzu kuan	cystic uterus, endometritis, metritis, hypotrophy of uterus, rheumatism of lumbar region
37. GB-26	Pung kung yu	cystitis, urine retention, bladder spasm, hematuria
38. ST-25	Tien shu	enteritis, diarrhea, abdominal pain, intestinal spasm
39. CV-12	Chung wan	acute gastritis, gastric disorders, vomiting, indigestion, anorexia
40. SI-11	Kung tzu	neuralgia, paralysis and sprain of shoulder; paralysis of scapula nerve, rheumatism of shoulder
41. TH-14	Chien ching	neuralgia, paralysis and sprain of shoulder and foreleg
42. LI-15	Chien juan	same as above
43. TH-10	Chou yu	arthritis, neuralgia, paralysis and sprain of elbow and foreleg

Number	Name	Indications
44. LI-11	Chih shang	sprain, neuralgia and paralysis of foreleg, paralysis of brachia and radial nerve
45. LI-10	Chih chu	same as above
46. TH-12	Ch'ing feng	general anesthesia, nervous disorders of forelimb
47. TH-9	Chien san li	paralysis of radial and ulna nerves, neuralgia and rheumatism of foreleg
48. TH-5	Wai kuan	same as above
49. TH-4	Yang chi	sprain of digits, neuralgia and paralysis of forelimb
50. SI-6	Yang chu	neurologic disorders of thoracic limb, sprain of carpal tendons, paralysis of radical nerve
51. SI-5	Wan ku	same as above
52. (extra point)	Pa feng	sprain and paralysis of digits
53. P-8	Nei kuan	neurologic disorders of thoracic limb, stomach and intestinal spasm, colic
54. GB-30	Huan tiao	posterior paralysis, neuralgia and paralysis of pelvic limb, sciatica, paralysis of femoral nerve
55. ST-34	Chi shang	Neurologic disorders of pelvic limb
56. BL-54	Chi hou	same as above
57. ST-35	Chi shia	sprain, neuralgia, arthritis of knee
58. GB-34	Hou san li	posterior paralysis, neuralgia and paralysis of pelvic limb, gastroenteritis, intestinal spasm and colic
59. ST-41	Chih shi	sprain, neuralgia and paralysis of hindfoot
60. LIV-4	Chung fong	same as above
61. K-6	Hou kon	same as above

Cat Acupuncture Body Map[6]

Home Acupuncture Treatment

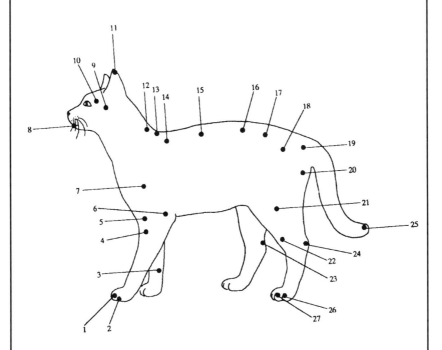

To use this chart, locate the general area which corresponds to your cat's problem. When a point is in need of pressure, the cat will respond by showing slight pain during palpation of the acupressure point. Massage gently for 1-10 minutes. This technique can be used as often as desired to provide relief to the cat. Use massage; only a trained acupuncturist can use needles. Home acupressure treatment cannot replace the advice of a veterinarian. (See key on the following pages.)

Cat Acupuncture Body Map Key

1. Located between front paw webbing. Used for front leg paralysis.

2. Same as No. 1. Used for front leg paralysis and deafness.

3. Local point pain.

4. One inch below No. 5 in the crease formed by the muscle. Used for local joint pain, constipation.

5. Located in the crease formed by the elbow. Local pain, paralysis of front limb, constipation, dermatitis, itching, cough.

6. For local pain.

7. Located in the shoulder joint, used for shoulder pain.

8. Located in the middle of upper lip. Used for emergency and shock. Apply acupuncture by pinching with thumb and index finger.

9. Used for difficulty in mastication and local pain.

10. Used for eye problems.

11. Tip of ear. Used for eye problems.

12. One inch behind the ear. Used for cervical problems and deafness.

13. Located on center line one inch inward and below No. 12. Uses are the same as for No. 12.

14. Located in front of scapula one inch from center line (spinal column). Used for cervical pain, arthritis in any joint, bone problems in general.

15. Behind scapula one inch out from spinal column. Thoracic pain, infections, cleansing of the blood.

16. Located opposite the navel on the spinal area and one inch out from that midline. Used for thoracic-lumbar pain, urinary problems, kidney and sexual disorders.

17. In front of the ilium one inch out from spinal midline. Used for lumbar-sacral pain, pain at the hips, and constipation.

18. Located at the crease formed by the head of the femur and hip joint. Used for hip pain.

19. Located one inch up and 45 degrees out from crease of tail. Used for hip, sacral pain, and constipation.

20. Located below the head of the femur. Used for lumbar pain, sacral pain, and stifle (knee) pain.

21. Located behind the crease formed by flexing of the knee. Used for hind leg paralysis, local knee pain, and any other weakness of lower limbs.

22. Located one inch below the patella (kneecap). Used to increase appetite, for paralysis of hind limbs, tonic to entire systems.

23. Used for urinary problems, and as an aid in the delivery of kittens.

24. Used for local pain and lumbar pain.

25. Located at the tip of the tail. Used for all back problems, constipation and hind leg paralysis.

26. Located in hind paw webbing. Used for hind leg paralysis, urinary problems, and as a tonic to give strength to lower limbs.

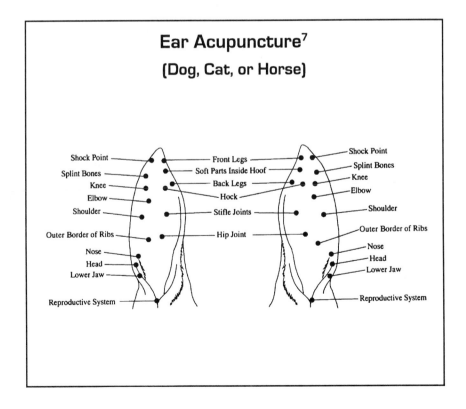

Ear Acupuncture[7]

(Dog, Cat, or Horse)

Diagnostic Points in Dog or Cat[8]

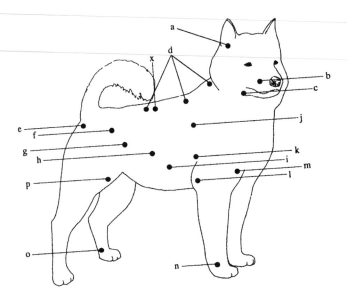

Pressure on these points elicits a pain response:

a. ear-otitis or ear canal infection
b. tooth abscess or gum infection
c. pharyngitis or tonsillitis
d. along back-intervertebral disc luxation, arthritis
e. anal gland infection or impaction
f. hip arthritis or dysplasia
g. cystitis or bladder infection or obstruction
h. abdominal pain-foreign body obstruction, infection, peritonitis
i. chest region-low abdominal pain-hepatitis, pancreatitis
j. chest region-pleurisy, pneumonia
k. heart region-pericarditis, endocarditis
l. elbow-arthritis, bursitis
m. shoulder-arthritis
n. forepaw-foreign body, cyst or referred pain from l, m, k, or d
o. hindpaw-foreign body, cyst or referred pain from p, f, g, or d
p. knee-patella dislocation or torn cruciate ligament
x. kidney region-nephritis

Note: Dr. Gloria Dodd, DVM, adds to (i): from low to *high* abdominal pain for liver, pancreas (right side), spleen (left), stomach, gall bladder and bile ducts.

Dog or Cat Acupuncture Body Map[9]

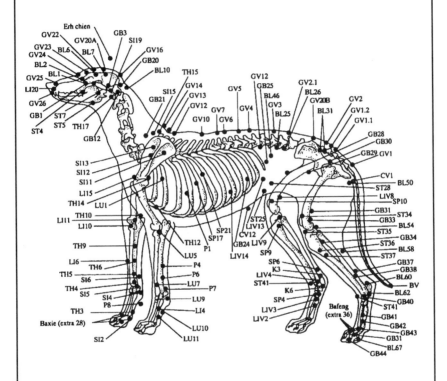

Dog or Cat Acupuncture Body Map[10]

Dorsal Aspect (Top of Body)

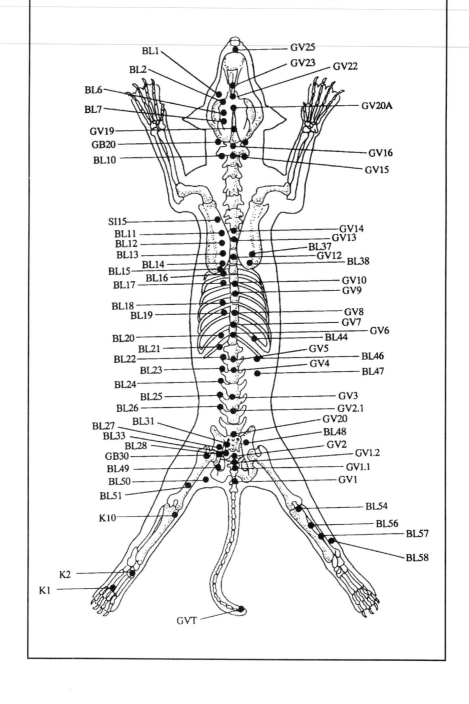

Dog or Cat Acupuncture Body Map[11]

Ventral Aspect (Underside of Body)

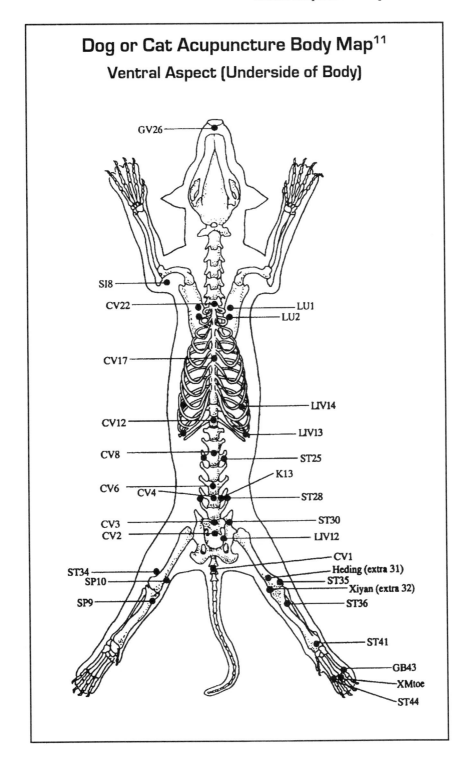

Specific Meridians[12]
(Dog or Cat)

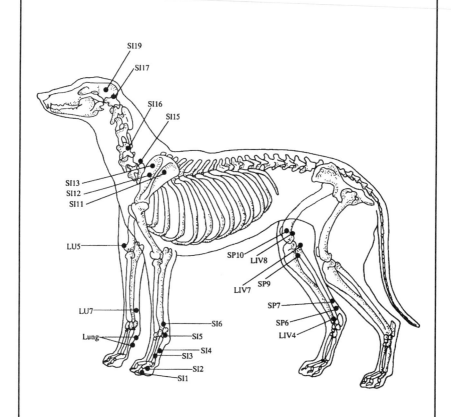

Key:
LIV - Liver
LU - Lung
SI - Small Intestine
SP - Spleen

Specific Meridians[13]
(Dog or Cat)

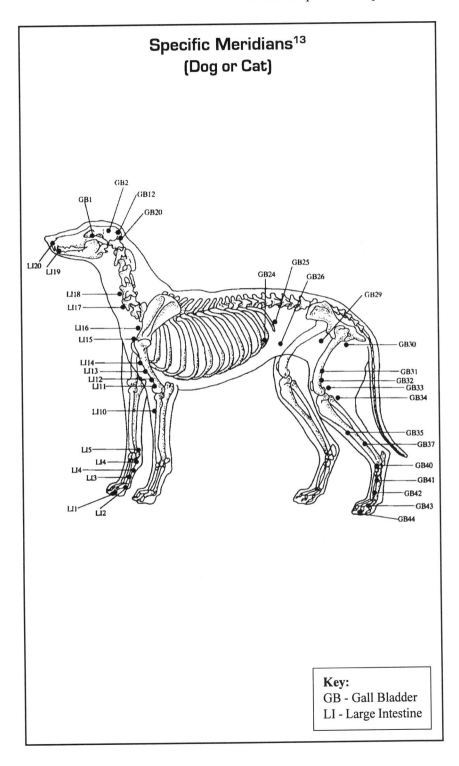

Key:
GB - Gall Bladder
LI - Large Intestine

Specific Meridians[14]
(Dog or Cat)

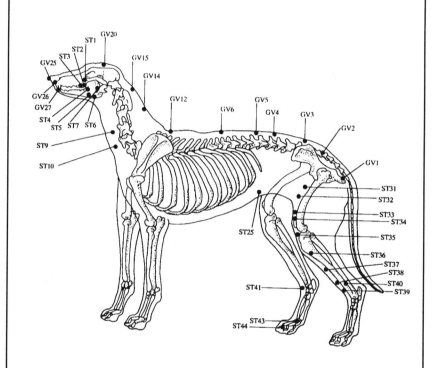

Key:
ST - Stomach
GV - Governing Vessel

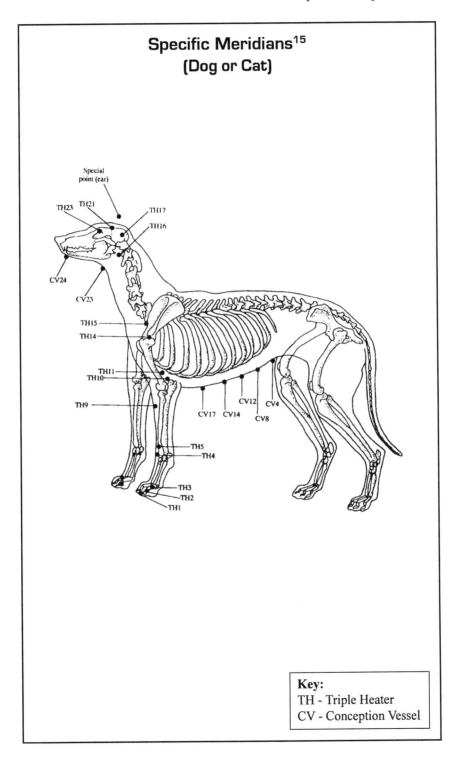

Specific Meridians[15]
(Dog or Cat)

Key:
TH - Triple Heater
CV - Conception Vessel

Specific Meridians[16]
(Dog or Cat)

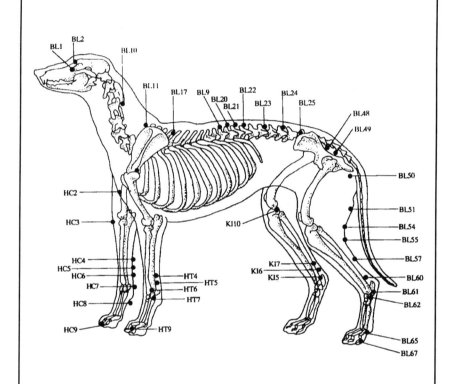

Key:
BL - Bladder
HC - Heart Constrictor
KI - Kidney

Acupuncture Map (Dog or Cat)[17]

The Paws-Hindlimb

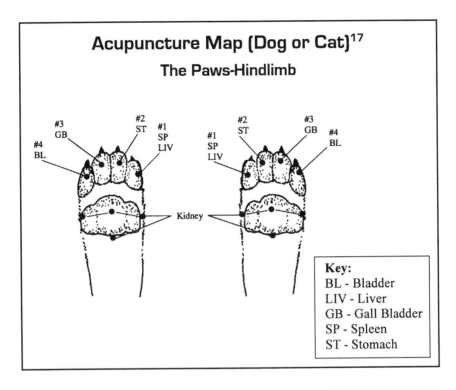

Key:
BL - Bladder
LIV - Liver
GB - Gall Bladder
SP - Spleen
ST - Stomach

Acupuncture Map (Dog or Cat)[18]

The Paws-Forelimb

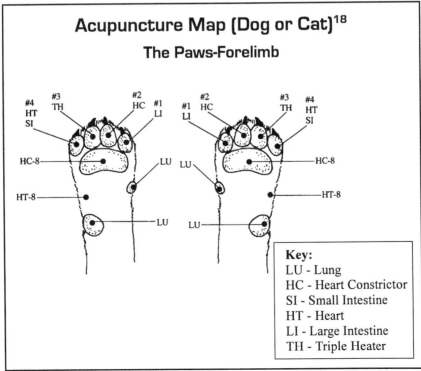

Key:
LU - Lung
HC - Heart Constrictor
SI - Small Intestine
HT - Heart
LI - Large Intestine
TH - Triple Heater

Emergency Resuscitation[19]
(Shock, Heart Failure, Respiratory Arrest)

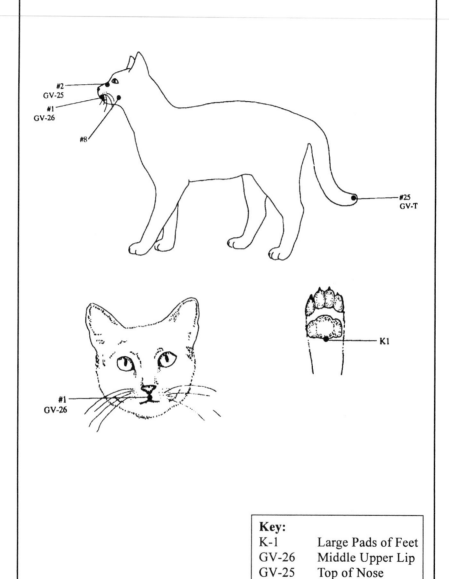

Key:

K-1	Large Pads of Feet
GV-26	Middle Upper Lip
GV-25	Top of Nose
GV-T	Tip of Tail
Erh chien	Lower Jaw

Acupressure Points for
Immune Stimulation—Bilaterally[20]
(Dog or Cat)

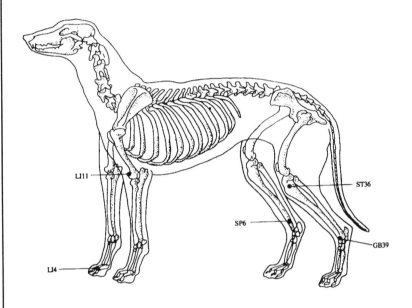

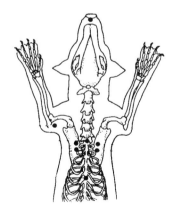

Key:	
L-I	Large Intestine
ST	Stomach
SP	Spleen
GB	Gall Bladder

Press each point with thumb or forefinger for about 60 seconds 1-2 times daily as needed, both right and left sides of animal.

[1]IVAS, *The International Veterinary Acupuncture Society* (Chester Springs, PA: IVAS), undated pamphlet, p. 5.

[2]Nancy Scanlan, DVM, "Animal Acupuncture," in *Natural Pet Magazine*, February, 1993, p. 7.

[3]Nancy Scanlan, DVM, "Needles for Cats, or How I Saw the Light and Became Holistic With the Help of Acupuncture," in *Tiger Tribe Magazine*, March-April, 1993, p. 16.

[4]Alan M. Klide, VMD, and Shiu K. Kung, Ph.D., *Veterinary Acupuncture* (Philadelphia, PA, University of Pennsylvania Press, 1977), p. 209.

[5]Sheldon Altman, DVM, *An Introduction to Veterinary Acupuncture*, pp. 131-136; and Alan M. Klide, VMD, and Shiu K. Kung, Ph.D., *Veterinary Acupuncture*, pp. 113-118. Altman adds meridian designations. Material is abbreviated.

[6]Judy Fireman, *Cat Catalog* (New York, Workman Publishing, 1976), p. 240.

[7]Linda Tellington-Jones, *The Tellington TTouch* (New York: Viking Press, 1992), p. 121.

[8]Dr. Michael Fox, *The Healing Touch*, (New York: Newmarket Press, 1981), p. 99.

[9]Sheldon Altman, DVM, *An Introduction to Veterinary Acupuncture* (Monterey Park, CA: Chan's Corporation, 1981), p. 148.

[10]Sheldon Altman, DVM, *An Introduction to Veterinary Acupuncture* (Monterey Park, CA: Chan's Corporation, 1981), p. 150.

[11]*Ibid.,* p. 149.

[12]Alan M. Klide, VMD, and Shiu K. Kung, Ph.D., *Veterinary Acupuncture* (Philadelphia, PA, University of Pennsylvania Press, 1977), p. 203.

[13]*Ibid.,* p. 204.

[14]*Ibid.,* p. 205.

[15]*Ibid.,* p. 206.

[16]*Ibid.,* p. 207.

[17]*Ibid.,* p. 208.

[18]*Ibid.,* p. 208.

[19]Sheldon Altman, DVM, *An Introduction to Veterinary Acupuncture* (Monterey Park, CA: Chan's Corporation, 1981), p 155; and Shin Dog Chart, pp. 131-136.

[20]Gloria Dodd, DVM, © 1987.

VII - Flower Essences
for Cats and Dogs

Flower essences go beyond homeopathy or acupuncture/acupressure in reaching the non-physical bodies for healing; in effect they do different things. Like homeopathic remedies, flower essences carry an energy imprint only of their foundation substance; in this case, the substance (flower petals) begins with a very high vibration rate. The methods of this book have progressed from physical level healing (nutrition, naturopathy, vitamins, herbs) to mental-emotional healing (homeopathy), with acupuncture an energy bridge via the etheric double between the two. Flower essences and gemstones go further into the outer vibrational bodies, providing healing that reaches the mental, emotional, and spiritual levels. They also provide a bridge to bring healing from these levels into the etheric double and physical body. They have less direct effect on the physical body than on the outer vibrational layers.

Energy in healing moves through the bodies in specific order. Healing may begin in the outer energy bodies and move toward the physical. It passes from the spiritual body's three layers (upper, middle, and lower spiritual bodies), through the two layers of the mental body (higher and lower, or creative and conscious mind). Then it moves through the single layer of the emotional body and into the etheric double, which is the energy twin of the physical body. Changes in vibration then manifest in the physical body.

Healing can also progress in the opposite direction, beginning first in the physical body and moving through the non-physical levels. A laying on of hands or Reiki healing, where the healer uses her hands to transmit energy through the person or animal receiving it, are examples of this. So is healing a strictly physical level or physically caused disease—malnutrition for example, which has a clearly physical body cure. (Most healers believe that every physical level dis-ease also has a cause or coordinating emotion in one or more of the upper layers.)

Healing begins at the pet's or person's physical body and moves vibrationally outward. Energy originates at the physical level, then passes into the etheric double, the emotional body, the lower and higher bodies, and through the three spiritual body layers. A dis-ease that is physical level in origin would have to progress very long and far to dis-ease the spiritual body levels.

Flower essences vibrate at a very fast energy rate; this is what gives them access to all of the bodies. Some essences seem to work more fully on the outer levels, some on the etheric bridge to the physical body, and some more fully on the emotional and mental body layers. Their energy moves freely and goes to where the healing needs to happen in the vibrational system. Some individual essences work with the etheric-located chakras, while others go all the way out to the vibrational blueprint that directs the outer bodies on the spiritual level.

Flowers are fragile and beautiful. They are the reproductive organs of plants and are plants' finest expression—in their colors, delicate shapes, short lives, and unique fragrances. The fragrances also have healing properties. They are the plants' expression of creativity and beauty. Each bloom is a wonder of the Earth and a gift of the Goddess. The flowering jacaranda in Florida is just another lovely tree until it blooms vividly and briefly in the spring and turns the tree to purple fire. Flowers are more-than-ordinary expressions of life on Earth.

Pets and people, like flowers, have their more-than-ordinary physical expressions in the non-physical bodies. These unseen parts fulfill the complexity of life and existence. They are how we feel and think, who we are, and why we have incarnated at this time. Animals have these complexities as fully as humans do. Physical level healing methods are needed for the earth plane physical body, but they do not meet the complexities of the unseen layers whose energy expresses the individual's or pet's Be-ing. Flowers that are almost non-physical to begin with become the bridge to these complexities when their vibrations are released in the essence-making process.

A drop of flower essence placed on the pet's or person's tongue has a non-physical vibration rate similar to but finer/faster than that of homeopathic remedies. Like homeopathics, they have very little or no physical substance, only an energy imprint of a flower that was barely physical at all. Each flower essence has its own rate of energy, as does each person, dog, or cat. A disruption in that pet's or person's vibration also has its own energy rate, and the disruption may occur in any of the bodies, moving into the physical manifestation (dis-ease) through the layers.

When a person or animal tests by a pendulum or Kinesiology for a particular flower essence that is a specific energy rate and form, she matches the disruption vibration in her aura bodies to the healing vibration in the essence that will correct it. She will not test "yes" for an essence that does not make this energy match. On taking the essence, its vibration moves outward from the physical through the unseen bodies until it reaches the place of the energy imbalance. When it reaches that place, the match of energies brings the disruption back to balance, disorder back to order, and healing begins. The disrupted vibration pattern healed, a ripple effect occurs. The healing/correction/return to order moves through the energy level bodies, finally manifesting in physical level wellness. The healing may travel as far as the spiritual level life blueprint, if it has to, but will eventually end at correcting the physical body.

Flower essences made from higher level plants such as the many rose species or the lotus tend to reach higher levels and aura layers than flowers of more common plants. Essences like dandelion or the flowers of garden vegetables and fruits tend to stay closer in vibration to the Earth and therefore work on closer-to-physical levels and healing issues. These might do most of their work on the emotional or mental bodies. The Traditional Flower Remedies (Bach Remedies) tend to focus on this emotional-mental level for humans and pets, and it is on this level that the first research on flower essences for healing was done. *Walnut* flower remedy, for example, helps in times of transitions like moving, going to a new home, or when another animal or person joins the family. The *Gruss an Aachen* rose essence, in contrast, stabilizes the fusion of the physical and unseen body levels.

Different flower essences have different uses and definitions. Some are very general, while others are highly specific. As an example of a general use essence with a wide range of application, *Crab Apple* is for cleansing and detoxification. It is used after surgery or during illness and is also useful for pets detoxing in a fast. Use it for animals or people with arthritis, kidney or liver dis-ease, abscesses, ear infections, or intestinal worms—any dis-ease requiring internal cleansing. *Crab Apple* essence is positive for an animal that has just been vaccinated or has been on chemical medications. A detoxifying essence has innumerable uses.

Another wide-range general flower essence for pets is *Snapdragon*, which is used for healing the mouth, head, neck, and face of animals or people, and for healing the teeth, jaw, and gums. *Snapdragon* is also for pets who use their mouths in negative ways—biting, chewing unusual things (plaster, linoleum, shoes, stones), or gnawing on people's fingers. Use it for teething puppies and kittens, for adolescent destructive chewing sprees, and for pets with behavioral problems involving chewing or biting. Use it also for aging pets with gum dis-ease, tooth decay, jawbone deterioration, or for mouth/jaw injuries or sores at any age. Both of these remedies can have a wide range of uses at different times in a cat's or dog's life.

Traditional Flower Remedies from Ellon:
The 38 Flower Remedies of Dr. Edward Bach[1]

Indications for Use

Agrimony: Mental anguish behind a "brave face."

Aspen: Vague unknown fears. Anxiety and apprehension.

Beech: Critical and intolerant of others.

Centaury: Unable to say "no." Easily imposed on.

Cerato: Unable to make decisions without advice from others.

Cherry Plum: Fears losing control of thoughts and actions.

Chestnut Bud: Needs to learn by experience; repeats same mistakes over and over.

Chicory: Always knows just what's "right" for others. Possessive.

Clematis: Dreamy, absent-minded, lack of attention and concentration.

Crab Apple: Poor physical self-image. Feelings of shame and uncleanliness.

Elm: Temporary feelings of inadequacy, overwhelmed by responsibilities.

Gentian: Easily discouraged, often with self-doubt. Pessimistic.

Gorse: Hopelessness and despair.

Heather: Obsessed with own troubles; overtalkative, unhappy when alone.

Holly: Suspicious, envious, vengeful; those who hate.

Honeysuckle: Dwells in the past, of what was, and could have been.

Hornbeam: Tiredness, and fatigue; gets things done, but feels need to be strengthened.

Impatiens: Impatient, fast-paced, irritable.

Larch: Lack of self-confidence; anticipates failure.

Mimulus: Fear of known things; heights, the dark, being alone, etc.

Mustard: Deep gloom, which comes and goes. Melancholia.

Oak: Workaholic. Nose to grindstone syndrome, can neglect own and needs of those close.

Olive: Complete exhaustion; weariness.

Pine: Dissatisfied with own accomplishments; feelings of guilt. Perfectionist.

Red Chestnut: Overconcern and worry for others, fearing the worst may happen.

Rock Rose: Terror, extreme fright, and panic. Nightmares.

Rock Water: Overly rigid, strict adherence to a particular belief or lifestyle.

Scleranthus: Indecisiveness, forever in between choices.

Star of Bethlehem: Past traumas not fully recovered from.

Sweet Chestnut: Extreme anguish; having reached the limits of one's endurance.

Vervain: "Must always be right." High strung philosophizer easily incensed by injustices.

Vine: Natural leaders; in extreme can be dominating and tyrannical.

Walnut: Stabilizes during periods of transition; eases process of letting go and beginning anew.

Water Violet: Loners, proud and aloof; difficulty developing close relationships.

White Chestnut: Persistent unwanted thoughts, mental chatter and associated sleeplessness.

Wild Oat: Feeling life is passing by; dissatisfied with career but undecided what else to do. Feeling life is passing by.

Willow: Resentment and bitterness at having been treated unfairly.

Nature's Rescue/Rescue Remedy: The Emergency Rescue of Dr. Edward Bach—Gentle, calming, and stabilizing in a wide range of stressful situations.

Nature's Rescue/Rescue Remedy Cream: Relief of pain and swelling due to minor burns, cuts, bruises, skin irritations, insect bites, acute muscle stiffness; and simple headache.

Traditional Flower Remedies from Ellon
for Use with Dogs and Cats[2]

Most animal personality traits, behavioral patterns, and emotional reactions bear striking resemblance to those same patterns in humans. After studying the indications for Remedy use, put yourself in the animal's place, feel what s/he feels, sense what s/he senses, then determine which of the indications most closely fit your animal's behavior patterns, personality traits, and/or emotions.

Leslie J. Kaslof, author of *The Bach Flower Remedies: A Self-Help Guide.*

General Uses for Pets

Agrimony: Helps ease the mental anguish that accompanies a slow healing wound or injury.

Aspen: For "skittishness." Very nervous and easily frightened.

Cherry Plum: For very aggressive animals that may seem to be uncontrollable.

Chestnut Bud: For those having difficulty in being trained; for animals that keep making the same mistakes over and over.

Chicory: Can be helpful for animals that demand attention. Can become possessive or jealous.

Clematis: Can be used for animals that are lethargic.

Crab Apple: Good for cleansing after an illness, accident, or surgery.

Larch: Effective in helping animals that lack self-confidence. Low animal in "pecking order."

Mimulus: For fears of specific non-threatening things such as water, cars, other animals, strangers, etc. Generally very timid.

Rock Rose: For animals that tend to panic easily or who have just had a really frightening experience. Terror.

Scleranthus: Helps alleviate car sickness.

Star of Bethlehem: For abused animals or those that have suffered trauma or serious injury. Can ease the grief of losing a human or animal companion.

Vervain: For hyperactive animals (also consider *Impatiens*).

Vine: For the "Boss" animal, leader of the group.

Walnut: Helps in adjusting to a new animal in the environment, change of routine, etc.

Water Violet: For the aloof animal or those that tend to be loners. Many cats are this type.

Remedies and Your Feline Friends[3]

Aspen: For the "fraidy cat" that is always slinking from "safe" place to "safe" place, never quite at ease. Startles easily at any sound, even non-threatening sounds it has heard before. (Note: In some cases such behavior is due to abuse or trauma in the past; for this use *Star of Bethlehem.* When in doubt, use both *Star* and *Aspen.*)

Beech: For the cat who has no tolerance for another animal or certain people. Effective with *Walnut* to assist in keeping the peace between two cats who always seem to be fighting.

Chicory: For the extremely affectionate cat that can be possessive and jealous, always near you wanting to be held, petted, and fussed over.

Clematis: Any time a cat appears stunned or experiences unusual, prolonged patterns of sleeping beyond the typical cat-nap. Used to help in regaining consciousness following an accident or operation. Can be used in conjunction with *Nature's Rescue (Rescue Remedy)* to help newborn kittens wake up and breathe. One tiny drop can be repeated every few minutes.

Honeysuckle: For the cat who has lost a person or another animal she has been close to. *Star of Bethlehem* can be used as well to address this condition. Also useful along with *Walnut* to help the cat adjust to moving to a new location.

Hornbeam: For fatigue. The strengthening remedy. Can be helpful in assisting runts or to build up any sickly animal.

Larch: Especially useful for the cat low in the pecking order, perhaps the runt. For the cat with little or no self-confidence. Self-esteem is an important part of feline well-being and is radiated by a balanced cat most of the time.

Mimulus: For fear of particular things or circumstances such as thunderstorms, vacuum cleaners, trips to the vet, visits by small children. In cases when fear turns to terror, use *Rock Rose* or *Nature's Rescue (Rescue Remedy)*.

Nature's Rescue/Rescue Remedy: Appropriate for any kind of accident, illness, or injury your cat may experience. *Nature's Rescue* can also be used in cases of pregnancy and queening, at cat shows, or car trips, while boarding, during a long absence, before and after surgery, or whenever a cat seems to be experiencing the effects of unusual stress. Do not neglect to seek the services of a veterinarian in all serious cases.

Star of Bethlehem: For all trauma, past and present, physical and psychological. For recuperation from surgery, queening, car trips, injury, weaning, boarding, and other traumas that affect your cat's dignity, freedom, health, or security. For cats adopted from shelters.

Vine: For the "Boss Cat." One who rules the roost and the household.

Walnut: Very helpful for any sort of changes that a cat may experience, such as new babies or new pets in the house, moving, weaning, heat cycles. Eases adjustment to house guests and holidays.

Water Violet: A constitutional remedy for most cats. Helps them keep their instinct for solitude in balance with their enjoyable interactions with people and other animals in their environment.

Traditional Flower Remedies and Your Dog

Aspen: For the nervous dog, fearful especially in new circumstances. This dog often carries its tail between its legs and may be a submissive wetter. Can assist dogs who have been harshly disciplined in the past.

Chestnut Bud: Helpful in training situations. Useful in teaching a puppy to make a distinction between right or wrong. For example: the difference between papers for paper training and today's paper on the sofa, or a rawhide bone and your shoes. Used in conjunction with effective behavior modification (for you and your dog).

Chicory: For a dog that follows you around and is constantly underfoot, becoming extremely upset when left alone. Can become jealous. For the extremely affectionate dog who must always be in your lap.

Clematis: Dogs will sometimes need *Clematis* when kept indoors in adverse weather, when waiting for a beloved person to come home, etc. If they are drowsy, not really asleep. Also useful following surgery to help with waking up from anesthesia. It may be used in combination with *Nature's Rescue (Rescue Remedy)* the moment puppies are born to help them wake up and breathe.

Holly: For the angry dog who threatens to attack or actually does attack without provocation. Remember that any major personality changes should always be checked out with a vet. In addition, *Holly* can be useful in treating aggressive behavior often due to abuse or trauma in the past. *Star of Bethlehem* should always be given in conjunction with *Holly*.

Honeysuckle: For the dog whose primary person has been permanently removed from its life. If a dog acts withdrawn, subdued, and unenthusiastic toward people. To be used in conjunction with *Star of Bethlehem*, especially if primary person has died. For homesickness while at a kennel or if left home alone for a prolonged period of time.

Mimulus: For the dog with a particular fear of known things such as loud noises, thunderstorms, vacuum cleaners, trips to the vet, visits by small children. When fear turns to terror, you can use *Rock Rose* or *Nature's Rescue (Rescue Remedy).*

Olive: For the dog who is totally exhausted, ill and/or traumatized. This remedy may lend a measure of strength and comfort to seriously ill dogs along with *Star of Bethlehem.*

Scleranthus: Can be helpful in case of car sickness, used along with *Nature's Rescue (Rescue Remedy).*

Star of Bethlehem: For the physically or emotionally traumatized dog, either currently or in the past. Nearly always indicated for dogs that have been in a pound. For abused animals.

Vervain: For highly strung dogs with a great deal of nervous energy, for those who are hard to keep from jumping or barking. While enthusiasm goes with the species, this remedy can help in slowing them down.

Water Violet: This Remedy is helpful for the dog who is aloof, self-reliant, intelligent, and a loner. It is useful for dogs that were socialized comparatively late in life and who seem very standoffish. Often an excellent choice for dogs who are part wolf, coyote, dingo, among others, or who have wild ancestry like the husky.

Essential Essences

Angel Essence (Sky Vine, white)—soul level healing

Angelic Grace Essence (Angel Face Rose, lavender)—universal love, heart healing

Ariel's Essence (Sky Vine, white)—heals aura damage

Astarte Essence (Perfume Beauty Rose, pink)—love and union

Aura Essence (Hibiscus, yellow)—aura cleansing and healing

Aura Cleansing Essence (Allemanda, purple)—spiritual healing

Beloved Essence (Confederate Jasmine, white)—love's consummation

Brede's Essence (Sky Vine, blue)—spiritual growth and transformation

Changing Woman Essence (Mandevilla, pink)—emotional healing and release

Channeling Essence I (Angel Trumpet Datura, white)—spiritual awareness

Channeling Essence II (King's Mantle, purple)—psychic balance

Detox Essence (Allemanda, yellow)—detoxification on all levels

Healing Love Essence (Crepe Myrtle, pink)—love and self-love

Hope Essence (Pandora Vine, lavender/pink)—hope for one's life

Inner Change Essence (Peace Rose, cream/pink)—stability during change

Inner Child Essence (Plumbago, blue)—inner peace

Kali Essence (Royal Velvet Rose, red)—supports life purpose

Life Essence (Passion Flower, red)—spiritual protection

Light Body Essence (Gardenia, white)—core soul healing

Lovers' Essence (Crepe Myrtle, red)—manifesting love on the earthplane

Mary Magdalene Essence (Sonia Rose, salmon pink)—comfort, hope, patience

Mind Travel Essence (Morning Glory, indigo)—mind expansion and telepathy

Moonflower Essence (Moonflower, white)—psychic awareness

Old Soul Essence (Angel's Trumpet Datura, purple)—karmic growth

Oneness Essence (Passion Flower, purple/blue)—oneness with all life, dreamwork

Psychic Shield Essence (Gold Badge Rose, yellow)—energy protection

Pure Love Essence (Pascali Rose, white)—love and union

Star Woman Essence (Angel Trumpet Datura, peach)—star wisdom

Transcendence Essence (Princess Tree, purple)—opening to Goddess

Trust Essence (Hibiscus, pink)—heals betrayed trust

Women's Body Essence (Tropicana Rose, orange)—reproductive healing

Women's Healing Essence (Hibiscus, red)—women's all-healer

Essences for Animal Care[4]

Using flower essences with animals can quickly instill a belief in the effectiveness of the remedies, even in the most hardened skeptics, since the "placebo effect" is hardly applicable. Skillful flower essence application with animals does involve careful and sensitive observation. Most of us have been accustomed through cultural attitudes to see animals more as things than as living beings. Developing an imaginative understanding of the feeling life of the animal is the key to effective flower essence selection. If you are the owner of a pet, don't forget to examine your own feelings with regard to the animal. Are you overly possessive, non-caring, cruel, or harsh? Sometimes cases with animals are best cleared up by using flower essences for the caretaker as well as for the pet!

The following are essences which practitioners have reported to be of benefit in working with animals. We welcome your insights and contributions.

Aspen: For unknown fear or terror in an animal; especially indicated when treating wild animals; enhanced when used in combination with *Red Clover.*

Borage: Good for lifting the spirit of an animal that may be depressed because of illness, old age, or a recent transition.

Chamomile: Has been used very effectively with *Rescue Remedy* for barking dogs, for any emotional upset accompanied by stomach distress such as gas or vomiting.

Cherry Plum: Often used as part of *Nature's Rescue* (*Rescue Remedy*), but also effective when used alone for cases of extreme tension or stress, such as a scared or frightened animal that is trapped.

Chestnut Bud: To help train animals and instill effective learning; seems to stimulate the animal's emotional memory, such as with toilet training.

Chicory: Especially indicated for younger animals such as whining puppies or kittens; also indicated when the illness may be psychosomatic, to get attention.

Dill: Good to include in any situations which involve being overwhelmed or confused, such as during travel or upset of schedule.

Holly: Used very successfully for jealous pets, especially when jealousy involved another pet vying for the attention of the caretaker.

Mimulus: For "nervous" conditions in animals; good for "jittery" horses. *Impatiens* should also be considered in the mix.

Penstemon: Good as a supplement to other treatments for illness or trauma; gives inner strength during adverse circumstances. Where there has been injury be sure to add *Arnica.*

Pink or White Yarrow: Effective in helping pets who take on or mirror the emotions of their human caretakers. (Essences for the owners should also be used!)

Self-Heal: One of the most commonly used and popular of flower essence treatments for animals; stimulates the inner healing forces of your pet; good to add to any standard medical applications, either external or internal; excellent in a cream base.

Perhaps the widest-ranging general remedy and probably the best known is *Nature's Rescue (Rescue Remedy,* and also called *Five-Flower Remedy),* which is used at any time of trauma, emotional or physical. The remedy is made from a combination of five flowers: Star of Bethlehem, Rock Rose, Clematis, Cherry Plum, and Impatiens. It is used in any upsetting situation or where resuscitation is required, to awaken newborns, after surgery or accidents, after any injury, for fear or fright with any cause, for abused and panicked animals, for calming stress of any sort, and for shock. It comes in a liquid dilution and also in a first-aid skin cream. When a cat or dog needs *Nature's Rescue/Rescue Remedy,* her guardian usually needs it, too. *Arnica* essence or *Comfrey* have similar indications for shock and trauma on any level. I keep *Nature's Rescue* on hand at all times, traveling or at home.

There are four major sources for obtaining prepared flower essences in the United States, other than by making them yourself. These are the Traditional Flower Remedies from Ellon (Bach Flower Remedies), Perelandra Rose and Garden Essences, the Flower Essence Society, and Essential Essences. The Traditional (Bach) Flowers are called remedies rather than essences as they are homeopathically prepared, and are also known as English Remedies. They were researched by homeopathic physician Edward Bach (1890-1936), who determined uses for thirty-eight remedies before his death. These Traditional Flower Remedies were the first marketed flower remedies and are the best known and understood. The literature on them lists mental and emotional uses but not specific physical dis-eases, though these also apply. They are the most easily available and are sold in many health food stores. They can be ordered direct from Ellon USA, Inc., 644 Merrick Rd., Lynbrook, NY 11563, (800) 433-7523. A new line of remedies for pets is in the works.

The Flower Essence Society of California is the major researching agent currently continuing Bach's work, and primarily researching American plants. The Society offers a selection of seventy-two flower essences, plus twenty-four that are still in the research state (of about two hundred being investigated at the center). They sell single essences and kits, aromatherapy oils and products, and reference books, including a comprehensive *Flower Essence Reperatory* (dis-ease index). Write for their catalog at FES, POB 1769, Nevada City, CA 95959, (916) 265-0258 or (800) 548-0075.

One further source for flower essences is Machaelle Small Wright's Perelandra Center for Nature Research in Virginia. The Perelandra flower essences include two sets of Rose Essences (eight remedies each) and eighteen Garden Essences made from the flowers of garden vegetables. They also sell Wright's books. Ask for their catalog from Perelandra

Center for Nature Research, POB 3603, Warrenton, VA 22186, (703) 937-2153 (twenty-four hour machine).

Essential Essences are made by me, and marketed via the *Essential Reiki Journal*, POB 1436, Olney, MD 20830-1436, (301) 570-1990.

If the plants needed are native and available, flower essences are easy to make at home. This is done simply by floating the flowers in pure water in full sunlight, then storing the water in dark bottles with an alcohol preservative. Making contact with the nature devas of the flowers and asking their help, and thanking them, make for the most powerful essences. To make a gemstone elixir you will need a sterilized simple glass bowl large enough to hold about one quart of fluid. You will also need distilled water. All implements should also be sterilized before using.

First wash the glassware in hot soapy water and rinse thoroughly. Take the glass bowl outside on a sunny morning and place it on the ground (not on concrete) near the growing flowers. Fill the bowl with pure water. Pick the healthiest blooms from several plants of the same type and put them on top of the water, touching them as little as possible (use sterilized scissors or tweezers). Cover the whole water surface with the flowers if you can; if not, a single bloom can make the essence. Leave the bowl and flowers in the sun for three hours, longer on a cloudy day or if you start after early morning. It is best to prepare essences as early in the day as possible, and on sunny, cloudless days in spring or summer.

After three hours, fill up to half of each storage bottle with good quality brandy. Remove the flowers and any debris from the water without touching—use a cup to pour. Pour the water into the bottles through the funnel, filling them the rest of the way, and label the bottles. Make only one essence at a time or wash your hands between handling different bowls and be careful not to confuse them in the labeling. A crystal grid or a pyramid or Reiki symbols can also be used—make sure the crystals have been cleared.

This process results in what is called the Mother Tincture, similar to the Mother Tincture in homeopathy. Once in the storage bottles, the Mother Essence may be homeopathically potentized by shaking, tapping, or striking the bottle sharply against your hand or a padded chair arm twenty or thirty times. A Stock Bottle is next made by taking 5–9 drops of the potentized Mother Essence and placing it in a one-ounce dropper bottle filled one quarter or one-half full of brandy or white vinegar and the rest with pure water. Potentize it again. This is how flower essences are sold. They can be used directly from this Stock Bottle, which I recommend, or further diluted.

The essences can be diluted once more into a Dosage Bottle, which may contain several different flower remedies for use over a period of time. Place 5–10 drops from the Stock Bottle of each essence chosen in a one-ounce brown eyedropper bottle of pure water with one-third vinegar or brandy. The dog, cat, or person is dosed from this bottle, though I personally prefer to dose directly from the Stock Bottle. Unlike homeopathic remedies, flower essences do not grow more potent with each dilution, and the second dilution to me seems more effective. If using a Dosage Bottle, I also recommend using more than at least 5–10 drops of each Stock Bottle remedy. Take them several times a day. Use only a few essences together at a time, generally three to five in a Dosage Bottle. Stock Bottle essences are single essences.[5]

The brandy, or other food-grade alcohol 60 proof or higher, is necessary as a preservative to keep bacteria from growing in and contaminating the essences. They keep the flower essence potent indefinitely, and as the essences are used by the drop, there is very little alcohol actually ingested. Flower essences can be preserved with white vinegar, but are less stable or permanent that way, similar to herb tinctures made with vinegar. Stock and Dosage Bottles are made in light-proof glass eyedropper bottles, with glass droppers. The bottles are usually brown but can also be amber, green or blue. They can be bought at pharmacies or from flower essence sources for under a dollar each. Make sure to label the bottles. This includes Dosage Bottles, which may contain several remedies for one pet (while a second bottle for another person or yourself contains a different list of essences). As in other holistic methods, the same remedies used for people are used for cats and dogs. When dosing, if the eyedropper touches the animal's mouth, rinse it off before returning it to the Stock or Dosage Bottle to prevent contaminating the remedy with a sour algae-like scum. If this happens, the remedy or dilution needs to be replaced.

There are several possible ways to choose which flower essence or essences are needed for your pet at any given time. The easiest method, though possibly the least effective, is by the definitions given for the remedies from each ordering source. (See listings in my book, *Healing with Flower or Gemstone Essences*, the *Flower Essence Repertory*, or any of the other flower essence books or literature.) These can do the job, but each dog or cat is an individual and there may be something going on vibrationally that is different from what the pet's guardian can observe. As flower essences are vibrational, a vibrational method of testing for them is more accurate than choosing them locally, though the literature is still usually the place to start.

Using a pendulum and muscle testing (one-person or two-person method) are ways of asking the animal's own energy bodies to choose the correct remedy. The essences tested for a particular pet may surprise you but when you use the essences, the results will confirm the pendulum and muscle testing. These forms of applied kinesiology testing also are useful with homeopathic remedies, in determining which of a couple of remedies is the closest match, and whether or when to repeat a dose. For example, a pet that is clinging, overly affectionate, and jealous of other animals or people in her family probably needs *Chicory* essence, but may instead or also test for the underlying cause of her behavior—*Bleeding Heart* or *Comfrey* flower essence for healing past abuse and insecurity.

A pendulum is my preferred way of testing for flower essences. It is my most used tool for every aspect of healing. A pendulum can be made from any object that swings from a cord, even a button on a string or any necklace on its chain. I prefer to make mine from a small (three-quarter inch to one inch) crystal on a five-inch length of fine-linked silver jewelry chain. A bead or small wire-wrapped gemstone at the holding end makes it comfortable to the fingers. If using crystals or gemstones, make very sure that the stones are cleared before using the pendulum, or erratic responses may result. Ask if one of your spirit guides would be willing to direct the pendulum's answers for a much more accurate tool.

In using a pendulum for the first time, establish the answers to expect from it. There will be a clear "yes" and "no," plus a "maybe or undetermined" response, but what these look like can vary from user to user. Everyone's energy flow is different, and it is this energy flow that directs the response. To begin, hold the pendulum by the smaller end with the crystal swinging freely from its cord or chain. Ask in your mind to see a "yes" swing and think "yes" without other interfering thoughts. In a few moments the pendulum will begin a distinctive motion—my "yes" swings forward and back. Then ask to see a "no" in the same way; the resulting swing is different—my "no" moves in a circle. When these are clear, ask for a "maybe or undetermined" and watch the results— mine for this is a crystal that hangs steady, with little or no movement at all. Practice these responses until you are comfortable with them.

Next ask some evident questions of the pendulum. "Is my dog's name Kali?" "Is Copper shedding?" "Is the cat indoors?" The questions must have clear "yes" or "no" answers, and phrasing them so the answers are totally unambiguous is the key to using pendulums in an accurate and meaningful way. Don't ask, "Which of these flower essences does Copper need?" Ask instead, holding one essence in your other hand at a time, "Does Copper need this essence now?" Test for flower essences in just this way, holding each one available in your hand and asking, "Does my pet need this essence now?"

In choosing which essences to order from a list, ready the list and definitions first, then using the pendulum ask about each one, one at a time. You can begin by asking, "Do I need to have any essence in this row?" and only if there is a "yes" for the row, test each bottle in the row. If the essences are for a specific animal, try to be touching her while you test and invite her higher self in for the session. If you are testing for a specific need for that cat or dog, using the pendulum, ask: "Is this essence helpful for Kali's hyper behavior?" I prefer to ask if the animal needs the essence overall, rather than for only one use. When the essence bottles can be held in your hand, test again.

A person or pet will test for different essences at different times. Some persons or pets will test for a particular essence more often, some seldom or never, some just once, and some every day over a long period of time. Because of this, I prefer to have the kits on hand rather than only one or two essences. Before testing your animal from an essence kit or selecting single essences, test yourself. This clears your own energy so your needs do not interfere with test accuracy. Since dogs and cats so closely absorb their guardian's emotions, stress, and illness, you probably need the essence (or others in the box), too. Why not heal everyone in the household along with the cat? The more you work with a pendulum, the more useful and accurate a tool it becomes. It is my preferred way of testing for flower essences and other remedies for my animals and myself.

Muscle testing is the next way to choose essences, homeopathics, supplements and vitamins, or to discover food allergies for people or pets. When used for someone else or a cat or dog, the process is called surrogate testing.

In the basic muscle testing method, a woman emotionally close to the dog or cat touches the pet with one hand, holding her other arm out straight. A second woman puts a flower essence bottle into the extended hand, then presses down gently on the extended arm just above the wrist. As she does this, she asks to be connected to the animal's higher self as well as to her own higher self. Then she asks, "Is this remedy good for Kali?" "Does Kali need this remedy?" As she does so she asks the other woman to "hold." The woman touching the pet tries to keep her arm steady against the pressure behind her wrist. If the essence is not needed by the animal, the arm goes down, indicating a "no" answer. If the essence is needed, the woman's arm remains firm, indicating a "yes." Do only gentle pressing, no force. There are only yes and no answers in muscle testing. For best results, the woman who is touching the pet goes through the essence testing process for herself first, taking what she needs of the flower essences before testing the cat or dog.

Muscle testing can also be done by one person working alone, using the thumb and little finger of one hand touching as the resistance to pulling apart by the thumb and first finger of the other hand. For a "no" with this method, the fingers of the "hold" hand separate easily and for a "yes" they remain together and resist the pressure. For more on this process, see *Natural Healing for Dogs and Cats*. With any of these methods, the results are best when you can have physical contact with the pet being tested. With experience in the testing methods, however, and an ability to hold the animal clearly in your focused mind, it is not always essential to have the animal present to choose her essences accurately. Always invite in the pet's higher self to help.

Surrogate Muscle Testing[6]
(Two-Person Method)

Testing the dog in the clear

Surrogate Muscle Testing[6]
(Two-Person Method)

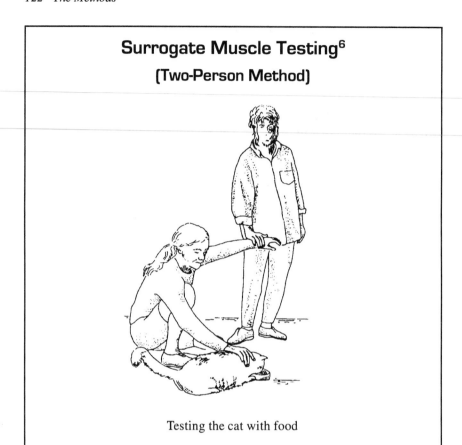

Testing the cat with food

Once chosen for the dog or cat, flower essences can be given in several ways. One is to place a drop from the Stock Bottle or a few drops when using a Dosage Bottle onto the pet's tongue or into her cheek pouch by pulling out her lip and dripping it in from the eyedropper. Another way is to place several drops in the pet's water daily or twice a day, whenever you refill the bowl. This method is more useful for dogs than cats, however, as some cats drink very little water at all. Flower essence drops can be placed on food or in a treat, or even be placed on the animal's skin—rubbed into her inside earflap or other hair-free area. Essences in a crisis can be given as often as every five minutes, if needed, until the crisis clears. Once an hour or half hour is not too often in acute, non-crisis situations. In general, I test and administer flower essences once a day, and put them on the animal's tongue.

Surrogate Muscle Testing[7]

(Kinesiology Self-Testing Steps)

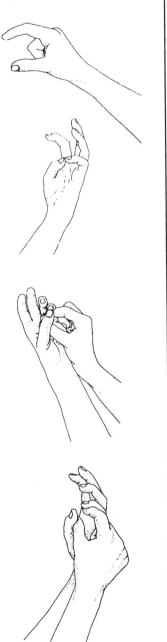

1. The circuit fingers: if you are right handed: place your left hand palm up. Connect the top of your left thumb with the tip of the left little finger (*not your index finger*). If you are left-handed: place your right hand palm up. Connect the tip of your right thumb with the tip of your right little finger . . . .

2. The test fingers: to test the circuit . . . place the thumb and index finger of your other hand inside the circle you have created by connecting your thumb and little finger. The thumb/index finger should be right under the thumb/little finger, touching them. Don't try to make a circle with your test fingers....It will look as if the circuit fingers are resting on the test fingers.

3. Keeping this position, ask yourself a yes/no question in which you already know the answer to be yes . . . . Once you've asked the question, press your circuit fingers together, keeping the tip-to-tip position. *Using the same amount of pressure*, try to pull apart the circuit fingers with your test fingers. Press the lower thumb against the upper thumb, the lower index finger against the upper little finger . . . .

   If the answer to the question is positive, you will not be able to easily pull apart the circuit fingers . . . . Important: Be sure the amount of pressure holding together the circuit fingers is equal to the amount pressing against them with your testing fingers. Also, don't use a pumping action in your testing fingers when trying to pry your circuit fingers apart. Use an equal, steady and continuous pressure.

4. Once you have a clear sense of the positive response, ask yourself a question that has a negative answer. Again press your circuit fingers together and, using equal pressure, press against the circuit fingers with the test fingers. This time the electrical circuit will break and the circuit fingers will weaken and separate . . . .

The effects of flower essences can be subtle or dramatic. I have seen *Nature's Rescue/Rescue Remedy* combined with homeopathic *Arnica* bring a puppy out of shock and back to consciousness in seconds. More usually, the essences work over longer periods of time—days, weeks, or months, depending on the individual—to balance an animal or person's energy, create positive behavioral changes, calm an anxious animal, and clear and stabilize physical health. I use flower remedies along with other forms of healing, including all the other methods of this book, plus veterinary/medical care. From taking them myself and observing their effects on both dogs and cats, I know they work, and they work on levels that most other remedies cannot reach. For physical body healing, they are best not used alone but combined with other methods. They often heal on levels beyond what can be directly observed, and I have seen evidence of this as well.

The flower essence choices of this book are only suggestions to be verified by testing the individual cat or dog. The essences are available from the sources listed above. Flower Essence Society and Pegasus Products have the largest selection, while the Traditional/Bach Flowers are the most readily available. The cost per bottle is well under ten dollars, and kits start at about twenty-five dollars. The choices given for pet diseases in this book are derived from a variety of sources, including the catalogs of each of the essence companies. Other sources include Diane Stein's *Healing with Flower and Gemstone Essences* (The Crossing Press, 1997); Flower Essence Society's *Flower Essence Repertory* (Patricia Kaminski and Richard Katz); and several Ellon USA pamphlets on using Traditional Remedies for pets. These include "Animals and the Bach Flower Remedies," "Remedies and Your Feline Friends," and "The Bach Remedies and Your Dog." All are published by Ellon USA, Inc.

[1]Ellon USA, Inc., 644 Merrick Rd., Lynbrook, NY 11563, (800) 433-7523. Used by permission.

[2]Leslie J. Kaslof, "Put Yourself in the Animal's Place," in *The Bach Remedies Newsletter*, vol. 05, Spring 1991. Used by permission.

[3]Sharon Scott, "Remedies and Your Feline Friends" and "The Bach Remedies and Your Dog," (Lynbrook, NY, Ellon USA, Inc., undated pamphlet). Used by permission.

[4]Flower Essence Society, POB 459, Nevada City, CA 95959. Used by permission. (handout sheet)

[5]Diane Stein, *The Natural Remedy Book for Women* (Freedom, CA: The Crossing Press, 1992), pp. 79-80.

[6]Priscilla Kapel, *The Body Says Yes* (San Diego, CA: A.C.S. Publications 1981), p. 53.

[7]Wright, Machaelle Small, *Flower Essences* (Jeffersonton, VA, Perelandra Ltd., 1988), p. 58-61.

VIII - Gemstones for
Animal Healing

The addition of gemstones to any healing program is as positive for dogs and cats as it is for people. These Earth minerals maintain a rapid vibration rate that affects wellness from the unseen bodies by way of the chakras. They are used with pets by attaching them to the animal's collar, on a crystal halter (Gloria Dodd, DVM; see her Appendix in *Natural Healing for Dogs and Cats*), large specimens placed in a room with the pet, placed in the animal's water bowl, or made into gemstone elixirs. These elixirs and gemstone healings work very similarly to flower essences in matching and correcting a dis-ease pattern in the energy aura of the non-physical bodies.

Gemstones affect pet or human health through the chakras. These are a series of energy centers on the etheric double, the energy twin of the physical body. The chakras are vortexes that extend into both the outer bodies and the physical body organs. They are gateways of protection, a final attempt in the energy bodies to heal dis-ease before it manifests physically. Dis-ease can be evident in the chakras and etheric double before it reaches the physical body, because the chakras are energy balancers and regulators. They are filters that screen dis-ease from the physical if it is possible to do so. By healing and clearing negative energy vibrations from the chakras, physical dis-ease can be prevented or released, and the pet or human body revitalized.

Animals and people both have extensive chakra energy systems. In people there are usually considered to be seven major chakras on the physical/etheric body and one above the crown of the head that connects the individual's etheric body to the other unseen levels. This last center is called the Transpersonal Point; it is the point where physical consciousness connects with the Goddess. The chakras have designated colors, and the colors of gemstones match and balance the colors of each chakra. Along with eight major chakras, there are a number of minor chakras. There are differing estimates of how many of these there may be in people—some sources say forty-nine. Chakras also run in octaves; the eight major (and many minor) centers of the etheric body are repeated in each of the other unseen bodies. There are a set of major and minor chakras in the etheric double, the emotional body, both layers of the mental body, and all three spiritual body levels.

The major chakras for humans are indicated in the following chart:

Chakra	Location	Unseen Body Level	Color
I. Root	Base of Spine; Gateway of Life, Vagina; Adrenals, Uterus	Physical/Etheric Double	Red/ Black
II. Belly	Just Below Navel; Sexual Center; Spleen, Ovaries	Emotional Body	Orange
III. Solar Plexus	Center, Lower Ribs; Energy Assimilation; Stomach, Pancreas	Lower Mental Body Conscious Mind	Yellow
IV. Heart	Center of Breastbone; Universal Love; Heart, Thymus	Higher Mental Body Creative Mind	Green
V. Throat	Base of Throat; Communication; Thyroid, Parathyroids	Lower Spiritual Body	Light or Silver Blue
VI. Brow/ Third Eye	Center of Forehead, Behind and Above Eyes; Psychic Awareness; Pituitary Gland	Middle Spiritual Body	Indigo or Dark Blue
VII. Crown	Top of Head; Life Purpose	Higher Spiritual Body	Violet or Purple
VIII. Transpersonal Point	Above Crown; Connection to Unseen Levels/ Goddess; No Body Coordinates	Goddess Connection	Clear or White and All Colors

Animals have as complex a chakra system as humans do, but it is only beginning to be mapped. However, human chakras run in a straight line down the center of the body (front and back), whereas the chakras of pets do not; they run in energy flow patterns instead. Human chakras are standardized—everyone has all of the chakras, and all are at least minimally active; animals' chakra development can be highly individual, not only in the minor chakras, but also in what might be considered the major centers. Some centers may be developed in people but not in a particular dog or cat.

The Heart center, for example, that is so important for humans may not even exist in a pet. This is not because animals are "heartless," but because they are "all heart" and have no need of one specific center to express it. The Throat center is a highly important center for humans, as people usually communicate by speaking. Cats and dogs do not speak, so their throats are less developed, but they use body language and have high sensory abilities, and there are chakras for these purposes in their energy makeup. Animals also speak telepathically, so their Brow chakras are highly developed.

Whereas people with awareness work hard at developing their Crown and Brow chakras for psychic ability, ability to know, connection to Source/Goddess, and awareness of purpose in life, these are the most developed centers in pets. Whereas people work hard at making Earth connection and at grounding, sexuality, and vitality (Root, Belly, Solar Plexus), these are highly developed in pets without effort. Marion Webb-DeSisto lists four major chakras for cats and dogs—the Crown/Brow (combined), Solar Plexus, Belly, and Root centers. A number of minor chakras are also more developed in pets than in people. These are on the paw pads (feet in humans), for connection to the Earth, and at the sensory centers of the nose, eyes, whiskers, and ears. Animals are far superior to humans in sensory development.

There are a number of minor chakras listed for dogs and cats that either don't exist or haven't been mapped for humans. In human metaphysics there is very little discussion of the minor centers, although some, like those on the hands and feet, are quite important. Laurel Steinhice has mapped these in pets. In dogs and cats there is a pair of centers at the hips that directs an animal's Self-Preservation instinct; in a well cared for domestic animal this chakra may not be active, but it may need balancing in an animal that has been through abuse. The Digestive chakra helps animals to determine what is safe food; it protects from poisoning. In a dog that raids garbage cans this chakra may be atrophied, but in most cats this chakra is more developed. There is a Dependence center

Location and Colors of Chakras for Pets[1]

Major Chakras	Location	Color:	Marion DeSisto	Laurel Steinhice
I. Root	Base of Tail		Dark Red	Red
II. Belly/Sexual Progression	Belly, Internal Organs		Bright Red	Orange
III. Solar Plexus	Back, Mid-Spine		Golden or Orange	Yellow Gold
IV. Heart	Chest		(Inactive or Minor in pets)	Green (Active only in some individuals)
V. Throat	Throat		Blue (Bud Chakra)	Blue (Active only in some individuals)
VI. Sensing Chakra	Bridge of Nose		(None Listed- Bud Chakra)	Silver Blue
VII. Third Eye/Brow	Brow, Head		Indigo or Green	Indigo
VIII. Crown	Top of Head		Violet	Violet

Minor Chakras	Location	Color:	Marion DeSisto	Laurel Steinhice
1-2. Self-Preservation	Hip Joints		(Not Listed)	Red
3. Reproductive	Sexual Organs		(Not Listed)	Red-Orange
4. Digestive	Tip of Liver			Rust Red
5. Respect/Recognition	Spine above Internal Sex Organs		(Not Listed)	Golden
6. Dependence	Underbelly		(Not Listed)	Citron Yellow
7-8. Body Language	Linked to Throat		Blue (Throat)	Blue
9- 10. Eyes	Eyes		(Not Listed)	No Color Given (Vary with individual development)
11-12. Base of Ears	Base of Ears		Pale Yellows, Become Aqua or Blue when developed	None Given
13. Nose	Tip of Nose		(No Color Given)	None Given
14-15. Whiskers	Face, Beside Mouth		(Not Listed)	None Given
16-19. Paws	Bottoms of Feet		Ruby	None Given
20. Tail Tip	End of Tail/Spine		Dark Red	None Given
21. Oversoul linkage (Transpersonal point)	Base of Skull		Part of Crown	White/Grey/Silver

NOTE: Chakra development is individual in animals; some chakras will be developed and others will not be, particularly in the Minor/Bud centers. For gemstones for the feet, black stones are appropriate (grounding).

The Chakra System[2]
(Dog or Cat)

by Marion-Webb DeSisto

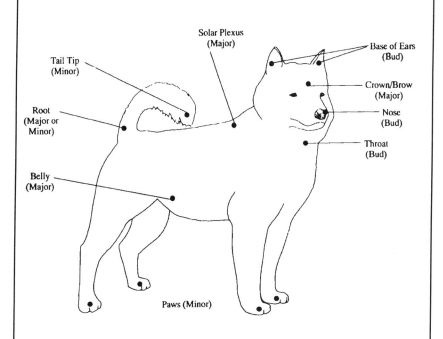

Major Chakras

Crown/Brow - Head
Green, Blue, Purple

Solar Plexus - Back
Orange or Golden

Belly/Belly - Root
Bright Red

Minor Chakras

Paws - *Ruby*

Tail Tip - *Dark Red*

Bud Chakras

Nose Tip

Throat

Base of Ears -
*(Pale Yellows,
become Aqua or
Blue when
developed)*

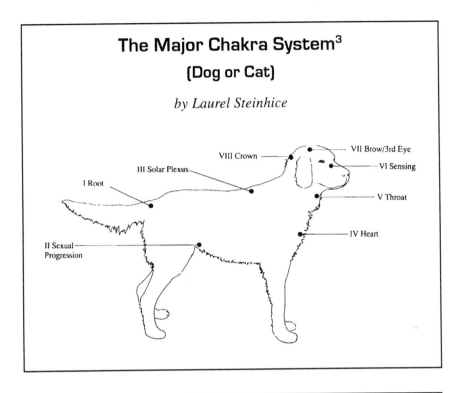

The Major Chakra System[3]
(Dog or Cat)
by Laurel Steinhice

VIII Crown
VII Brow/3rd Eye
VI Sensing
III Solar Plexus
I Root
V Throat
IV Heart
II Sexual Progression

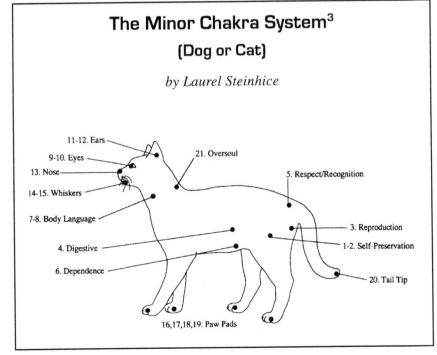

The Minor Chakra System[3]
(Dog or Cat)
by Laurel Steinhice

11-12. Ears
9-10. Eyes
13. Nose
14-15. Whiskers
7-8. Body Language
4. Digestive
6. Dependence
21. Oversoul
5. Respect/Recognition
3. Reproduction
1-2. Self-Preservation
20. Tail Tip
16,17,18,19. Paw Pads

for knowing one's place in the family or pack. Trust and obedience are governed there. This is also an important center for companion animals.

Gemstones are used to balance these centers, with each chakra color activated by stones of the same color. For example, the dark red of Root chakra is activated, given more energy, with dark red stones like garnet or ruby (or a garnet or ruby gem elixir). In a very hyper or stressed animal, root stimulation is not needed, but calming and grounding are in order. The balancing/calming color for red is black, and black gemstones or elixirs like hematite or black tourmaline can be used to soothe. The primary color for each chakra activates and stimulates, while the balancing color calms. The complementary/opposite color also decreases and balances chakra activity. If there is too much red in the cat's or dog's makeup, she is probably deficient in green, which is red's opposite. Colors are listed in the following chart:

Complementary Chakra	Activating Color	Balancing Color	Opposite
Root	Red	Black	Green
Belly	Orange	Brown	Blue
Solar Plexus	Yellow	Yellow-Green	Violet
Heart	Green	Rose	Red
Throat	Blue	Aqua	Orange
Brow	Indigo	White	Orange
Crown	Violet	White	Gold
Transpersonal	Clear	Clear	Clear[4]

Each pet or human dis-ease has references to a particular chakra and part of the body, so gemstones that match the chakra help to release the dis-ease. Their colors and mineral composition activate or balance to heal the disruption of energy in the chakra. The charts of this chapter reference dis-eases to the chakras, colors, and gemstones. Using a gemstone or gem elixir to match the cat's or dog's condition helps to release that dis-ease from her chakras and etheric body. That clearing has to happen for physical body healing to occur, and gemstones can effect the change, or speed or act as a catalyst for the process. Each dis-ease in the remedy section of this book provides a selection of gemstones that are a healing vibration match. To choose which of these stones to use on a particular pet, go by what is available and also test the pet with a pendulum or muscle kinesiology.

Gemstones for the Chakras[5]

Root	Belly	Solar Plexus	Heart	Throat	Third Eye	Crown
Black	Carnelian	Citrine	*Rose*	Chrysocolla	*Indigo*	*Violet*
Smokey Quartz	Red Coral	Topaz	Rose Quartz	Turquoise	Lapis Lazuli	Amethyst
Blk Tourmaline	Agate	Tiger Eye	Kunzite	Blue Topaz	Sodalite	Violet
Hematite	Jacinth	Hawks-Eye	Pnk Tourmaline	Blue Lace	Sapphire	Tourmaline
Tourmaline Qtz	Brown Jasper	Malachite	Pnk Jade	Agate	Azurite	Garnet
Black Agate	Fire Agate	Peridot	Rhodochrosite	Celestite	Dk Aquamarine	Zircon
Apache Tear/	Phantom	Amber	Rhodonite	Aquamarine	Star Sapphire	Fluorite
Obsidian	Calcite	Golden Beryl	Dolomite	Amazonite	Blue Spinel	Jade
Onyx	Fire Opal	Yellow Jade	Pnk Carnelian	Blue	Blue Zircon	Sugilite
Jet	Red Quartz	Chrysoberyl	Watermelon	Tourmaline	Kyanite	Alexandrite
Elestials	Wulfenite	Apatite	Tourmaline	Aventurine	Iolite	
Boji Stone	Salmon Jade	Yellow	Morganite	Gem Silica	Bl Fluorite	Lepidolite
Tektite	Pecos Quartz	Calcite	Pink Silica	Eilat Stone	Holly Blue	
Red		Tourmaline	*Green*	Andean Blue	Agate	
Garnet		Zircon	Aventurine	Silica		
Ruby		Fluorite	Green Jade	Angelite	*White*	*Clear*
Bloodstone		Green	Dioptase	Larimar	Moonstone	Quartz
Red Jasper		Calcite	Emerald		Moss Agate	Diamond
Red Jade		Tourmaline	Grn Tourmaline		White Agate	Zircon
Red Spinel		Zircon	Chrysoprase		Chalcedony	Herkimer
Red Quartz		Fluorite	Grn Quartz		Selenite	Diamond
Realgar		Sunstone	Jadeite		Cl Fluorite	Rutile
Red Phantom Quartz		Moldavite	Nephrite		Opal	Phenacite
			Grn Obsidian		Aragonite	
			Unikite		Pearl	
			Dendritic Agate		Ivory	
					Phantom Qtz, Snow Quartz	

Chakra Correspondences[6]

Chakra	Body	Color	Healing Issues
Root	Physical/ Etheric Double	Black	Anxiety, grounding, addictions, fear, pain, colitis, diarrhea, abortion/miscarriage recovery, menopause, moving forward, karma, death, reincarnation, past lives
		Red	Uterus, menstruation, fertility, life force, red blood, circulation, warmth, AIDS, leukemia, cancer, constipation
Belly	Emotional	Orange/Brown	Ovaries, spleen, sexuality, orgasm, fertility, asthma, allergies, epilepsy, arthritis, menstruation, impressions, visualization, ovarian cysts, endometriosis, coughs
Solar Plexus	Lower Mental	Yellow/ Yellow/Green	Assimilation, nutrition, ideas, energy, psychic, diabetes, digestion, eating disorders, ulcers, apathy, tiredness, will-power, visualization, depression, urinary
Heart	Higher Mental	Green/Rose	Heart dis-ease, blood circulation, immune/thymus, love, loneliness, self-image, trust, abused childhoods, giving, compassion, receiving love, imagination, infections
Throat	Lower Spiritual	Blue/Aqua	Anger, communication, expression, creativity, voice, burns, sore throats, laryngitis, choking, headaches, migraines, rape and incest recovery, inflammations, swellings, ears
Third Eye/Brow	Middle Spiritual White	Indigo/	Endocrine balancing, menstrual cycles, eyes, senses, multiple sclerosis, headaches, degenerative dis-eases, white blood cells, immune system, colds, flu, sinuses, psychic development, clairvoyance, mental, pneumonia
Crown	Higher Spiritual	Violet	Degenerative dis-eases, vision, immunity, white blood, headaches, insomnia, anxiety, calming, head, brain, stress
Transpersonal Point	Spiritual	Clear	Connection with Goddess, all-aura healing, channeling, knowledge, unifying, clearing, vitalizing, protection

Different gemstones do different things, as do different stone types in the same chakra color (and individual stones within a type). Of the Brow chakra white stones, for example, moonstone is feminine and a gentle awakener whereas aragonite is a reality check that can be a rather harsh correction. Different animals that need Brow chakra stones will test for different types of white gemstones. They may also test "yes" for one piece of moonstone and "no" for another. In black stones, obsidian opens karmic and survival issues for clearing and healing, while black tourmaline is calming, grounding, and places a protective shield around the person or pet that uses it. A formerly abused animal could test for either stone, depending on what she is ready to heal. In the Solar Plexus yellow stones, amber is an energy balancer and calmative, while yellow topaz heals the cat or dog in times of transition—which can be anything from moving to a new home to passing over. Every chakra color has stones with a variety of uses. No two stones are alike. Guidebooks list these gemstone uses, but pendulum or muscle testing can determine more directly what a particular pet needs at a particular time. A large crystal cluster or gemstone specimen can affect the energy of an entire room, and if the dog or cat needs a particular energy/gemstone, everyone in the human family may benefit from it as well.

Stones also heal all the body levels, because they match the chakras, each of which corresponds to one of the unseen aura body layers. The etheric double corresponds to the Root chakra, the emotional body to the Belly chakra, and the lower mental body to the Solar Plexus center. These are all highly developed energy centers and levels in cats and dogs. The higher mental body corresponds to the Heart chakra, and the lower spiritual level to the Throat center. Neither of these is usually developed in pets but can be in some individual pets. However, they are important issue centers for people, developing love and communication—two areas of awareness that companion animals have already achieved. The middle and higher spiritual bodies—the Brow and Crown centers—are already highly developed in dogs and cats, and are things that people are struggling to awaken in themselves. We have much to learn of spirituality from our pets.

By selecting a gemstone energy that matches the chakra and unseen body level, and that corrects a disruption or boosts a positive quality, healing is facilitated. Animals are aware of the energies of crystals and gemstones and pets will often pick the stones they need themselves from a pile shown to them. One dog that I had, Tiger, did this regularly and loved to sleep with a crystal or gemstone between her front paws. She loved rose quartz. My other dogs have been uninterested in stones, although Kali likes to bounce them around the room and chew them. A stone placed in her waterbowl will reappear later in her toy box. Cats are attracted to the sparkle of stones and like to hoard them away in special places. Merely by being around the gems' energy, the animals are being healed by the stones.

The colored gemstones have specific uses matching a chakra, aura body, and dis-ease. Clear quartz crystals can be programmed to either magnify the effects of colored stones or to act in their place. First clear the crystal (more on clearing below), then program or charge it for a specific purpose. "Heal Copper" is specific enough for a charge. Then use that crystal for healing by placing it in the pet's bed or water, attaching it to her collar if it is small enough, leaving it in the room with the pet if it's large enough, or making it into a gem elixir. The energy of the stone must be within the animal's aura to be effective, so place it as close to the animal's body as possible. A clear crystal programmed in this way will take the place of a colored stone.

All gemstones and crystals must be cleared before using them for healing people or pets. Stones often absorb negative energy and the vibration of dis-ease into themselves, and this must be released. A stone will also bond with the energy of the person or pet using it, so it should be cleared before someone else uses it. A crystal that has been programmed for healing Kali should be cleared and reprogrammed before using it for healing Copper. Stones also become tired and drained from use and need to be revitalized to remain effective. An uncleared stone can cause energy disruption instead of energy rebalancing and healing, and a stone left uncleared too long may even shatter.

Clearing stones is very simple and can be done in a number of ways. Probably the easiest way is to bury it in a ceramic or glass container (not plastic or metal) filled with dry sea salt overnight. If a stone has been used for a long time or to heal serious illness the clearing can take longer—use your pendulum to check what's needed. Check with the pendulum to verify that the stone is completely cleared before removing it from the salt. Other methods are to place the stone in a sea salt and water solution or a lemon ammonia and water solution; outdoors in the sunlight, rain, or moonlight; bathe it in ocean water or rain water; or smudge it with the smoke of burning sage or cedar. Stones will clear when placed in a bowl of dried sage herb, mugwort, or rose petals, and when buried in the ground or in the soil of a potted plant. There are flower essence combinations available at metaphysical stores for gemstone clearing that are very effective and can clear stones quickly.

Leave a crystal or gemstone on a cat or dog for no more than twenty-four hours, then clear it again. One way is to leave the stone on the pet all night while the animal is quiet; in the day when she is active and likely to lose it, take it off for clearing. A stone that is not kept clear will be less effective and can even cause harm. When using stones in the water bowl, or as the basis for a gem elixir it is particularly important to start by clearing the stones. Do not use a gemstone or crystal that your pendulum does not verify as completely cleared of negative, disrupted, dis-ease vibration energy. Also do not use any stone that the pendulum or muscle testing does not verify to be what the pet or person needs.

Gemstone elixirs are a very powerful way to use gem and crystal energy for healing animals and humans. They are made in the same way as flower essences (see the previous chapter), and used by placing the drops on the dog's or cat's tongue, or in her water bowl. If your dog takes her stones from the water bowl to bounce them across the living room as Kali does, gem elixirs are a good alternative. They are perfect for the cat or dog that seems to lose stones off her collar as fast as you can fasten them onto it (like Copper). They concentrate the healing energy of the stones, as well.

When making a crystal or gemstone elixir, first make very sure that the stone to be used is fully cleared. The stone can be raw or tumbled, cut and faceted, or otherwise polished. Only a very small piece is needed. Place the cleared stone in a clear glass bowl outdoors on a sunny morning. Pour pure water over the stone to fill the bowl, then leave in the sun for about three hours. Bottle as for flower essences, using brown bottles up to half filled with brandy and pouring the essence liquid to fill up the bottles. Remove the stone from the liquid; it can be reused as often as needed. Place these Mother Tincture bottles in a crystal grid for a further two hours to strengthen them or charge them with Reiki.

The Mother Essences can be potentized homeopathically by succussion—shaking, tapping, or striking the bottle against your hand or a padded chair arm twenty to thirty times. Make a Stock Bottle by placing 5–9 drops of the Mother Essence in a brown eyedropper bottle filled thirty to fifty percent with brandy or white vinegar and the rest with pure water. A Dosage Bottle can also be made, but I prefer using my gem elixirs and flower essences from the Stock Bottle. To dose, place one drop on the cat's or dog's tongue or inside her cheek pouch or several drops in her water bowl once or twice a day.

Gem elixirs can also be made more simply by placing the cleared stone in a clear glass of pure water on a windowsill in the sun for an hour or two. Then pour this glass of gemstone-charged water, minus the stone, into the pet's water bowl. Do this daily; it is an effective essence and can be very strong but must be used that day. The brighter the sunlight the

Essential Gemstone Essences

Amber—all-aura healing

Amethyst, Rutile—clears energy flow

Angelite—emotional stability

Aquamarine—core soul repair and healing

Aventurine, blue—regeneration

Azurite—intense transformation

Celestite—flowing with life

Citrine, natural—energy cleansing and balancing

Clear Quartz Crystal—all healing

Dioptase-Malachite—heals past life betrayals

Elestial Quartz—life path transition

Emerald—purification

Herkimer Diamond—pure love

Jasper, Leopard Skin—access to herstory

Kunzite, pink—emotional balance, compassion

Kyanite, blue—communication with all life forms

Lapis Lazuli—releases negative thought patterns

Moldavite—other-planetary contact

Moroccan Red Quartz—life force, sexual stimulant

Phenacite—information/light

Rose Quartz, gem—heart healing

Selenite—clears the aura bodies

Sulfur—spiritualizes intellect

Tourmaline, pink—compassion, universal love

Vanadanite—women's reproductive healing

Zincite—spiritual purification

stronger the essence and the less time it takes to transfer the gem energy into the water. When used directly like this, chrysocolla or malachite gemstones should be left in the water no longer than half an hour.

These essences can be very powerful. Watch the animal for signs of detoxifying and don't overdo it. Test with the pendulum each day to see if the dog or cat still needs the essence and how often in the day to dose. These can work more quickly than flower essences. Test the cat or dog to choose which gemstones are useful for her healing on a daily basis. If you have an awareness of what stones work with each chakra and healing need, and what stones are available to you at the time, this is not a long process. Small pieces of gemstones that are raw or tumbled are perfect for making elixirs and are available very cheaply at gem shows, metaphysical stores, and lapidary shops.

You can purchase gem elixirs from Essential Essences, and from many metaphysical stores and gemstone shops. A comprehensive written guide to making such elixirs and using them is Diane Stein's *Healing with Gemstones*. The suggestions on gemstones in this book come primarily from my many years of using gemstones and crystals and my gemstone book. Also refer to my previous books, *All Women Are Healers* and *The Natural Remedy Book for Women* (The Crossing Press, 1990 and 1992), and *The Women's Book of Healing* (Llewellyn Publications, 1988). Gemstones are a healing method I recommend highly; I have watched their effectiveness for myself and my dogs for a very long number of years.

[1]From the work of psychics Marion Webb-Former and Laurel Steinhice. See Diane Stein, *Natural Healing for Dogs and Cats* (Freedom, CA: The Crossing Press, 1993), pp. 23-32.

[2]Marion Webb-Former, Personal Communications, March 18, 1992, and April 5, 1992.

[3]Laurel Steinhice, "Energy Centers in Dogs and Cats," Personal Communication, 1992.

[4]Diane Stein, *All Women Are Healers* (Freedom, CA: The Crossing Press, 1990), pp. 20-21.

[5]From Diane Stein, *The Women's Book of Healing*, p. 284; and Katrina Raphaell, *Crystal Enlightenment*, pp. 162-164. Also in Diane Stein, *All Women Are Healers* (Freedom, CA: The Crossing Press, 1990), p. 26. Additions have been made.

[6]See *The Women's Book of Healing* for more detailed chakra correspondences. From Diane Stein, *All Women Are Healers* (Freedom, CA: The Crossing Press, 1990), p. 22.

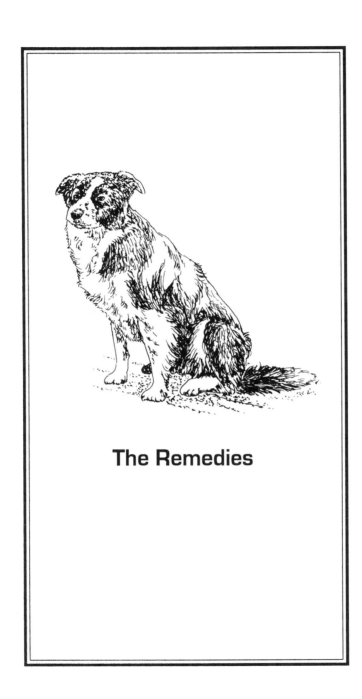

The Remedies

How To Use This Section

The pages that follow offer healing remedies for fifty common pet dis-eases. They utilize the eight methods discussed in the previous chapters. For each of the methods, information on one (or more) is given, along with how to use. When no directions are given, I have already covered that material in the early part of this book. Combinations of remedies will be listed as such, otherwise, each suggestion is an individual alter-native. For example, if there are several herbs listed in the herbal sec-tion, choose only one unless it is stated specifically to combine several. Herbs can be used in combinations safely, but one or two together is usually enough. I feel that potions using a dozen different herbs are re-dundant, expensive, and unnecessary. With homeopathic remedies, pick the one that most closely fits the dog's or cat's symptom picture. When one method or choice within a method is considered to be the most im-portant or most effective, I indicate it as such.

All of the dis-eases require use of a preservative-free pet food or natural homemade diet plus supplements. Full health and healing cannot happen on commercial dog and cat foods, and an animal healing any dis-ease needs an optimal diet as her body's best support. Remember also to use a few days of fasting for any animal with a fever-bearing dis-ease, infectious viral or bacterial dis-ease, or digestive upset. Before using any remedy, know how best to use that remedy for animals. When choos-ing vitamin C for your cat's feline leukemia, for example, read the method chapter on vitamins and minerals along with the section on feline leuke-mia before proceeding. Always place the animal on an optimal diet first.

You may choose to combine methods, using vitamins and minerals, herbs, homeopathy, acupuncture/acupressure, etc. This is perfectly safe and can be a valid way to go, but is not always necessary. Use one pri-mary method with any other that offers secondary support. There is no need to go out and buy a remedy from each method for your pet. Try one method, and if it is ineffective, try something different; each dog or cat is an individual with her own needs. At least one physical level method should be used for any physical level dis-ease; these methods include naturopathy, vitamins and minerals, and herbs, with homeopathy or acu-puncture/acupressure as the highly successful methods that bridge the physical and non-physical levels. An additional non-physical level rem-edy makes a good balance—a flower essence, gem elixir, or gemstone. When the animal's dis-ease is fully non-physical (emotional or behav-ioral rather than physical), non-physical methods alone may be used if physical level causes have been ruled out. Flower essences and homeopathy are good choices here. Also use psychic communication to find out what the problem is. Always feed the natural diet.

Many healers of both animals and people work with only one remedy and have highly successful results. This is a valid choice, too. When using a combination of methods be careful not to overload the dog or cat, whose body is already working hard to heal her dis-ease. Use muscle testing or a pendulum to help you decide what remedy or remedies are best for the individual. Test also to see how many times a day to use each remedy and keep current on what the pet needs at any particular time. She may test for flower essences for a day or week, then not need them again. She may next need gemstones or a gem elixir, or a different herb or homeopathic remedy than the one she formerly had been taking. With homeopathy in particular, watch for changes; as the animal responds to her remedies, her symptoms will change, and so will the homeopathic she may need.

While determining dosage, follow the information given in the remedy section or in the earlier section discussing that particular healing method. If no information is given on exact amounts to use, go by one of the following procedures. Most or all holistic remedies list on the bottles an adult dose. These are based on a standard one-hundred-and-fifty pound person. Estimate your pet's weight and divide by a hundred and fifty, and this will give you the fraction to use. If a dog weighs fifty pounds, she would take a third of the general adult human dosage. Label dosages tend to be lower rather than optimal, however. There is another option. Use a quarter the human remedy dose for cats and small dogs, half the human dose for medium-sized dogs, and a full adult dose for large and giant breed dogs. This option applies primarily to vitamins, minerals, and other supplements.

For homeopathic remedies, the same dose is given for a dog, cat, or any size human. Take a few drops of liquid homeopathic preparation or crush a pellet or two and place the liquid or crushed pellets on the animal's tongue. Dosage is unimportant here; potency is what to look for (30C is my preference). For herbal tinctures, use two drops for a cat, and for a dog two to eight drops depending on the animal's size. Overdoses are unlikely with any natural remedy, when used with common sense. Flower essences and gem elixirs cannot be overdosed, but they are expensive and you don't want to waste them. A drop or two on the tongue is enough. The naturopathic foods also cannot be overdosed, but if an animal is detoxing on them, use these foods moderately. Too much detoxification too fast puts heavy strain on a pet's body. However, in poisoning cases you need to get the poison all out fast.

Remember also to be patient. Natural remedies work more slowly (and more thoroughly and deeply) than chemical drugs. They will not cause a change immediately like a shot of penicillin—unless you are using homeopathy and select the right remedy. Observe carefully. When you change your cat's or dog's diet to a natural one, the real changes take a month or so before they become noticeable. With herbs or vitamins it may take a few days to a few weeks before the healing becomes evident—or it can happen overnight. Continue to use the remedies and to observe the animal's physical and emotional changes. In an emergency, however, it may be necessary to use the rapid intervention of veterinary chemical healing. When the situation is life threatening, take your pet to a veterinarian. Use natural healing methods later to support her healing at home.

A further caution: no book can take the place of veterinary care, particularly if the dog or cat is injured or in an urgent situation. Sometimes the excesses of the veterinary/medical system are necessary, and in emergencies, or if a dis-ease has gone on too long, or if natural remedies are not working, it may be the only way. *Holistic* veterinary care is very much recommended, but if a holistic vet is far away or available only by phone, use whatever veterinary help is available in urgent situations. There are still too few holistic veterinarians out there.

Every method and remedy in this book is also valid for human use. I recommend natural healing methods for people as well as for cats and dogs; it is our most positive and successful option in an over-medicalized, over-chemicalized, and over-technologized society. It is also a way of honoring and living with the beauty of this green Earth, and is an attempt to heal Her as we heal our animals and ourselves.

A comment on footnoting. Every method and remedy in this book has been carefully researched and has also been used by me over a period of years for humans and pets. I have tried to keep the footnoting to a minimum in this book, in order to prevent dozens of distracting references for each dis-ease, method, and remedy. Many of the sources in any given method also overlap. Where information comes specifically from one expert, I have footnoted it. Otherwise, see the bibliography at the end of this book for further information and references. Much general veterinary information comes from Delbert G. Carlson, DVM, and James M. Giffin, MD, *Dog Owner's Home Veterinary Handbook* and *Cat Owner's Home Veterinary Handbook* (New York: Howell Book House, 1980 and 1983); general dis-ease information and descriptions from James F. Balch, MD, and Phyllis A. Balch, CNC, *Prescription for Nutritional Healing* (Garden City Park, NY: Avery Publishing Group, 1990). For further information, also see my previous books, *Natural Healing for Dogs and Cats* and *The Natural Remedy Book for Women* (Freedom, CA: The Crossing Press, 1993 and 1992).

Abscesses and Boils

An abscess is a pocket of pus under the skin surface. In dogs and cats it is usually caused by a small puncture wound that closes on the outside, but has bacteria or foreign matter trapped inside. Cats get these from claw and bite wounds in fights, and dogs from burr, sticktight, or other plant pieces that work their way under the skin. Cellulitis is an inflammation of the deep skin layers, and boils are primarily bacterial infections under the skin (staph infections) often caused by systemic toxicity and lowered immune function. A carbuncle is a spreading boil—there may be several infections in an area.

The signs of this infection include a painful, red, swollen area of skin that feels hot to the touch. In cellulitis the skin feels hard, and in an abscess there is fluid beneath the surface. If the infection grows, there may be evidence of swollen lymph glands or red streaks radiating from the sore. The animal may seem depressed or may become anorexic, refusing to eat. There may be fever and chills. To heal, the abscess or boil needs to be opened and drained; it must be cleaned of any foreign matter and pus. Healing occurs from the inside out, rather than from the surface. A boil or abscess that does not drain may need to be surgically lanced, but with the use of natural methods this is usually unnecessary.

An animal that is diabetic, has thyroid dis-ease, or a reduced immune system is more susceptible to recurring staph infections. Chronic constipation may be a cause, as well as allergies, stress, or poor hygiene.

Nutrition: Commercial pet foods, low in nutrients and high in chemicals and sugar, are often a cause of abscesses and boils. The poorer quality generic foods that contain little or no zinc are particularly suspect in dogs. A natural or preservative-free diet is necessary, as poor nutrition can be a source of both reduced immune system and systemic toxicities.

Naturopathy: Start with a detoxifying fast of a few days, especially if the dog or cat has fever. Lemon juice enemas during the fast are especially positive, and aloe vera juice internally functions as a laxative and a detoxifier. Use hot compresses or poultices three or four times a day for fifteen minutes at a time. Be careful that they are not so hot that they burn the pet. They can be made from a teaspoonful of salt or boric acid to a cup of boiled water; castor oil or tea tree oil; roasted and mashed garlic, onions, or an oven-heated lemon slice. Anitra Frazier uses a teaspoon of Betadyne solution and a half teaspoon of sea salt (not table salt) to a cup of pure water.

Once the abscess has opened, drained, and any foreign matter has been removed, the wound can be helped to heal from the inside. Anitra Frazier uses a second compress solution as above, replacing the Betadyne with a teaspoonful of calendula tincture.[1] The wound should not be allowed to close up as long as there is still pus or foreign matter remaining.

Kelp boosts the thyroid and adds essential minerals, and garlic is an antibiotic and immune builder. Bee products also boost the immune system. Also use honey or chlorophyll externally in compresses. Put a teaspoon of apple cider vinegar in the water bowl to speed healing.

Vitamins and Minerals: The supplements of the optimal diet are highly important, particularly the mineral powders. Deficiency in minerals may make a pet susceptible to the dis-ease. Give vitamin C to bowel tolerance for infection clearing, mixing it with the animal's honey water or herb teas during her fast and with food after. For cats and small dogs, Richard Pitcairn suggests 250 mg three times a day for at least three days; for medium-sized dogs give 500 mg three times a day, and for large dogs use 1000 mg per dose.[2] The animal may take much more. The deficiencies in zinc can cause abscesses and boils. Use zinc gluconate and C lozenges for small pets, non-chewable zinc when larger amounts are needed. Give about 5-10 mg of zinc per day for cats, 20-25 mg per day for a medium-sized dog, and 50 mg per day for a large dog.

Herbs: Dose the dog or cat with goldenseal and echinacea combination tincture or tea. Compresses can be made of this tincture or tea also, or of either herb. When using herbal antibiotics internally, do not stop until all infection has been cleared for several days, or symptoms may return. Usnea is another herb specific for staph infections. Comfrey root or leaf is an important infection-healing herb, used in poultices, compresses, and internally. Also burdock and red clover combined are good internal detoxifiers, as are chaparral, pau d'arco, or Oregon grape root. Horsetail grass taken internally reduces inflammation. Use slippery elm poultices hot until the pus has cleared, then cold to heal the wound.

Homeopathy: Try *Belladonna* in early stages when the skin is hot, red, and painful; used early enough it may stop an abscess from forming. After twenty-four hours, if the animal shows pain when the forming sore is lightly touched, go to *Hepar sulph.* Once pus has formed use *Mercurius.* When there is much redness and swelling around the abscess, which looks shiny and angry, the remedy is *Apis. Lachesis* is used when the skin looks purplish, the pus is dark and thin, and the lesion is tender; stop this remedy as soon as there is any improvement. If there is foreign matter in the abscess, or for recurring or persistent infections, use *Silica.* After the pus is expelled, *Calendula* tincture as a compress heals the wound.

Acupuncture/Acupressure: Use the Immune Stimulation sequence of Gloria Dodd, DVM, shown in the method chapter. On the Cat Chart, point #15 is for blood cleansing and infections.

Flower Essences: *Crab Apple*, *Allemanda* (Detox Essence), or *Tomato* essence detoxify, and *Dill* or *Garlic* flowers help to reduce inflammations. *Nature's Rescue (Rescue Remedy)* is useful in any acute situation. *Agrimony* is for slow healing wounds.

Gemstones: Elixirs of *Emerald* or *Malachite* are powerful cleansers and detoxifiers. When using *Malachite*, leave the stone in the water for no more than half an hour. *Obsidian*, *Smoky Quartz*, or *Bloodstone* are other choices. *Lapis Lazuli* is an anti-inflammatory, infection fighter, and all-healer. Use any of these in the dog's or cat's aura as well.

Aging

Companion animals today do not live as long as they did fifty or even thirty years ago. Natural healing methods help a dog or cat to live comfortably longer, without debilitating dis-eases. Delbert Carlson, DVM, and James Giffin, MD, list cat life expectancy at about fifteen years. Smaller dogs live longer than the large breeds, with large dogs reaching old age at ten years. Only ten percent of dogs live past age ten, according to these experts[3], even though animals in their twenties were not uncommon in my childhood. Something is changing for the worse, and commercial diets, over-vaccination, and chemical drugs are a major part of the problem.

Supporting a pet holistically through old age can add comfortable and pain-free years to her lifespan. While specific dis-eases are discussed in their own remedy sections, a few general tips may make a positive difference. Older pets are less able to assimilate food and absorb nutrients and vitamins from their diets. Therefore a quality preservative-free diet is essential. They need fewer calories because of decreased activity, and less protein is recommended for overworked aging kidneys. It must be noted that commercial diets can cause kidney failure in older dogs and cats, but natural diets do not.

Aging animals may become incontinent (watch for urinary infections in both cats and dogs), and are often constipated. Careful observation is needed here to prevent emergencies. Older animals are less able to throw off toxins from their bodies and because of this may develop skin problems, tumors, body odors, or appear matted and unkempt. Daily grooming and a gentle body massage weekly checks for problems and keeps the animal clean and comfortable.

Using holistic methods rather than harsh chemical drugs with side effects helps to strengthen older animals, lessens the degenerative effects of chronic dis-eases, and extends lifespans.

Nutrition: Aging pets do not need in their diets preservatives, sugar, salt, and poor quality food. A natural homemade diet, possibly chopped up small for easier digestion, is a must, or use a preservative-free pet food with supplements. Poor food has reduced our dogs' and cats' lives by half or more. Don't wait until your animal is old to start giving her good food, but don't hesitate to change an older pet's diet now.

Naturopathy: Digestive enzymes are highly important in helping an older pet to assimilate nutrients, both in foods and supplements. Feline or canine enzymes are available from several natural pet catalogs and an increasing number of pet shops; give a quarter teaspoon to a teaspoonful per meal. Human enzymes from a health food store are also positive: give one-half tablet per meal for cats and small dogs, more for larger pets. Kelp provides missing iodine and minerals, bee products and garlic build immunity, and garlic is an internal antiseptic. Give aloe vera juice with liquid chlorophyll daily to prevent constipation and help the aging animal detoxify. Chlorophyll is also a blood sugar balancer. Cider vinegar in the water bowl or on food acidifies the urinary tract, adds potassium and other minerals, and aids tissue repair and healing. A teaspoonful of wheat germ oil daily helps dribbling in older female dogs.

Vitamins and Minerals: Feed the supplements listed with the optimal diet, varied as below. Both elder dogs and cats require more of the B-complex vitamins and vitamin E, and less vitamin C in their daily diets. For dogs, use half the adult dog amount of vitamin C but double the E (see the method chapter on Nutrition for size and dosage tables). For cats, give 500-750 mg of vitamin C daily, and 50 IU of vitamin E.[4] Use a low potency human B-complex supplement (10-20 mg) that is yeast-free, or use brewer's yeast if the pet is not allergic to it, and don't forget the trace minerals powders. Additional B-12 is positive. Give 5-10 mg of zinc daily to aid the immune system. Give 10,000-25,000 IU of vitamin A with 400-800 IU of vitamin D weekly. Crush all tablets into food, and pierce gel capsules with a pin, squirting them into food.

Raw thymus glandular, germanium, and coenzyme Q10 all oxygenate the cells and support the heart and immune system. Raw kidney extract is positive for pets with reduced kidney function. Buy these for humans and use proportionate to your pet's weight.

Herbs: Hawthorn is a general circulatory system strengthener that helps the heart, balances blood pressure, and is a gentle protection from stress. It may be used daily long-term. It is recommended for pets with heart dis-ease. Ginkgo biloba may help in preventing or reducing senility. It also strengthens circulation, as does ginseng or ginseng with royal jelly. The best general herbal nutrient is alfalfa, which is also a detoxifier and helpful for arthritic joints and hip and bone problems. Yucca helps arthritis and is a natural steroid, and dandelion gently cleanses the liver. Horsetail grass adds silica and calcium for urinary problems and arthritis. For debilitated animals, slippery elm is a nutrient that may be used with honey or honey and water as a food.

Homeopathy: Remedies are given to fit specific symptoms; where there is a specific dis-ease, see that section. *Crataegus* (homeopathic hawthorn) may be used daily as a heart strengthener. Also for daily use try combination cell salts, called *Bioplasma*, in 6X or 12X potency. English homeopathic vet Francis Hunter suggests *Baryta carb* for senility in cats or dogs with incontinence. Give three times daily in the 30C potency for three or four days and repeat when needed.[5] *Aconite* or *Ignatia* may also help the senile pet that is upset or frightened with no apparent cause. Use *Carbo veg* for a coughing or wheezing animal that is exhausted, and has constipation with gas. It is also good in cases of collapse where the animal is overweight with poor circulation, little activity, and chronic dis-eases.

Acupuncture/Acupressure: Check the Diagnostic/Alarm points weekly during a gentle body massage; this can reveal and often release problems early. Be familiar with the Resuscitation points also shown in the method chapter. (This would be point #8 on the Cat Chart.) For specific dis-eases use the appropriate points on both charts. Cat Chart #22 is a systemic tonic.

Flower Essences: *Hornbeam* strengthens and *Peach* is for longevity. Essences specifically for aging are *Centaury, Beech, Holly* and *Penstemon.* Try Essential Essences Old Soul Essence (*Purple Angel Trumpet*). Transition Essence (*Easter Lily*) is for the death transition, as is Conscious Dying Essence (*Golden Chalice*). Brede's Essence (*Sky Vine*) or Light Body Essence (*Gardenia*) are comforters. *White Bougainvillea* is an aging essence.

Gemstones: Red stones for the Root and Feet chakras help to energize and revitalize. These include *Garnet, Ruby,* or *Red Jasper.* Pink or green gems strengthen the heart: *Rose Quartz, Pink Tourmaline, Kunzite, Aventurine,* or *Bloodstone. Jade* heals the kidneys, and *Amber* or *Citrine* the urinary and digestive tracts. Make any of these into elixirs or place in the pet's aura; test with a pendulum for what the animal needs.

Allergies

The immune system of a human or animal is finely tuned to defend the body from foreign substances and dis-ease bacteria or viruses. Sometimes it overreacts, and sometimes the immune response is so overworked from pollution and a chemicalized toxic environment that it reacts unnecessarily.

Holistic physician James F. Balch defines "allergy" as "the inappropriate response by the body's immune system to a substance that is not normally harmful."[6] Allergens are found in foods; inhaled as pollens, molds, dust, feathers; and transmitted by insect stings or flea bites (as when an allergy to flea saliva results in persistent itching rash), or by skin contact with irritants (detergents, flea collars, insecticides, petroleum products).

Any animal or person can become allergic to just about anything, including chemical medications and even herbs. An allergic cat or dog may scratch, break out into skin rashes, have runny eyes and sinusitis, cough, have recurrent urinary tract infections, vomit frequently or experience diarrhea and gas. Dogs with inhalant allergies will often chew their feet. At the extreme end of allergic emergencies is anaphylactic shock, a violent reaction that can be life-threatening.

Hyperactivity in pets may be a food-allergy reaction. About a third of pet allergies are food sensitivities, often to the chemicals, dyes, flavorings, and preservatives in commercial pet foods. Dogs and cats have low tolerance for chemicals, toxins and petroleum products, but are surrounded by them. Flea collars are made from the same chemical as nerve gas; it is no wonder that so many pets are allergic to them and to petroleum flea sprays and dips. A natural diet and the use of only natural products on and in pets goes a long way toward easing and preventing allergic reactions.

Nutrition: A change of diet to preservative-free pet foods or natural homemade diet with supplements may be the answer, and is certainly the place to start. Often this is all that is required for full pet health. In his book *Pet Allergies: Remedies for an Epidemic* (Very Healthy Enterprises, 1986), pet allergy researcher Alfred Plechner lists the following as primary allergens for dogs: beef, milk, yeast, corn, pork, turkey, eggs, fish and wheat. For cats, he lists beef, tuna, milk, yeast, pork and turkey.[7]

Naturopathy: Digestive enzymes are important here. Also daily detoxification using aloe vera with liquid chlorophyll. Bee products can decrease pollen reactions; start them about two months before the season begins for best results. A daily dose of garlic in the diet or apple cider vinegar in the water bowl may make a pet resistant to fleas. Kelp in the diet is important for any skin and scratching allergies. A few days' fast with warm-water enemas is helpful for detoxifying.

Vitamins and Minerals: Use one of the daily vitamin and mineral programs described in the "Nutrition" chapter; trace mineral powders or kelp are essential. Recommended vitamins are vitamin C with bioflavonoids 500-2,000 mg, daily or to bowel tolerance, B-complex (10-20 mg) and pantothenic acid (B-5). Give 5-10 mg of zinc and 100-400 IU of vitamin E daily. A pet multiple vitamin tablet can take the place of a B-complex supplement, but be cautious about using brewer's yeast for the B-vitamins. For pantothenic acid (B-5), the dose for a 150-pound adult human is up to 2,000 mg per day; use proportionately for animals according to body weight. B-vitamins are water soluble and non-toxic in any amount. Supplement vitamin A, using for cats a capsule containing 10,000 IU of vitamin A and 400 IU of D once a week. For larger animals use more often, or in higher amounts. (For my Siberian Huskies, I give 50,000 IU of vitamin A—without D—twice weekly when needed.) For zinc, use low-potency zinc gluconate with vitamin C throat lozenges.

Herbs: Liver-cleansing herbs like yarrow, yellow dock, dandelion or red clover are helpful, particularly during the fast. Licorice root, an herbal cortisone, often has rapid positive results, especially for spayed females who may benefit from its estrogen content. Instead of chemical flea collars, try an herbal collar scented with aromatherapy oils of pennyroyal, citronella, cedar or eucalyptus. Natural and non-toxic flea shampoos and sprays are beginning to reach the market. One that works even in Florida is Critter Oil, made from aromatherapy oils. Contact the SuDi Company, POB 12767, St. Petersburg, FL 33733, (813) 327-2356.

Anitra Frazier offers the following recipes as part of her extensive allergy protocol for cats. The same herbs in larger doses are fine for dogs.

> *For a stuffy nose*, give three drops in each nostril of warm saline nose drops. If you add two drops of goldenseal extract to 1/4 cup of the solution, it will kill germs and viruses and shrink swollen tissue. For red, itchy eyes, you can use the same solution as eye drops.

> *For itchy skin*, massage in Lemon Rinse, an herb tea made by pouring a pint of boiling water over a thinly sliced skin-and-all lemon; let stand twenty-four hours.

> *For diarrhea and/or vomiting*, give one teaspoon slippery-elm syrup before each meal,[8] or sprinkle the powder on food.

Homeopathy: See the sections that describe your animal's symptoms, i.e., "Skin and Coat Ailments," "Constipation," "Diarrhea," "Digestive Problems." Avoid using veterinary cortisone, as it inactivates homeopathic remedies. For runny, reddened eyes and runny nose with no other symptoms, try *Euphrasia*. Sudden blotchy rashes or swellings on the head or body respond to *Urtica urens*. *Rhus tox* is for the early stage of contact dermatitis, for itching, for burning rashes, and particularly for poison ivy exposure. Rashes of fine dry bumps, especially on the face, with the pet irritable and wanting to be left alone, respond to *Bryonia*. Bee strings or allergic reactions that look like bee stings—the skin is hot and dry with angry red lesions, and the dog or cat is depressed or irritable—respond to *Apis*. *Sulphur* may be helpful with any skin rash, particularly when other remedies fail.

First aid measures for anaphylactic shock include *Aconite* at first onset. This may end the attack if used immediately. Dr. Gloria Dodd also recommends *Apis* 6X and *Nature's Remedy* (*Rescue Remedy*) rubbed into the animal's gums; in acute cases, use every ten minutes for one hour, then hourly as needed. See the section on "Shock."

Acupuncture/Acupressure: For sinusitis and upper respiratory allergy symptoms, use Shin Dog Chart point #2 (GV-25) *Pi liang*, and #8 (not designated) *Erh chien*. When allergic symptoms are indigestion, diarrhea or lack of appetite, use #14 (GV-7) *Chung su,* #15 (GV-6) *Chi chung* and #30 (GB-24) *Wei yu*. For allergic shock, point #1 (GV-26) *Jen chung* is used for resuscitation. See the diagram on "Resuscitation" in the "Method" chapter.

Klide and Kung, again using the Shin Dog Chart, suggest points #26 (CV-1) *Chiao cho*, #44 (LI-11) *Chih shang*, #13 (GV-10) *Ling tai* and #30 (GV-24) *Wei yu* for hypersensitivity to foreign protein materials.[9]

In the Cat Chart, the shock/resuscitation point is #8; for itching, dermatitis or coughing, use point #5. Also see the information under "Skin and Coat Ailments."

Flower Essences: Use *Nature's Rescue* (*Rescue Remedy*) for allergic reactions, or anytime the pet is very uncomfortable. *Crab Apple* or *Allemanda* (Detox Essence) essences are body cleansers, as are Aura Essence (*Yellow Hibiscus*) or Aura Cleansing Essence (*Purple Allemanda*), and *Tomato* helps in throwing off toxins and in cleansing.

Gemstones: Elixirs of *Rose Quartz* and other pink gemstones soothe the skin; *Black Tourmaline* cools the digestive tract; and indigo stones like *Azurite*, *Azurite-Malachite* and *Lapis Lazuli* cleanse and balance the lymphatic system, and are astringent.

Anal Gland Impaction

The anal glands are two small sacs located just inside the dog and cat rectum. They are the animals' scent glands, used for territory marking and recognition. They normally empty when the pet has a bowel movement. Sometimes these glands do not empty properly and become impacted, and they may become infected or abscessed. This occurs most frequently with dogs, particularly small dogs, but also with cats, and with dogs who are overweight or chronically constipated. Older pets may also have difficulty with their glands. The symptoms of anal gland impaction include body odor, crying out during bowel movements and dragging the anus along the floor in an attempt to relieve the itch or pressure. Rashes, sores or hot spots on the pet's hindquarters may appear. These can break out all at once and look horrifying, but they heal quickly once the glands are expressed. For dogs, make sure they have the opportunity to relieve themselves several times a day; for cats, keep the litter box very clean.

Dog groomers empty anal glands routinely during a pet bath, and that is when to do it at home. When the glands express, a foul-smelling oily brown liquid or paste comes out of them. In dogs, the sacs are inside the anus at about five and seven o'clock; in cats, they are at four and eight o'clock. They are pea-sized in dogs; smaller in cats. In some dog breeds they may be too far inside the rectum for expression without using surgical gloves and inserting your finger.

To clear the glands, raise the dog's or cat's tail and grasp the skin around the lower anal opening from the outside with thumb and forefinger. Push in firmly while squeezing the fingers together. When the glands release, wash or wipe away the secretions. If there is blood or pus in the discharge, there is infection present; follow the directions in the section on "Abscesses." Done expertly, gland expression is finished before the animal has time to complain. Some animals need their glands expressed frequently, others never.

Nutrition: An animal on a natural homemade diet or preservative-free foods bought at the pet store is seldom obese or constipated, therefore unlikely to experience anal gland impaction.

Naturopathy: Fiber or bran in the diet helps tremendously here; add a teaspoon of bran daily to food for cats or small dog breeds, more for larger dogs. Add chopped-up vegetables or non-citrus fruits to the diet—prunes, apricots and figs are laxative, as is a teaspoonful of olive oil added to food. (Avoid mineral oil laxatives that deplete the body of vitamins.) Adding aloe vera juice with chlorophyll to the daily diet is very helpful. Garlic is an intestinal antiseptic.

Vitamins and Minerals: Use the daily vitamin and mineral supplements listed in the chapter "Daily Nutrition." Vitamins E and A heal the internal mucous membranes and aid colon health. Use vitamin D with vitamin A, 400 IU of vitamin D with 10,000 IU of A weekly for cats and toy-dog breeds, 25,000 IU of vitamin A with 800 IU of vitamin D weekly or twice weekly for respectively medium and large breeds.

Herbs: Dr. Richard Pitcairn suggests a hot compress of either calendula solution or red-clover infusion or tea to stimulate and soften the glands and make them easier to express. Do the expressing as soon as the compress is removed.[10] Juliette de Bairacli Levy uses diluted liquid witch hazel compresses, or a suppository of yellow dock leaves, for severe cases. Internally, she gives dandelion infusion or fenugreek. For the fenugreek recipe, soak two tablespoons of the seeds per cup of warm water for twenty-four hours; give the liquid to drink and mix the seeds into food.[11]

Homeopathy: *Hepar Sulph* is indicated when the glands have become infected; use it three times daily for a week. Where there is inflammation, irritation and the problem is chronic, try *Silica* three times daily for ten days or watch for response. *Chimaphilla umbellata* is used when there is swelling in the perianal area, difficult urination, and ropy mucous in the urine. *Arnica* may help inflammation and discomfort.

Acupuncture/Acupressure: On the Shin Dog Chart, use the following points for constipation: #19 (GV-2.5) *Kuan hou*, #22 (GV-2) *Wei ken*, # 23 (GV-1.2) *Wei chieh* and #24 (GV-1.1) *Woei kan*. If there is anal prolapse, use the following: #20 (GV-20B) *Pai hui*, #22 (GV-2) *Wei ken*, and #26 (CV-1) *Chiao cho*.

On the Cat Chart, points #4, #5, #17, #18 and #25 are for constipation. Where there is infection, use #15 for blood cleansing.

Flower Essences: *Crab Apple* or *Tomato* essences are for cleansing and for chronic conditions. Detox Essence (*Yellow Allemanda*) aids constipation. Also try Grounding Essence (*Bottlebrush Tree*) for intestinal cleansing and letting go. *Nature's Rescue* (*Rescue Remedy*) is always useful for an animal in distress.

Gemstones: Black gemstones tone the bowel and red ones aid constipation. Try such cleansers as *Bloodstone, Smoky Quartz* or *Obsidian*. Elixirs of *Malachite, Hematite, Coral* or any of the *Jaspers* are indicated for constipation. Elixir of *Emerald* detoxifies.

Anemia

An animal who is anemic will show some or all of the following symptoms: very pale gums and white (instead of pinkish) color inside the ears, loss of appetite and weight, depression and excess sleeping, fast pulse, fainting, listlessness, and general weakness. Anemia is caused by a deficiency of red blood cells, due to underproduction by the animal's body or to blood loss. Loss of blood may result from injury, internal bleeding, giving birth, poisoning or infestation by parasites including fleas, intestinal worms, coccidia or protozoa parasites. Inadequate red blood production—which accounts for most cat anemias—may be caused by viruses, chronic kidney dis-ease, iron deficiency, poor diet, toxins or poisons, and some veterinary drugs. In dogs most anemias not caused by injury are caused by parasites: intestinal worms, heartworm, coccidiosis or a severe case of fleas. An animal with heart dis-ease and poor circulation may also be anemic.

The first thing to do for an anemic cat or dog is to determine the cause and correct it if possible. Have a veterinary fecal test done to check for worms and parasites, a heartworm blood test, and make sure the pet is free of fleas. A checkup will determine whether heart or kidney dis-ease is present. An injured animal should always be checked for internal bleeding. When it is a result of viral infections, anemia is usually overlooked until the pet is past the crisis; once the infection ends, red blood cell production will usually increase. Feline leukemia or FIP (feline infectious peritonitis) are both chronic conditions and sources of anemia. Anemia from poor circulation can be counteracted by herbs (see the section on "Heart Dis-ease"), and anemia from nutritional deficiency is easily remedied. The following recommendations are for treatment of anemia resulting from poor nutrition, as well as for support of animals recovering from dis-ease, surgery, and the aftereffects of parasite removal.

Nutrition: Optimal nutrition is essential here, with the natural homemade or preservative-free diet and full supplement program. Add soft-cooked egg yolks, raw liver and dark green vegetables to the diet. Use brewer's yeast if the animal is not allergic. Avoid bran for constipation, and avoid mineral laxatives that drain nutrients from the body.

Naturopathy: Liquid chlorophyll is a blood builder and highly recommended for supporting the animal in recovery or chronic dis-ease. Add to it a few drops of liquid kelp (iodine) daily, or use kelp powder; the trace minerals are highly important. Blackstrap molasses, which contains iron and B-vitamins, as well as honey and bee products, are useful in treating anemia. Put cider vinegar in the water bowl or directly on food, and feed your pet digestive enzymes daily.

Vitamins and Minerals: Full vitamin and mineral supplementation—Cat or Dog Oil and Powder, Vita-Mineral Mix with A, D and E, or a daily multivitamin and mineral tablet with additional vitamins E and C. Vitamin C aids iron absorption; administer 500-3,000 mg, depending on the size of the pet. B-complex is extremely important; give it to your pet in brewer's yeast, a pet multivitamin tablet or in a 20-50 mg yeast-free human supplement. Give additional vitamins B-12 (cyanocobalamine), B-5 (pantothenic acid), B-6 (pyridoxine) and B-9 (folic acid). Increase the amounts of vitamins A and E, and make sure there is copper in the daily trace minerals or multivitamin tablet. Give 5-15 mg of zinc. Raw spleen glandular may help; get it from a health food store and divide the human dose according to the pet's weight; this may be used in combination with amino acids. If natural iron made from herbs and molasses is not enough, the supplement to use is Floradix from a health food store. Be careful not to use too much; and add iron only when actual iron deficiency has been determined.[12]

Herbs: A number of herbs are blood builders and iron supplements. Alfalfa is the place to start as a general tonic and nutrient that enhances the action of all other herbs and vitamins. Nettles or yellow dock are primary iron supplements. Other blood-building herbs include comfrey, dandelion, raspberry leaf and elderberry. Slippery elm is a nutrient; it can actually be used as a food for weak or anorexic pets.

Homeopathy: *Ferrum met* (homeopathic iron) is a general anemia remedy for a weak, lethargic animal with a poor appetite. This is an alternative to iron supplements, which cause constipation and may be toxic in overdose. *Silica* is recommended for the cat or dog recovering from dis-ease, injury, surgery or malnutrition; try a 200 C potency three times weekly for six to eight weeks for pets with chronic anemia. Where there are gastric symptoms, chronic anemia or anemia caused by hemorrhage, try *Arsenicum*. This is for a dog or cat who is restless, warmth-seeking, easily exhausted, who drinks water frequently in small amounts. For an obese animal who is anemic try *Calc phos*. When anemia occurs with slimy diarrhea and skin eruptions, the remedy is *Merc sol*, and for anemia in young puppies or kittens use *Trinitrotoluene, Ferrum iodum* or *China*.

Acupuncture/Acupressure: The Shin Dog Chart gives no specific points for anemia, but lists several meridians as appetite stimulants and tonics. These are #14 (GV-7) *Chung su*, #15 (GV-6) *Chi chung*, #17 (GV-4) *Ming men*, #30 (GB-24) *Wei yu* and #32 (GB-25) *Pi yu*. See the chart for the locations of the GV (Governing Vessel) and GB (Ball Bladder) meridians. The Cat Chart suggests point #22 for lack of appetite and as a general tonic.

Flower Essences: For recovery from blood loss, try *Stinging Nettles* or *Red Ixora*. In cases where anemia follows a dis-ease, use *Hornbeam*, *Penstemon* or *Saguaro* to strengthen physically and emotionally; *Zucchini* is for recovery states. Use *Clematis* for pets who are lethargic and sleeping extensively, and *Olive* for exhausted, ill or traumatized animals.

Gemstones: *Hematite* or *Bloodstone* are blood builders, as are *Red Jasper* or *Green Jasper*. Red or orange-red stones stimulate the life-force, circulation and red blood cell production. *Fluorite* in elixir stimulates the life-force, as well. Elixirs of *Coral, Diamond, Garnet, Herkimer Diamond, Tektite* or any of the *Tourmalines* are also recommended.

Appetite Loss

Cats are usually finicky eaters, but sometimes their fastidiousness goes too far; the animal gets thinner and thinner and refuses full bowls. Dogs do this too, though less often than cats; some breeds such as Siberian Huskies are notorious for being picky eaters. When a healthy pet refuses to eat there are two main reasons. Too much food may be available over too long a stretch of time. Leave the bowl down for half an hour, then take the rest away until the next mealtime. Or there may be a need for internal cleansing and detoxification. Try a few days' fast with cleansing herbs.

Loss of appetite is also a sign of illness. An animal with a fever, with bacterial or viral dis-ease, or with digestive upset will refuse all food. This loss of appetite may save her life. She should not be forced to eat; honor her need for a few days' fast and support her in her illness. Refusal to eat and weight loss can also be a sign of diabetes, pancreatitis, kidney dis-ease, hyperthyroidism, urinary tract infection (FUS), constipation, bowel blockage, tooth or gum dis-ease, or severe intestinal worms. (Voracious eating may also be a worm or diabetes symptom, or a symptom of hyperthyroidism.)

Dehydration from these or other causes will make an animal stop eating. This needs to be corrected immediately. Vomiting or diarrhea that lasts for more than twenty-four hours in a grown pet may cause dehydration if the animal is not taking in enough fluids to replace the loss. This becomes serious for infant animals within a few hours. Cats in particular are subject to dehydration. When a dog or cat stops eating completely and illness is apparent, the cause must be found and expert help sought.

Anitra Frazier gives five tips for fattening up the starved street cat (or dog) who has now found a home. Another reason for an animal to be underweight is malnourishment. 1) Feed only a small amount at a time; 2) make the animal eat slowly by spreading a little food out on a large plate; 3) serve food at room temperature; 4) serve only natural, preservative-free food; and 5) add digestive enzymes for at least the first month.[13] The following information is for the underweight dog or cat who has no serious health problem or illness.

Nutrition: Use a preservative-free or natural homemade diet with the usual supplements. Remove all food between meals, leaving the bowl available for only a half an hour at a time. Serve all food at room temperature. Keep the animal as calm, loved and stress-free as possible.

Naturopathy: For healthy pets, except for starving strays, start with a few days' liquid fast. Juliette de Bairacli Levy suggests three to seven days of fasting for a healthy dog or cat, using detoxification and internal cleansing methods (herbs, enemas, honey). Aloe vera juice with liquid chlorophyll is a good detoxifier and laxative. Once the pet is eating again, kelp (iodine and minerals) helps thyroid balance, and honey or other bee products are excellent nutrients. For the debilitated pet, royal jelly with ginseng is a good tonic. Include cat or dog digestive enzymes with each meal (a quarter teaspoonful of feline enzymes or half a health food store human tablet for cats). Put a teaspoonful of apple cider vinegar in the water bowl to provide hydrochloric acid. Also see the section on Anemia.

Vitamins and Minerals: Offer the full complement of daily vitamins, minerals and oils described in the "Nutrition" chapter. Add 10,000 IU of vitamin A with 400 IU of D weekly or twice weekly for cats and small dogs; 25,000 IU of A with 800 IU of D weekly for medium dogs; the same twice weekly for large breeds. Give vitamin E (50-400 IU daily), vitamin C (500-2,000 mg), and zinc (5 mg of zinc daily for cats and small dogs, 10-15 mg daily for medium dogs, 25 mg daily for large-breed dogs). Zinc stimulates taste and sense of smell—an animal that cannot smell will not eat—and zinc deficiency has been implicated in human anorexia. Supplement B-complex in a pet multiple and mineral tablet, as brewer's yeast or in a yeast-free human 10-20 mg B-complex tablet. Make sure the pet multiple contains a trace amount of copper, but do not supplement copper individually without expert direction.

Herbs: Alfalfa tea is the best herbal nutrient, containing all of the vitamins and minerals. Peppermint, fennel, ginseng, gentian, chamomile or watercress are appetite stimulants. Ginger, dill, chamomile or papaya leaves aid digestion; burdock and dandelion are detoxifiers. Try Swedish Bitters from the health food store, adjusting dose to body weight, and serve it in honey.

Homeopathy: Lack of appetite from simple indigestion responds to *Carbo veg*, and from constipation or indigestion to *Nux vomica*. These two may be alternated for use with finicky pets. If the animal seems interested in eating, but then changes her mind, try *Arsenicum*, also for restless animals who walk to and from the dinner bowl. When the appetite is erratic, varying from voracious to not eating at all, the remedy is *Ferrum phos*.

Acupuncture/Acupressure: Several acupuncture points are listed for appetite enhancement. These are from the Shin Dog Chart and include #14 (GV-7) *Chung su*, #15 (GV-6) *Chi chung*, #17 (GV-4) *Ming men*, #30 (GB-24) *Wei yu* and #32 (GB-25) *Pi yu*. In the *Cat Catalog* cat acupressure chart, point #22 is for appetite loss and is a general tonic.

Flower Essences: Anorexic pets may respond to *Comfrey*, *Corn* or *Zucchini* essences. Try any of the *Rose* essences for love and reassurance. *Crab Apple*, *Tomato* or *Allemanda* (Detox Essence, Aura Cleansing Essence) are detoxifiers. For recovery after trauma or dis-ease, use *Zucchini*.

Gemstones: Yellow gemstones balance and aid appetite. Test for *Citrine, Amber, Amber Calcite* or *Yellow Jade*. Yellow-green *Apatite* is a digestive stimulant as well.

Arthritis and Hip Dysplasia

Large breed puppies and dogs are more susceptible to arthritis, hip dysplasia and joint dis-eases than are cats or small dog breeds. Small dogs, especially miniature poodles, often have luxating patellas (kneecaps that don't stay in place). Pure breed show kennels routinely euthanize animals who show these conditions, while puppy mills breed from affected stock. Such tragedies are all too frequent, particularly since hip dysplasia and most other joint and bone dis-eases are fully preventable by proper breeding practices and good nutrition. Adding vitamin C to the diets of pregnant females and puppies from birth prevents joint and hip dis-ease, even when the problem is hereditary. For animals who have already developed those problems, and for the pet who develops osteoarthritis with old age, holistic methods and good food offer full and comfortable lifespans. Avoid dosing with aspirin, steroids or butazolidin; natural methods are effective without destroying the animal's immune system or causing stomach ulcers.

In dogs, the most common joint dis-eases are hip socket malformation (hip dysplasia), dislocating kneecaps caused by malformation of the legbones, degeneration of shoulder joints, popping hock (ankle) joints, swelling and pain in the leg joints of young dogs, and arthritis or dysplasia of the elbow. Both dogs and cats may develop rheumatoid or osteoarthritis. Septic arthritis is more common in cats than in dogs, is treated as a bone infection and is only briefly covered in this section. The following methods are positive for all forms of arthritis and joint dis-ease.

Nutrition: The natural diet is essential with some variations. Dr. Richard Pitcairn suggests using as little meat as possible, a vegetarian diet, or nearly so, for dogs, and no yeast. Increase the amount of bone meal in the Dog Powder Mix, but replace the brewer's yeast with a human yeast-free B-complex tablet. Feed your pet grated raw vegetables, especially carrots, beets and celery, which are liver cleansers.[14] Avoid the nightshade vegetables—potatoes, tomatoes, peppers and eggplant. Avoid sugar in the diet, milk products, cayenne pepper, citrus fruits, salt and any chocolate whatsoever.

Naturopathy: Provide sunshine and exercise. The weekly one-day fast, as well as a fast during arthritis attacks (with additional detoxifying methods) are highly important. Use aloe vera juice with liquid chlorophyll daily, garlic, cider vinegar in the water bowl, and bee products. Kelp offers pain relief, bone minerals and iodine, and is highly recommended, as are digestive enzymes. Shark cartilage, one capsule per eleven pounds of body weight daily, may work wonders, but is expensive. Reishi mushrooms have been helpful in some cases.

Vitamins and Minerals: Vitamin C to bowel tolerance (500-3,000 mg per day or even higher of sodium ascorbate C with bioflavonoids) is the key. This alone can result in full cures for young animals and major relief for older ones. It is also used for septic arthritis and any joint or bone dis-ease. Wendell O. Belfield, dog and cat vitamin researcher, equates hip dysplasia with subclinical scurvy, the vitamin C deficiency dis-ease. Use daily a yeast-free health food store B-complex tablet instead of yeast in the Dog/Cat Powder, in the size of about 10 mg for cats and small dogs, 20 mg for larger dogs. Give half the amount of Dog Powder/Cat Powder Mix when the yeast has been deleted. Feed 10,000-25,000 IU of vitamin A with 400-800 IU of vitamin D weekly, 100-600

IU of vitamin E daily, and 5-15 mg of zinc daily. Calcium, magnesium, copper and silica are other important minerals (in bone meal or trace mineral powders), as are supplements of vitamins B-6, B-5 and PABA. Germanium, Coenzyme Q10 or SOD are pain-relievers; divide the human dose according to weight. Do not use iron supplements.

Herbs: Add a teaspoon to three tablespoons of alfalfa to the daily diet, or use it as a tea. A good herb infusion for arthritis is a combination of alfalfa, comfrey and burdock. My dogs eat comfrey leaves eagerly from my hand. Juliette de Bairacli Levi also recommends comfrey with chopped raw parsley, and rosemary or nettles tea. She uses an external massage oil made of four tablespoons olive oil, one tablespoon linseed or sunflower oil, and half a teaspoonful eucalyptus oil. She also suggests Vicks Vapo-Rub for massage/liniment.[15] Both of these are greasy; avoid Vicks for animals that lick their coats.

Yucca has been gaining increasing attention among dog guardians for its steroid and pain-relief properties for arthritis, hip dysplasia, and bone or joint discomfort. Licorice root is an herbal cortisone, and horsetail grass adds silica and aids calcium absorption. Nettles or chaparral detoxify, as does burdock or celery seed. For pain relief, try valerian root (severe pain, sedative), scullcap or St. John's wort (nerve pain, relaxant), chickweed, or feverfew. Black cohosh and devil's claw are also arthritis herbals. For septic arthritis, strong herbal antibiotics include echinacia and goldenseal together. Also feed garlic.

Homeopathy: When the animal is sore and stiff upon getting up, but moves more easily after, try *Rhus tox*. In the opposite case, when pain seems worse following movement (and the animal is lame), the remedy is *Bryonia*. This may be a younger pet that doesn't want to move. *Arnica* is for swelling, bruising or pain—try one pellet three times per day for a few days. When there is swelling in the joints, with pain, sudden onset and reddened skin, the dis-ease may respond to *Apis. Kali carb* is a joint fluid and lymphatic drainer.

Caulophyllum is used where smaller joints are affected, particularly in feet and neck. This is targeted for female animals with a history of genital and reproductive problems. *Actea racemosa* (also listed as *Cimicfuga*) is for arthritis and rheumatism that affects the whole body, joints as well as surrounding muscles, when the dog's or cat's movement is slow and heavy. *Conium* is used in advanced dysplasia when there is difficult movement of the hindquarters, loss of body control, painful stiffness, and the hind legs tend to sway. Use *Arnica* for pain or *Hypericum* where there has been nerve damage. Where other remedies fail, try *Sulfur*.

Acupuncture/Acupressure: There is extensive information for arthritis and other hip and joint discomfort in the Shin Dog Chart. General points for rheumatism include #10 (GV-14) *Ta chui*. Points for the loin area include #16 (GV-5) *Hsuan shu* and #17 (GV-4) *Ming men.* For lumbar rheumatism use points #33 (BL-23) *Shen yu* and #36 (BL-26) *Tzu kuan.* For arthritis, neuralgia, or paralysis of elbow and forelimb see points #43 (TH-10) *Chou yu,* #44 (LI-11) *Chih shang* and #45 (LI-10) *Chih chu.* For the shoulders use #40-42; for hip dysplasia use #55 (ST-34) *Chi shang* and #56 (BL-54) *Chi hou.*

For hip dysplasia, Klide and Kung suggest that when one hip is involved use points #37 (GB-26) *Pung kung yu,* #37C (not designated), #41 (TH-14) *Chien ching,* #41C (not designated) and, on the other side only #59 (ST-41) *Chih shi.* For dysplasia of both hips, the suggested points are #38 (ST-25) *Tien shu,* #38C (not designated), #40 (SI-11) *Kung tzu,* #40C (not designated), #59.1 and #59.2 (ST-41) *Chih shi,* and #46 (TH-12) *Ch'ing feng.*[16]

In the Cat Chart, use points #3 and #4 for joint pain, and #14 for arthritis and cervical (neck) pain. Lumbar pain and the hips respond to points #16-20 and #24.

Flower Essences: Anitra Frazier suggests using the following three traditional remedies together for arthritis: *Crab Apple* to detoxify, *Hornbeam* and *Larch* to increase strength and confidence. Try *Dill* for arthritis and stiffness; and *Stinging Nettles* for cleansing the blood and aching limbs. *Comfrey* and *Self-Heal* are inner healers, and *Tomato* is for throwing off toxins and cleansing.

Gemstones: Orange and orange-red stones are traditionally used for arthritis and other joint dis-ease, as well as the white stones for lymphatic drainage and calcium. These include *Carnelian, Coral, Red Jasper, Pecos Quartz* and *Fire Agate* of the orange, and *Chalcedony, White Quartz, Pearl, Ivory* and *Clear Fluorite* of the white stones. Indigo gems are detoxifier/drainers. Aqua stones are pain relievers and anti-inflammatory; these include *Lapis Lazuli, Azurite, Turquoise* and *Aquamarine.* (Use pendulum testing to determine which stones are effective.) Use them in the animal's aura, or make them into an elixir.

Asthma

An allergic dog or cat can develop asthma, which homeopaths believe originates as a skin rash in a young animal that has been suppressed by cortisone/steroids and gone deeper into the lungs. Animals with pushed-in faces—Pug dogs and Persian cats—are more at risk. Asthma attacks are characterized by a sudden onset of breathing difficulty, with wheezing and coughing. The wheezing is heard when the animal exhales; the lack of oxygen may turn gums and mucous membranes to a bluish color. The pet may lie on her chest with her mouth open, trying to breathe, or she may sit with her shoulders hunched up. Attacks range from mild and short to severe, life-threatening and requiring hospitalization. More cats than dogs develop asthma, with pollens or other airborne allergens the most frequent triggers. Heart dis-ease can result in cardiac asthma. In the veterinary/medical system, cats are treated with cortisone, adrenalin and bronchodilators; the antihistamines used for dogs are not used on cats. Calming the pet is important, and holistic methods can help tremendously. Chemical steroids are not considered a positive treatment by holistic practitioners; they depress the immune system and suppress the dis-ease deeper and deeper. Holistic treatments release it completely from the bodies.

Anitra Frazier connects asthma in cats with hypoglycemia and lists it as a symptom of low blood sugar.[17] Holistic physician James F. Balch indicates that magnesium deficiency or a lowered ability to utilize magnesium are factors. Asthma attacks are caused by spasms in the muscles surrounding the small airways of the lungs;[18] magnesium is the classic remedy for muscle spasms anywhere in the body. He suggests a hypoglycemic diet for asthma sufferers. Sulfite food preservatives and secondary cigarette smoke are high risk factors for asthma sufferers. A cat or dog with asthma needs to live in a non-smoking home. Be aware of allergen foods and avoid feeding beef.

Nutrition: The diet, including any table scraps or treats, needs to be preservative-free. Look for preservative-free dog or cat goodies, and avoid the ones sold in supermarkets; also, avoid rawhide bones for dogs unless they are totally preservative-free. Use a hypoglycemic diet, which means high protein, small meals several times a day, sugar-free, and no by-products or chemical additives. Totally avoid the semi-moist packet foods; a homemade diet is best. Use more whole raw foods and fewer carbohydrates. Add the daily vitamin-mineral supplements—particularly minerals, but both are essential. Avoid cold foods, dairy products, beets and carrots.

Naturopathy: Liquid chlorophyll is highly important for calcium metabolism; it is also a powerful blood-sugar balancer. Use it daily with aloe vera juice for detoxifying. (See the "Naturopathy" chapter for dosages.) Bee pollen is important for the animal allergic to airborne pollens; start about two months before the pollen season and give honeycomb, bee pollen or raw honey daily in increasing amounts. (Animals like the sweet taste.) This builds the immune system and desensitizes the animal to the allergen. Garlic builds the immune system and is an internal anti-septic. Kelp, bone meal or trace-mineral powder is highly important to provide calcium and magnesium,, both of which stop spasms. The weekly fast helps to detoxify the pet's body. Give digestive enzymes with each meal.

Vitamins and Minerals: Use one of the vitamin-mineral programs in the "Nutrition" chapter, along with preservative-free food. Vitamins A and E are important antioxidants and lung healers; A is for tissue repair and immunity; E heals scar tissue and protects the lungs from irritants. Give a B-complex supplement or brewer's yeast, with additional vitamin B-5 (pantothenic acid), B-6 (pyridoxine) and B-12 (cyanocobalamine). Magnesium chelate or asporotate may stop an asthma attack; James Balch's *Prescription for Nutritional Healing* lists 750 mg of magnesium to 1,500 mg of calcium for adult humans;[19] for pets, divide the dose by body weight. Sodium ascorbate C with bioflavonoids, about 250 mg per meal for cats or to bowel tolerance for dogs, helps build the immune system and detoxifies.

Herbs: Licorice root or yucca are natural steroids that are safe and effective. They can replace the pet's need for cortisone. Lobelia, comfrey and peppermint together as a tea are used during attacks, as is mullein. Too much lobelia will cause vomiting. What comes up is the fluid in the lungs that needs to be released. It is safe. Lobelia can also be made into an herb elixir or used as a homeopathic. Elecampane sweetened with honey is another herb of choice for asthma attacks. Use some in a steam tent or inhalation. Blue-violet leaf taken long-term helps dry lung moisture, and is also a cleanser and slight calmative. Nettles is a cleanser, and pau d'arco or echinacea are antibiotics. Horsetail grass is an herbal mineralizer. Avoid alfalfa.

Homeopathy: *Aconite* is for the first onset of attacks which often involve fear and may begin after exposure to cold wind or drafts. Exposure to cold wind or drafts may precipitate attacks. *Arsenicum* is for attacks that improve with heat or warmth; the animal is restless, anxious and exhausted, and her condition is worse between midnight and 2 a.m. Try *Chamomilla* when attacks follow anger, when the pet is whiney and restless. *Carbo veg* comes with gagging and vomiting of mucous, wheezing, long coughing attacks and weak exhaustion; the animal's skin is blue and cold.

When breathing is labored and wheezy, there is degenerative damage to the lung mucous membranes; try *Phosphorus*. For loud, rattling cough with nausea and vomiting, use *Ipecac*. Attacks that occur between 3 a.m. and 5 a.m. respond to *Kali carb*. *Lobelia* is available as a homeopathic remedy (see above).

Acupuncture/Acupressure: The following points on the Shin Dog Chart are for bronchitis, pneumonia, cough and lung disorders: #10 (GV-14) *Ta chui*, #12 (GV-12) *Shen chu* and #27 (LU-1) *Fei yu*. Klide and Kung used the following sequence successfully for a dog with bronchial asthma: K-27, K-26, GV-1, BL-12 and BL-13. After six treatments, the attacks, which had been happening daily, did not recur. They treated cardiac asthma with the following points: ST-9 *Jen Ying* and CV-22 *Tien Tu*; persistent coughing was treated with ST-9 and CV-22. After a few sessions, the attacks stopped and did not return; the cardiac asthma was a residual of heartworm treatment.[20]

In the Cat Chart, acupressure point #5 is for coughing, #15 is for blood cleansing and thoracic pain, #16 is for thoracic pain, and #22 is a general tonic.

Flower Essences: Use *Nature's Rescue* (*Rescue Remedy* or *5 Flower Remedy*) frequently during attacks, and use *Crab Apple, Tomato* or Detox Essence (*Allemanda*) for cleansing and chronic conditions. Anitra Frazier suggests four flowers for hypoglycemia: *Crab Apple, Larch, Clematis* and *Hornbeam. Larch* is for animals who expect to fail and give up easily; *Clematis* is for drowsy dreaming pets; *Hornbeam* is for animals who need encouragement and strengthening.[21] *Bird of Paradise* (Paradise Essence) also balances blood sugar.

Gemstones: Aqua stones like *Turquoise* or *Chrysocolla* soothe and repair the lungs. *Amazonite* aids calcium balance. Also use *Angelite*.

Burns and Scalds

Dogs and cats often get underfoot, especially when you are making dinner. Burns or scalds from hot spills can happen in the most careful household. Cats have been known to climb a hot stove, and dogs to steal dinner from inside the oven. Walking on a hot pavement or hot metal roof can burn their paws. Young animals sometimes find electrical cords attractive, and bite or chew on them. A burning candle flame also looks like something to play with. Light colored animals with pink or white skins and thin fur are susceptible to sunburns, especially on their noses or earflaps. Large double-coated dogs whom their guardians insist on shaving in summer also may get sunburned. Burns may be caused by heat, chemicals, electric shocks or radiation. (Sunburn is a radiation burn.) All burns are painful; serious burns can lead to shock or death. Use the following first aid techniques, then determine whether veterinary care is required.

There are four degrees to burns in increasing seriousness. In a first-degree burn, the skin looks pink to red and when you touch the burn, your finger will produce a white spot; blisters may be prevented by quick treatment. In a second-degree burn there is blistering and the skin is redder. The burned area may be swollen and very painful. In third- or fourth-degree burns, the skin looks white or charred, the hair comes out easily, and there will be either severe pain or no pain if the nerve endings are destroyed. If more than fifteen percent of the body surface is burned, the animal may not survive. In serious burns the skin may ooze. First- or second-degree burns that do not cover a large area may be treated at home; third- and fourth-degree burns or large-area burns require emergency veterinary care.

For immediate first aid, place cold-water compresses or ice packs on the burned area and keep changing them for twenty minutes. If possible, submerge the animal in a tub of cold water deep enough to cover the burn and hold her there for twenty minutes. This stops further tissue damage and may prevent blistering in second-degree burns. With chemical burns it washes away the toxin. For chemical burns from acid, wash the skin with baking soda and water (four tablespoons to a pint of water) to neutralize the acid; for alkali burns, wash with cider vinegar in water in the same proportions. Do this immediately. Clip away the hair over a burn before applying anything other than the above. If you are going to the vet, keep a cold compress on the skin along the way[22] and do not apply any salves. Avoid touching the burn.

Nutrition: A pet recovering from burns needs all the support and help she can get; burns take a long time to heal. Feed the optimal homemade or preservative-free diet with supplements; additional vitamins, minerals and nutrients are listed below.

Naturopathy: Aloe vera juice or gel is a classic burn remedy. Apply it after the water soak; it can be mixed with propolis, royal jelly, chlorophyll or vitamin E. Witch hazel, cider vinegar, castor oil, baking soda and water, diluted lemon juice, or a salted raw onion slice are other good compresses and poultices. Juliette de Bairacli Levy does the following: first bathe the burn with apple cider vinegar for ten minutes, then spread raw honey thickly over the area (clip the hair). Keep changing the compress until the animal seems out of pain, then bandage the honey compress into place and leave it on.[23] Vitamin E can be added to the honey. She also uses poultices of grated raw potato pulp. Put cider vinegar in the water bowl while the pet is healing.

Vitamins and Minerals: Add extra bone meal powder or calcium/magnesium (one human tablet for a fifty-pound dog) to the pet's food as a pain reliever until the burn is healed. Give 10,000 IU of vitamin A daily and 100 IU of vitamin E daily for three weeks, substituting the A plus D capsule once a week for cats.[24] For dogs give 10,000-25,000 IU of vitamin A and 200-1,000 IU of vitamin E. E internally and externally is a burn healer and prevents scarring; for external use, pierce a vitamin E capsule with a pin and squirt it onto the burn. Use vitamin C to bowel tolerance, plus zinc and essential fatty acids, or the Dog/Cat Oil Mix.

Herbs: A mixture of aloe vera and vitamin E is a primary burn remedy. Calendula tincture heals burns quickly and reduces pain; put five drops into a cup of sterile saline solution as a wash or compress. Comfrey is another burn remedy; use the crushed raw leaves as a poultice, or use an infusion of comfrey leaves as a compress. Comfrey leaves can also be mixed with calendula, vitamin E, liquid chlorophyll or honey. If the burn becomes infected, use a compress of five drops of goldenseal tincture to half a cup of sterile saline solution; also give goldenseal with echinacea internally. A drop or two of cayenne tincture placed on the tongue or gums is helpful for treating shock.

Homeopathy: First give *Arnica* or *Aconite* for stress, fear and shock. *Urtica urens* is for stinging burns, usually first or second degree, with *Calendula* tincture or salve externally. *Urtica* tincture (Stinging Nettles) can be used externally—two drops of tincture to an ounce of water—as a compress. For second-degree burns after blisters form, make a compress of *Hypericum* tincture (St. John's wort). Use *Urtica* or *Cantharis* internally. After the blisters break—don't break them yourself—wash with *Calendula* tincture and saline solution two or three times a day. With third-degree burns, give *Cantharis* internally, with external *Calendula* only after healing begins. *Phosphorus* is for electrical burns, given two to three times a day for several days. *Ruta grav* is for scalds with pain in sinews and tendons. *Calendula*, *Urtica* and *Hypericum* all come in salves and salve combinations.

Acupuncture/Acupressure: Check the chart for Resuscitation and Shock and use those points. On the Dog Chart these include #1 (GV-26) *Jen chung*, #2 (GV-25) *Pi liang*, #8 (not given) *Erh chien*, and #25 (GV-T) *Woei chien*. Use point #28 (P-1) for mental stress.

On the Cat Chart, #8 is for shock, #15 is for infections and blood cleansing. Never use pressure directly on a burn.

Flower Essences: Begin with *Nature's Rescue* (*Rescue Remedy*) for any crisis, trauma, shock or stress. *Rock Rose* is for trauma and terror, and *Agrimony* eases the anguish of slow healing. *White Lightnin'* is for trauma, and *Gruss an Aachen* stabilizes the aura bodies. A flower essence of *Comfrey* will aid cell regeneration. Comfort Essence (*Lisianthus*),

Comfort Essence II (*Lagerfield Rose*) or Brede's Essence (*Sky Vine*) are highly comforting. *Nature's Rescue (Rescue Remedy)* or other essences may also be used directly on the skin; add them to compresses, or use the *Nature's Rescue* cream.

Gemstones: Green, blue or aqua gemstones soothe and cool while reducing pain. Try *Chrysoprase, Turquoise, Aquamarine, Chrysocolla, Angelite* or *Celestite,* or any of the *Agates* for cell regeneration. Use them in the aura or as elixirs. *Amethyst* in the environment is a soothing calmative.

Cancer and Tumors

As toxins increase in the environment and in pet (and human) foods, cancer is increasing in dogs, cats and people. One veterinarian told me as I was losing my third Siberian Husky in ten years to cancer that about half of non-accidental pet deaths are now from some form of cancer. Cancer is the cause of one in three human deaths in the United States today, and the numbers are increasing. A hundred years ago—before the era of refined sugar and white flour, processed foods with dyes and pre-servatives, automobile exhausts, chemicalized tobacco smoke, high-tension electrical wires, TV, nuclear testing, ozone damage, toxic wastes, insecticides and PCBs—cancer was rare, and people and animals lived far longer than they do now. In earlier days, when people and pets died young, infectious dis-eases were most often the cause.

The medical/veterinary response to cancer is a horror of increased suffering and unquiet death. Surgeries remove organs and body parts, some of them vital, leaving the animal or human barely able to function, in chronic pain and debility. Radiation and chemotherapy treatments are a misery of burns, nausea, inability to eat or digest food, hair loss, pain and other side effects. When humans are faced with a cancer diagnosis, they may envy pets, who can be euthanized rather than having to face medically managed, prolonged suffering. Holistic healing offers a far gentler way of dealing with cancer and a far gentler progression to death. Used from the beginning, holistic healing *may* clear a cat or dog of ma-lignancy; if it cannot, it will slow the growth and spread of the dis-ease and keeps the pet far more comfortable until the end.

Use the following information alone or in tandem with veterinary methods, but better results can be expected when no chemical drugs are used. Cortisone and other veterinary/medical drugs inactivate homeopa-thy, and chemotherapy destroys the immune system just when it is needed most. For cats with feline leukemia, see that section as well. For any animal with cancer, find a holistic veterinarian and follow her advice.

Nutrition: An optimal diet without preservatives is probably the best cancer preventive. If your pet already has the dis-ease, change her diet as soon as possible and be generous with the supplements. Many of the dyes, preservatives and chemicals in commercial pet foods are known carcinogens. Additionally, a nutritionless commercial diet gives the animal no strength to fight so serious a dis-ease. Feed raw liver (organic) and sweetbreads (thymus) and use filtered water.

Naturopathy: Detoxification is central to any cancer program; do fasts with coffee enemas under expert supervision if the pet is debilitated. Beet, carrot and celery juices (or natural grape, black cherry, or black currant juices) are liver cleansers. Other detoxifiers include aloe vera juice used daily with liquid chlorophyll, garlic or onions, and cider vinegar in the water bowl. Bee products or shiitake mushrooms are immune-system builders. And both are nutrients. Kelp (iodine) balances the thyroid and is particularly important in breast tumors. Use digestive enzymes, raw thymus glandulars and mixed glandulars from a health food store. Shark cartilage is a hopeful new development; give one capsule per eleven pounds of body weight per day.

Vitamins and Minerals: Feed the daily recommended supplements, doubling the amounts of vitamins A and B-complex, and using four times the usual amount of vitamin E. Give vitamin C with bioflavonoids to bowel tolerance, 2,000-6,000 mg per day.[25] Selenium and zinc are important immune-system builders; use proportionate to weight. Pat Lazarus lists the following amounts for a medium-sized dog: C to bowel tolerance, 5,000 IU of A daily with 400 IU of vitamin D, B-complex 20 mg, 400 IU of E, 50 mg selenium, 5-10 mg zinc, plus digestive enzymes. She also reports success with laetrile (vitamin B-17), and recommends raw thymus extract and evening primrose oil.[26] Calcium/magnesium is a pain reliever, and vitamins B-6, B-9 and B-12 may reverse precancerous conditions.

Herbs: Blue-violet leaf and red clover used together twice daily in a strong infusion or extract can clear tumors from anywhere in the body. They must be used over a period of time, possibly several months. Richard Pitcairn recommends goldenseal tincture made into an elixir and used in the homeopathic manner. Other anti-cancer herbs, most of them liver cleansers, include pau d'arco, chaparral, Jason Winters' Tea (chaparral and red clover), echinacea, black radish, Oregon grape root, dandelion, yellow dock, burdock or periwinkle (vinca). Some herbalists strongly recommend using milk thistle extract (silymarin) with any other cancer treatment, as it cleanses and repairs the liver, which is key to this dis-ease.

Another herbal recipe for cancer, leukemia and other immune-system disorders is called Essiac. This is a human recipe that may also be used for dogs and cats. The formula requires 6 1/2 cups burdock root, 16 ounces powdered sheep sorrel (the active ingredient; make sure it is sorrel and not a substitute), 1 ounce powdered turkey rhubarb root and 4 ounces powdered slippery elm bark. Make the infusion as follows:

In a stainless steel pot, bring five gallons of sodium-free distilled water to a boil. Stir in one cup of the Essiac formula and boil for ten minutes. Turn off stove. Scrape the herbs from the pot sides, cover and steep for twelve hours. Then turn on the stove for twenty minutes at full heat. Strain the liquid twice, pour it hot into dark bottles and refrigerate. For a medium-size dog, heat a tablespoon of distilled water in a stainless steel pot and add a tablespoon of Essiac. Give once daily on an empty stomach. For more information and the recipe source, contact Dr. Gary Glum, Silent Walker Publishing Company, P.O. Box 92856, Los Angeles, CA 90009, (310) 271-9931.

Another new herb offers hope for solid-tumor cancers, but not leukemias. Dr. Helmut Keller of Germany is researching *Carnivora*, the Venus flytrap plant. *Natural Health Magazine* (September/October 1992) reported on his work, and the guardian of a dog with jaw cancer contacted him. In the May/June 1993 issue, the name-withheld guardian reported complete clearing of the dis-ease. The herb is not approved for sale in the United States but under FDA laws may be obtained by a veterinarian direct from the researcher for compassionate use. Contact: Helmut Keller, MD, The Chronic Dis-ease Control and Treatment Center, Am Reuthlein 2, D-8675, Bad Steben, Germany, Phone 011-49-9288-5166 or FAX 011-49-9288-7815. This is very expensive, a 50 ml vial costing about $318.[27]

Homeopathy: For malignant or benign warty tumors, try *Thuja* first; this remedy antidotes vaccination reactions, which may be the cause. Breast tumors respond to *Phytolacca decandra*, which Richard Pitcairn uses in a 1C elixir made from poke root herb tincture. In older animals where the tumors are accompanied by lymphatic swelling and muscular weakness of the hindquarters, try *Conium*; there may be chronic ulcers with discharge. Use *Iodum* for too-thin animals with great appetite and small, hard lymph glands. The dog or cat seems shriveled-looking and the tumors may be superficial. *Bellis perennis* is the remedy when the growth was caused by an injury. Dr. Gloria Dodd suggests reducing hard, stone-like tumors with *Baryta carb*, followed by nosodes of the specific tumor/cancer and lymph drainers.

Use *Hydrastis* for cancer in general. The following are 6X cell salts recommended by Richard Pitcairn, but use them in 30C potency instead: *Kali mur*, where there are soft tumors sensitive to pressure; *Kali phos*, where the tumors discharge a smelly secretion and the animal is high-strung or exhausted; *Silica*, where there is pustular discharge and hard swelling.[28] Cancer nosodes include *Schirrhinum* or *Carcinosinum* in 30C or 200C potency. See a homeopathic veterinarian to obtain these.

   Acupuncture/Acupressure: This method of healing is not recommended for cancer or tumors.

   Flower Essences: *Crab Apple, Allemanda* (Detox Essence, Aura Cleansing Essence) or *Tomato* are for cleansing and throwing off disease; *Celery* or Aura Essence (*Yellow Hibiscus*) restores immune balance; *Cucumber* or *Pandora Vine* (Hope Essence) is for depression. *Hornbeam* strengthens, and *Apricot* essence both strengthens and releases miasms.

   Gemstones: *Bloodstone* is a cleanser, *Carnelian* strengthens and *Rhodochrosite* in crystal form helps cancer directly. Also, try *Rose Quartz* crystals or the stone in its usual non-crystalline form.

Cataracts

Cataracts are considered common in old age for humans and pets, but they are another indication of the pollution we live in. Environmental and internal toxicity are causes of this dis-ease, which is preventable and may be reversible by holistic methods if they are started early enough. Malnutrition is a factor in cataract formation: commercial pet foods leave our animals malnourished amid full bowls. If human sugar substitutes (sorbitol) have been implicated in cataract formation in people, what about the sugars and other chemicals and flavorings in pet foods? Galactose—milk sugar—intolerance is another factor, and most dogs and cats are intolerant to cow's milk. Other causes include food allergies, fatty-acid intolerance, high cholesterol (increasing in pets), improper calcium assimilation, hormone imbalance, liver dis-ease, chronic constipation, heavy metal toxicity (lead and aluminum in pet foods), electromagnetic pollution, x-ray and radiation exposure, many chemical drugs, adrenal exhaustion, trauma, poor circulation, spinal misalignment, diabetes (also increasing in pets) and free-radical damage from pollutants.[29] With all of these factors in the environment and with the "ordinary poor health" of our dogs and cats, is it any wonder that cataracts occur as frequently as they do?

Nutrition: Adequate nutrition is a must, as several vitamin deficiencies have been linked to cataract formation. Feed the preservative-free or homemade natural diet with supplements. Dogs and cats both require meat as a central item in their diets; a lack of protein amino acids contributes to cataracts, and lack of the amino acid taurine causes blindness in cats. See the information under Vitamins and Minerals below.

Naturopathy: Dr. Richard Pitcairn reports cataract reductions or cures simply from placing a drop of eucalyptus honey in the animal's eye twice daily over a period of several weeks.[30] Raw cucumber juice used twice daily as an eyedrop or bathing the eyes with a few drops of cold black tea and a drop of raw honey[31] is recommended by Juliette de Bairacli Levy. Castor oil is an effective cataract eyedrop. A poultice of grated raw potato applied twice daily is also effective. Aloe vera juice with chlorophyll and beet juice is an important internal cleanser. Or you can use aloe vera juice as an eyedrop. Detoxifying fasts with enemas are extremely important for moving toxins out of the body.

Vitamins and Minerals: Cataracts have been traced to deficiencies in vitamin A, vitamin C and bioflavonoids, vitamin B-2 (riboflavin) and several of the amino acids. All these are provided in the Optimal Diet With Daily Supplements. Give vitamin C with bioflavonoids to bowel tolerance, B-complex (10-20 mg), vitamin E (100-300 IU daily), selenium (50 mcg), vitamin A (10,000-20,000 IU), and zinc (5-10 mg). (The vitamin amounts above are for a medium-sized dog; use smaller or larger doses according to your pet's body weight.) The amino acid lysine or a health food store amino acid combination supplement is also important. Health food store eyedrops of vitamin B-15, zinc ascorbate or Conjunctisan A used twice daily may clear cataracts; the drops are proving hard to locate in Florida, however. Potassium is important; use cider vinegar in the water bowl rather than a supplement. Calcium/magnesium is a heavy metal detoxifier; find it in the trace-minerals powder or bone meal.

Herbs: Herbal eyedrop favorites include infusions of greater celandine, cineraria, rue or sage tea, with celandine as the most recommended; place a few drops into the eye twice daily. Eyebright tea is a favorite also, used both internally and externally; add half a teaspoonful of sea salt to a pint of eyebright infusion for an eyedrop, but celandine may be more effective. Internally, give bilberry extract to detoxify the eye, chaparral as a strong general detoxifier, rose-hip tea for vitamin C and bioflavonoids, or alfalfa as a detoxifier and general nutrient. Black currant oil, which contains an essential fatty acid, may be helpful.

Homeopathy: For older, weakened animals whose vision is dim and is worse in artificial light, *Conium* may help; there may be excessive tearing and sunlight sensitivity. *Phosphorus* is a possibility for cataracts, glaucoma and retinal degeneration; check the *Materia Medica* to see if the picture fits your pet. *Silica* delays the progress of mature cataracts, but use *Natrum mur* in early stages of the dis-ease. *Euphrasia* (eyebright) drops help tearing, but will not remove the cataract. *Cineraria* in the Mother Tincture can be diluted by one drop to nine drops of pure water and used as an eyedrop daily for about two months.

Three of the cell salts are listed by several sources; use them in the full 30C potency. In early stages of the dis-ease, use *Calc fluor* for about two weeks to prevent further degeneration. *Natrum mur* is used when the cataracts also accompany kidney dis-ease; the dog or cat is thirsty and run-down. Give one dose daily for three weeks in 30C potency. *Silica* can resorb scar tissue and is recommended in 200C potency, one dose weekly for eight weeks. (Silica is Dr. Gloria Dodd's first preference for mature cataracts.)

Acupuncture/Acupressure: Eye dis-eases in general respond to point #29 (LIV-14) *Kan yu*. Cataracts, retinitis, conjunctivitis, or atrophy of the optic nerve refer to #7 (ST-1) *Cheng chi* on the Shin Dog Chart.

The Cat Chart lists points #10 and #11 for eye problems. Also note #15, used for blood cleansing.

Flower Essences: *Crab Apple*, *Tomato* or *Allemanda* (yellow or purple) are for cleansing, and try *Bird of Paradise* (Paradise Essence) when the cataracts come with diabetes. *Tomato* is for cleansing and throwing off dis-ease.

Gemstones: *Malachite*, *Turquoise* or *Solution Quartz* are elixirs for cataracts; when using *Malachite*, leave it in the water for no longer than half an hour. Place *Amethyst*, *Moonstone*, *Lapis Lazuli* or *Malachite* in the animal's aura, as well.

Constipation

A bowel movement once or twice daily is normal for most dogs and cats. A pet who does not eliminate regularly, who strains at eliminating hard, dry stools, or produces stool that is blood-tinged, or watery and brown, may have a fecal impaction in the lower rectum. A poor-quality diet with

too much meat and not enough fiber is the usual cause of chronic constipation. It may also be caused by the animal eating bones, or the bones,
hair and feathers of outdoor prey. Cat hairballs, as well as hair consumed
by shedding long-haired dogs, cause constipation too, which daily grooming helps prevent. Worm infestation may produce constipation symptoms, and animals who get too little exercise are often constipated.

A cat will refuse a dirty litter box and become constipated by withholding her eliminations; a dog who cannot go outdoors often enough
will do the same. Elder pets may develop sluggish bowel function; soft-
ening their dry foods with water and adding digestive enzymes and bran
ease elimination. Aluminum toxicity is an increasing cause of chronic
constipation in people and pets, and commercial pet foods tested for aluminum and other heavy metals have shown high enough toxicities to
cause this. Tap water in many or most cities is also high in heavy-metal
toxicity. Stress, anemia, hypothyroidism, food allergies, spinal problems,
liver dis-ease and not enough water are other causes of constipation.

Chronic constipation is a toxicity dis-ease that can lead to bowel
cancer if left uncorrected for a long enough period of time. When waste
does not leave the body quickly, it is reabsorbed into the blood stream
and toxins are reabsorbed with it. Bad breath, body odor, skin problems,
gas, obesity, indigestion, irritable bowel syndrome and diverticulosis are
only a few of the results of constipation. Mineral-oil laxatives should be
avoided, as they deplete vitamins from the body and result in laxative
dependency.

Nutrition: The optimal diet—with its balance of protein, whole grains
and vegetables, and its supplemented nutrients—is necessary to correct
chronic constipation. The change of diet may be all that is needed. Feed
bran, fresh-chopped fruits, raw green vegetables (feed vegetables and
fruits separately) and whole-cooked grains. Prunes, apricots, figs, apples,
raisins and berries are all laxative and most pets learn to like them; use
whenever needed, fresh or dried.

Naturopathy: Start with a few days of fasting and with an enema
daily, or every other day, to clear the body of toxins as quickly as possible. Feed aloe vera juice with liquid chlorophyll, a gentle laxative that
soothes and heals the internal membranes of the bowel, on a daily basis.
Digestive enzymes are helpful for the constipated dog or cat, and essential for the elder one. Garlic is an intestinal antiseptic; bee products are
laxative. Add a teaspoonful of bran to the diet occasionally for medium-
sized dogs; for cats, Anitra Frazier uses half a teaspoonful of bran with
half a teaspoonful of butter.[32] Do this for a few days, but not every day.
Use filtered or bottled water, and make sure the pet is drinking enough.
(Cats drink very little water—this is normal.)

Vitamins and Minerals: The vitamins, minerals and oils in the Dog/Cat Powder and Oil Mix are important for their essential nutrient values; the minerals are cleansers, and the oils lubricate the system. Calcium/magnesium is a heavy-metal detoxifier, and magnesium is slightly laxative; these are in the mineral mix. Vitamin C is a detoxifier, antiseptic and natural laxative in high amounts; use 500-3,000 mg per day to bowel tolerance. Zinc is also important; use 5 mg per day for cats and small dogs, 10 mg for medium-sized dogs and about 20 mg for a large dog. Increase the daily amounts of vitamin E.

Herbs: Ground psyllium seed is a recommended laxative for dogs or cats; use one eighth teaspoonful with two tablespoons of water once per day for cats, at least half an hour before a meal or giving other vitamins; increase the amount for larger dogs. Senna pods, cascara sagrada and rhubarb are other herbal laxatives, as is licorice root, but the aloe vera juice with chlorophyll listed under Naturopathy is still my first choice of remedies. Comfrey with pepsin is helpful for digestion and is also laxative. Alfalfa is a cleanser and detoxifier. There are a number of herbal laxative combinations on the market for human use; divide the dosage according to weight for pets.

Homeopathy: An irritable dog or cat that strains to eliminate but doesn't produce much responds to *Nux vomica*, which is the basic constipation remedy. *Bryonia* is used when stools are large, hard and dry—almost burnt-looking—and the mucous membranes are dry. The animal prefers not to move. *Lycopodium* is for ineffectual urging with small, hard, incomplete stools, and for constipation when the animal is pregnant. If constipation goes with skin problems, try *Sulfur*, and if there is gas with simple constipation, try *Carbo veg*. *Natrum mur* is especially useful for cats when there is excessive thirst, sores in the mouth, and general weakness, and when the stool seems dry and hard to expel, but there are other watery discharges (watery eyes, watery vomiting, heavy salivation or urination). Try *Silica* when the dog or cat cannot seem to expel the bowel movement. Where constipation and diarrhea alternate, try *Graphites*.

To treat aluminum-toxicity constipation, Dr. Gloria Dodd uses *Alumina*, along with lymphatic drainers *Zinc cyanatum* and *Agaricus musc* for brain and nervous system clearing. In aluminum poisoning, which is common, there is chronic constipation with messy or sticky stools.

Acupuncture/Acupressure: Three points are listed on the Shin Dog Chart for both constipation and diarrhea: #22 (GV-2) *Wei ken*, # 23 (GV-1.2) *Wei chieh* and #24 (GV-1.1) *Woei kan*. For constipation only use point #19 (GV-2.5) *Kuan hou*.

The Ottaviano Cat Acupressure Chart lists points #4 and #5 for simple constipation, and #17, #19 and #25 for constipation with hip pain or spinal involvement.

Flower Essences: *Crab Apple, Tomato, Allemanda* (Detox or Aura Cleansing Essence) or *Bottlebrush Tree* (Grounding Essence) are essences for clearing and detoxifying; *Vine* helps the animal to relax. When digestive upsets leading to constipation can be linked to emotional causes, *Chamomile* or *Aspen* helps.

Gemstones: *Emerald, Bloodstone, Picture Jasper* and *Sulfur* are laxative and the metal copper in elixir. Yellow or yellow-green gemstones stimulate the digestive system and aid in elimination.

Coughing

Coughing can be a symptom of an infection (viral, bacterial, fungal, or parasitic), an inhalant allergy, asthma, heart dis-ease, a foreign object in the lung, or pressure on the larynx from tight collars or growths. Worm larvae in the respiratory system can cause coughing. "Kennel cough" is an infectious dis-ease of dogs characterized by a harsh, dry cough that sounds more frightening than it usually is; this type of cough in cats may indicate bronchitis. A cough with fever, sneezing and runny eyes indicates a viral respiratory condition. A high, weak, gagging cough with swallowing and lip-licking in dogs or cats usually means a sore throat or tonsillitis. A moist, bubbly cough indicates fluid or phlegm in the bronchial tubes—from infection, asthma, bronchitis or allergy. Prolonged spasmodic coughing after exercise indicates heart dis-ease. Wheezing coughs accompany asthma or allergic bronchitis.

Given so many possibilities, a coughing cat or dog needs veterinary diagnosis and care. If the cough is due to heart dis-ease, see the section in this book on that ailment. For asthmatic coughs and viral dis-eases, see those sections in this book when local irritation is the sole source of the cough, or when veterinary information suggests that symptomatic relief is indicated, the remedies listed below may be used. Kennel cough responds to these remedies also—but again, work with your holistic veterinarian. A cough is caused by irritation to the air passages, and continued coughing increases the irritation. The irritation dries the mucous membranes lining the lungs and throat, and this causes more irritation and more coughing.

The following remedies help to break the coughing cycle; they may be used with other holistic or veterinary/medical methods to offer relief.

Naturopathy: If the animal has any form of infectious dis-ease or fever, she must be fasted on liquids with enemas for detoxification. A pet with this type of dis-ease will usually refuse food, and this is positive. During the fast give honey or other bee products. Garlic is an important antiseptic here. Anitra Frazier uses Delicious Garlic Condiment, mixing 1/4 teaspoon raw crushed garlic with 1/8 teaspoon each of distilled water and tamari soy sauce. Let stand two to five minutes, then mix with the pet's dinner or liquids;[33] use higher amounts for animals larger than a cat. The D.C. Jarvis cough remedy is a good one for pets: boil a lemon for ten minutes, juice it, put the juice in a glass with an ounce of vegetable glycerine, stir well and fill the rest of the glass with raw honey. Apple cider vinegar may be substituted for the lemon juice. Use as needed in teaspoon doses, stirring the mixture before administering it.[34] Compresses to the throat and chest of cider vinegar, castor oil or oil of eucalyptus (one teaspoon per cup of warm olive oil) may be used.

Vitamins and Minerals: Very high amounts of vitamin C are essential for any respiratory dis-ease. Go to bowel tolerance, mixing sodium ascorbate C with whatever liquids you are giving. C is also used intravenously, in the amount of 200-500 mg per pound of body weight twice a day. Vitamin A heals the mucous membrane; give 10,000-25,000 IU daily short-term, using the A with D once or twice a week. Zinc boosts the immune system and may also be crushed into liquids; use 5-20 mg of zinc gluconate according to body size. Wendell Belfield, DVM, also suggests selenium and raw thymus glandular for dogs with kennel cough.[35] Black currant oil in addition is positive and increased vitamin E.

Herbs: Mullein is the classic herb for coughs, sore throats and respiratory irritation from infections or any other cause. Wild cherry bark, blackberry, thyme, coltsfoot, elder, sage, peppermint, licorice root and/or slippery elm are also used. Juliette de Bairacli Levy says sage is the best choice. St. John's wort controls coughing and stimulates sweating to break fevers. Where there is a respiratory dis-ease, use goldenseal as an antibiotic with or without echinacea. Cayenne in very small amounts breaks up congestion, and ephedra is a bronchodilator, also used in very small amounts.

Make an herbal cough syrup of a strong licorice-root decoction, with a teaspoonful of raw honey added to each tablespoon of decoction given. (One teaspoonful of pine needles or borage may be added to the licorice.) Another recipe takes one tablespoon of black currant jam (preservative-free only, from a health food store or homemade), stirring it into a cup of water; add honey as you did to the licorice root.[36] With health food store herbal cough syrups, use the infant dose for cats, the child's dose for medium dogs, and the adult dose for large dogs.

Homeopathy: A dry, hacking cough which is worse at night after eating or drinking, or from moving around or from entering a warm room from outside, responds to *Bryonia*. This is the most likely remedy for kennel cough and for some cat coughs. Try *Spongia* for heart cough, or a dry, harsh cough that ends in retching. *Crataegus* also helps heart coughs. For a dry, harsh cough from a tickling sensation in the larynx, the remedy is *Phosphorus*; the cough is worse at night and when entering cold air. For violent spasmodic coughing to the point of retching and when the animal can't catch her breath, use *Drosera*. Use *Kali bich* when stringy mucous is expectorated with the cough, or *Antimonium tart* when there is rattling mucous and frothy discharge. Try *Rumex crispus* where the cough is accompanied by much mucous, and seems better at night and in the evening. Use *Aconite* at the first onset of coughing due to any causes; it may stop it from progressing further.

Coughs due to respiratory infections—where there is sneezing, runny nose, fever and raw throat—respond to *Gelsemium*. Use *Eupatorium* with distemper symptoms and fever. *Ipecac* is for moist, rattly coughs with choking and nausea. All these require holistic veterinary supervision.

Acupuncture/Acupressure: On the Shin Dog Chart, points #2 (GV-25) *Pi liang*, #3 (GV-16) *Ta feng men* and #12 (GV-12) *Shen chu* are for distemper. Point #10 (GV-14) *Ta chui* is for bronchitis; #12 (GV-12) *Shen chu* is for bronchitis, pneumonia, and distemper; and #27 (LU-1) *Fei yu* is for bronchitis, pneumonia and coughing. Try these bronchitis points for kennel cough as well. For cough due to heart dis-ease, use #28 (P-1) *Shin yu*. See also the sections on "Asthma" and "Allergies."

On the Cat Acupressure Chart, #5 is for cough; #15 for chest pain, infections and blood cleansing; and point #16 is for the chest.

Flower Essences: Anitra Frazier suggests *Crab Apple* to help cleanse, *Mustard* for gloom and *Hornbeam* to strengthen. Other cleansers include *Allemanda* (Detox Essence), *Yellow Hibiscus* (Aura Essence), *Tomato*, *Pennyroyal* and *Stinging Nettles*. *Celery* restores the immune system.

Gemstones: Light blue or aqua stones soothe the throat and upper chest; indigo stones are astringent and lymph drainers. Pink-rose gemstones aid the immune system and heart. Try *Chrysocolla* or *Lapis Lazuli* as all-healers, or *Turquoise, Blue Lace Agate, Celestite* or *Blue Topaz*. *Azurite* or *Azurite-Malachite* are immune/lymphatic cleansers and drainers; they also dry mucous. *Rose Quartz, Kunzite* and *Pink Tourmaline* calm and boost the heart and lungs. If making *Chrysocolla* into an elixir, leave it in the water for no more than half an hour.

Diabetes

This is a dis-ease almost unknown in dogs and cats until fairly recently when the quality of nutrition declined and the level of chemicals, preservatives and sugars in commercial pet foods rose. Diabetes is a dis-ease given to our pets (and ourselves) by corporate greed. Stress and shock can also act as catalysts to the beginning of a diabetic state. Juliette de Bairacli Levy places part of the blame on the systemic shock of vaccinations.[37] Cortisone therapy may also produce a diabetes-like reaction.

Diabetes is more common in dogs than in cats, but it is becoming more frequent in both. In cats, watch for dehydration. In dogs, totally avoid the semi-moist commercial food packets; their high levels of sugar and preservatives cause diabetes.

Early signs of diabetes in cats and dogs include excessive water drinking with frequent urination, and large appetite with weight loss. In more developed cases there is vomiting, weakness, an acetone (nail polish remover) smell on the breath, dehydration, labored breathing, lethargy and coma. Laboratory tests reveal high blood-sugar levels, as well as sugar and acetone in the urine. The diabetic animal is losing many of her vitamins and minerals in the frequent urinations and, unable to metabolize sugar, she becomes malnourished despite the high food intake.

Diabetes is a glandular malfunction of the pancreas. A number of dis-eases are complications of diabetes. These include cataracts, liver and kidney dis-ease, artery and heart dis-ease, obesity, retinitis (inflammation of the retina in the inner eye), increased infections (including urinary infections and ringworm), slow healing, and gangrenous sores. Such complications are prevented or reduced by adequate nutrition and lowering of blood-sugar levels.

Holistic veterinary assistance is required with diabetes; natural methods can reduce or eliminate the need for insulin. Keys to healing are the optimal diet, keeping the pet free of stress and maintaining a rigid routine (the same amount of exercise at the same time every day, the same food in the same amounts, etc.). When using any healing method with diabetic pets, start gradually, monitor blood-sugar levels carefully and frequently, and use the method consistently. Stopping and starting—of insulin, an herb, a supplement, or any other factor—can result in the pet's death.

Nutrition: The natural preservative-free diet, especially the homemade one, is essential here, with additional supplements. Trace minerals are important, as is yeast for non-sensitive pets. Reduce the Dog or Cat Oil formula to a quarter cup each of vegetable oil and cod liver oil, and serve only half a teaspoon of the Mix daily, with the usual amount, or more, of vitamin E. Specific whole grains helpful in lowering blood sugar include millet, rice, oats, cornmeal and rye bread. Vegetables include green beans, winter squash, dandelion greens, alfalfa, corn, parsley, onions, garlic and Jerusalem artichokes. Use raw foods, cooked grains and vegetables. Fresh fruits are fine, but feed them separately.[38] Grated carrots, brussels sprouts, cucumber and avocados are also recommended. No sugars or preservatives.

Naturopathy: Begin treatment with a few days fasting—under holistic veterinary supervision only—then switch to the optimal diet. Feed high amounts of garlic as a cleanser, blood sugar balancer and antiseptic. Liquid chlorophyll is highly important in balancing blood-sugar levels; it may be used more than once a day. Goat's milk helps overacidity, and the iodine from kelp is important. Digestive enzymes are highly recommended.

Vitamins and Minerals: Give the recommended daily supplements described in the "Nutrition" chapter of this book, with the changes indicated above. Trace minerals are highly important; chromium, zinc and manganese help to balance blood sugar. Essential fatty acids and calcium/magnesium are important, and are provided in the daily Dog/Cat Oil and Powder Mixes. Vitamin B-complex (10-20 mg) lowers the need for insulin and helps to detoxify stress; use a low potency tablet if not feeding yeast, or give a pet multiple vitamin-mineral supplement. Add additional B-6 to prevent artery dis-ease. Give double the usual amount of vitamin E, with vitamin C (500-3,000 mg per day) or to bowel tolerance, and liquid lecithin in the amount of half a teaspoon to one tablespoon per day. Raw pancreatic glandular is helpful. A chromium supplement (glucose tolerance factor) from the health food store, with dosage reduced according to body weight, may decrease insulin need significantly.

Anitra Frazier's recipe for cat diabetes follows. Increase the amounts for use with the larger dogs.

Add to Each Meal:

1 teaspoon Vita-Mineral Mix
1 teaspoon chopped alfalfa sprouts
250 mg vitamin C powder
1/16 teaspoon potassium chloride (salt substitute)
1 drop stevia extract

Daily: 100 IU vitamin E
(After two weeks reduce to 400 IU of E weekly.)

Weekly: 10,000 IU vitamin A and 400 IU vitamin D[39]

Herbs: The gentle yellow herb yarrow has a chemical composition similar to insulin. Increase amounts gradually, monitor blood sugar carefully, and use consistently if positive effects result. Alfalfa is a nutrient, detoxifier and blood-sugar balancer important for this dis-ease. Other herbs for diabetes include dandelion, parsley, buchu, mullein and periwinkle. Goldenseal can reduce blood-sugar levels significantly, but is not for daily dietary use. Stevia, a chocolate-tasting herbal sweetener, is a blood-sugar balancer. Ginseng is a stabilizer, energizer and balancer of blood-sugar; use the weaker teas rather than concentrates. Anitra Frazier along with the recipe above suggests giving cats a teaspoon to a tablespoon of a tea of dill seed or horsetail grass with each meal.

Homeopathy: The primary homeopathic remedy for diabetes is *Syzygium*, whose remedy picture describes all the symptoms of the disease. Dr. Gloria Dodd uses this in combination with *Diabetogenic factor* (a nosode), and *Cactus grandiflora* as a lymph drainer. If the pet has very low energy and body discharges, add *Carbo animalis*, or *Carbo veg* if the animal is fat and lazy. *Senna* is recommended if the skin is very dry, along with the *Syzygium* combination. For diabetes with skin involvement, a homeopathic preparation of *Insulin* may also be indicated. The Boericke *Materia Medica* suggests this in a 3X to 30X potency.

Uranium nitricum is for diabetes with emaciation and dropsy (skeletal thinness and fluid retention, usually in the abdomen), frequent urination, prominent abdominal bloating and dry mucous membranes. Dropsy, which indicates liver and kidney involvement, requires this remedy. George Macleod suggests a 30C potency for cats or dogs, used three times a week for six weeks. *Iris versicolor* is a general pancreatic disease remedy; the pet has loose yellowish-looking stools. *Iodum* is used when the urine is yellowish green with a milky appearance, and the stool is light colored and loose, sometimes frothy. When there is great debility, *Phosphoric acid* may help. If there are diabetic cataracts, try *Calc fluor* or *Silica* in 30C potency. As with all holistic remedies for this disease, the remedies must be used carefully and consistently.

Acupuncture/Acupressure: Two meridian points in the Shin Dog Chart apply: #34 (BL-46) *Yi yu* for pancreatitis, indigestion, chronic diarrhea and diabetes; #17 (GV-4) *Ming men* for hormonal imbalances.

The Cat Chart lists two indirect numbers: #15 (blood cleansing) and #22 (systemic tonic).

Flower Essences: *Bird of Paradise* (Paradise Essence) may help for sugar dis-eases and addictions. Use *Tomato* or *Red Ixora* (Blood Cleansing Essence) for the circulatory system and blood cleansing. Traditional flowers to reduce stress include *Mimulus* for fear and *Hornbeam* for strengthening and self-confidence.

Gemstones: *Moss Agate, Amethyst* or *Rhodochrosite* are the gem elixirs. *Rhodochrosite, Malachite, Citrine* or *Amber* may be placed in the water bowl or aura.

Diarrhea

Diarrhea is a symptom rather than a dis-ease. It usually means that the dog or cat has eaten something spoiled, toxic or inedible. With my dogs, these things have included garbage can contents, a long-dead squirrel, a two-pound brown bag of raw almonds (bag and all) and an empty plastic bag. Cats are more likely to eat spoiled and dead things. Cow's milk will cause diarrhea in most adult dogs and cats, as will too much food or fruit, a sudden change, eating bones or eating allergenic foods. Toxins in flea collars and flea dips can cause diarrhea or vomiting. Remove the collar and, in the case of dips, wash the animal with soap and water. Intestinal parasites can cause diarrhea as the pet attempts to rid her lower bowel of them. Animals sometimes eat plants that cause diarrhea to rid their bodies of wastes. Once the causative factor has moved through the intestines or once the toxin has been removed, the diarrhea usually stops.

Some diarrhea is more serious. If there is blood in the stool or the stool is black and tarry, there may be intestinal-tract bleeding that needs veterinary attention. If there is violent diarrhea, abdominal distention, projectile vomiting, dehydration, fever or respiratory symptoms, or if there are signs that the animal is actually sick (as opposed to detoxifying), expert evaluation is needed. Diarrhea with no other symptom should be allowed to continue for a day or two to rid the body of causative toxins. This is for adult cats and dogs only; in young kittens and puppies diarrhea is serious; the resulting dehydration can cause death within a few hours. If diarrhea continues for more than four hours, take the young animal to your holistic veterinarian quickly.

Nutrition: If diarrhea is a chronic condition, changing the animal to a natural diet with supplements may be the entire answer in a way that the veterinary I/D diets are not. Sensitivities to preservatives, dyes, chemicals or allergen foods are the likely cause when no worms or dis-ease are present. Begin with a few days fasting or change the diet gradually—but change it. Remember to include the nutritional supplements. For pets who are highly food sensitive, there are hypoallergic natural diets on the market.

Naturopathy: Support the animal in her attempt to detoxify by removing all solid food for two or three days, but make no attempt to stop the bowel action. Keep fresh water available at all times, and feed liquids that keep salt and potassium levels up to prevent dehydration. This is done by placing a teaspoon of apple cider vinegar in the water bowl and feeding clear broths with a bit of soy sauce or tamari, or use kombu broth added. Broths can be made of vegetables, rice and meat, but feed your pet only the liquid.[40] Add lots of garlic to the soup. Juliette de Bairacli Levy offers honey-lemon juice with garlic at first, then organic apple juice and/or raw honey. She recommends laxatives to clean the bowel quickly during the fast.[41]

Liquid chlorophyll is an intestinal antiseptic; use it with aloe vera juice, a laxative that heals the bowel membranes. Once on solid foods again, digestive enzymes are recommended. When changing to a natural diet does not end chronic diarrhea in a pet with no serious dis-ease, this can be the other half of the solution.

Vitamins and Minerals: Stop the use of these during the fast; an animal with diarrhea is not absorbing them. After, make sure to supplement with B-complex, lack of which may cause diarrhea, and feed the suggested daily supplements. Diarrhea drains vitamins and minerals from the animal, and chronic or long-lasting diarrhea may result in severe deficiencies. Be aware that too much vitamin C will cause diarrhea, sometimes suddenly and even after the amount has been right for a period of time. As a pet becomes stronger and needs less C, her bowel tolerance level decreases; this can be the diarrhea source. During infectious diseases with diarrhea, use high levels of C, dissolving sodium ascorbate powder in other liquids during the fast. (With dis-ease, the need for vitamin C increases drastically and lowers again as the pet heals.) Give a teaspoon of liquid acidophilus (lactose-free) to restore intestinal flora balance.

Herbs: Give slippery elm syrup or the powder mixed with honey or water, or carob powder mixed with honey and water, give half a teaspoon to two teaspoons three times per day for three days. Add to these a quarter teaspoon of cinnamon; it is binding. Blackberry tea, easily found in supermarket teabags, also stops diarrhea; cinnamon can be added to this as well. Use catnip tea for dogs but not for cats. Sage mixed with honey stops diarrhea, as does raspberry, strawberry leaf, chamomile, ginger or black elder.

Activated charcoal tablets are good for absorbing toxins and poisons (food poisoning, garbage can raiding) but they interfere with normal digestion. Use one-half to one teaspoon of the powder, or one to three tablets, every two or three hours for twenty-four hours only. Allow the pet to detoxify on a fast for at least twenty-four hours before attempting to stop the diarrhea.

Homeopathy: *Arsenicum* is the remedy when diarrhea is accompanied by vomiting which may be frequent. The animal is extremely restless and feels cold to the touch; she is thirsty, but vomits back water almost immediately. When there is frequent diarrhea with straining but no vomiting, try *Merc cor.* For dysentery (bloody diarrhea with abdominal pain and sometimes fever) with vomiting, try *Ipecac. Phosphorus* is the remedy for copious, chronic, debilitating diarrhea; it was the remedy that healed Copper. Use *China* when there has been great loss of body fluids and debility after a long diarrhea attack. Use *Colocynthis* when diarrhea comes with colic and pain. The cat or dog is extremely irritable and angry. *Croton tig* is for chronic diarrhea that is frequent and watery; give the dose three times daily for up to a week; the course may need repeating. Where there is blood in the stool, try *Merc cor.*

Acupuncture/Acupressure: The Shin Dog Chart lists several meridian points for diarrhea but none are given in the Cat Chart. Use #15 (GV-6) *Chi chung,* #16 (GV-5) *Hsuan shu* or #26 (CV-1) *Chiao cho* for simple diarrhea. For chronic diarrhea, the points are #32 (GB-25) *Pi yu* and #34 (BL-46) *Yi yu.* (The latter is for diarrhea with diabetes.) Enteritis responds to #17 (GV-4) *Ming men* (chronic), #30 (GB-24) *Wei yu* and #38 (ST-25) *Tien shu.*

Flower Essences: Anitra Frazier suggests *Crab Apple* for cleansing (or use *Tomato* or *Allemanda*), *Vine* to relax and *Aspen* to calm fears.[42] *Bottlebrush Tree* detoxifies environmental contaminants and poisons. *Sweet Bell Pepper, Chamomile* or *Vervain* eases diarrhea caused by stress or emotional upset. *Celery* or *Tomato* builds the immune system and throws off toxins and dis-ease.

Gemstones: *Beryl* in an elixir is for diarrhea, and the metal *Copper* is for dysentery. *Emerald* elixir or *Malachite* are powerful detoxifiers. Place *Black Tourmaline, Tourmaline Quartz* or *Smoky Quartz* in the aura.

Digestive Problems

Cats and dogs get upset stomachs, just as people do. The cause may be overeating, eating what they shouldn't eat (rubber pieces from squeaky toys, chewed wood or plaster, etc.), eating spoiled food (garbage-can raiding, that lovely bird killed last weekend), swallowing hair, or ingesting common poisons like fertilizers and weed killers (see the section on "Poisoning"). Worms and diabetes cause gastritis symptoms, as do liver and kidney dis-ease, medication reactions, fear and stress, reaction to flea products used externally, infectious dis-eases and motion sickness. Much chronic gastritis is due to food allergies and intolerances, nutritional deficiencies or shortage of digestive enzymes. Gastritis may also be caused by ingestion of foreign objects; if it is not easily passed by vomiting, see a veterinarian quickly. Bloat is a form of gastritis not covered in this section; it is a medical emergency.

The main symptoms of indigestion/gastritis in dogs or cats are vomiting, which may be accompanied by diarrhea, abdominal pain, gas, appetite loss, depression and listlessness. Salivation can also indicate nausea in cats or dogs. The pet reacts when you touch her abdomen, and may hide after eating or within an hour or so after eating. Attacks, usually from something ingested, may be sudden and acute; vomiting or diarrhea serve to remove the cause, and the dis-ease ends. With an infectious dis-ease other symptoms appear including fever. Chronic indigestion, or sporadic attacks of vomiting with no seeming connection to meals, may be caused by diabetes, liver or kidney dis-ease, by worms, or by food allergies or enzyme deficiency. Vomiting may also be from stress. Where indigestion is chronic and change of diet does not remedy it, or where vomiting is projectile, or contains blood, worms or foreign objects—holistic veterinary help is needed.

Nutrition: Chronic indigestion is usually the first thing remedied by changing to a preservative-free or natural homemade diet with supplements. Dogs and cats often have food allergies to the ingredients in commercial pet foods, and intolerances for the chemicals and preservatives. Raw meat in the diet offers digestive enzymes that cooked and processed foods lack. Pets with internal organ weaknesses are much eased by a natural diet; the liver, kidneys and pancreas are overworked when they must filter out commercial food toxins and when they must function on too-low levels of nutrition.

Naturopathy: In cases of acute indigestion or gastritis, begin with a few days of fast. A vomiting animal should never be fed solid food, which she will probably only vomit back up again; instead, allow her to detoxify and rest her digestive system until all toxins are removed. Give her liquids by freezing them into ice cubes and feeding her the cubes; liquid chlorophyll is an antiseptic, and aloe vera juice is a laxative and internal cleanser and soother. Return to the normal optimal diet with supplements slowly. Keep water available at all times, but if it induces more vomiting, limit the pet to frequent ice cubes. Offer the herb teas listed below, and offer honey or bee products.

Once returned to solid food, digestive enzymes are a must for chronic digestive problems. The combination of the natural diet and enzymes should clear the dis-ease if no infection, worms, foreign objects or organ damage is the cause. Digestive enzymes also help healing after acute indigestion.

Vitamins and Minerals: When the animal is eating again, return to using the supplements listed with the optimal diet. Deficiency of B-complex vitamins, particularly folic acid (B-9) and B-12, can be a cause of chronic digestive upsets. Give a 10-20 mg B-complex, in liquid form if necessary, if not supplementing with yeast (watch for allergy), or a pet multiple vitamin-mineral tablet. Give vitamin E, vitamin C in sodium ascorbate non-acid form, and calcium/magnesium if not using the trace minerals powders. Vomiting and diarrhea drain nutrients from the body; the pet may be deficient temporarily or long-term, and supplements are highly important.

Herbs: Chamomile tea is the gentlest and best of the liver cleansers and anti-indigestion herbs. Use it during the fast, frozen into ice cubes if necessary. Peppermint, ginseng (powder from the tea or a capsule, not the strong extract), catnip (for dogs only), parsley, fennel, dandelion or slippery elm are digestive healers. Other choices include comfrey, burdock, agrimony, dill, lovage or raspberry leaf. Alfalfa or slippery elm are nutrients; St. John's wort helps cramping, abdominal pain and colic; ginger, raspberry leaf or peppermint aid motion sickness. Chamomile is the first choice, or use chamomile with peppermint for any gastritis or indigestion; it is available in supermarkets in teabags. Goldenseal or garlic are helpful for chronic indigestion, as antibiotics and as intestinal antiseptics.

Homeopathy: *Nux vomica* is the classic indigestion and overindulgence remedy, usually for acute cases where there is no marked increase in thirst and the pet is highly irritable. When, along with vomiting and diarrhea, the pet wants frequent small drinks of water and vomits after drinking, use *Arsenicum*. *Merc cor* is also for vomiting after drinking, but in this case the pet wants large amounts of water instead of small sips, and she vomits some time later; there may also be diarrhea with vomiting and blood in the stool. Give *Ipecac* for repeated vomiting; use *Phosphorus* where the stomach is emptied soon after eating food, or when foreign objects have been ingested. *China* may be used with other remedies if there has been significant loss of body fluids. *Cocculus* is for motion sickness. Also see the section on Diarrhea. Give remedies frequently in acute cases, watching for response and decreasing as symptoms ease. Once every hour or two is not too often in the acute phases.

Acupuncture/Acupressure: No points are listed on the Ottaviano Cat Chart, but a number of points are indicated on the Shin Dog Chart for use with both dogs and cats. Point #25 (GV-T) *Woei chien* is for gastroenteritis; #30 (GB-24) *Wei yu* is for gastritis, stomach distension, indigestion, enteritis and lack of appetite, as is #32 (GB-25) *Pi yu*. Point #31 (LIV-13) *Shiao chung yu* is for enteritis, diarrhea and intestinal spasm. Point #34 (BL-46) *Yi yu* is for pancreatitis and diabetes, with chronic diarrhea and indigestion. Point #38 (ST-25) *Tien shu* is for enteritis, diarrhea, abdominal pain and intestinal spasm; point #39 (CV-12) *Chung wan* is for acute gastritis, gastric disorders, vomiting, indigestion and anorexia.

Flower Essences: *Agrimony* is for indigestion due to stress. *Aloe Vera* flower essence is for indigestion. *Dill* or *Sage* essence is for food assimilation; *Sage, Crab Apple, Allemanda, Bottlebrush Tree* and/or *Tomato* are cleansers. *Gruss an Aachen Rose* stabilizes the aura bodies. Use *Nature's Rescue (Rescue Remedy)* frequently in acute illness. Test for Essential Essences Rose combinations for calming and security.

Gemstones: *Beryl* elixir aids indigestion, as does an elixir of any of the agates, particularly *Moss Agate. Malachite* or *Chrysocolla* in elixirs is positive; leave in the water for just half an hour. In the aura, use *Malachite, Green Tourmaline, Amber, Amber Calcite, Peridot* or *Topaz.*

Doggy (or Kitty) Odor

The skin is the largest organ of elimination in the dog, cat or human physiology, although sweat glands are limited mainly to feet and nose in dogs and cats. The skin releases toxins from the rest of the body, cleansing it and clearing it of dis-ease. Body odor in a pet is a sure symptom that the animal is eliminating a lot of toxins, more than her body can handle comfortably, and she needs some additional help.

The pet with body odor may have an obvious cause for it—she needs a bath or has fecal material clinging to the hair at her hindquarters. If the odor is primarily from the mouth, the cause may be gum dis-ease, tartar accumulation or tooth decay. Internal odors come with skin problems (oily coat, eczema type dis-eases and rashes, dandruff), constipation and consequent need for intestinal cleansing, blocked anal glands, dirty or infected ears, and worm infestations. Odors can be caused by more serious conditions, such as liver or kidney dis-ease, diabetes, thyroid disorders, intestinal disorders, infections, and respiratory infectious dis-eases. Odors often come with the inefficient metabolism of old age.

If the problem is obvious—like needing a bath, ear cleaning, anal expression or laxative—do the obvious. A cat or dog with tooth or gum dis-ease can have her teeth checked and cleaned by a veterinarian under light anesthetic for a reasonable cost. Skin problems, constipation, gum dis-ease and many metabolic disorders respond well to the natural diet. This alone may be enough to clear the toxicity and the odor. An animal with infections or internal-organ pathology needs holistic veterinary care, with the optimal diet and supplements to support it. Once the cause is understood and treated, holistic methods work wonderfully to clear the pet's body of toxins and odor—and keep it clear.

Nutrition: The preservative-free or natural homemade diet with supplements is usually the key to body odor from internal toxicity. Avoid allergen foods like beef, yeast, corn and milk; if using a prepared pet food try a hypoallergenic one. These are usually made from lamb and rice, and are available for both dogs and cats. The supplements, particularly the mineral powders, are extremely important.

Naturopathy: Begin with a few days of liquid fasting with laxatives or enemas, then switch to the optimal diet. Detoxification is the key here, using aloe vera juice with liquid chlorophyll daily (in and out of fasting), and placing a teaspoonful of cider vinegar in the water bowl. Garlic is an intestinal cleanser and disinfectant, and kelp can be the answer for pets with low thyroid metabolism. Digestive enzymes are highly important once the animal is returned to solid food. Plain yogurt helps to balance intestinal flora. Raw carrot helps the liver. Use chopped dried fruits for laxatives. It is important to leave food available for half an hour at a time only; then remove it out of smelling reach until the next meal. Observe the weekly one-day fasts for pets not otherwise debilitated.

Vitamins and Minerals: Feed the daily supplements, particularly the mineral combinations. Adding zinc to the diet can do the trick, using 5-20 mg daily depending on body weight. Dogs readily take zinc gluconate with vitamin C throat lozenges from your hand; for cats, crush the tablets into food. Vitamin C is the healer for gum dis-ease, and is an all-body cleanser and antiseptic; use 500-3,000 mg per day, or go to bowel tolerance. Joan Harper uses a recipe for doggy odor that is also valid for cats: Take 10 mg of zinc and 50 IU of vitamin E, mixed with half a teaspoon of liquid lecithin, "liberal sprinkles" of sodium ascorbate C, and garlic flakes.[43] Use daily along with the mineral supplements and kelp. She reports the odor gone within a week or so. Calcium/magnesium—also found in the mineral mixes—detoxifies and reduces or removes odor. Give vitamin A.

Herbs: Juliette de Bairacli Levy gives an infusion of rue for pets with bad breath.[44] Goldenseal and Myrrh tincture diluted with a little water is a gum treatment. Goldenseal, an herbal antibiotic, is indicated where there are intestinal dis-eases or skin problems. Add alfalfa to the diet as an all-round cleanser, nutrient and mineralizer. Horsetail grass gives important minerals. Dandelion, burdock or yellow dock are liver cleansers. See the sections on "Constipation," and "Anal Gland Impaction," "Ear Infections," and "Skin Problems." After a bath using mild soap, add a few drops of lemongrass essential oil, lemon juice (one part juice to eight parts water) or cider vinegar to the rinse.

Homeopathy: For bad breath or body odor with constipation and irritability, try *Nux vomica*. *Merc sol* is used for gum dis-ease, when the gums are red and swollen, receded from the teeth and there is bad breath. Bad breath from intestinal digestive causes responds to *Nux vomica* or *Carbo veg* (if there is gas and rumbling sounds); the two remedies can be alternated. *Kali phos* is for the nervous pet with greasy hair, offensive smell and itching. *Natrum mur* is for the pet with thyroid imbalances; she has greasy, oily skin with itching, odor and irritation. Where the pet has dry, flaky, itchy skin with odor, and fleas, or when other remedies have failed, try *Sulfur*. *Psorinum* may be the remedy when there are skin problems with odorous discharges; the animal seeks warmth and is sensitive to cold; the hair may be dry and matted.

Acupuncture/Acupressure: See the sections on "Digestive Problems," "Constipation," "Diarrhea" and "Skin Problems." No specific points are listed on either the Shin Dog Chart or the Cat Chart for body odor or bad breath. Point #15 on the Cat Chart, for blood cleansing, may help. Do an all-over body massage to stimulate metabolism and organ function.

Flower Essences: The essences for cleansing are key here, particularly *Crab Apple*, *Allemanda* (Detox Essence, Aura Cleansing Essence) and *Tomato*. Use Grounding Essence (*Bottlebrush Tree*) to clear the digestive tract of toxins. Aging Essence (*White Bougainvillea*) helps in conditions related to old age.

Gemstones: The minerals *Magnesium* or *Sulfur* in elixir aid body odors. Try any of the *Agates* for digestive disorders leading to odors, or for gum dis-ease. *Emerald* made into an elixir is a very powerful detoxifier, as is *Malachite*. Place Malachite in the aura, as well.

Ear Infections

Head shaking, pawing or scratching at the ears, odor, brown discharge, and redness or swelling inside the earflap indicate an infection. This may be caused by injury or by foreign bodies in the ear (ticks or plant matter from running through high grass), by bacterial or fungal infections, or by mites. Flop-eared dogs are very prone to this ear infection, particularly cocker spaniels. In my dog-grooming days, I don't think I ever groomed a cocker with healthy ears. Fungus infections inside the ear can be caused by leaving bath water inside them, or from too many treatments with antibiotics. Chronic ear infections that are bacterial or fungal are signs of a reduced immune system and may also come from food allergies. Bacterial infections may be the result of injuries from fights. Ear mites are tiny parasites that cause a crumbly dark-brown discharge and intense itching; suspect them if both ears are infected, particularly in cats. Mites are contagious to other pets in the family, and may travel to the body of the animal. When ear mites are suspected, treat the ears, then bathe the pet with an anti-flea preparation. Natural preparations are based on citrus oils or aromatherapy oils, and they work. Bathe once a week for three weeks, even after the mites have been treated with repeat ear treatments.

Many flop-eared dogs have hair growing inside the ear canals; groomers are able to remove this air-blocking hair with forceps. Doing so helps to prevent ear infections by allowing moisture that is inside the ear canals to dry. The hair strips off with little protest from the pet. After removing it, wipe the inside of the ear with a cotton ball soaked in witch hazel or hydrogen peroxide half diluted with water. With cockers, poodles and other flop-eared dogs with ear problems, periodically use a clothespin to hold the animal's earflaps together (by the hair, not the skin). This exposes the insides of the ears to air and helps heal infections. Put cotton balls soaked in olive oil inside the ears when bathing dogs or cats. Foreign bodies in the ear canal may require removal by a veterinarian.

Nutrition: What you feed your pet definitely makes a difference. Within three weeks after switching Copper to preservative-free dry food and a pet multiple vitamin-mineral tablet, his four-year chronic ear problem disappeared. I definitely recommend the preservative-free or natural diet with supplements.

Naturopathy: Detoxification methods are useful here, with a few days of fasting and internal cleansing. Start by cleaning out the ears with cotton balls soaked in apple cider vinegar, white vinegar, hydrogen peroxide, or witch hazel. Anitra Frazier uses Betadyne diluted in water to the color of weak tea, followed by diluted vinegar. Use cotton balls soaked in the solution, or fill the ear from an eyedropper. Do not use Q-tips; they go too deep for safety and may injure ear-canal walls.

Pat McKay combines aloe vera with hydrogen peroxide for ear infections, wax buildup and ear mites. To two ounces of aloe vera juice or gel, add one teaspoon of three percent food-grade hydrogen peroxide. Put this in a spray bottle or eyedropper bottle, or on cotton balls. Fill each ear with the solution, massage gently at the ear base for one or two minutes (hear the squishing sound), then let the animal shake it all off.[45] Do this daily until the problem is cleared and no further brown discharge appears, then repeat weekly for two to three weeks to catch any newly hatched mites and break the cycle permanently. With mites, also bathe the cat or dog weekly for a few weeks.

Vitamins and Minerals: Vitamin E (puncture the capsules) makes a soothing and healing ear medication. Use it after cleaning the ears with vinegar, peroxide or witch hazel, or alternate the cleaning with vitamin E. This vitamin taken internally, plus vitamin A, helps to heal internal and external skin membranes. The daily vitamin-mineral supplements boost the pet's immune system and help rid the body of infections.

Herbs: Mullein-and-garlic ear oil, available from health food stores, works as well in pets' ears as it does in people's. Clean the ear canals of discharge and wax daily before using. Garlic oil is especially useful when the infection is due to fungus or yeast, usually from chronic wetness inside the ears.

Make an infusion of rosemary in olive oil instead of water and use it for cases of foreign bodies in the ear. Use daily until the irritation clears; the plant piece dissolves and floats out. When Kali came to me with something deep inside her ear canal, I first cleaned the ear with peroxide, then with a cotton ball wet with echinacea tincture. The next day I put vitamin E oil in the ear. Alternating these, it took about ten days to clear her infection.

Dr. Richard Pitcairn offers an extensive herbal protocol for ear mites in dogs or cats. Use Formula One for the first three days, then do nothing for three days. On days seven to nine, use Formula Two. Wait ten days and repeat the sequence.

Formula One

Place the following in a one-ounce dropper bottle:

3/4 ounce almond oil
1/4 ounce olive oil
400 IU vitamin E (puncture a capsule)

Refrigerate. Warm before using by setting the bottle in a bowl of warm water. Use on days 1, 2, 3.

Formula Two

2 teaspoons ground dried rue
5 teaspoons witch hazel extract
1 cup boiling water

Steep the rue in boiling water for fifteen minutes, then strain and add the witch hazel. Refrigerate. Warm before using by setting container in a bowl of warm water. Use on days 7, 8, 9.[46]

Homeopathy: When the ear is very inflamed and sensitive to the touch try *Hepar sulph*, or use *Graphites* where there is much smelly discharge. Where pain is extreme and the animal yelps on touching the ear, the remedy is *Chamomilla*. *Merc sol* is used when the earflap and top of the canal have a wet, sore, red appearance. *Merc cor* or *Rhus tox* is for chronic ear infection cases. For dry skin, watery discharge and restlessness—especially when the animal is worse at night—use *Arsenicum*. If the surface of the ears is scaly with scabby edges, the remedy is *Kali bich*. For blood blisters (hematomas) on the external earflap, use *Arnica*.

Acupuncture/Acupressure: No meridian points for ear infections are listed on the Shin Dog Chart or John Ottaviano Cat Chart. See the chart for Immune Building in the acupuncture method chapter. Also use point #15 on the Cat Chart for infections and blood cleansing.

Flower Essences: Cleansing and detoxifying are important, so again use *Crab Apple*, *Tomato*, *Allemanda* or *Bottlebrush Tree* essence. *Dill* and *Garlic* are for inflammations.

Gemstones: *Kunzite* or *Rose Quartz* elixirs help the ears, light blue stones clear infections. Try *Chrysocolla*, *Turquoise* or *Lapis Lazuli* in the animal's aura.

Epilepsy

Seizure disorders may be hereditary or acquired, and are more frequent in dogs than in cats. An injury resulting in the animal losing consciousness may later become epilepsy, as may poisoning, a blow to the head, nervous-system damage from distemper or other infectious dis-ease, brain tumor or encephalitis. Some conditions can mimic epilepsy but do not recur or end when the cause is removed. These include hypoglycemic attacks, convulsions caused by heavy worm infestation in puppies, insect-sting reactions, laryngospasm, heart dis-ease, malnutrition or food sensitivities, and anxiety attacks. A diagnosis of epilepsy is made when seizures are recurrent and follow a similar pattern each time. The seizure itself lasts less than five minutes (continuous seizures lasting longer are veterinary emergencies), with a recovery phase that can last for several hours. In an epileptic animal, seizures may be triggered by fatigue, fever, overexcitement or anxiety, bright or flashing lights, loud noises, hyperventilation or estrus.

During a seizure put a blanket over the animal and keep her from injury. Otherwise do not interfere. Speak calmly and reassuringly to her; she may sense your presence and benefit from hearing your voice. There may be bizarre behavior, then the seizure itself, then the recovery phase. During the recovery phase, let the animal rest quietly. Some dog breeds—including St. Bernards, poodles, beagles and German shepherds—are prone to seizure disorders. When a cat has epilepsy, it is usually the result of injury, malnutrition or a nervous system dis-ease rather than heredity.

Veterinary medical drugs are used to control seizures but do not heal them, and may have long-term side effects like anemia and liver dis-ease, or daily side effects like lethargy and dopiness. Try holistic methods before resorting to drugs; holistics cause no further damage and may remove the source of the problem. A pet with epilepsy needs protection from pollutants and toxins; lead or aluminum poisoning may be the cause of the condition.

Nutrition: Pet allergist Alfred Plechner reports cases in which both dogs and cats on heavy medication for uncontrollable seizures were able to stop medication after dietary change. He placed the animals on hypoallergenic diets—low protein and no preservatives—and nothing more was needed. He recommended a vegetarian diet for the dog, and homemade chicken and rice diet for the cat.[47] An organization called PETA has a book on vegetarian diets for dogs; call them at (301) 770-8950. Feed vitamin-mineral supplements, replacing the brewer's yeast with a yeast-free B-complex tablet. When going vegetarian, proceed very carefully, and use one of the vegetarian pet-supplement products. Try a chicken and rice diet, or lamb and rice first. Cats cannot live as total vegetarians. Some of the holistic dog foods are without meat; again, use adequate supplements. Allergies to foods, or to chemicals in commercial foods, are implicated in many epilepsy cases; avoid tuna and beef.

Naturopathy: Epileptic pets or people must avoid constipation. Feed aloe vera juice with liquid chlorophyll as part of the daily diet. Kelp, alfalfa and/or the trace mineral powders are important; they help to detoxify heavy metals from the body. Kelp adds iodine to boost the thyroid. Use only totally chemical-free foods, flea products, insecticides and environmental products, and give filtered or bottled water. The epileptic pet needs a non-smoking environment. Soured milk products like plain organic yogurt are positive, as are organic vegetables and vegetable juices, seaweed, eggs, red grapes, beet tops, raw goat cheese and carrots.[48] Use digestive enzymes. Lemon juice enemas are helpful; use with detoxifying fasts.

Vitamins and Minerals: The full daily dietary supplements are required. Instead of brewer's yeast, give a yeast-free 20-50 mg B-complex with additional B-6 and B-3, and half a teaspoon of lecithin daily. Wendell Belfield uses 50 mg each of B-6 (pyridoxine) and B-3 (niacinamide form only of niacin) for an average-sized dog, 100 mg of each for large breeds;[49] for cats use 25 mg each. B-6 deficiency alone may cause seizure disorders. Seizures in cats are often traced to chemical poisoning from insecticides; remove all flea collars and give vitamin C to bowel tolerance, with the B-vitamins listed above and zinc.[50] Vitamins B-9 and B-12 are also positive for both dogs and cats. The amino acids taurine and tyrosine are recommended supplements for humans with epilepsy. (Taurine is familiar as the amino acid without which cats cannot survive.) Divide the adult human dose (500 mg three times daily) by pet body weight. Vitamins A and E are important antioxidents. Raw thymus and raw thyroid glandulars are also indicated.

Herbs: Scullcap, a calmative and a nervous-system repairer, is recommended for epilepsy by virtually all sources. Use a strong infusion or tincture twice daily. Other recommended herbs include black cohosh, hyssop, lobelia, wood sage, rue, hops, rosemary, blue vervain and oatstraw. Passionflower, valerian or hawthorn are also calmatives. Use black walnut if worms are the suspected cause; see the section on "Worms" in this book. All parasites must be removed. Alfalfa is recommended, and may be used with any other herbs.

Homeopathy: *Belladonna* may be the first remedy to try; use it for attacks with dilated pupils and throbbing pulse, when the pet feels hot. *Cocculus* used regularly over several months may prevent seizures. *Ignatia* is used when hysteria or loss of consciousness accompany attacks. *Artemisia* (mugwort) is used for petit mal seizures, sometimes brought on by a head blow or fright; the pet may be overexcited or irritable before onset. *Bufo rano* is for impatient, nervous animals; there may be agitation, howling or biting with attacks, or the pet may hide. *Cicuta virosa* is indicated for grand mal seizures, with the dog or cat acting delirious afterwards. When there are violent convulsions with rigid body, locked jaws and foaming at the mouth, the remedy is *Oenanthe crocata*.

Dr. Richard Pitcairn suggests all of these in 6X potency; George Macleod uses 30C for all but *Ignatia*, *Cocculus*, or *Oenanthe*, which he recommends at 6C. Give the dose after each attack, except for *Cocculus*, which is used on a regular (pendulum test for frequency) basis. Attacks come less and less frequently, except when the matching dose is first used; then it may bring on an early attack; after this initial aggravation, expect significant improvement, and do not give another dose until the attack has subsided. If there is warning of an incipient attack, a homeopathic dose given at that time may prevent it.[51]

Acupuncture/Acupressure: First use the Shock and Resuscitation points shown on the chart in the "Method" chapter. Klide and Kung in *Veterinary Acupuncture* describe a number of cases successfully treated, some with implants at the points for permanent stimulation. Commonly used points included GV-20, GV-21, GV-22, GV-23, GV-24, GB-13, GB-14 and GB-15.[52] See a veterinary acupuncturist.

Flower Essences: Give *Nature's Rescue* (*Rescue Remedy*) or Comfort Essence (*Lisianthus* or *Lagerfield Rose*) first, as often as every five minutes if needed. Rub it onto the animal's gums and nose (do not block breathing), or inside the ears if necessary, and continue through the recovery period in decreasing frequency. *Comfrey* regenerates the nerves; *Gruss an Aachen* or other *roses* stabilize the aura bodies, and *Scullcap* is another nervous system flower essence. Use *Clematis* for returning to consciousness, *Olive* for recovery. The pet guardian will need *Nature's Rescue* (*Rescue Remedy*), too. Brede's Essence (*Sky Vine*) stabilizes.

Gemstones: *Picture Agate, Diamond, Jet, Kunzite, Malachite, Amethyst, White Opal* or *Sugilite* are all recommended as elixirs. Place *Amethyst* in the pet's aura and a large cluster in the room; *Sugilite* balances the hemispheres of the brain.

Fading Newborns

One day you have a healthy, active litter of newborn puppies or kittens; the mother is happy and everything seems okay. The next day you find a baby dead in the nest, the next day another one, and the next. There seems to be nothing wrong—no dis-ease, no discomfort in mother or infants—but the babies are dying. This fading newborn syndrome happens usually in the first week of life, although puppies and kittens are highly fragile for longer than that. Quality nutrition in the mother can prevent some or most of these deaths as nutritional deficiencies can be the cause. Lead poisoning in the mother has been recently implicated in human Sudden Infant Death Syndrome (crib deaths). Bacterial infections like brucellosis in dogs, or FIP (feline infectious peritonitis) and (FeLv) feline leukemia in cats, are causes of newborn deaths. Diarrhea is also an infant killer. Simple stress is an enormous factor in depleting new lives.

Puppies and kittens are completely helpless at birth, with no hearing or vision and no automatic regulation of their body temperatures. A chilled newborn loses strength and the ability to nurse; the baby goes into shock, and dehydration and death come soon after. Birth defects, environmental stresses, infections, maternal neglect and toxic mother's milk are other causes of newborn deaths. It is vital to watch the litter carefully for any sign of stress or illness or failure to thrive. Early intervention is their only chance. Prevention of problems by bolstering the mother's and babies' nutrition, by preventing chilling and dehydration, and by intervening immediately in diarrhea or infections, gives many kittens and puppies the chance to grow up.

Nutrition: Start with the mother, as newborns take their nutrition from her milk. Feed the dam the optimal diet, with increased supplements for pregnancy and lactation. See the chapter on "Nutrition" for vitamin and mineral amounts. Additional vitamin C, zinc and B-complex are essential; give vitamins A and E, with minerals. If the babies are ill, the mother needs treatment. And treating her helps the newborns. Start the newborns from weaning on the optimal diet.

Naturopathy: Use by eyedropper the following emergency remedy for diarrhea at any sign of dehydration or watery stools. Dehydration is indicated when, in lifting the skin at the scruff of the neck, the skin remains up instead of sliding back into place as you let go. A newborn can die of dehydration within a few hours. Dissolve half a teaspoonful of salt, two teaspoons of sugar or glucose (available from drugstores) and two teaspoons of honey in a cup of boiled water. (This is a universal remedy, but for human babies omit the honey.) The boiled water can be replaced by barley water. Cool to body temperature and feed by the drop every few minutes. Warm the newborn if chilled by holding her against your own skin until she becomes active again, give the drops every few minutes, then place her with her mother or on a hot water bottle wrapped in a towel (not too hot).[53] If diarrhea continues after a few doses, or if the newborn remains chilled, go to the veterinarian. (Pedialyte for babies may also be used.)

Conversely, for constipation in new puppies or kittens, give the *mother* aloe vera juice. Use the amounts listed in the Naturopathy chapter.

Vitamins and Minerals: Give vitamin C pediatric drops for all newborns from birth, and supplement the mother with increased amounts of this vitamin. The drops are available from pharmacies and the amounts to use are listed with the daily nutritional supplements in the "Nutrition" chapter. According to Wendell Belfield, DVM, this alone prevents the infections that can cause diarrhea, chilling and newborn deaths. The information comes from research on human crib deaths, where vitamin C supplements to babies and nursing mothers have been shown to virtually eliminate the heartbreak of sudden-death babies.[54] From weaning continue vitamin C, and add B-complex and vitamins A and E. Crush them into food or use liquid vitamin supplements for children. Put the drops from an eyedropper into the cheek pouch of the pet. Iron, selenium, calcium/magnesium or vitamin D deficiency have also been suspected as crib-death causes in humans. Feeding the mother the optimal natural diet with supplements is essential, along with starting the babies after weaning on the optimal diet.

Herbs: At any sign of infection, give the dam garlic and echinacea with goldenseal tincture. Echinacea is a specific for streptococcus infections, as is usnea. These reach the babies through her milk. Give the mother an infusion of raspberry leaf or bilberry (more vitamin C, in herb form); these help diarrhea. You can also use blackberry leaf tea specifically for diarrhea. Raspberry is helpful for the mother throughout pregnancy and nursing. Slippery elm is a food herb that may be used for weaning; it also reduces diarrhea. Alfalfa should be part of the mother's diet during pregnancy and nursing.

Homeopathy: *Carbo veg* is the primary remedy where the baby feels cold and clammy and breathing is depressed. Homeopathic *Echinacea* or *Pyrogen* is used for septicemia infections in newborns, and a nosode of *Streptococcus* is given to the mother. To dose infants, crush the pellet and place it in a teaspoonful of spring water; use an eyedropper to put a drop into the cheek pouch. For diarrhea in kittens or puppies, where stools are watery, yellow and expel forcefully, try *Podophyllum. Aloe* is used where feces are jelly-like and may contain blood; they dribble out, sometimes with spluttering. Where there is lethargy and small, watery, foul-smelling stools, use *Arsenicum. Aconite* is for shock and collapse, and *Carbo veg* for collapse. *Merc cor* is used when diarrhea is the only symptom.

Acupuncture/Acupressure: Newborns should be handled as little as possible; however, the points for "Shock and Resuscitation" may be important. See the chart in the "Acupuncture" chapter, and also try the Immune Stimulation points. On the Cat Chart, try #22 as a tonic, #15 for infections and #8 for shock. Work very gently here. Advice from an expert is recommended.

Flower Essences: If unable to dose by mouth, these may be placed on the baby's skin at the back of her neck or on her belly. Give *Nature's*

Rescue (*Rescue Remedy*) as frequently as needed as a primary remedy. *Gruss an Aachen, Cauliflower* or Light Body Essence (*Gardenia*) stabilize the aura bodies. *Olive* is for exhaustion, trauma and illness. Use *Penstemon* with other essences for strength.

Gemstones: *Fluorite* elixir stimulates the life force. Red stones are life-force stimulants; and pink ones are particularly soothing to newborns and young animals. Place *Rose Quartz, Kunzite* (pink, blue or purple), *Pink Silica* or *Pink Tourmaline* in the nest. Purple stones calm stress.

Feline Leukemia

Feline leukemia is the number-one killer of cats today. Where many cats are crowded together, nearly one hundred percent will be infected. In cities, twenty-five to sixty percent of free-roaming cats have the disease; in sparsely populated rural areas, the incidence can be as low as five percent.[55] The virus that links to feline leukemia is transmitted via cat-to-cat contact; kittens can be infected in gestation, or from an infected mother's milk. It is contagious to other cats with repeated exposure to infected animals—not by saliva, urine or feces. An exposed cat may be totally unaffected, may become ill, or may become a carrier with or without becoming ill.

Most feline leukemia deaths come indirectly, from other dis-eases resulting from lowered immunity. Some of these include FIP (feline infectious peritonitis), cancer (usually lymphosarcoma), feline infectious anemia, feline viral respiratory dis-ease complex, bacterial infections and FUS (feline urologic syndrome).

The dis-ease depresses the cat's immune system, causing leukemia or cancer. The original illness lasts from two weeks to four months, and is diagnosed by a blood test. Symptoms include fever, apathy, appetite and weight loss, constipation and/or diarrhea, vomiting, anemia with pale mucous membranes, or enlarged lymph nodes. There may be tumors, fluid accumulation in the chest or abdomen (FIP), depression, persistent infections and failure of wounds to heal.

Leukemic cats seek warmth and need to have it provided. They also need protection from all toxins and environmental pollutants, including chemicals of every sort, food additives, flea products and insecticides, household cleaners, cat litter treated with chemical deodorizers, cigarette smoke, and radiation from TVs and microwave ovens. Anitra Frazier implicates vaccinations as a source of immune system malfunction and a possible cause of feline leukemia.[56] While the veterinary/medical system offers no hope and directs infected animals to be euthanized, cats treated with holistic methods have been known to revert to negative status and become totally free of the dis-ease—and this in more than a few cases. Cats who eventually will die of feline leukemia live longer and far more comfortably with holistic treatment, and they die without pain.

Nutrition: Optimal nutrition is essential, with the full range of daily vitamins and minerals. Absolutely no preservatives or chemicals are allowed. Feed the homemade natural diet with a little less meat. Anitra Frazier suggests *fifty percent meat* (raw hamburger, organic chicken and organic egg yolk; or lightly cooked chicken, beef, lamb, turkey, liver; tofu and egg white), *twenty percent grain* (soaked oat bran or oat flakes; cooked Wheatena, oatmeal, teff, amaranth, quinoa) and *thirty percent vegetables* (raw grated carrot or zucchini are recommended).[57] Prefer organic foods. Be aware of allergy-causing foods.

Naturopathy: Along with vitamins and minerals, digestive enzymes are important. Aloe vera juice with liquid chlorophyll daily is a stomach calmative, particularly useful when vomiting is a symptom; it is also a detoxifier and antiseptic. Garlic is an important immune booster and anti-viral. Juliette de Bairacli Levy recommends it, along with a teaspoon each of raw honey and molasses daily, and organic red grape juice.[58] Kelp and alfalfa add iodine and minerals. Use raw thymus glandular, raw spleen or combination raw glandulars, and combination amino acids. Detoxification is important, but never fast a debilitated cat without expert supervision.

Vitamins and Minerals: Wendell Belfield's work with feline leukemia has produced consistent successes, with sick cats becoming well and cats testing positive for the dis-ease reverting to negative blood status. The protocol is simple and inexpensive. Along with a pet multiple vitamin-mineral supplement (or the Cat Oil and Cat Powder Mixes, or Vita-Mineral Mix with A, D and E), feed vitamin C to bowel tolerance 3,000-5,000 mg daily. (An animal with lowered immune system will accept much more vitamin C than usual.) Use sodium ascorbate C powder and divide it into two doses mixed into meals. Start small and increase gradually.[59] Add to this the contents of a capsule of liquid calcium (or 1/4 teaspoon extra bone meal) with each meal, and the goldenseal listed below under "Herbs." Once the cat tests negative, which may happen in ten to twelve weeks in asymptomatic cats (symptomatic/sick ones take longer), she still needs to remain on the supplements lifelong. Avoid the use of cortisone and steroids. This information has saved the lives of many cats.

Anitra Frazier adds other vitamins to the C and calcium. With each meal, give a teaspoon Vita-Mineral Mix, a tablet of Bioplasma (homeopathic combination cell salts), a quarter teaspoon digestive enzymes, 10 mg coenzyme Q10, an eighth teaspoon olive oil, 10,000 IU vitamin A or half a teaspoon cod liver oil, 2-3 mg zinc, and a teaspoon of chopped alfalfa sprouts. Give 400 IU vitamin E once weekly.[60] If not feeding yeast, add a 10 mg B-complex.

Herbs: Place two drops of goldenseal tincture (or use the elixir or homeopathic) with each meal. If the cat's symptoms worsen, stop until they improve again; most cats show consistent improvement. Anitra Frazier suggests an infusion of Korean white ginseng and dill seed in equal parts, a teaspoonful to each meal. Juliette de Bairacli Levy depends primarily on raw garlic for this dis-ease, but also suggests herb infusions of cleavers with watercress or nettles. Milk thistle (silymarin), an important liver healer, is recommended. Black radish, dandelion or chaparral are liver cleansers; yellow dock adds iron and also aids the liver. Echinacea, goldenseal and pau d'arco are antibiotics, and red clover with violet or chaparral are cancer detoxifiers. The following mushrooms are immune builders: somastatin, reishi, shiitake.

Goldenseal is the primary herbal, perhaps with milk thistle or yellow dock. Essiac may be important (see "Cancer" section).

Homeopathy: Richard Pitcairn uses homeopathic goldenseal, *Hydrastis canadensis*, in the 1C potency, one drop twice a day. Follow his protocol under herb elixirs in the chapter on herbs. Go to higher potencies, especially once the animal's improvement remains constant on the lower potencies. He also suggests two of the cell salts used together: *Natrum mur* for a weak cat with severe anemia and dehydration, one tablet three times a day; and *Calc phos*, one tablet a day. Again, I find better results with higher potencies dosed by observation. Dose the two cell salts separately.

George Macleod suggests that some cases respond to a nosode of FeLv infected blood, and others to a nosode of homeopathically prepared lymphosarcoma tissue. One cat with a lymphosarcoma tumor responded to a combination of the nosode and *Phosphorus*. *Calc fluor* or *Silica* may be useful for swollen lymph glands. Lymphosarcoma (tumors) are often seen with feline leukemia. Newton Laboratories offers a "Feline Leukemia" combination that is a helpful support.

Dr. Gloria Dodd offers the following protocol: She says that feline leukemia becomes extremely difficult to treat if the animal has been on cortisone. Cats who have reverted to negative status (or sick, or positive-status cats) break out again with the dis-ease if stressed with x-rays, steroids or vaccinations, including the FeLv vaccination, and these must be strictly avoided. Do not let a recovered cat outdoors, both as a precaution against her transmitting the dis-ease to other animals, and to limit stress to the infected animal. Along with vitamin therapy, color and gem therapy, and acupuncture, Dr. Dodd uses homeopathy:

> My treatment for corticosteroid depressed FeLv cats was detoxification, stimulation of the immune system and supportive therapy for the involved organs. Detoxification of the steroids by the homeopathic steroid, weekly administration of potentized homeopathic FeLv with weekly increased potencies (I may start at 30C and go up to 10M before completely ridding the cat of the virus). I also used the EAV to detox with nosodes for Rabies Vaccination, FDVRTC combination vaccines, any pesticides and drugs found. A homemade clean diet detoxed by Parcell's method of clorox soaks, ozone injections, and I used at the setting of 50 gauss-2 cycles per second frequency at 30 minutes . . . .

> All heavy metals were also detoxed with nosodes. In my practice these were very sick cats, some almost comatose and it took many months to bring a good majority back. Some didn't make it, but the ones that did live became completely FeLv free—and even bred and had FeLv negative (and viral-free) kittens.[61]

EAV refers to Electroacupuncture. According to Voll, this is a method of acupuncture therapy as well as an accurate diagnostic. FDVRTC refers to the upper respiratory-distemper combination vaccine for cats.

Parcell's solution is used to remove the pesticides and contaminants from fresh fruits, vegetables and meats by soaking the food in a solution of half a teaspoon of Clorox to a gallon of water for about an hour to remove these toxins. This is similar to the hydrogen peroxide soaks recommended by Pat McKay: Take one tablespoon of three percent food-grade hydrogen peroxide to six ounces of purified water and pour over meat to marinate for an hour. For vegetables and fruits, McKay uses a ten to fifteen minute soak in water with a tablespoon of raw apple cider vinegar.[62] Either of these methods helps greatly to decontaminate food for people and pets.

Acupuncture/Acupressure: The information here is also from Dr. Dodd; see the chart titled "Immune Stimulation" in the method chapter. She uses the immune points bilaterally. Use LI-4 (Hoku), ST-36, SP-6, LI-11 and the Voll point for bone marrow, GB-39. Work with an experienced acupuncturist.

On the Cat Chart, use point #15 for infections and blood cleansing and #22 for a systemic tonic.

Flower Essences: Anitra Frazier suggests *Mimulus* for fears of illness, *Aspen* for fear of the unknown, *Crab Apple* for cleansing and *Hornbeam* as a strengthener. *Celery* is for immune balance, and *Tomato* is for throwing off dis-ease; *Cucumber* aids depression. Old Soul Essence (*Purple Angel Trumpet*) or Light Body Essence (*Gardenia*) stabilize the life force as well as *Sonia Rose* (Mary Magdalene Essence).

Gemstones: *Emerald* in elixir is a deep cleanser and detoxifier. Dark blue/indigo stones balance the glandular and lymphatic systems: *Lapis Lazuli, Azurite, Azurite-Malachite* and *Sodalite. Pink Tourmaline, Kunzite* (pink or purple) or *Rose Quartz* boosts the immune system via the thymus. In the environment or aura use *Sugulite, Amethyst, Lapis Lazuli* or *Pink Tourmaline.* Red stones boost the life force; use *Ruby, Red Spinel* or *Garnet* in the aura, or as elixirs.

Fleas

Fleas, ticks and (more rarely) lice are more of a problem on pets with "ordinary poor health" than on pets who are naturally raised and optimally healthy. Fleas are a summer nuisance, generally disappearing in northern states around November, only to reappear again in late summer. In the South, the hot, damp climate is a breeding ground year-round; there isn't enough cold weather to significantly reduce the pest population.

The increasing problem of these parasites is a reflection of the out-of-balance state of the Earth. Chemical collars, tags, dips and insecticides seemed a great idea twenty or thirty years ago, but today we find that the insects have mutated, becoming immune to one chemical after another. Each succeeding innovation in flea control is more lethal—to the host animal, not the fleas. Today's crop of insecticides causes cancer, heavy-metal poisoning, blood poisoning, leukemia, skin rashes, vomiting, and nervous system damage, along with seizures, lung problems, respiratory arrest, liver damage and allergies. But fleas, ticks and lice are still with us.

If your dog or cat has fleas, it is important to remember that only one-tenth of the fleas present are actually on the pet. The rest are in the carpet, in the drapes, in the upholstery, breeding more fleas. When bathing your pet for fleas, also wash the bedding, vacuum the house and furniture thoroughly (get into all the cracks), and keep the grass in the yard cut low. If your house or grounds are overrun with fleas, it's best to let a professional exterminator do the job at least once. Take the pet and yourself out of the house for four hours, and bathe the pet that day. Natural products are becoming more available and are recommended. Heavy chemical baths and dips are unnecessary; a simple bath in blue dishwashing liquid will kill the fleas on the pet—suds her up and let the soap stay on for ten minutes before rinsing. Never use dog flea products on cats, and never mix products—combining them can be deadly.

For the most part, natural methods do as well as chemical ones in controlling fleas—and they don't kill your pet along with the bugs.

Nutrition: A healthy, unstressed animal with a strong immune system is less likely to have fleas than one who is stressed or malnourished. The optimal diet is necessary for true good health. Feed the preservative-free or natural homemade diet with supplements, groom your pet daily using a flea comb, and keep your pet and her environment clean; fleas, ticks and lice will be much less of a problem. This reduces tapeworms, too, as they are carried to dogs and cats by fleas. Sugar is a flea attractor.

Naturopathy: A good part of the answer for flea and other skin-parasite control lies in this section. Double the amount of brewer's yeast during flea season, and feed two cloves of raw crushed garlic (not deodorized) daily for a medium-sized dog. Give a teaspoon of yeast daily for cats and small dogs; use a tablespoon for a fifty-pound dog. (For alternatives to yeast, see below.) These must be fed daily without missing a day to be effective. As it may take three or four weeks daily feeding for these to become effective, start before flea season begins. Brewer's yeast can be used externally as a flea powder, too.

Apple cider vinegar in the water bowl, or a teaspoonful daily on food, makes the pet's blood inhospitable to fleas. Royal jelly, a bee product, boosts the immune system and is recommended for pets with heavy infestations. Make a spray of a teaspoon of three percent food-grade hydrogen peroxide and two ounces of aloe vera juice, and spray on the pet. This helps to repel fleas, plus eases flea-allergy dermatitis.[63] Timson, an enzyme cleaner for dairy milk pails, makes a soothing and safe rinse for flea-irritated skin (although it will not kill fleas themselves); buy it at feed stores.

For the house, make a mix of half a cup each of boric acid or borax, salt, and talcum or diatomaceous earth, and put it in a salt shaker. Use it on furniture, on rugs and floors, and in pet bedding to kill fleas safely. Borax or diatomaceous earth can also be used in a fertilizer spreader to control fleas outdoors.[64] Diatomaceous earth may be used as a flea powder on even newborn puppies and kittens; it is totally non-toxic, except to fleas.

The following lemon rinse can be used as a flea spray on dogs or cats, as well as in the house and yard. Add the skins, or skins and fruit, of lemons, oranges and grapefruits to a large pot of water and boil down. Use at least one whole fruit per pint of water. (In Florida we drag pounds and pounds of fallen fruit to the garbage every day all winter.) Strain out the residue and place it in a sprayer. It works and is completely safe;

plus it gives your animals and house a nice citrus smell. There are a number of variations to this Recipe. It can also be made as a sun tea.

Vitamins and Minerals: Dogs and cats with high levels of vitamin B-1 (thiamine) in their blood stream are intolerable to fleas. Along with either brewer's yeast or a yeast-free (10-25 mg) B-complex tablet daily, add a low-potency B-1 supplement. Alfred Plechner found that pets supplemented adequately with trace minerals and zinc had far fewer fleas and far fewer flea allergy skin problems; feed the daily recommended supplements. Essential fatty acids, contained in the Dog/Cat oils, are also important. Give vitamin C as a detoxifier and immune builder, particularly if insecticides are being used in the environment. Vitamin B-5 and Oil of Evening Primrose are also helpful for pets with flea allergy skin problems.

Herbs: The primary herbs for flea control—juniper, bergamot, eucalyptus, citronella, geranium, cedar and lavender for dogs, lavender oils or a prepared pet-safe combination for cats—are concentrated into aromatherapy oils. These need to be diluted. Put a few drops in a spray bottle of water and shake well before each use. The oils can be rubbed undiluted onto a rope collar as repellents; renew the oils weekly. These are all for external use. For dogs use essential oils of juniper, bergamot, eucalyptus, citronella, geranium, cedar or lavender. Pennyroyal is used in most natural flea collars, but is thought by some to cause liver problems. For cats use lavender oil only or a prepared cat-safe combination.

Critter Oil is an herbal product made from aromatherapy oils of lemon, cedarwood, grapefruit, pennyroyal, eucalyptus, sage and other herbs. It is added to water for a flea or house spray, or to dishwashing soap and water as a shampoo, and used straight on collars safely. Write to the SuDi Company, POB 12767, St. Petersburg, FL 33733, (813) 327-2356. It works and smells wonderful, is inexpensive, and is totally safe for both dogs and cats.

Try a collar of eucalyptus nuts as a flea repellent; it works as well as chemical flea collars, but is absolutely safe. An herb called Canadian fleabane (erigeron) is available from holistic pet catalogs.

Homeopathy: *Sulfur* 30C may be the most likely remedy for flea-bite allergies; the cat or dog has dry, flaky skin and scratches. *Apis* is for redness around bites with swelling and a blotchy appearance. Where the pet scratches until the hair is gone, leaving sticky-wet skin patches, try *Merc sol.* For chronic scratching with dry, rough, scaly and sometimes inflamed skin, try *Arsenicum.* There may be inflammation and the pet is restless. *Mezereum* is for itching rashes over bony areas of the body; there may be large scabs on the head. For frantic scratching with angry looking little pimples, especially around the genitals, the remedy is *Cantharis. Urtica* is for itching rashes, often from allergy to flea collars.

A nosode made from fleas themselves, called *Pulex*, is available. See also the sections on "Allergies" and "Skin and Coat Ailments."

Acupuncture/Acupressure: On the Shin Dog Chart, the following are points for allergy to foreign protein materials: #26 (CV-1) *Chiao cho*, #44 (LI-11) *Chih shang*, #13 (GV-10) *Ling tai* and #30 (GB-24) *Wei yu*. On the Cat Chart use point #5 for dermatitis and itching, #15 for blood cleansing. The Immune Stimulation points are also positive.

Flower Essences: *Garlic* flower essence helps to repel fleas and ticks, but takes about three weeks to become effective. *Crab Apple*, *Allemanda* or *Tomato* for cleansing are also helpful.

Gemstones: A piece of *Amethyst* in the water bowl may help to repel fleas. Elixirs of any *Agate*, *Garnet*, *Jade* or *Herkimer Diamond* heal the skin, and *Sulfur* mineral is an insect repellent.

Food Addictions

Any human or pet can be allergic to just about anything, and food allergies—which are prevalent in pets—can also be the source of food addictions. What the pet is allergic to is just the thing she craves. She may crave it to the point where she will eat nothing else, starting a spiral of digestive problems, skin problems, chronic discomfort and general poor health. An animal who scratches constantly with not a flea in sight (or, conversely, suffers from chronic flea and parasite overruns)—or who has chronic skin problems, chronic diarrhea that may contain jelly-like mucous or blood, or vomiting that usually occurs about two hours after eating—probably has food allergies. Many of these allergies—some of them functioning as addictions—are due to the chemicals and preservatives contained in commercial foods. Pet-food companies notoriously include ingredients that cause and encourage food addictions, thus ensuring themselves a market for their product. The dog or cat refuses anything else, occasionally even to the point of real starvation. The sugar content in semi-moist dog food packets fosters sugar addictions—along with diabetes, hypoglycemia and heart dis-ease. In cats, the biggest problem is propylene glycol, with the same results as sugar in dog foods. The semi-moist foods are the worst of the never-positive commercial feeding options.

Some foods that seem wholesome and are themselves whole foods can be the source of both allergy and addiction. Hormones and chemicals fed to meat animals, along with chemical fertilizer residues in plants, may be causes. Major pet allergen foods include beef, horse meat, pork, fish, turkey, wheat, corn, milk products, yeast and eggs. Other likely allergens include peas, beans, nuts, shellfish, fish oils, fruit, broccoli, cabbage, cauliflower, chard, tomatoes, grapes, pineapple, spices and mushrooms.[65] Chocolate is highly addictive and can be fatal to cats or dogs. This is also true of beer, wine and other alcoholic beverages.

Cats can easily become "tuna junkies." This is another item that cat-food companies include for the purpose of creating addiction (and therefore sales). Too much fish in the diet robs the body of vitamin E, creating a deficiency dis-ease called steatitis, as well as contributing to heavy-metal poisoning. Chronic urinary tract infections, damage to liver, kidneys and pancreas, and skin and digestive problems all come from tuna. Unfortunately, some cats will eat nothing else.

See the sections on "Allergies" and "Skin and Coat Ailments" for more of what allergies can do to pet health. The focus of this section is on how to break the addictions and put pets on a diet of real foods.

Nutrition: Obviously, the answer to food addictions lies with a quality diet. Feed the preservative-free or natural homemade diet with supplements, and watch skin and digestive problems disappear. Alfred Plechner states that "more than thirty percent of the ailments I treat in my practice are directly related to food." Usually the food the pet has eaten every day for years is the source of the problem.[66]

Naturopathy: A major detoxification to remove the allergen from the pet's blood, organs and body tissues comes first. Start with a few days of fasting, which will also make the animal more likely to accept the new diet when the fast ends. Use aloe vera juice with chlorophyll to aid detoxification, and give enemas if needed. When starting the new diet, there are two ways to approach it. One is by offering food for half an hour, then removing the bowl completely if the animal doesn't eat. Never leave food out between meals. Offer no treats until real eating is established, and remember that most treats are full of sugar. Use natural treats only. If the pet refuses food, let her continue her fast a little longer.

The other method is to mix old and new foods together, gradually increasing the amounts of the new and decreasing the old. This takes longer than "cold turkey" and I don't recommend it, but do it if your pet won't eat otherwise. Another alternative, even less recommended, is to bribe your cat with a bit of something she loves—tuna (add some vitamin E) or whatever the addictive food may be. In any case hold out and be strong in making the change; the animal's quality and length of life depends on your success. The optimal diet is worth working for.

Garlic, bee pollen and cider vinegar are positive during the changeover and after. Beet juice is a liver detoxifier; use in very small amounts increased gradually. Digestive enzymes are important.

Vitamins and Minerals: Follow the supplement protocols that are part of the natural diet. Give vitamin C with bioflavonoids to bowel tolerance as a detoxifier. Quercetin, a bioflavonoid, helps reduce addictive reactions and clear the body of toxins. Give increased amounts of B-complex (10-25 mg), with additional B-5 (pantothenic acid) and B-12 (cyanocobalamine). Pantothenic acid reduces allergic reactions and detoxifies; B-12 is for energy, red blood cells and reducing stress. Use these in yeast-free forms. Vitamins A with D (10,000-25,000 IU of A with 400-800 IU of D) and vitamin E are important antioxidants. Cats addicted to fish need more E. Coenzyme Q10 may be helpful and 5-10 mg of zinc per day. Use the trace mineral powders in the daily diet.

Herbs: Liver-cleansing herbs, including dandelion, burdock, pau d'arco, and red clover—aid and speed the elimination of addictive substances. Herbs that help in releasing addictions are scullcap and chamomile. Milk thistle (silymarin) heals and repairs livers damaged from chemicals and toxins, as do comfrey and yellow dock. Yarrow is another liver detoxifier; it lowers blood sugar and is especially recommended when the addiction has been to sugar. Alfalfa contains almost all known nutrients, and increases the potency of other herbs and vitamins. Swedish Bitters, a couple of drops added to each meal, is a digestive stimulant.

Homeopathy: Alternate *Carbo veg* with *Nux vomica* for the picky eater who refuses new food; try this twice a day for a few days. *Calc phos* stimulates appetite and aids food assimilation. When there is complete loss of appetite, the remedy is *Rhus tox*; give the dose half an hour before meals. When the cat or dog seems to want food but rejects what is in her bowl, *Arsenicum* is the remedy; the animal is restless and walks back and forth to the bowl. For the overly affectionate animal who whines and complains but still won't eat the new food, the remedy may be *Pulsatilla*. (This is usually a pet of light coloring who acts childlike.) Also see the section on "Appetite Loss."

Acupuncture/Acupressure: There are several points on the Shin Dog Chart for appetite enhancement. They include #14 (GV-7) *Chung su*, #15 (GV-6) *Chi chung*, #17 (GV-4) *Ming men*, #30 (GB-24) *Wei yu* and #32 (GB-25) *Pi yu*.

On the Cat Acupressure Chart, #22 is for appetite and is a general tonic; try #15 for blood cleansing.

Flower Essences: For releasing addictions to sugar, *Bird of Paradise* is the essence. *Rescue Remedy* or Comfort Essence (*Lisianthus* or *Lagerfield Rose*) aid in the process. *Crab Apple*, *Allemanda* and *Tomato* are detoxifiers.

Gemstones: Yellow gemstones balance and aid the appetite and detoxify the liver, pancreas and upper digestive system. *Amber, Citrine, Amber Calcite, Jade, Yellow Jade,* yellow-green *Apatite* and *Peridot* or green *Jade* are also positive. *Emerald* in elixir is a detoxifier and cleanser. *Kunzite* calms and balances the pet emotionally through the dietary transition process.

Grief
ঔ——ঌ

Dogs and cats have highly developed emotional bodies, with less developed mental levels. They feel, and feel deeply, although they may not always understand just what the problem is or why something has happened to them. When the human they have bonded with suddenly leaves or dies, or when an animal friend moves away or dies, a pet can be overwhelmed with grief. If the cat or dog must then adjust to living with a new family, the grief, confusion and emotional upset are increased. If the animal suddenly finds herself in a shelter and all alone, she may experience pain that becomes difficult to heal in the most caring new home. Dogs and cats experience anger, depression, apathy, lethargy, loss of the will to live, fear, terror, and may also place blame on others—rightly or not. Where understanding of causes is limited, these emotions can be worsened and acted out in negative behaviors. Dogs bond totally and for life. Cats, who are more loners and place oriented, are less sociable. They react deeply to stress and change.

When Tiger died, Dusty looked for her in cupboards and under furniture for months. When Dusty died, Copper blamed me for her not returning home from the vet's; he was angry and shy of me for weeks. At any mention of her name, he still goes looking for her through the house. An animal brought from a shelter may be missing her first family, wondering where they are and why they left her. When Kali came to me, she showed me pictures of having been pushed out of a moving car, but she missed the people who had pushed her and was angry that they didn't come and take her home. A pet whose guardian moves may follow her on foot for hundreds of miles, determined to find her or die. An animal whose guardian dies has lost an important part of her own heart.

The person living with these stricken pets must do healing work with them even though she may be grieving the loss herself. She must offer more and more love and attention, and be patient with the animal's emotions and behavioral aberrations. Most pets will bond again; grief eases with time and love.

Nutrition: The preservative-free or natural homemade diet is important for any animal; for a pet under stress it is essential. Hypoglycemia, allergies, malabsorption or thyroid imbalances add greatly to depression. Turkey, with its high tryptophan content, calms and aids depression, and complex carbohydrates (whole grains) are mood-elevating foods. Although the B-complex vitamins contained in brewer's yeast are highly important in raising grief and depression, be sure that your pet is not allergic to yeast (see below).

Naturopathy: The prescription here is not for foods or remedies, but love. Do full body massages, Tellington TTouch (see my book, *Natural Healing for Dogs and Cats*), and give lots of quality time and attention. Take dogs for long walks and trips in the car. For dogs or cats, use psychic communication. Ask how the animal is feeling. Ask her what she needs and what you can do to help. Clear up any misinformation she may have. (Some of this will surprise you.) Tell her you are grieving, too, if that is the case. Give lots of strokes and caring. Chlorophyll and bee products give energy, and kelp (iodine) balances the thyroid.

Vitamins and Minerals: Feed the supplements that go along with the Optimal Diet. Calcium/magnesium are relaxants, zinc boosts the immune system, manganese and chromium help energy and mood. All these are in the trace mineral powders and Mixes. Give at least 500 mg of vitamin C per day. The most important vitamins for emotional healing are the B-complex, particularly B-6 (pyridoxine), B-9 (folic acid) and B-12 (cyanocobalamine). If yeast is an allergy concern, give a 10-20 mg yeast-free human B-complex tablet daily or even twice daily, crushed into food. Essential fatty acids, such as black currant oil or evening primrose oil are positive energy and optimism. Try a combination amino acids.

Herbs: Alfalfa adds nutritional support and increases the action of other herbs. Simple calmatives and stress reducers include chamomile, scullcap, passionflower and hops. Hawthorn and motherwort are stress reducers, and valerian is for the cat or dog that is highly agitated. Try ginseng to increase energy in an apathetic animal, using the powdered tea rather than the stronger liquid concentrates. Dandelion is a liver cleanser and energy booster.

Homeopathy: *Ignatia* is the classic remedy for any dis-ease or behavior with grief as its basis, including hysteria and behavior aberrations. For the pet who is so dejected she seems to drag her feet when she moves, the remedy is *Calc carb*. Where there is severe depression and the animal seems to forget how to do things she has always done, try *Calc phos*. A melancholy, peevish animal may respond to *Lycopodium*;

she is afraid to be alone and may have digestive or urinary symptoms. *Nux vomica* is for the irritable dog or cat who blames others and does not want to be touched. With *Arsenicum*, there are periodic episodes of anger, panic or restlessness, and the animal feels cold to the touch. For behavior problems that occur when the animal is left alone, especially in light colored clinging pets, try *Pulsatilla*.

Acupuncture/Acupressure: The Shin Dog Chart lists no specific meridians for grief, but #20 (GV-20B) *Pai hui* is for nervous disorders, and #28 (P-1) *Shin yu* is for mental stress. In the Cat Chart, try #22, which is a general all-body tonic.

Flower Essences: *Star of Bethlehem* with *Honeysuckle* helps pets who are grieving the permanent loss of a person or animal friend; also try Essential Essences Grief Essence (*White Peony*). *Walnut* aids adjustment to a new home or environment. Where there are emotional and digestive symptoms from grief and loss, the essence to use is Aura Essence (*Yellow Hibiscus*). *Angelica* is for extreme behavior changes from difficulty in adapting to a new family. *Clematis* is for the lethargic dog or cat, *Cucumber* or *Pandora Vine* (Hope Essence) is for depression, and *Bleeding Heart* heals the heart and emotions.

Gemstones: Pink stones, particularly *Rose Quartz*, are traditional for easing grief. Place a piece in the pet's environment and on her collar, making sure to clear the stone frequently. *Jet* and *Onyx* are traditionally stones of mourning and recovery from loss. Pink, purple or blue *Kunzite* or *Lepidolite* are mood-raisers and emotional balancers. Make any of these into gem elixirs.

Hairballs

Cats and even some long-haired dogs ingest quantities of fur that must be removed routinely from their digestive systems. This is especially a cat problem, as cats with their barbed tongues are unable to spit out the hair in their mouths and therefore must swallow it. Most hair is expelled by vomiting, but hair that reaches the intestines may wad up there, causing impactions that can become veterinary emergencies. (I knew a cat that died of this.) The vomiting of sausage-like wet hair masses is unaesthetic, but is normal and positive, as it removes the hair before it creates a problem. Vomiting hair, foam without hair in it, or gagging attempts to vomit are all signs of hairballs. There may be hair in the stools, and this is normal—but if the cat suddenly has diarrhea followed by constipation, then stops producing stool, stops eating and becomes lethargic, take her to the veterinarian.[67]

Though hairballs are routine and usually harmless, the best treatment is prevention. Daily grooming removes the loose shedding hair so the cat (or dog) doesn't take it in by licking. Some Persian cat breeders recommend bathing cats weekly to remove the loose hair; they teach guardians to do this even with kittens. Heavy-shedding dogs like Siberian Huskies who also lick themselves like cats can have problems with furballs, too, but this is mostly a cat dis-ease. By starting from babyhood, animals learn to accept and like grooming and bathing. Maintaining the pet's digestive system in top form by good nutrition and prevention of constipation helps the animal to pass hairballs before they become a problem. Good nutrition also helps prevent excessive or year-round shedding.

Nutrition: The optimal diet keeps a cat's or dog's digestive system working well, so that ingested fur is expelled easily or moves through the intestines without difficulty. The daily supplements are important; oils help lubricate the digestive tract and move the hair through.

Naturopathy: Daily aloe vera juice with liquid chlorophyll prevents constipation and keeps the intestines moving and clear of toxins. Garlic is an antiseptic for the digestive system; try Anitra Frazier's Delicious Garlic Condiment: mix one-eighth teaspoon each of pure water and tamari soy sauce with one-quarter teaspoonful of crushed raw garlic. Let stand two to five minutes, then give one-eighth teaspoon in food three times a week to cats.[68] Digestive enzymes are important as well.

Grace McHattie suggests feeding cats oily fish once a week and keeping grass available for eating.[69] In *Cats Naturally*, Juliette de Bairacli Levy recommends frequent feeding of sesame, sunflower or corn oils. Remember fasts and enemas.

Vitamins and Minerals: Feed the daily supplements, including the Cat Oil Mix or Vita-Mineral Mix with additional vitamins A, D and E. These contain the essential fatty acids for lubricating. Add a teaspoon of bran per pound of food to prevent or ease constipation and move hair through. Vitamin C to bowel tolerance is laxative and a detoxifier; supplement with zinc (5-10 mg) and vitamin E. See the section on "Constipation."

Avoid mineral-oil laxatives as they drain vitamins and nutrients from the body; aloe vera juice is much more positive. In using hairball preparations, look for those that do not contain benzoate of soda. If the cat or dog requires removal of furballs by the veterinarian, give one charcoal tablet after, and for two weeks add half a teaspoon of liquid lactose-free acidophilus to food.[70]

Herbs: Along with bran, psyllium seed is a good laxative for cats; give one-eighth teaspoon with two tablespoons of water once a day, at least half an hour before a meal. Herbal laxatives include senna pods, rhubarb or cascara sagrada; licorice root is also a laxative. Alfalfa is a cleanser and detoxifier, though not strictly a laxative. Aloe vera juice with chlorophyll is still my primary choice of laxative for pets. It works gently and reliably, and heals the intestinal membranes as it works. There are a number of hairball preparations available from pet stores and veterinarians. Additionally, herbal laxatives for humans may be divided into pet dosage according to the animal's weight.

Homeopathy: The primary remedy that helps a cat or dog expel ingested hair is *Nux vomica*. Use it twice a day for a few days, or by the observation method, to help remove hair by vomiting or through the stools. If vomiting seems to cause the animal pain, try *Phosphorus*. Also see the remedies under "Constipation."

Acupuncture/Acupressure: No specific points on the Dog or Cat Charts are designated for eliminating hairballs. For constipation use point #19 (GV-2.5) *Kuan hou*. For constipation or diarrhea use #22 (GV-2) *Wei ken*, #23 (GV-1.2) *Wei chieh* and #24 (GV-1.1) *Woei kan*. The Cat Chart lists points #4 and #5 for constipation.

Flower Essences: *Crab Apple* and *Tomato* are cleansers and detoxifiers. Grounding Essence (*Bottlebrush Tree*) clears the digestive tract, and *Yellow Allemanda* (Detox Essence) aids elimination.

Gemstones: *Beryl* or *Malachite* strengthens the bowel and aids elimination; use them in elixirs, leaving *Malachite* in the water for no more than twenty minutes. *Green Jasper* and *Picture Jasper* are laxatives, and *Emerald* is a cleanser. Place a piece of *Malachite* on the pet's collar to remove toxins within.

Heart Dis-ease and Hypertension

These are "human dis-eases" almost unknown in pets until just a few decades ago, the results of high-stress living and poor nutrition, of damage from pollutants, toxins and chemicals. In dogs, heart dis-ease usually takes the form of valve and muscle weakness, while in cats it most often consists of a dilation of one or both sides of the heart. Congenital (born with) weaknesses like heart murmurs may occur, as well as heart arrhythmias (irregular pulse). While hypertension (high blood pressure) occurs more often in dogs and people than in cats, the most frequent form of cat heart dis-ease, cardiomyopathy, produces low blood pressure. (In most veterinary clinics, blood pressure is not routinely measured.) Hardening of the arteries occurs only rarely in pets, but heart failure is increasing in both dogs and cats.

When failure occurs in the left side of the heart, pulmonary pressure builds, resulting in lung congestion and pulmonary edema (fluid build-up in the lung sacs). The animal coughs after exercise, may bring up a bubbly red fluid, is out of breath, and her tongue and gums may look bluish. The pulse is rapid, weak and irregular, with heart murmurs. When the dis-ease is advanced there may be anxiety or fainting spells. Coughing at night and after exercise or excitement are early symptoms. When the failure is on the right side, pressure backs up in the veins, resulting in congestive heart failure. The animal is lethargic, with shortness of breath, heart murmurs, rapid pulse and lack of appetite. In later stages there is weight loss, spleen and liver enlargement, kidney failure and fluid in the abdomen.

In cardiomyopathy in cats the heart wall either thickens and stiffens, or thins and balloons out. There is low blood pressure, resulting in not enough blood to nourish the organs. Organ failure occurs, and blood clots may cause strokes. In dogs, parasite damage from heartworm dis-ease also may result in congestive heart failure. A deep, soft cough is the most frequent early symptom, made worse by exercise. Many dogs and cats with heart dis-ease live full lives with early diagnosis and supportive care. Holistic methods are often more positive than the side effects of veterinary drugs.

Nutrition: Feed the optimal preservative-free diet, of course, with supplements. This diet emphasizes no salt, and uses only a small amount of meat. Feed half to one ounce of raw beef, turkey or chicken daily, but use more tofu, eggs and dairy products.[71] Feed three or four small meals per day instead of one or two big ones. Whole cooked grains and raw vegetables are important. Use bottled water without chlorine or fluoride for drinking. Keep exercise gentle and reduce stress.

Naturopathy: Apple cider vinegar in the water bowl or on food is a potassium supplement for pets on diuretics; it may make a veterinary potassium medication unnecessary. Raw honey and/or bee products strengthen the heart, and are tonics and nutrients. Garlic lowers high blood pressure and cholesterol levels. Kelp lowers blood pressure and eases angina pain. For cats with cardiomyopathy's low blood pressure, substitute trace mineral powder for the kelp in the Vita-Mineral Mix.[72] Richard Pitcairn suggests substituting dolomite powder for the bone meal in the Dog/Cat Powders. Be careful of lead contamination in dolomite if you choose to do this; a trace mineral powder is preferred. Give digestive enzymes daily with meals.

Vitamins and Minerals: Pets on veterinary heart medications need increased amounts of all vitamins and minerals. Diuretics in particular wash nutrients from the body. Use vitamin C in the salt-free ascorbic acid form, going to bowel tolerance. Vitamin E is primary in all forms of heart dis-ease and hypertension. Give 100 IU daily for cats and small dogs, 200 IU for medium and large dogs and 400 IU for the giant breeds. Give 10,000-25,000 IU of vitamin A daily, with 400-800 IU of vitamin D once a week. Both vitamins A and E come in emulsified dry forms that are easier to assimilate and make overdoses impossible. Pat Lazarus suggests adding vitamin E only after the pet's heart is stabilized. She also suggests magnesium to regularize the heart rate and potassium (as cider vinegar).[73] Other minerals include 5-10 mg of zinc daily (important), and chromium and selenium in the trace mineral powder. Give a daily complete B-complex in higher amounts than usual (20-50 mg), with additional B-6 and B-3 (niacinamide form only). Coenzyme Q10 helps bring oxygen into the cells and tissues. Essential fatty acids, such as evening primrose or black currant oil, may prove helpful.

Herbs: Hawthorn berry is the most frequently recommended herbal for the heart; it is a tonic, strengthener and heart muscle repairer, and may be used daily long-term. Start with three drops of the tincture three times a day for five days. If there is no improvement, increase to six drops three times a day for five days. Increase again if there is no improvement; the correct dose is reached when the heart cough stops and the pet's energy is good. Actual dose will vary from animal to animal. Do not skip doses. Hawthorn may also be given as a tea/infusion, or made into an elixir. The major heart drug digitalis was synthesized from the foxglove plant, and a similar herbal—considered safer—is lily of the valley flowers. Use either of these only under expert supervision, or as homeopathic remedies (see below).

Juliette de Bairacli Levy recommends rosemary tea with honey as her central herbal for heart dis-ease and heart weakness. Give one level teaspoon of pure raw honey to every tablespoon of rosemary infusion.

In addition, use dandelion and/or watercress in one meal per day as a diuretic and for mineral contents. Heartsease (wild pansy) is another heart tonic herb[74]. Parsley or dill seed tea also makes excellent herbal diuretics and can take the place of medical drugs. Uva ursi (bearberry), juniper and buchu are other herbal diuretics. Alfalfa increases the action of other herbs taken along with it; it also regulates blood pressure and reduces cholesterol. Scullcap is a safe calmative, as is peppermint tea. A combination of scullcap, cayenne and goldenseal is a heart strengthener (but tastes awful—put it into capsules).

Homeopathy: *Crataegus*, homeopathically prepared hawthorn, is the remedy for an animal with extreme breathlessness on exertion, when she has an irregular, weak or intermittent pulse, when symptoms worsen as the environment worsens, when she has high blood pressure and is nervous and irritable. The remedy may be used daily long-term in low potency (lX, 6X), or use the 30C when needed. *Convallaria majalis* (lily of the valley) increases heart action and regulates heart rate; it is recommended when there is difficulty breathing, dropsy, angina, palpitations from the least exertion, and lung congestion. *Digitalis* (foxglove) is used after faintness or prostration following exertion; the pulse or heartbeat is abnormally slow; the animal may collapse; she may have a blue tongue; and there may be liver involvement. Give one tablet after each attack to decrease frequency and severity of future attacks.

Apis is indicated when there is edema (water retention, dropsy); use a 6X potency three or four times a day for ten days. *Strophanthus hispidus* is for heart weakness due to valve problems (murmurs); there is a weak, irregular pulse and difficult breathing. The pet may be obese and have skin problems. *Carbo veg* aids breathing; give in 200C daily for seven days, or as needed. *Spongia* is for dry, gasping heart coughs; dose in 30C once per day for ten days.

In case of an actual heart attack (rare in pets—most deaths come from lung congestion), *Aconite* is a first aid measure. Give *Cactus Grandiflorus* for emergencies and for general heart dis-ease symptoms; the animal may respond to *Cactus* where other remedies fail. *Crataegus* and *Cactus* are the two primary remedies for pets or people with heart dis-ease.

Acupuncture/Acupressure: On the Shin Dog Chart use #28 (P-1) *Shin yu* for heart dis-ease and #27 (LU-1) *Fei yu* for cough and pulmonary congestion. Emergency points that can resuscitate an animal in crisis are #1 (GV-26) *Jen chung*, #2 (GV-25) *Pi liang*, #8 (not given) *Erh chien* and #25 (GV-T) *Woei chien*. The Cat Chart lists #8 as an emergency shock point.

Flower Essences: *Oak* is for pets who need patience during illness, *Impatiens* is for the "type A" nervous cat or dog, and *Hornbeam* is for strengthening and fatigue. *Hawthorn* aids vitality, blood cleansing and chronic conditions. *Bleeding Heart* (Bodhisattva Essence) enhances emotional heart healing and the ability to accept love. Try *Sweet Bell Pepper* for inner peace.

Gemstones: The pink and rose stones are traditional heart healers. Use *Rose Quartz, Kunzite, Pink Tourmaline,* or *Lepidolite* in the aura, or as elixirs.

Heatstroke

Heatstroke is an emergency situation that requires quick first aid to save an animal's life. The first remedy is prevention—keeping pets cool and quiet in hot weather. Never leave a cat or dog in the car in temperatures over sixty degrees; a closed-up vehicle, even with open windows, rapidly becomes an oven. Concrete runs without shade in hot weather can also lead to sunstroke. Being muzzled under a hair dryer at the groomer's, overexertion in the heat, or being confined in crates or carriers with too little ventilation are all to be avoided. Fresh water must be kept available always, with cider vinegar, in hot weather.

Flat-faced animals—pugs, bulldogs and Persian cats—are more susceptible to heatstroke, as are pets with heart or lung dis-ease, or other breathing difficulties. Watch all overweight pets. On hot days, your cat or dog needs to be indoors with the same air-conditioning you require; keep animals quiet, calm, and cool.

Rapid, harsh breathing is the first symptom of overheating. The animal's mucous membranes and tongue become bright red, and the dog or cat drools. Cats lick themselves, spreading thick saliva on their coats in an attempt at cooling by evaporation (this is mostly ineffective). Dogs and cats frequently vomit. Unrelieved, the animal becomes unsteady and begins to stagger, getting progressively weaker and often starting a bloody diarrhea. Tongue and mucous membranes next turn bluish, and the animal may collapse into coma and die. Internal body temperature can reach 106°F. There may be swelling in the throat that further impedes breathing and heat release.

Remember that pets do not have sweat glands over the entire body surface as we do; they have few ways to cool themselves and thus overheat more easily and rapidly than humans do. See below under Naturopathy for first aid.

Nutrition: Beyond the Optimal Diet with supplements that all pets need to be on, heatstroke is not a dis-ease preventable by nutrition. After a heatstroke emergency ends, rest the animal completely in an air-conditioned room, giving mineral-rich broths on at least a one-day liquid fast. Put a bit of soy or tamari sauce into the liquids, and apple cider vinegar (two teaspoons per pint) into the water bowl to replace lost salt and potassium, and for electrolyte balancing. These are important. Replacement liquids like Gator-Ade may be used as well. Heatstroke is the one case where salt replacement is necessary. Honey strengthens the recovering animal. As cats are not big drinkers, IV fluids and veterinary help in administering them may be necessary.

Naturopathy: Here is the first aid for heatstroke; it must be done immediately to bring down internal body temperature, prevent brain damage, and save the cat's or dog's life. First take the animal from the sun into shade, or place her in an air-conditioned room if possible. If the body temperature is above 104°F or the animal is staggering, immerse her in a tub of cold water, taking care that her nose stays unsubmerged. If a tub is not available, wrap the animal in cold wet towels and/or use ice packs around her head and body (particularly around the head). Wetting with a cold garden hose is also positive—anything to bring the temperature down quickly. If the pet has collapsed or is near to it, give a cold water enema for even more rapid drop in temperature. This cooling needs to be done even before seeking veterinary help; there is no time to waste. Once the rectal/internal temperature drops to 102°F (not lower), seek veterinary care. Continue the cold water and cold packs on the way.

Vitamins and Minerals: After the emergency ends, and the pet is rested, fasted and returned to a normal diet, she needs an increased amount of B-complex vitamins for at least a week. If not supplementing daily with yeast, give a yeast-free B-complex tablet, 10-25 mg. Double the amounts of vitamins E and A for a few days, and give vitamin C with bioflavonoids to bowel tolerance. All these help reduce and repair internal damage. Calcium/magnesium helps potassium balance, and potassium must be supplemented (use cider vinegar). Continue the tamari as a salt replacement for a few days. An amino acid combination may be helpful. Protect the dog or cat from heat—after a sunstroke episode she will always be hypersensitive to temperature changes.

Herbs: Mineral replacement is important, and alfalfa is an all-mineral balancer. Horsetail grass may be added, as well. Dulse, kelp or watercress add much needed potassium; barley water and soured milk products like plain natural yogurt or buttermilk are recommended. Barley offers energy and the soured milk products rebalance the intestinal flora.

Ginseng with royal jelly, available in glass tubes at health food stores, is a strengthener.

Homeopathy: Use these during the water treatment, or as soon as possible. *Belladonna* is the generally recommended remedy for heat-stroke; the animal has a dry, hot, flushed skin, dilated pupils and strong pulse, with thirst and red membranes. *Glonoine* is for the pet who develops spasms after application of cold packs, and for the aftereffects of the heatstroke incident. If the dog or cat acts intoxicated, try *Gelsemium*. *Aconite* is for the pet who is anxious, or acting dull and delirious, i.e., for shock. For heat prostration rather than sunstroke, where dehydration is the cause and the skin feels cold and clammy (instead of hot and dry), the remedy is *Veratrum album*; there is gum pallor, nausea, weakness and sometimes rapid pulse. Also see the Shock and Resuscitation Chart in the method chapter. Use points #1 (GV-26) *Jen chung*, #2 (GV-25) *Pi liang* and #25 (GV-T) *Woei chien* for shock, sunstroke and resuscitation; use #8 (not given) *Erh chien* for shock, resuscitation and spasms. In the Cat chart, use #8 for shock.

Flower Essences: *Nature's Rescue* (*Rescue Remedy*) is first, used as often as every five minutes while needed. Other emergency essences include *Comfrey*, *St. John's wort*, *Penstemon*, *White Lightnin'*, or *Gruss an Aachen*. *Self-Heal* and *Sunflower* are specifically for sunstroke. *Hornbeam* strengthens, and *Scullcap* strengthens the nervous system after the emergency. Give *Clematis* for lethargy, disorientation and shock.

Gemstones: Blue, indigo, aqua or green stones cool the body and regenerate. Try *Celestite*, *Chrysocolla*, *Chrysoprase*, *Aquamarine*, *Turquoise*, *Lapis Lazuli*, or *Aventurine*. Place them in the tub of water that is cooling the pet.

Hyperactivity

The barking, obsessive, irritable, biting, overexcited or all-over-everyone dog—or the nervous cat who refuses to be handled, who hides, hisses, bites or scratches—is no fun to live with. The animal may have periods of hysteria (genetic in cocker spaniels), erratic and unpredictable personality, or negative behaviors difficult to understand or bear. No training seems to help, and today's Popular Mechanics style of dog training is ineffective and often inhumane. Bad breeding can cause these traits genetically, as can boredom, or simple lack of stimulation or exercise. Vaccination reaction can also be a cause; see the section on "Vaccination/Vaccinosis." A pet with a physical problem may show negative behaviors that are a result of fear or pain. The animal may be trying to tell you she's unhappy; use psychic communication to understand the source. When a pet has been adopted from a shelter she may come traumatized to a new home. Realize that it takes six months to a year of gentle care for these animals to heal.

Dogs and cats also react emotionally to the energy in their household. If the people are upset or the home is disrupted, the pet may respond with actions that mirror the energy in the household. (This behavior tends to occur just when the people are least able to tolerate more stress.)

Cats and dogs are also highly sensitive to psychic energy. If there are spirit attachments or other negative energies in the environment, they may affect the animal first. Any agitated energy, including electromagnetic pollution, can cause hyperactivity in pets.

Hyperactivity can be, and often is, chemical. The findings on this in children carry over to pet behavior. Hyperactivity in cats or dogs may be caused by food allergies, or sensitivities to dyes, preservatives, colorings and other chemical additives. The preservative BHT, frequently used in pet foods, has been implicated. A diet too high in copper or in phosphorus (too much meat with not enough calcium/magnesium) has also been implicated. Lead toxicity is a cause of hyperactivity in children; commercial canned pet foods contain dangerous levels of this heavy metal. Other heavy metals, phosphates, sulfites, nitrites, along with toxins in the air, water or environment, are sources of hyperactive behavior. Secondary smoke from cigarettes can affect pets this way, too.[75] Too many dogs and cats are put to death for negative behaviors that could be stopped with a change in diet.

Protecting pets from pollutants, negative energy, allergens and food preservatives can lead to marked changes in the behavior of hyper dogs and cats.

Nutrition: Obviously, the preservative-free or natural homemade diet with full supplements is essential here, and may be all that is needed. Use slightly less meat (about ten percent less) and proportionately more whole grains, and no sugar.

Avoid treats with sugar or those that are not preservative-free. For dogs, avoid rawhide bones (that may use cyanide as a preservative). Avoid allergen foods—beef, tuna, wheat, corn, yeast, pork and milk products. They may be tried after the pet has calmed down, one at a time, watching for reactions. Turkey, for the non-allergic pet, is a calmative food, as are wholegrain oats and barley. If feeding prepared foods rather than cooking, look for the hypoallergenic blends usually made with lamb and rice.

Naturopathy: Start with a few days fasting, using enemas if the pet is not eliminating, then switch to totally preservative-free food. Give aloe vera juice with liquid chlorophyll as a detoxifier. Algin (sodium alginate) from health food stores detoxifies heavy metals, as does adding kelp or alfalfa sprouts to food. Use one-half to two teaspoons of sesame or sunflower seeds daily, adding calcium and magnesium.[76] Juliette de Bairacli Levy suggests raw honey as a curative for hysteria and hyperactivity. She also uses black currant syrup or rose hip syrup (for essential fatty acids and vitamin C) with the natural diet.[77] Digestive enzymes are important, especially in the first month of changeover to the new food. Garlic is a detoxifier and reduces high blood pressure, which can also be a cause of nervousness.

Vitamins and Minerals: Complete supplementation of Dog/Cat Oils and Powders is important for B-complex, calcium/magnesium, vitamin A and trace minerals. If the pet is yeast sensitive, replace the brewer's yeast with a B-complex tablet that is higher in potency than usual (20-50 mg). Extra vitamins B-5, B-6 and B3 (niacinamide form only) may be helpful. Give one teaspoon to one tablespoon of lecithin granules daily. If not using bone meal, give a calcium/magnesium tablet. Use vitamin C 500-3,000 mg or to bowel tolerance, and 5-15 mg zinc. Give vitamin A with weekly D and E. The amino acid GABA can solve many nervous disorders, but try the dietary changes first for a period of at least one month before trying GABA. Also, if one month on a clean diet makes no difference, go to home cooking or try a different preservative-free brand with no beef.

Herbs: Alfalfa is an important heavy-metal detoxifier that increases the potency of other vitamins, minerals and herbs. Oat tincture is a calmative and can be used long-term. Scullcap repairs the nervous system and is a calmative; blue vervain aids depression in pets; chamomile helps the clinging, whining pet; and valerian root (the strongest of these) is for hypersensitivity. Try any of these for a week, watching for response; increasing the doses may be necessary (see "Heart Dis-ease" directions for hawthorn). If an herb works, use it for two to three weeks, then taper off. Start again when needed.[78] Other calmative herbs include hops, rosemary, lime blossom, passionflower, wood betony and catnip (for dogs only). Scullcap and valerian are the two most often used.

Homeopathy: For high-strung, unruly and destructive pets, try *Scutellaria* (scullcap), Francis Hunter's remedy of choice for four-footed juvenile delinquents. He suggests using this twice daily for up to a week— unless the situation is aggravated—then evaluating the results. However, he describes a case in which the first dose resulted in a worsening (aggravation) of behavior, then the problem disappeared with no further doses needed.[79]

When there are rapidly changing mental states and nervousness, sometimes hysteria, try *Ignatia*. This remedy is also useful when there are spirit attachments that need releasing. Attacks of panic or misbehavior with restlessness and anger respond to *Arsenicum*; the animal feels cold to the touch. Spasmodic attacks of hysteria respond to *Cuprum met*. The cell salt *Kali phos* is recommended by Richard Pitcairn for genetically hyper animals, as well as for those with psychological disturbances. For the pet toxic from pollutants and preservatives, use *Calc sulph* and *Natrum sulph* together twice a day for several weeks. These are low-potency cell salts, usually 6X strength. Newton Laboratories has a hyperactivity combination that is highly effective.

Acupuncture/Acupressure: The Shin Dog Chart lists #20 (GV-20B) *Pai hui* for nervous disorders and #28 (P-1) *Shin yu* for mental stress. Klide and Kung use the following sequence for "thunder nerves," animals who respond to thunder or Fourth of July fireworks with distress and hysteria: LU-19, GB-20, B-10, GB-3, B-13 and GV-15.[80] No points are listed on the Cat Acupressure Chart.

Flower Essences: Behavior is the central specialty of flower essences, and good results come from choosing the one/s that closest match the animal's behavior. Remember to use pendulum testing to pick the remedies. *Crab Apple* or *Tomato* helps to clean out toxins. *Allemanda* detoxifies environmental contaminants.

Vervain is the hypersensitivity essence. *Chicory* is for possessiveness; *Holly* for jealousy and aggressiveness; *Impatiens* for irritable, impatient pets, *Mimulus* eases fears of specific stimuli (thunder, other animals); and *Rock Rose* is for panic attacks. *Comfrey* and *Dill* help the pet that has suffered past abuse. *Aloe Vera* is for behavioral problems due to stress. Where human stress is transferred to pets, use yellow, pink or white *Yarrow*. Try *Snapdragon* when the animal barks, bites or chews negatively. *Angelica* helps extreme behavior changes, and *California Poppy* calms and aids behavior problems. Inner Change Essence (*Peace Rose*) or Comfort Essence calms.

Gemstones: *Rose Quartz, Kunzite, Lepidolite*, or *Amethyst* calms and balances the emotions. Try an elixir of *Emerald* to detoxify, or use elixirs of *Angelite, Sugulite, Amber, Smoky Quartz, Black Tourmaline, Blue Tourmaline*, or *Rhodochrosite*. Place a piece of *Amethyst* in the pet's aura or water bowl to balance the nervous system and detoxify, and keep a large cluster in the home.

Immune System Building

The immune system is the body's defense against outside interference, especially against bacterial, fungal and viral dis-eases. When it is functioning optimally, these dis-eases that surround us and our pets constantly pass by without notice or harm. When it is functioning at low or deficient levels, infectious dis-eases ranging from abscesses to cancer result. Other immune deficiency dis-eases in pets include feline leukemia, feline infectious peritonitis, distemper, strep or staph infections, ringworm, warts, and other skin fungus dis-eases, wound infections or poor healing ability, pneumonia, infectious hepatitis, ear infections, kennel cough, toxoplasmosis, and the respiratory dis-eases of dogs and cats. Autoimmune dis-eases are those in which the body overreacts and attacks itself, as in allergies, asthma, hives, some forms of arthritis, and lupus. Diabetes onset (a new epidemic in pets) often occurs after an infectious dis-ease or trauma. Cancer seems to be the primary reaction to weakened immunity.

The human or animal immune system is designed to take much less stress and toxicity than it receives today. Pets and people are under constant bombardment from chemical and heavy metal toxins, food additives, water contaminants, air pollution, and from low-level radiation (microwaves, TV sets, ELF waves and high-tension electrical wires). The pet immune system is confused and often derailed by the many vaccinations given all at once, some of which trigger the dis-eases they are supposed to prevent. It is further hampered by food quality that borders on malnutrition, and by the high stressed, unnatural way of life common to cats and dogs living indoors in cities.

Immune system dis-eases were only defined as a concept in the 1950s, and were almost unknown before that. Having reached epidemic proportions among humans, they have now also reached dogs and cats; our pets are dying of dis-eases that were unknown a hundred years ago. The information in this section is an attempt to bolster the health of the at-risk pet and make any animal stronger for longer life on a depleted Earth.

Nutrition: Reducing toxins that overload pet immune systems begins with a fully nutritional diet free of chemicals and preservatives. Feed a preservative-free or homemade natural diet with supplements, as described in the "Nutrition" chapter of this book. Where it is possible to use organic foods for animals and people, do so. Each ingredient in the optimal diet is designed to balance pet immune systems by giving quality nutrition with less immune system stress and by filtering toxins from the body. The diet pays off in longer life and fewer veterinary bills. You will have a healthier, happier, more beautiful pet.

Naturopathy: Begin with a few days of fasting with enemas if needed, then change to the whole-foods diet with fasting one day a week. Aloe vera juice with chlorophyll in the daily diet and during the fast helps to detoxify the intestines and move wastes out of the body quickly. Garlic is an immune builder, and is anti-viral, anti-fungal and anti-bacterial. Kelp boosts the thyroid, which in turn balances the body's entire glandular system and raises immunity; the minerals it provides detoxify pollutants and heavy metals. Bee products are major immune builders that help the dog or cat recover from stress, and honey is a complete nutrient. Apple cider vinegar, one teaspoon per pint in the water bowl or one teaspoon per day on meals, is also an immune builder, supplementing potassium and other minerals. Digestive enzymes aid in nutrient assimilation and digestion.

Vitamins and Minerals: Give the daily supplements listed with the optimal diet. Brewer's yeast may be replaced by a 10-20 mg yeast-free B-complex tablet for yeast-sensitive pets. The B-vitamins are essential for healing the stress that is a major immune system weakener. Feed raw liver once a week (organic if possible) to maintain these vitamins in the system, and supplement with vitamins B-6 and B-9 (pyridoxine and folic acid). Calcium/magnesium and trace minerals—provided in the Dog/Cat Powders, bone meal or trace mineral powder—reduce pain and stress, and detoxify heavy metals from the body. Vitamin C with bioflavonoids, 500-3,000 mg per day or to bowel tolerance, is the best immune builder available. Give vitamins A and D (10,000-25,000 IU of A with 400-800 IU of D) weekly; give vitamin E, 50-400 IU per day or fed weekly. These are antioxidants that protect against and heal pollution damage. Zinc, 5-15 mg per day, boosts the immune system and all body healing. Essential fatty acids—evening primrose oil or black currant oil—are helpful, as are combination raw glandulars, especially raw thymus. For animals who are stressed or in pain, add coenzyme Q10, selenium and/or amino acids.

Herbs: Herbal antibiotics fight infections and build the immune system, but these are to be used only when actually needed. Use echinacea, goldenseal, pau d'arco, St. John's wort, or chaparral. Burdock, red clover, yellow dock, yarrow, dandelion, milk thistle and blue violet cleanse the lymphatic system and liver. Nutrient herbs that provide minerals include alfalfa, oatstraw, horsetail grass, chlorophyll and wheatgrass. Alfalfa increases the effectiveness of any other herb used with it. For immune deficient cats or dogs, try the anti-viral mushrooms like shiitaki or reishi. Ginseng or ginseng with royal jelly are immune builders and strengtheners.

Homeopathy: This system of healing works on symptoms, rather than specific dis-eases or conditions. The two remedies that follow are universals. Try combination cell salts, *Bioplasma* 6X or 12X, twice daily as an all-nutrient for pets. Give *Thuja* 30C now and after the yearly vaccinations to antidote the negative effects, but not the protection of vaccinations. Dose daily for a week unless or until there are aggravations—which may include skin problems, recurrence of old symptoms or behavior aberrations—then stop. Many immune system dis-eases are being traced to vaccination reactions. For specific dis-eases, see the sections in this book that apply, and see a homeopathic veterinarian.

Acupuncture/Acupressure: Work the Immune Stimulation points shown on the map in the Acupuncture/Acupressure method chapter. Use them daily or weekly, while checking the Diagnostic points in an all-over body massage. Releasing congested meridians found in the massage may release pending dis-ease before it reaches the physical level; it also warns the pet guardian when something is developing. The Immune Stimulation points are also a general strengthener. Make the massage a time of love and attention, fun for person and pet.

Flower Essences: *Tomato* helps in throwing off toxins and dis-eases. *Salvia* boosts immunity during stress. *Hornbeam* strengthens, and *Crab Apple* or *Allemanda* (purple or yellow, Detox Essence, Aura Cleansing Essence) are cleansers. *Agrimony* aids slow healing.

Gemstones: Any of the following in elixir are immune system builders: *Emerald, Jade, Picture Jasper, Amethyst, Blue Quartz, Rose Quartz, Ruby, Blue Tourmaline, Pink Tourmaline, Kunzite, Rhodochrosite.*

Incontinence

This chapter is not about the puppy or kitten in training, but about the older dog or cat who has been house-trained for years and now has accidents. She can't quite make it to the litter box or out the door, wakes up from a nap in a puddle of her own urine, or dribbles when excited. The animal may not notice at first, and then is upset; the guardian doesn't know whether to act angry or not. Punishment is out of the question, of course—for some pets, even acknowledging mild disappointment by voice is too much embarrassment. She is not doing it on purpose. The first thing to do is have the pet checked for bladder or kidney infection and make sure the litter box is kept clean. Spinal cord or disc dis-ease or arthritis stiffness can be other causes of incontinence. When the cat or dog is also manifesting behavior problems and the wetting indoors or outside the box starts, it may be a different story. A pet acting out of fear, insecurity or emotional stress may leave surprises—right on your bed or pillow, if she is angry enough. She needed to get your attention. Try psychic communication, not punishment, to find out what's bothering her; relieve the source and ease the dog or cat's anger, fear or unhappiness.

Usually, however, incontinence is not a behavior problem but a physical one. Elderly animals lose muscle control or become confused and can't get to the right place in time. These animals need more frequent trips outdoors or litter boxes placed nearer to them—one in the house may no longer be enough. Even if there is no bladder infection, the problem in cats may be due to repeated infections (FUS) and catheterizations that cause muscle weakness and loss of control. Dogs, particularly older females, develop bladder-control problems as a result of spaying; males can develop it from enlarged prostates. This is traceable to a hormone deficiency from lack of estrogen, indicated by dribbling, strong urine and a scalded, red look around the vulva or penis. Modified spays that leave the ovaries intact would prevent this in females. The veterinary/medical system gives the hormone DES, a known carcinogen, to correct incontinence in both female and male dogs. Holistic methods are safe and can work just as well.

Nutrition: The natural diet with supplements is essential, as chemicals and preservatives can cause further irritation to a sensitive bladder, and allergies to these can also cause incontinence. Eliminate dry foods totally and use the homemade diet or preservative-free canned foods. Avoid feeding milk products, liver, other organ meats or yeast; give egg yolks, raw vegetables, and a few drops of tamari sauce to add amino acids.[81] See the diet under "Urinary Tract Infections." The supplements are important.

Naturopathy: For dribbling older dogs, add a teaspoon of wheat germ oil to the diet daily. A teaspoon of honey added to a cup of barley water each day soothes the bladder.[82] D.C. Jarvis also lists honey as a virtual cure for children with bedwetting problems, which may indicate usefulness for animals as well.[83] Apple cider vinegar placed on food or in the water bowl is a urinary tract antiseptic and supplements needed potassium. Some positive vegetables to feed, along with raw meat and cooked whole grains, include carrots, parsley, asparagus, squash, broccoli, zucchini, dandelion greens, yams and green beans.

Vitamins and Minerals: Feed the supplements listed below with the natural optimal diet, replacing brewer's yeast with a yeast-free B-complex tablet of 10-20 mg. Vitamin C with bioflavonoids is important—go to bowel tolerance or give 500-3,000 mg daily. Calcium/magnesium is important; if not feeding your pet the mineral powders, give a human tablet of about 300 mg for a medium-sized dog (half a tablet for a cat or small dog) with vitamin C only. Vitamins A and D or cod liver oil are important for bladder-muscle function and for healing internal organs and membranes. Double the usual amount of vitamin E for internal healing and to reduce bladder scars. Zinc improves bladder function; supplement 5-15 mg. Evening primrose oil is a hormone balancer. Nutritionists James and Phyllis Balch recommend as primary for children's incontinence a vegetable source protein supplement, used daily to strengthen the bladder.[84] Find this in a health food store and divide the human dose.

Herbs: The following are specifically for the pet who is hormone deficient. Licorice root, dong quai and wild yam are natural estrogens that make hormone injections unnecessary. When the uterus and ovaries are removed, estrogen production must move to the adrenals, and these herbs aid that change. Start with 2-4 drops of the tincture in meals, increasing gradually at five day intervals until the incontinence stops. Remain at that dose for a few weeks, then decrease gradually; if symptoms return, start again. Try this for at least a month before resorting to chemical hormones. Herbs that encourage the bladder to empty completely when the animal voids include oatstraw, marshmallow, parsley, plantain, buchu, nettles or dandelion leaves. Also see the sections on "Aging" and "Urinary Tract Infections."

Homeopathy: For incontinence where age is not a factor the remedy is *Calc fluor*; where age is primary and the animal may be senile, use *Baryta carb*. Try *Apis* for the dog or cat who just can't seem to make it outdoors or to the litter box; she is full to bursting. Where there is false pregnancy (a hormone imbalance) with incontinence, the remedy is *Pulsatilla*. Give *Merc cor* where the pet seems to void more than she has drunk, or *Sulfur* for incontinence and frequency. Try *Causticum* for pets who dribble from excitement and seem unaware of it while it's happening; use it also for animals who urinate soon after falling asleep. Male cats or dogs who spray after neutering—usually soon after—or females who spray may be helped by *Staphisagria*, and homeopathic preparations of female estrogenic hormones may help neutered pets with incontinence; these include *Folliculinum*, *Ovarium*, or *Estrogen*. With any of the above remedies dose daily until there is an aggravation, or until the problem stops. Repeat courses may be needed.

Acupuncture/Acupressure: Both charts offer points for incontinence. In the Shin Dog Chart, #33 (BL-23) *Shen yu* is for urinary disorders and sexual hormone imbalances. Point #35 (BL-25) *Huan cho* is for hormone insufficiency disorders, and #37 (GB-26) *Pung kung yu* is for cystitis, bladder spasm and urine retention. Points #17-19 (GV-4, GV-3, GV-2.5) are for urinary disorders and hormone balancing. See the chart for the meridians for spinal problems and sphincter muscle paralysis (points #20-26).

In the Ottaviano Cat Acupressure Chart, point #16 is for urinary problems, and #26 for urinary problems with hind leg paralysis (spinal involvement).

Flower Essences: *Chaste Tree Flower* essence or *Squash* balance hormones. *Centaury Agave* or Old Soul Essence (*Purple Angel Trumpet*) eases problems of old age. *Dill* eases arthritis stiffness and kidney problems, and *Agrimony* is for the animal who may act out jealousy by urinating.

Gemstones: *Garnet* or *Kunzite* in elixir aids hormonal imbalances; and *Amber, Yellow Jade, Green Jade* or *Peridot* heals the bladder, along with other yellow or yellow-green gemstones. Use them in elixirs or in the pet's aura. Try a natural or rutile *Citrine* cluster in the water bowl or room.

Injuries: Cuts, Sprains and Abrasions

Minor injuries happen to cats and dogs about as often as they do to children, and most treatments for children will work for dogs or cats, as well—with a few notable exceptions. Aspirin or aspirin-derivative products (Tylenol, Motrin, white willow bark, white oak bark) can actually kill cats. Remember too, that the skin of dogs and cats is very sensitive, more so than human skin, and needs gentle treatment. Tincture of iodine, for instance, so popular as a disinfectant when I was growing up— is not recommended for cuts and scrapes on animals *or* people; it is too strong and further damages lacerated tissues.

Pets have allergic reactions to insect bites in the same ways that people do, but probably have them more often. (See the section on "Shock.") They also tend to get into fights, which result in puncture wounds with risk of abscess and other infection. The remedies used on dogs and cats, particularly cats, must be safe to ingest, as the animals are sure to lick them off.

Here are some safe holistic ideas for treating minor sprains and other wounds, injuries, and for fast healing and prevention of infection. For deep or extensive wounds, heavy bleeding, shock, allergic reaction with facial swelling or unresponsive infections, take the animal quickly to a veterinarian. A Red Cross course in animal CPR is interesting, inexpensive and recommended: it may save your cat or dog's life.

Nutrition: The pet receiving optimal diet with supplements has far better healing resources than the dog or cat fed commercial chemical-laden, nutrient-poor food. A naturally fed pet heals more quickly, develops fewer infections and abscesses, and bounces back more rapidly from traumas of any sort. If surgery is necessary, the animal goes into it with much better chances of survival. Avoid using chemical flea collars on pets; if an anesthetic is used, the collar's chemicals can seriously complicate the animal's chances for recovery.

Naturopathy: For any but the most minor wounds and injuries, start with at least a one-day liquid fast, using organic red grape juice and water, raw honey with water, or barley water. Honey and other bee products, especially propolis, boost the immune system, reduce pain and speed healing. Use aloe vera juice with liquid chlorophyll internally to detoxify, externally for burns, cuts and other minor wounds. Externally, put a teaspoonful of three percent food-grade hydrogen peroxide in two ounces of aloe vera juice or gel. This can be dabbed on or sprayed from a bottle. For open wounds and rapid tissue healing, substitute calendula tincture for the peroxide.[85] If there is pus in the wound, use the peroxide until the infection is clear, then heal the skin with calendula and aloe vera together. The wound should not be allowed to close up until all pus and infection are gone. Garlic in the diet boosts the immune system, speeds healing, and is anti-bacterial and anti-viral; it prevents infections and helps heal them. Kelp aids bone healing, and the iodine it contains boosts the thyroid. A teaspoon of boric acid in a cup of boiled and cooled water makes a compress for pus wounds, infections or inflamed bites.

For strains or sprains, confine the animal to a cage or small space to keep her as immobile as possible, unless the pet's temperament causes her to be more stressed when confined. Use ice packs with an Ace bandage for the first twenty-four to thirty-six hours. Make sure not to cut off circulation, and have the pet checked for broken bones. Give digestive enzymes in the diet.

Vitamins and Minerals: The daily dietary supplements are important, with the following specifically to aid healing of external or internal injuries. Vitamin C (500-3,000 mg) with bioflavonoids reduces bruising and bleeding, prevents infections and reduces inflammation. Double the amount of vitamin E, using it daily for at least a week; this vitamin induces healing of skin and internal tissues, and prevents scarring. Give additional vitamin A, 10,000-25,000 IU daily for a week, with 400-800 IU of vitamin D weekly. Zinc is necessary for all wound, burn and tissue healing; it boosts the immune system to speed recovery and prevent infections; give 5-10 mg daily. Where there has been shock, trauma or bleeding, the B-complex vitamins are also important. If not supplementing with brewer's yeast, give a 10-25 mg yeast-free human B-complex tablet daily. All of the above are even more important if the pet has had surgery or has lost much blood. If there are sprains, strains or broken bones, use the above plus a calcium/magnesium tablet for bone healing, and to reduce spasms and pain. Vitamin C is extremely important for sprains. If the pet is in much pain, give germanium.

Herbs: Stop the bleeding of wounds by sprinkling goldenseal or cayenne pepper powder into the cut. Adding goldenseal tincture to water (about five drops to a cup or less of pure water) makes a good antiseptic wound rinse. Hydrogen peroxide in water (about half a teaspoon to a cup of pure water), or witch hazel straight, can also be used as an antiseptic wash and is good where there are infections or abscesses. Use echinacea or goldenseal internally when cuts have become infected and also as external compresses. Keep the animal on these herbal antibiotics internally for a few days after the infection has healed. Hypericum/St. John's wort tincture taken internally eases pain and speeds healing where tissues have been torn or nerves damaged; it is good for wounds, bruises, sprains and strains. Alfalfa, horsetail grass or oatstraw taken internally add needed calcium for sprains or broken bone healing. A poultice of comfrey leaves works wonders, with comfrey or burdock tea internally, for sprains or strains and after a broken bone has been set. A number of soothing herbal wound creams are available.

Homeopathy: *Aconite* is the first aid remedy for any trauma, shock or injury; use it immediately. Its primary indication is fear. *Arnica* is for bruising, falls, blows, soreness, bleeding wounds and septic conditions, and for sprains, strains or broken bones. The dog or cat fears touch or being approached; she wants to be left alone; she is nervous and hypersensitive. Take the homeopathic Arnica internally, but the Arnica Mother Tincture is only for external use on unbroken skin. *Hypericum* is used for any injuries affecting the nerves and tissues; it also prevents tetanus in puncture wounds. The main symptom is extreme pain; it is used after surgery, after animal fights that have resulted in bite wounds, and for crushed toes or tail tips. The pet is melancholy and may be in shock.

Ledum is for insect bites, animal bites and other puncture wounds if the wounded part feels cold. This remedy antidotes spider poisons, to which many pets have allergic reactions. *Hepar sulph* is for painful wounds and prevents them from becoming infected. *Hamamelis* is for wounds with dark, oozing blood that won't stop, and *Ferrum phos* is for wounds bleeding bright red. *Urtica* is for burns (see "Burn" section). For the first few days after sprains use *Rhus tox*, then switch to *Ruta grav. Ruta grav* is for strains or sprains with injuries to ligaments, tendons, bone covering (periosteum) and for lameness or body pain; the dog or cat is highly restless, or lethargic, weak and despondent.

Acupuncture/Acupressure: Never place pressure over an injury site, wound or sprain. On the Shin Dog Chart, point #28 (P-1) *Shin yu* is for relief of mental stress. Consult the "Shock and Resuscitation" chart if needed. (Most of the points are for strains and sprains.) See the Dog Chart in the method section and use the meridians that apply. The Ottaviano Cat Acupressure Chart lists several points for pain in various parts of the body, as well as #8 for shock. Again, see the chart itself in the method chapter. No specific listings are given for injuries or wounds.

Flower Essences: Use *Nature's Rescue* (*Rescue Remedy*) immediately after trauma and as frequently as needed thereafter. *Arnica* is for trauma and bruising, *White Lightnin'* for trauma, *Salvia* for stability during stress, and Light Body Essence (*Gardenia*) for accidents and first aid. *Comfrey* regenerates nerves and is another first aid essence. Use *Grapefruit* for spinal injuries from falls and *St. John's wort* essence to release pain and fear. *Rock Rose* is for extreme fear, *Star of Bethlehem* for trauma and injury—both are in *Nature's Rescue*. *Penstemon* or *Self-Heal* is a good addition to the other flowers.

Gemstones: For pain or tissue healing use *Herkimer Diamond, Kunzite, Sugulite, Boji Stone* or *Black Tourmaline. Amethyst* is a calmative and pain reliever after any trauma; place a cluster near the animal's bed or attach a piece to her collar. *Rose Quartz* heals the skin.

Lick Granulomas

Dogs and cats do the strangest things—like lick at one spot on a leg, ankle or foot until it develops first a hairless, shiny pink spot and then a serious sore. Sometimes a minor irritation, like a flea bite, starts the animal licking. Other times there is no apparent cause. The spots may come in pairs, one on each leg in about the same place. Cats can develop a granuloma on the lips or mouth, where it is called a "rodent ulcer," and on dogs the sores are often found between the foot pads. Standard veterinary sources list this as frequent in larger short-coated dog breeds, especially bird dogs, Labradors, Great Danes and Dobermans. Veterinary/medical treatment involves runs of antibiotics, cortisone shots, radiation treatment or cobra venom injections. Vets insist that lick sores only happen to middle-aged animals who are bored and inactive, but this is not always the case. It can be a systemic bacterial infection.

I've had my own experience with granulomas with Kali, a one-year-old Siberian Husky puppy. First came lots of scratching, then intensive licking with no fleas. Then I discovered an inflamed open sore between the pads of a hind foot. We went to the veterinarian, who gave her a two-week run of antibiotics and an external spray (which Kali hated). The sore went away, only to reappear as soon as the antibiotics were finished. We went back to the vet and repeated this three times. Each time sores returned within a week of stopping the medication, or Kali licked new ones in different places.

Finally I started holistics, going first to homeopathy to stop the itching. This actually closed up the lesions overnight. I started her on herbs and kelp, and changed her brand of preservative-free pet food (details below). The sores return occasionally now, less severely each time. Treated holistically, they disappear within a few days. The non-holistic veterinarian wants to know what I use—and I tell him!

Nutrition: Feeding a preservative-free or natural homemade diet can be all that is needed to clear up granulomas, which are toxicity based. The daily supplements are extremely important, not only for general good health but specifically for the skin. If your dog's or cat's sores don't improve within a month, go to the homemade diet or switch preservative-free brands to a hypoallergenic one without beef. Many pets have food allergies, and changing brands seemed to make a difference for Kali. Be aware of the major allergen foods and avoid them. Many pet skin problems are caused by the toxins in commercial foods, and by a lack of necessary oils and nutrients which the optimal diet provides.

Naturopathy: Use detoxification methods, starting with three to seven days of fasting with lemon juice enemas if the animal is not eliminating. Feed aloe vera juice with liquid chlorophyll to remove toxins from the body, and use the gel externally on the sores. Adding kelp to Kali's diet made a major difference in reducing her sores from large bleeding ones to minor skin abrasions. (I added three drops of liquid kelp to food daily; she weighs fifty-five pounds.) Sources disagree about the need for oils like safflower, sunflower and cod liver oil—Dr. Pitcairn recommends them, Dr. Belfield says no. My opinion is that for pets with dry skin they are useful, but add extra vitamin E. Brewer's yeast is recommended for pets who are not allergic to it. Garlic is an antibiotic food and highly recommended. Cider vinegar in the water bowl adds potassium and minerals.

Beet juice is a liver cleanser and detoxifier. Start with a very small amount of grated raw beets or organic beet juice. Give only a little to prevent too much cleansing too fast. Increase to about a teaspoonful for cats and small dogs, to two tablespoonsful for a hundred-pound dog. Use this only once a week. Beets change the pet's urine to red, a temporary and harmless effect.[86]

Vitamins and Minerals: Give the daily recommended supplements with oils and, most important, trace minerals. Put vitamin C powder on the food, 500-2,000 mg or to bowel tolerance. I find that at 500 mg I can give this to Kali for a couple of weeks at a time, then must stop for a while. Give 5-20 mg of zinc daily, an important vitamin for skin healing. Calcium/magnesium is also recommended—in the mineral powders, or use in tablet form with vitamin C. Vitamin A, 50,000 IU twice a week for a couple of weeks, also made a significant difference; adjust the amount for body size and double the daily amount of vitamin E. For Kali I used 400 IU daily for a couple of weeks; Pat Lazarus describes using 200 IU daily for two and a half months, but does not indicate the size of the dog.[87] Vitamin E seems to be the primary vitamin for these kinds of lesions; also use it externally as a salve. If not supplementing with brewer's yeast or a multi-tablet, give a 10-20 mg yeast-free B-complex tablet daily. Kali's standard vitamins consist of a pet multiple vitamin and mineral tablet, along with zinc, liquid kelp, and additional C and E when needed. She eats preservative-free, hypoallergenic dry food.

Herbs: This also made a great difference. When my veterinarian wanted to start cortisone shots on Kali, I began giving her six drops a day of licorice root tincture, and started her on homeopathy (see below). The dog liked the taste of the licorice, sucking it from the eyedropper eagerly. Her sores disappeared literally overnight. I've continued the licorice in an attempt to balance her adrenals. Another time, I placed her on goldenseal and echinacea tablets for about three weeks to pick up where the veterinary antibiotics left off. These are herbal antibiotics, and the licorice is an herbal "steroid." Yucca is another herbal steroid/

cortisone alternative; usnea is another antibiotic herb for systemic bacterial infections. I put comfrey tincture on a cotton ball and dabbed the sores twice daily, leaving the ball wedged between her toes. (She ate it.) Horsetail grass used internally is an herbal silica.

Homeopathy: The first homeopathic I tried that worked for Kali was *Arsenicum* which relieved the itching and stopped her constant licking for a while. It needed repeat doses in decreasing frequency. Symptoms here are a highly restless, irritable pet who frequently returns to the water bowl for small sips, symptoms worsening at night, and raw, burning skin. I alternated this with *Silica* for ulcers, abscesses or bumps under the skin, weak lower spine (she came to me injured), cracks and sores between toes, skin blotches, and seeking warmth (also *Arsenicum*). After twenty-four hours on these (two doses of Arsenicum and one of Silica) the sores disappeared. I continued dosing in decreasing frequency for about three weeks as symptoms returned. When the sores started again later, I gave a dose of each, then started Kali on silica in cell salt potency (6X) twice daily, then once a day. I use a pendulum to help me determine when to repeat the dose.

Other remedy possibilities include *Sulfur* for dry skin lesions with itching, also for bacterial skin infections. *Hepar sulph* is the choice for lesions around the mouth, rodent ulcers in cats with thin blood-stained discharge and extreme touch sensitivity. Also try *Nitricum acidum* for rodent ulcers. Try *Calc sulph* for lesions on limbs when sensitivity is less, but pus has formed. *Natrum phos* shows shiny red skin lesions, occurring especially at the ankles and feet. *Ferrum phos* is for the early stages of lick granulomas that appear mostly on the right side of the body; there is inflammation, pain and redness.

Acupuncture/Acupressure: There are only two books in English at present on veterinary acupuncture, and both describe remarkable changes in skin dis-eases while offering specific points only for allergies. The Shin Dog Chart has no specific meridian information for lick granuloma. On the Cat Chart, point #5 is for dermatitis and itching, #15 for blood cleansing. Also notice the various points for local pain. See a veterinary acupuncturist; this is the type of illness most applicable to the method.

Flower Essences: Try a few drops of *Nature's Rescue* (*Rescue Remedy*) in the water bowl; it helps in any situation. *Crab Apple*, *Allemanda* and *Tomato* are cleansing essences. *Red Ixora* is a blood cleansing essence. When environmental contaminants cause hair loss, *Yellow Hibiscus* (Aura Essence) is another cleanser. Try *Snapdragon* for negative licking and mouth sores. Where licking may be from boredom or a nervous behavior, *Nasturtium*, *Chicory*, *Mimulus* or *Aspen* may help. *Agrimony* is for slow-healing sores or wounds.

Gemstones: *Rose Quartz* and other pink stones heal the skin. *Amethyst* is a cleanser and calmative. Use lots of *Amethyst* in the house, water bowl and on the pet's collar. Other pink stones include *Pink Tourmaline, Lepidolite, Kunzite, Pink Silica* or *Rhodochrosite*. Where sores are on the mouth, try indigo gemstones (*Lapis Lazuli, Iolite, Sodalite, Blue Sapphire*) in elixir; these are also antiseptic for inflammations on the rest of the body.

Liver Dis-ease

Liver dis-ease in pets was once solely the result of viral hepatitis and leptospirosis, two ailments rare now with routine vaccinations. Today's liver problems are more insidious, resulting primarily from the accumulation of toxins, chemicals, metals and poisons entering the body through the environment. They come from chemicals like carbon tetrachloride, insecticides like Chlordane, household cleaners and deodorizers, bathroom cleaning products, cat litter deodorizers, mothball or paint fumes, automobile exhausts, and secondary cigarette smoke. Heavy-metal poisoning by lead, aluminum, copper and mercury accumulation causes liver damage. Lead comes from canned commercial pet foods, tap water and insecticides; aluminum from aluminum cans, cookware and bowls, foil and tap water. Mercury toxicity comes from insecticides, pesticides and chemical fertilizers (all used in agriculture) and from canned fish, medical drugs and latex paints; copper from water pipes, meat (feed additive), copper pots, hormones and water-softening chemicals. Some veterinary/medical drugs including anesthetics, antibiotics, sulfa drugs, diuretics, anticonvulsants and steroids—can cause liver dis-ease with overdose or overuse. Food additives, dyes and preservatives contain liver-damaging chemicals that build up in the body over time. Ethoxyquin and BHA/BHT in pet foods have been implicated in liver damage and liver cancers, as have nitrites/nitrates, sodium benzoate and propyl gallate. Nutritional deficiencies in chlorine or magnesium, as well as diets too low in protein and too high in fats and sugar, also cause liver damage.[88]

Symptoms of impaired liver function include lethargy and weakness with appetite loss, weight loss, vomiting and diarrhea. There may be yellow, fatty stools, vomited yellow foam, frequent flea and ringworm infestation, and allergic reactions. Later in the dis-ease the dog or cat displays the symptoms of jaundice: the whites of the eyes turn yellow, she has tea-colored urine and ascites (fluid accumulation in the abdomen).

Spontaneous bleeding is a sign of advanced liver damage; the animal drinks water excessively and displays pain when her abdomen is touched. If the damage has not gone too far, and if the cause can be determined and removed, holistic methods support the body and help the liver to heal and regenerate.

Nutrition: The diet needs to be totally free of preservatives and chemicals, high in lean meat, raw vegetables and cooked whole grains, and very low in fats. The homemade diet with supplements is best, feeding three or four small meals per day rather than one or two large ones. Cottage cheese and eggs are positive, but if giving other milk products, only soured ones like yogurt and kefir are allowed. When using Dr. Pitcairn's Dog/Cat Powders and Oils, eliminate the oils until the pet is healed, then return them gradually, but give Vitamin E. If using Anitra Frazier's Vita-Mineral Mix, use the following altered recipe for cats (fine for dogs, too), giving a teaspoon per meal plus a quarter teaspoon of cod liver oil:

Vita-Mineral Mix for Liver Dis-ease

1-1/2 cups yeast
1/2 cup kelp or trace mineral powder
2 cups lecithin
2 cups bone meal, calcium lactate or calcium gluconate[89]
1-1/2 cups bran

Use bottled or filtered water for drinking; don't use tap water. Give barley water frequently, or as a plain-water substitute.

Naturopathy: This is a toxicity dis-ease, and the healing begins with a fast of a few days, particularly if the pet has a fever. Use enemas of lemon juice, wheatgrass, liquid chlorophyll, or coffee and water. Start the cat or dog on daily aloe vera juice with liquid chlorophyll—constipation is to be avoided in this dis-ease. Give grated raw organic beets or beet juice in the diet, starting slowly and increasing gradually to a teaspoon for cats and up to two or three tablespoons for dogs. Also give grated carrots. Dr. Richard Pitcairn suggests using this daily, but work up to it very slowly to prevent too intensive a detox too fast. Fresh parsley is also recommended by Dr. Pitcairn, one to two tablespoons daily.[90] Digestive enzymes are important with the meals, and Anitra Frazier adds a quarter teaspoon of liquid acidophilus daily, lactose free. Garlic is positive, as are kelp and cider vinegar. If using honey or bee products, feed half the usual amount for easier digestion.

Vitamins and Minerals: Feed the daily supplements of the optimal diet, altered as given above. Vitamin C with bioflavonoids is important for detoxifying and regenerating the liver; give 500-2,000 mg per day or go to bowel tolerance. Give a low-potency yeast-free B-complex tablet, with additional lecithin, and a liquid liver extract from a health food store. Combination amino acids, or a liver-designated amino acid mix with cysteine, glutathionine and methionine, protect the liver and aid detoxification; several of these liver combinations are available. Increase the amounts of vitamins A and E: Anitra Frazier suggests for cats 200 IU of vitamin E and 10,000 IU of vitamin A three times a week for three weeks, giving 400 IU of vitamin D once weekly. Coenzyme Q10 oxygenates and is a liver protector. Pat Lazarus recommends vitamin B-15 (pangamic acid).

Herbs: A number of herbs are liver cleansers. The most gentle and reliable is dandelion, but milk thistle also repairs the liver; use the two together. Other liver herbs include celandine, rosemary, burdock, black radish, Oregon grape root, horsetail grass, chamomile, clover, echinacea, goldenseal or yellow dock. Juliette de Bairacli Levy recommends bitters: gentian root, wormwood, southernwood, centaury, blue pimpernel, St. John's wort or rhubarb.[91] Swedish Bitters is a liver tonic available in health food stores; these must be mixed with honey for a pet to accept them. Raspberry or strawberry leaf clears liver congestion, and agrimony helps jaundice. Remember, dandelion and milk thistle are the primary herbs.

Homeopathy: For jaundice when the animal also has alternating diarrhea and constipation, and vomiting, try *Nux vomica* very four hours for a few days. *Chelidonium majus* (celandine) is the most recommended liver and jaundice remedy, again given every four hours until the jaundice disappears, or by the observation method. Give *Phosphorus* when there are clay-colored stools, gum hemorrhages and vomiting soon after eating or drinking; the dog's or cat's abdomen is too tender to touch. When the animal can eat only a little at a time, and the symptoms are worse in the late afternoon and early evening, the remedy is *Lycopodium*. This is usually a thin, older pet, prematurely grey. *Berberis* is used when the cat or dog vomits early in the morning, has poor appetite and pain over the back with weak legs. Give *Chionanthus* when other remedies fail and there is jaundice and putty-like stools. *Phosphorus* was the remedy that saved Copper's life. Liver dis-ease is serious; consult an experienced veterinary homeopath.

Acupuncture/Acupressure: On the Shin Dog Chart, meridian point #13 (GV-10) *Ling tai* is for hepatitis, #29 (LIV-14) *Kan yu* for hepatitis and jaundice. Cat acupressure points have no specific liver coordinates; try #15 on the Ottaviano Cat Acupressure Chart for blood cleansing, #22 for lack of appetite and as a general tonic.

Flower Essences: Blood Cleansing Essence (*Red Ixora*) detoxifies the liver from pollutants and contaminants as do yellow or purple *Allemanda* (Detox or Aura Cleansing Essence); *Water Lily* is for toxicities and all healing, but is best used with other essences. *Dandelion* strengthens and regenerates the liver. Anitra Frazier suggests *Crab Apple* for cleansing, with *Hornbeam* to strengthen, plus one of the following: *Impatiens* for the irritable, touchy animal who is easily angered; *Aspen* for an animal fearful for no apparent reason; *Scleranthus* for the dog or cat with mood swings.[92]

Gemstones: Place in the cat or dog's aura a piece of *Citrine* (natural if possible), *Yellow Topaz*, *Apatite* or *Turquoise*—making sure to clear the stone frequently. Use any of the following in elixir: *Azurite-Malachite, Amber, Calcite, Malachite, Citrine, Herkimer Diamond, Lapis Lazuli, Peridot* or *Sugulite*. When using *Malachite*, leave it in the water for no more than half an hour.

Mange and Ringworm

These are dis-eases of a stressed and weakened immune system. Mange in dogs may be hereditary (genetic immune deficiency), and although veterinary books declare it rare in cats, it is becoming more frequent in both animals, with nursing young often inheriting mange mites from their infected mothers. Ringworm is a common fungal dis-ease and mange is the result of a skin mite parasite. With ringworm, immune function is again the key.

Both dis-eases are treated in the same ways holistically, and both require persistence. Keeping the animals, their bedding, and their environment clean is essential. Also, keep yourself and your own environment very clean, as both dis-eases can be passed from animals to people (and vice versa in the case of ringworm). The cat or dog mange mite cannot reproduce on human skin and is thus self-limiting; ringworm will usually only spread to people when resistance is low. Humans, including children, and pets with liver dis-ease or diabetes are especially susceptible. Bathe the animal in Betadyne solution weekly, and use chlorine bleach in laundry and housecleaning water. The treatments below are recommended for both mange and ringworm, and may be used on people as well.

The first symptom of both dis-eases is skin lesions. In ringworm there are circular bald patches, usually starting on the head; the skin is grey, red or scabbed and it may or may not itch. Cats who have not yet begun to show lesions can carry ringworm to people. There are two types of mange mites—sarcoptic and demodectic. Sarcoptic mange is more contagious to humans and other pets, but probably more responsive to treatment; its main symptom is itching and scratching of red welts or bumps. Demodectic mites appear as bald patches, usually on the face or head, and are less transmissible. Again there is itching, but unless the patches spread to a large area of the body, this type of mange may be self-limiting. Demodectic mange may be itch-free.

Avoid the veterinary/chemical drugs for these dis-eases if possible. Besides being highly toxic, they haven't in my experience worked, but only prolonged the dis-ease. The drugs for demodectic mange cause damage to the liver, kidneys and nervous system (behavior aberrations), and further weaken the immune system. The drugs for ringworm cause vomiting, vertigo, reduction in white blood cells, lethargy, brain and nerve damage, and more. The thing my vet didn't tell me about an adolescent Siberian puppy's localized demodectic mange was that even without the drugs it would probably have just disappeared. With persistence, ringworm is more easily treatable than mange. Holistic methods would have saved a great deal of pet and human misery—and an animal's life.

Nutrition: Feed the holistic diet, a preservative-free pet food or homemade diet with supplements. A major part of the treatment for these dis-eases lies in boosting the immune system and in clearing the liver of toxins—both processes promoted by the natural diet. If using the Pitcairn Dog/Cat Oil and Powder Mixes, double the amounts of cod liver oil and brewer's yeast, then add lecithin and the vitamins listed below. If using the Vita-Mineral Mix, use the altered recipe suggested in the "Liver Dis-ease" section and feed the liver dis-ease diet. Give vitamin A daily. Feed raw liver (organic if possible) and egg yolk once a week, and avoid all milk products and fats other than those in the daily oils. A raw foods diet is important.

Naturopathy: Begin with a three- to five-day liquid fast using beet or celery juice as a detoxifier, then switch to the optimal diet. Use antibiotic herbs during the fast. Give aloe vera juice with liquid chlorophyll. Aloe with hydrogen peroxide can also be used externally. Bathe the animal weekly, or even daily, soaping twice with an herbal flea shampoo or Betadyne (non-soapy) scrub. Leave the second soaping on for ten minutes before rinsing thoroughly, then use the Lemon Rinse recommended in the "Fleas" section to soak the cat's or dog's coat, making sure to wet the sores. Use this solution daily while dabbing pure lemon juice (or iodine, only if the sores are few) onto the lesions. For ringworm, clip the hair around the lesions—it prevents them from spreading—and make sure the cat's or dog's feet and claws are soaped thoroughly— scratching spreads the dis-ease.[93] Juliette de Bairacli Levy also paints ringworm, but not mange lesions, with fingernail polish, which suffocates the fungus.

Add lots of garlic to the animal's diet, and put apple cider vinegar into the water bowl. Digestive enzymes are helpful, and the iodine and minerals in kelp are important. Cider vinegar, garlic juice (not oil) or Betadyne may be used externally on the sores. Essential oils of juniper and lavender diluted in herb infusions, water or other liquids (about three drops of each per ounce of liquid, mixed thoroughly), may be used externally as well. Make sure these are pure oils, not perfumes.

Vitamins and Minerals: Along with the daily supplements, vitamins C, E and zinc are the important ones. Give vitamin C to bowel tolerance, 500-3,000 mg—a pet with a weakened immune system will take a surprising amount of C without diarrhea. Give 5-20 mg of zinc, depending on body size, and give a bit more than usual as an immune system builder. Vitamin E amounts should be doubled—on my puppy I went as high as 800 IU per day for a couple of months. Even on a small cat give E daily for a while, then go to weekly. Use the dry emulsified E to prevent any risk of overdose. An alternative to high levels of vitamin E is vitamin A, giving 10,000 IU daily to a cat or small dog and more for larger dogs; give with 400-800 IU of vitamin D once a week. Vitamin A also comes in an emulsified form that prevents any risk of toxicity, but if the pet starts vomiting on either, cut the dose. Add lecithin to the diet, one-half to three teaspoons, and if not feeding brewer's yeast give a yeast-free B-complex tablet in higher potency than usual, about 15-30 mg. Vitamin pioneer Adele Davis attributes ringworm to B-complex deficiency.[94] She also recommends, as does Anitra Frazier, daily liquid acidophilus for ringworm.

Herbs: Give goldenseal with echinacea from the start of the fast through the complete healing of mange or ringworm, being careful to continue for at least ten days after symptoms disappear. These herb tinctures can also be used on the lesions directly, and in infusions or tinctures mixed with the lemon rinse. Plantain or lavender also kills mites when used externally. The classic herbal for external and internal use is black walnut hulls available in tincture. Other useful herbs include wormwood, butternut bark, and/or sage, all externally. Juliette de Bairacli Levy recommends a combination of wormwood, red clover and violet leaf, used externally in a strong infusion.[95] These are for both mange and ringworm. Tea tree oil can also be used externally; use clover, sage or chaparral internally. Again, the primary choices here are goldenseal and echinacea internally, with these and/or black walnut on the lesions. Levy also strongly recommends kelp in the diet. Tea tree oil must be diluted if used as a full-body rinse.

Homeopathy: The primary remedy for mange is *Sulfur*, lower potencies administered twice a day until there are aggravations or improvements, then by the observation method. Some homeopathic veterinarians use *Sulfur* in increasingly higher potencies—30C, 200C, 1M, 10M. It may be alternated with *Arsenicum* to relieve the furious itching. Where Sulfur and Arsenicum fail, try *Psorinum*. *Sepia* is for the animal in convalescence. It may take some time with these to begin seeing results.

For ringworm, the primary remedy is *Bacillinum*, going to *Sepia* if this fails, or one of the other remedies that follow. Use *Sepia* when there are circular patches, more on the body than on the head. *Kali arsenicum* is for the early itching stage, or a restless pet that thirsts for small sips of water; here, symptoms worsen after midnight. Also try *Arsenicum* for itching and restlessness. *Chrysarobinum* is for scaly, crusty eruptions around the eyes or ears. Try *Tellurium* when lesions appear equally on both sides of the body. *Hypericum* ointment eases itching.

Acupuncture/Acupressure: See the chart on Immune Stimulation and work those points. On the Cat Acupressure Chart, #5 is for dermatitis and itching, #15 for blood cleansing, #22 is a general tonic.

Flower Essences: *Red Ixora* is a blood cleanser. *Self-Heal* aids in all healing and in cleansing the skin of toxins. *Crab Apple*, *Allemanda* and/or *Tomato* are cleansers, and *Salvia* and *Celery* support the immune system under stress. Use *Snapdragon* when lesions are primarily together around the mouth. Anitra Frazier suggests *Crab Apple*, *Aspen* and *Gorse* for mange mites; and *Crab Apple*, *Mimulus*, *Aspen* and *Holly* for ringworm. Use these as combinations: *Crab Apple* to cleanse, *Aspen* to calm the nerves, *Gorse* for hopelessness, *Mimulus* to ease fears, and *Holly* for pets who lash out.[96]

Gemstones: Use natural or rutile *Citrine* as an elixir or in the water bowl, in the environment and on the pet's collar; it cleanses the skin of toxins and regenerates tissue. *Bloodstone* is similarly positive. Make an elixir of *Emerald* for deep cleansing and detoxifying. *Lapis Lazuli* and *Sugulite* balance the endocrine system and raise immunity; *Emerald*, *Jade* or *Blue Tourmaline* also builds immune function. Test with a pendulum.

Moving

Other than acquiring a new guardian, or being out on the streets on her own, moving is the highest stress point in a cat's or dog's life. She watches the space that has been her whole world being torn apart and packed away into boxes. There is dust in the air. Her guardian is distracted and not thinking of her. She feels ignored and has no idea what's coming (unless they have moved before). There are new smells in the air, dust that irritates, and nothing is where it belongs. Her guardian appears and disappears, and is stressed in a way that the dog or cat can only worry about—she doesn't know what to do. Her guardian is going away. Is the pet coming along? Where will they go? What if she is left behind in this torn-up house? No one is paying attention to her. Is she still wanted? What did she do wrong? Is she being punished?

The guardian is stressed and busy, but the pet is not in danger. She is moving to the new house too, but how is the pet to know that? And if there is a long distance to travel—a cross-country trip in the car, a plane ride—there are even more traumas to come. Dogs and especially cats like their daily routines uninterrupted, and changes distress them deeply. Cats are particularly rigid in this.

The following are some tips to help ease the fright and make moving a less scary time for your pet. First, use psychic communication, showing her the new house and pictures of her living there with you. Tell her how nice it will be, how much bigger, with new spaces to play in. Show her all her toys there, and even a fenced-in yard. Show her how she will get there, step by step; rehearse it in pictures and psychic talking, answering her worries and fears. Repeat the session nightly until the move, always reassuring the cat or dog that she is coming with you, and that you will take care of her. If the new place is local and the pet an explorer, take her for a trial visit before the move.

Tip number two is the safe carrier. For pets who are crate-trained, this is easy. For animals new to it, it is wise to get them used to the carrier early. Leave the box open where the pet can explore it, and put some catnip or biscuits, as well as her favorite toy or her blanket, inside. Feed her in the crate and gradually close the door for short periods, turning a deaf ear to protests. Praise her when you let her out. Then start taking the dog or cat for short trips in the carrier. For a larger dog, put the crate in the car, then the dog in the crate—but get her used to being in the carrier first. This training is especially important for the pet who must travel by air or long distance, and for the pet who has never been crate-trained. If traveling by air with the cat or dog, the airline will give further instructions.

The third important tip is that during the moving process and for at least two or three weeks after, keep a very careful watch over the animal. With her home disrupted, a nervous cat or dog may try to bolt out the door. On the actual moving day, place the pet in her carrier while people and furniture are going in and out, and place the carrier in the quietest possible place. Make sure the pet has water and frequent toilet access. When traveling long distance by car, make sure to only open the crate in a closed-in space. Let the dog or cat out in her new home after all the fuss is done, and you and she can be alone. Hold her and stroke her and show her how nice this is. Show her where she goes outside or where her litter box is. Show her where her food and water bowls are, and her toys. Show her these things often, until she has gone to them on her own volition. In the new home, be careful that the dog or cat does not run off—she may try to go back to her old home, no matter how far away. Keep the pet's daily schedule as normal as possible, and give lots and lots of love.

Nutrition: Your dog or cat should be placed on the optimal natural diet long before moving; a time of stress and upheaval is not the time to switch diets. Pets under stress tend to lose appetite, so tempt your cat or dog with things she likes, things that are good for her. If bribe foods are necessary at this time, be a little lenient. The daily supplements are very important at moving time to maintain healing for pets who are often under trauma and change. Feed raw organic liver about once a week.

Naturopathy: In the new home, rub a bit of butter on all four paws of your cat or dog. By the time the butter is licked off, some of the pet's smell has mingled with the new environment and the animal can claim the new house as home. This trick is especially effective with cats. To make male dogs feel at home, take the animal on a leash around the outside perimeters of lawn and house, letting him sniff and urinate to his satisfaction. The act of urinating is an act of claiming territory, and once the dog has marked the property as his, he will accept it as home. Female dogs, although less territorial, also need this introductory walk.

Give digestive enzymes, garlic, bee pollen, kelp and cider vinegar. Chlorophyll balances energy.

Vitamins and Minerals: Keep up the daily supplements, even amid the chaos of moving. Give additional B-complex or brewer's yeast, as these vitamins heal the negative effects of stress and fear. Positive additional B-vitamins include B-3 (niacinamide form), B-5 (pantothenic acid) and B-6 (pyridoxine). Give vitamin C, at least 500 mg per day, as another stress management supplement; zinc is recommended (5-15 mg per day) to maintain the immune system. Calcium/magnesium is a calmative; use it only with vitamin C. Vitamins A and E can be increased slightly and given daily for a week, then return to the once-per-week routine with vitamin D. Amino acids GABA or tyrosine are calmatives, as is germanium.

Herbs: Avoid veterinary tranquilizers; they have unpredictable results, add toxins to the body and negatively affect the immune system. Instead, give calming herbs. Scullcap is most recommended, or use valerian root for the extremely frantic animal. Other calming herbs include chamomile, passionflower, rosemary, hops or catnip (for dogs only). Siberian ginseng calms and stabilizes energy, but give it only in very small amounts. Alfalfa and kelp are the best all-round nutrients and herbal supports. For the pet who refuses food, try mixing a little honey and water into slippery elm powder—it's delicious and tempting.

Homeopathy: *Aconite* is for fear and apprehension related to any shock or trauma; also use it for the frightened pet who is travel sick. Give *Gelsemium* to the animal who is literally shaking with fear, and may have wet the floor or her carrier. *Ignatia* helps a dog or cat accept new surroundings. *Scutellaria*, homeopathic scullcap, is the remedy when a pet's nature and behavior seem to change radically during a move. For travel sickness, give a dose of *Cocculus* before starting and repeat if needed. If there is vomiting, use *Ipecac*.

Acupuncture/Acupressure: Treat the dog or cat to a nightly all-over massage or Tellington TTouch session before seeking specific meridian points. Do an ear massage, too. These are stress reducing measures that calm both pet and guardian. For specific meridians, on the Shin Dog Chart use point #20 (GV-20B) *Pai hui* for nervousness and #28 (P-1) *Shin yu* for mental stress. On the Cat Chart, point #22 is a general tonic and increases appetite.

Flower Essences: Put a few drops each of *Nature's Rescue* (*Rescue Remedy*) and *Walnut* in the water bowl daily, starting as soon as packing begins and continuing for about a month in the new house. *Walnut* aids in accepting changes and transitions; *Nature's Rescue* is for trauma. These are the two primary essences. *Aloe vera* is for behavioral problems due to stress, and *Yarrow* is for emotional protection. *Chamomile* is for animals with digestive upset from nervousness. *Dill* helps pets overwhelmed by travel, and *White Lightnin'* is for trauma and fear. *Impatiens* helps the nervous, high-strung cat or dog. *Scleranthus* is for motion sickness.

Gemstones: *Amethyst* is the central gemstone, a total calmative. Place a piece in the water bowl and as many in the environment as possible, or make an elixir. Other calming stones include *Rose Quartz, Kunzite, Pink Tourmaline, Lepidolite, Sugulite, Celestite, Aquamarine* or *Turquoise*. The colors are pink, violet or light blue.

Overweight

The dog or cat who is overweight is probably starving. She is seeking nutrients from foods that have too little nutritional value, and therefore is eating too much. Commercial pet foods are filled with things an animal doesn't need—sugar, salt, waste fillers, chemicals. These same foods lack what is required for animal health—vitamins and minerals, enzymes, proteins, vegetables, grains. Malnutrition and/or malabsorption are important factors in animal and human obesity, as are food allergies and sensitivities. Other factors include glandular malfunction, boredom and habit, lack of exercise, competition for food with other pets, and guardians who substitute food for love. Spaying or neutering does not have to result in overweight. Guardian common sense is needed here, too, as overweight animals are more likely to develop heart dis-ease, hypertension, diabetes, cancer, and liver and kidney dis-ease. Being overweight reduces lifespans.

Nutrition: Obviously, we are talking about a nutrition problem, and the optimal diet is essential in reducing weight in pets. This doesn't mean using a reducing diet, or even limiting food intake, but offering quality nutrition with supplements so the animal can get what she needs while taking less food. For the first few days on the preservative-free or natural homemade diet with supplements, the cat or dog will actually increase her food intake. Allow this, even to the point of offering an additional meal—but give no food between meals and take the bowl away out of smell-reach after mealtime. Once she has taken in the nutrients she so badly needs, the pet's appetite will balance out. Gradually, she will begin to lose weight and at the same time be more satisfied. Food allergies and food addictions may need to be dealt with, but the end result will be a sleek and healthy pet.

Anitra Frazier and Richard Pitcairn both suggest adding to meals supplements that make dogs or cats feel full sooner. These include extra bran (a teaspoon for cats and small dogs, up to about a tablespoon for large dogs), and especially filling or cleansing vegetables: zucchini, carrots, celery, broccoli, cabbage, onions, cauliflower, leafy greens or parsley.[97] Use the extra vegetables in the same amounts as the bran.

Naturopathy: Detoxification is important; start with a cleansing fast and enemas if needed. Many overweight pets are also constipated, and this needs correcting. Feed aloe vera juice with liquid chlorophyll during the fast and in the daily diet. Digestive enzymes are important. Kelp boosts thyroid function, a glandular insufficiency that may cause obesity. Put apple cider vinegar in the water bowl to supplement potassium. Watermelon is a diuretic, and garlic is an overall detoxifier.

Vitamins and Minerals: Feed the daily supplements with the following additions. Add half a teaspoon to two teaspoons of lecithin daily to meals, and give 500-2,000 mg vitamin C per day. Extra B-complex vitamins, especially vitamins B-5 and B-6, help to keep the spayed or neutered pet slim. Give vitamin E. Chromium in the trace minerals powder helps to balance blood sugar. Essential fatty acids (evening primrose oil or black currant oil) may be helpful. Also try a combination amino acids. A combination of raw glandulars may also be helpful.

Herbs: Juliette de Bairacli Levy suggests daily use of rosemary, as well as dandelion and parsley.[98] Chickweed, cleavers and/or pokeroot also burn fat; changes begin slowly, then are suddenly apparent after a few weeks. Stevia, a drop or two on food, tastes sweet and is an herbal blood-sugar balancer. Fennel or yerba maté decrease appetite and aid digestion. Licorice root balances blood sugar and is an herbal estrogen that may reduce obesity in spayed females. Senna or cascara sagrada are laxatives, but aloe vera is gentler.

Homeopathy: *Calcarea carbonate* is the remedy for overweight from impaired nutrition with pituitary or thyroid dysfunction; the animal may have heart dis-ease or anemia, and be sensitive to cold. The classic homeopathic remedy for obesity is *Phytolacca* berry given twice a day on a month's trial. *Natrum mur* or *Natrum phos* may be used twice weekly as other alternatives. Where there is chronic mucous congestion with obesity, try *Ammonium bromatum*. The cell salt *Natrum sulph* relieves water retention and aids weight loss.

Acupuncture/Acupressure: No points are given on either chart for weight loss or obesity. Point #35 (BL-25) *Huan cho* balances hormonal insufficiencies. Massage the ears for all-over balancing, and see a veterinary acupuncturist for specific help.

Flower Essences: *Crab Apple*, *Tomato*, yellow or purple *Allemanda* and *Yellow Hibiscus* are cleansers. *Bird of Paradise* aids blood sugar problems. *Roses* and other calmative flowers will help.

Gemstones: Yellow and yellow-green stones balance the digestive system and aid weight loss. *Citrine* is most recommended. Other stones include *Amber*, *Topaz*, *Amber Calcite*, *Apatite*, *Malachite* or *Peridot*. If making *Malachite* into an elixir, leave it in the water for no more than half an hour.

Pain Relief

Pain is a signal to the body that something is wrong. Once the problem has been treated, pain keeps an animal or human from overdoing it—from running on a sprained ankle and causing more damage, for example—before the healing is complete. Nothing hurts a pet guardian more, however, than watching an animal in pain. The dog or cat hides in a corner or in her bed, refusing to come out, refusing to eat, and nothing seems to gain a response. She has been treated by the vet, but is far from well. Dogs and cats take pain as a matter of course and, until it becomes excessive, go on with their daily lives. If a leg hurts, they lift it and run on three. When pain is severe animals do what they think they must to stop it. Animals caught in traps have been known to bite off the captured limb and similar things can happen in a nerve damage chronic pain situation. Mostly, however, pets take healing sleeps and wait for the pain to end. The pain remedies people resort to may be highly toxic to dogs or cats. Animals are drug sensitive, cats particularly so. Aspirin or Tylenol may be used occasionally for dogs, although they may cause stomach upsets, ulcers and internal bleeding over time. Cats and aspirin don't mix at all; as few as one per day over a few days can cause death from liver or bone marrow damage. This is also true for Tylenol, Motrin and other aspirin derivatives, including the herbs white willow bark and white oak. Pets have low tolerances for and exhibit erratic responses to tranquilizers and narcotics. Cortisone and other steroids remove symptoms temporarily, but drive the dis-ease deeper into the body and weaken the immune system. Even antibiotics, the most commonly prescribed veterinary/medical drugs, can cause temporary or permanent damage when overdosed or used for too long. All medical and over-the-counter drugs should be regarded as toxic for pets. The following are holistic alternatives for helping a cat or dog in pain. Be sure the source of the discomfort is known and that the animal receives holistic veterinary care as well.

Nutrition: If your pet has been on the natural diet with supplements, she has the best tools available to speed her healing and recovery. In time of pain, make sure the supplements are provided, especially brewer's yeast and minerals. Liver, yeast and dark green leafy vegetables are anti-stress foods. Keep salt to a minimum. Feed additional bone meal (a quarter teaspoon extra for cats and toy-breed dogs, to a teaspoon for larger dogs) and cod liver oil (one eyedropperful for cats and small dogs).[99] These add calcium and vitamin D, respectively. Keep the pet quiet and protect her from excitement and stress.

Naturopathy: A cat or dog who is ill or in pain will usually choose to fast for a few days; this is healthy, especially in cases of fever or wound healing, as well as with viral or bacterial dis-eases. Support the process with high-nutrient liquids like vegetable or chicken broth. Honey and other bee products are complete nutrients that reduce pain, build the immune system and speed healing. Liquid chlorophyll aids blood sugar balance and calcium uptake, and calcium is a major pain reducer. Kelp provides minerals and iodine that relieve pain. If the animal has been on many antibiotics or has experienced heavy bleeding, she may need help replacing vitamin K, which is produced in the intestines. Foods that do this include plain natural yogurt (health food store, not supermarket), kefir milk, acidophilus milk and lecithin.[100] Digestive enzymes are important when the animal is eating again. Put cider vinegar in the water bowl; potassium is a pain reliever. Oat or barley water during the fast and the cooked grains later are positive.

Vitamins and Minerals: Vitamin C with bioflavonoids, B-complex calcium/magnesium, and vitamin E are the primary pain relief and healing supplements. Give vitamin C to bowel tolerance, the powder mixed with the fasting broths (see Naturopathy, above) or placed on food. Much more will be needed than usual; expect to give from 1,000-6,000 mg per day. Animals with any infectious dis-ease, viral or bacterial infection, wound, sprain, or broken bone particulary need lots of C. The B-complex vitamins are other major pain relievers, helping the central nervous system to detoxify the effects of injury, fear or stress. Give a full yeast-free B-complex supplement (15-30 mg) if not feeding brewer's yeast, and give additional B-5 (pantothenic acid) and B-6 (pyridoxine). Vitamins B-1 (thiamine) and B-2 (riboflavin) are also positive. Double the amount of vitamin E for a week, and give additional vitamin A with D (or added cod liver oil—not both) for a couple of days, then go back to the weekly dosage. Both speed healing and vitamin E is especially needed after surgery. Give daily one calcium/magnesium tablet (human product) containing about 300 mg of calcium and half that of magnesium per tablet, along with some trace minerals; these are major pain relievers, and as long as vitamin C is also given, there is no risk of kidney stones. Essential fatty acids (black currant oil or evening primrose oil) also reduce pain and speed healing. Feed 5-10 mg of zinc per day. Germanium is a potent pain reliever.

Herbs: There are a number of pain relieving herbs that are safe and effective. St. John's wort is important for body pain from sprains, broken bones and arthritis, and from any nerve injury. Valerian is a general pain reliever and is quite strong; scullcap is another effective pain remedy; both are tranquilizing. Ginseng with royal jelly is a tonic and restorative. Arnica tincture may be used externally for local pain where the skin is unbroken. Alfalfa provides minerals and pain relief, and increases the effectiveness of other herbs. Slippery elm powder mixed with water or honey is a nutrient food, aids internal mucous membrane irritation, and can be used as a paste externally on sores, swellings, skin ulcers and insect bites. Use it with lobelia externally for blood poisoning, abscesses or rheumatism.

A number of herbs make good poultices or compresses. These include chaparral, dandelion, yellow dock or comfrey for skin ulcers, rashes and skin cancers. Use onion poultices for boils, or make a mustard plaster for inflammation, swelling, lung congestion and tense muscles—wrap it in gauze or a washcloth rather than placing mustard directly on the skin. Pokeroot or sage help mastitis or breast inflammations; mullein poultice is for inflamed tonsils or lung disorders. With mullein use four parts dry herb to one part hot vinegar and one part water in the poultice. Goldenseal and echinacea are good poultices or compresses for any inflammation.[101] Keep these hot, but be careful not to burn the skin. Place the poultice over the pain site.

Homeopathy: Dose with *Aconite* at first onset for fear, pain, shock or trauma, changing to other remedies later. *Hypericum* is for any injury involving nerve damage, especially pain in the feet. *Arnica,* used for blows, prevents bruising and stops bleeding; the remedy is used internally, the tincture externally on unbroken skin only. *Ruta grav* aids injuries to muscles, tendons and ligaments, where there is bruising over bone. *Calendula* cream heals cuts and skin abrasions quickly, and Hypericum also comes in salves. *Rhus tox* helps rheumatism and arthritis when the pet seems better after moving around; *Bryonia* is the opposite—for pain that worsens with movement. Use *Apis* where there is redness and swelling, as in bee stings or inflamed joints. Sudden acute pain may respond to *Chamomilla*, including mouth and toothache pain. For colic try *Colocythis*. See the remedies under specific dis-eases.

Acupuncture/Acupressure: There are a number of meridians for localized pain on both the Shin Dog Chart and the Cat Chart; use the ones that apply. This method of healing is extremely important for dogs or cats in chronic pain. If the animal welcomes it, do a full body massage or Tellington TTouch session daily—or, if possible, do a Reiki healing daily or more often. These transmit your love and caring, and give relaxation and relief. Never apply pressure over a wound or pain area, and respect the animal's signals as to what feels good and what doesn't. See *Natural Healing for Dogs and Cats* for more information on TTouch, massage and psychic healing.

Flower Essences: *Nature's Rescue (Rescue Remedy)* is the first remedy to use when a cat or dog is in pain or in crisis. Use it as often as every five minutes and put some in the water bowl, or give at least four times daily while the animal is healing. If unable to place the remedy on the pet's tongue, rub the liquid on her gums, nose or inner earflaps. *Self-heal* is a supporting essence for the healing process. Give *Comfrey* as first aid for accidents or injuries, *Yellow Ixora* (Ch'i Kung Essence) for meridian balancing. *Gruss an Aachen* stabilizes the physical and non-physical bodies; *White Lightnin'* is for trauma. For releasing fear and pain after injury use *St. John's wort* essence. *Hornbeam* is for fatigue, and *Olive* is for the dog or cat who is exhausted, ill or traumatized. For pets in pain and depressed due to illness, try *Pandora Vine* (Hope Essence). *Penstemon* gives strength and is good with other essences; use *Arnica* for injury.

Gemstones: The black stones are pain relievers, particularly *Black Tourmaline*, *Tourmaline Quartz*, *Smoky Quartz* and *Boji Stone*. *Chrysocolla* or *Lapis Lazuli* is an all-healer, while *Amethyst* is a pain reliever and calmative.

Poisoning

Along with chemical toxicity from the environment, which accumulates over time, direct poisoning is an ever-present danger for dogs and cats both in and out of the home. Deliberate intent is less often the cause than accidents or carelessness. Too many deadly chemicals, insecticides and rat poisons are designed to taste good to the vermin they are intended for, but attract dogs and cats instead. Baits are the major poisoning agents—rat and mouse baits, roach, ant, slug and snail traps. The chemicals they contain include arsenic, sodium fluoracetate, metaldehyde, lead, phosphorus, zinc phosphates and warfarin. Organophosphates and carbamates—used in dewormers, flea preparations and garden sprays—are also dangerous chemicals, as are the chlorinated hydrocarbons used in insecticides. Antifreeze tastes sweet to both dogs and cats, and is lethal in very small doses—one teaspoon is enough to kill a cat and little more will kill a dog. Petroleum products cause pneumonia if inhaled, and the corrosives and acids in household cleaners, drain openers and solvents burn animal mouths, esophagi and stomachs. When pets get into human medications, or their own, they can die from the results, another reason not to make these things taste good. Eating some houseplant species can also poison cats and dogs. Scavenging and garbage can raiding can result in food poisoning, and while this is more frequent in dogs, cats are scavengers too, and more sensitive to the results. Chocolate can be fatal to dogs.

If your animal has been poisoned, or you suspect she has, contact your local poison-control center, veterinarian, or veterinary emergency clinic after hours, or call the twenty-four-hour Toxicology Hotline for Animals. Read the material under Homeopathy below, and see the chart "Poison First Aid" on the following page. If you know the source of the poison, identify it and bring the container to the vet's after administering first aid. If you don't know the source, the pet's symptoms will usually make it clear to professionals. In most cases you will be told to immediately induce vomiting, unless the pet has been poisoned by petroleum products, by external chemicals, or by acids or alkalis. For chemicals on the skin, bathe the animal with plain soap and water. For ingested acids or alkali do the following: rinse out the animal's mouth, then for acids give an antacid—Milk of Magnesia, Pepto-Bismol or Maalox, one to two teaspoons per five pounds of body weight. For alkali, give an acidic—cider vinegar diluted with one to four parts water, or lemon juice. Then *take the pet to the veterinarian*. The next steps are delaying absorption by coating the intestinal tract, and finally giving herbal laxatives to remove the remaining poison from the body.

Obviously, prevention is the best treatment. Make very sure that rat, slug and insect baits are where animals cannot reach them. If antifreeze spills, hose it down thoroughly until all traces are totally gone, and keep pets indoors while using antifreeze. Keep kitchen cleaners, medications (yours and your pets') out of reach, along with houseplants that are toxic. Give the pets greens in their diet so the houseplants are less tempting.

Never use dog flea or other insecticide products on cats; these include shampoos, collars and sprays. And a plea for pet safety from poisoning, cars and many other hazards: never allow animals to run loose.

The Digestion Recognition Chakra has totally atrophied in most dogs and cats; if they are unable to protect themselves, we must protect them. The following are some recovery tips for the cat or dog who has survived a poisoning experience.

Nutrition: Providing enough nutrition, vitamins and minerals in the daily diet keeps pets from looking for missing nutrients in unusual places. A dog that chews plaster, for example, is deficient in and looking for calcium and magnesium. When a pet is recovering from arsenic or other bait-type poisoning—after the several days of fasting that must follow any treatment—feed a diet high in sulfur and fiber to detoxify. Appropriate foods include bran for fiber; egg yolks, garlic, beans, legumes and onions for sulfur. A high protein diet with egg yolks and organic liver helps to heal liver damage. After phosphorus poisoning, keep the diet free of fats for several weeks to lessen strain on the liver. Activated

Poison First Aid[102]

Call: Your local poison control center or any hospital emergency room, your veterinarian, or the Toxicology Hotline for Animals.

Toxicology Hotline for Animals
    (800) 548-2423   ($30 charge on credit card)
    (900) 680-000   ($20 first five minutes, then $2.95 per minute on phone bill)

To Induce Vomiting—Most Toxins (Use One):

1. *3% Hydrogen Peroxide*—One teaspoon for cats, up to three teaspoons for dogs; give every ten minutes repeated three times.
2. *Salt*—One-quarter to one-half teaspoonful, placed dry at the back of the tongue.
3. *Syrup of Ipecac*—One teaspoonful per ten pounds body weight.

Do Not Induce Vomiting If Your Pet Does Any of the Following:

1. Swallows acid, alkali, solvent, or heavy duty cleaner.
2. Is severely depressed or comatose.
3. Swallows a petroleum product.
4. Swallows tranquilizers (which prevent vomiting).
5. Swallows a sharp object (which could lodge in her esophagus or perforate the stomach).
6. If more than two hours have passed since the poison was ingested.

Plan of Treatment

1. Eliminate the poison, usually be inducing vomiting.
2. Delay absorption by coating the intestinal tract by giving 1 gm activated charcoal to 4 cc. water, a teaspoon per two pounds of body weight. Thirty minutes later, give Glauber's Salt (one teaspoon per ten pounds body weight) or Milk of Magnesia (one teaspoonful per five pounds).
3. Laxatives to speed elimination of poisons from the body. Never give pets commercial human laxatives other than the Milk of Magnesia described above.

charcoal tablets or granules in water given every fifteen minutes are an emergency measure; stop them after the emergency, as they take needed nutrients from the body.[103]

Naturopathy: Keep the animal on a fast of several days until all toxins are removed from her body; when returning her to food, do it very slowly. Give laxatives or enemas twice daily, and use aloe vera juice with liquid chlorophyll. After emergency care, keep the animal on water only for two or three days, then give slippery elm syrup or the powder mixed with water or honey three times a day to heal the intestinal tract. Add barley water, and later the cooked barley grain. The whites of raw eggs whipped into foam alleviate internal burning and may be used for a few days but no longer; they interfere with biotin, a B-vitamin. Some emergency antidotes: for strychnine poisoning give half a teaspoon of permanganate of potash in half a pint of water; for phosphorus give baking soda and water, and Milk of Magnesia; for lead from paint or other sources give a teaspoon of epsom salts in a cup of water.[104] Garlic and kelp are important detoxifiers after emergency treatment and fasting. For food poisoning give cider vinegar, honey water, and liquid chlorophyll.

Vitamins and Minerals: Once the animal is eating again, the focus is to heal the damage as completely and quickly as possible. Vitamin C with bioflavonoids, in high amounts, is essential. The B-complex vitamins are also important, as brewer's yeast or as a yeast-free supplement, with additional B-2 (riboflavin) and B-5 (pantothenic acid). Both detoxify. Give higher than usual amounts of vitamin E, in the dry form if the regular isn't tolerated. Free-form amino acids or protein powder also help liver function, as does liver extract; find these in health food stores. SOD, lecithin, selenium or coenzyme Q10 are all positive, and the single amino acids cysteine, cystine and methionine. Remember the daily supplements of the optimal diet.

Herbs: Slippery elm soothes and heals burned and raw internal membranes, and is the first herb to use. When the cat or dog is eating again, go to mallow as another tissue healer and regenerator. Senna is a laxative (I still prefer aloe vera); Juliette de Bairacli Levy lists both rue and hyssop as antidotes for all forms of poisoning. After the crisis, silymarin (milk thistle) helps to repair liver damage. See the other remedies in the "Liver Dis-ease" section.

Homeopathy: Several homeopathic remedies are highly diluted forms of toxic substances like arsenic (*Arsenicum*), and strychnine (*Strychninum*). Where the symptoms match, or where the pet has ingested these toxins, give the matching homeopathic under the Law of Similars (like cures like). The remedy picture for *Arsenicum* is burning pain and restlessness; the animal wants small sips of water frequently, and has acute vomiting and/or diarrhea. Where there is liver damage and damage to mucous membranes, hemorrhages, jaundice, inflammation, vertigo, heavy vomiting and fetid, copious diarrhea, *Phosphorus* is the remedy; the animal is fearful and hypersensitive. (These are the symptoms of phosphorus poisoning.) Use *Strychninum* where there are convulsions and spasm, violent jerks in the spinal column and rigid neck and back, with violent vomiting. The animal is restless and irritable, hypersensitive, and may go into convulsions at the slightest sound or touch. Symptoms come suddenly and explosively, and at intervals.

Where there is burning red throat, abdominal bloating, green bilious vomiting and dysentery, give *Merc cor*. The cat or dog is delirious, the lips black and swollen, the face red and puffy. *Cuprum met* is for violent contractive pain with spasms and convulsions, foaming at the mouth, falling and unconsciousness; the face is distorted and the animal fearful. *Nux vomica* is a polycrest remedy (useful in many instances, like Arsenicum). Try it here for food poisoning or other types of poisoning where the animal is noticeably irritable and nervous and cannot bear noises, light, odors or being touched. There may be convulsions that are worse with moving or touch, along with light sensitivity, raw throat, bloody saliva, vomiting with much retching, or attempting to vomit with nothing coming up; if no other remedy is available, try this one. For bait-type poisonings try Arsenicum.

Acupuncture/Acupressure: Do the Shock and Resuscitation points first, as diagrammed in the "Acupuncture" method chapter. Then go to points matching the symptoms. If there is vomiting, diarrhea and gastritis, work the points listed under indigestion. Use #39 (CV-12) *Chung wan* for acute gastritis. If the pet is having convulsions, use point #3 (GV-16) *Ta feng men*. After the crisis the liver damage points may apply; see that section. It is inappropriate to stop diarrhea and vomiting until after the toxins are out of the body. On the Cat Chart, point #8 is for shock.

Flower Essences: Give *Nature's Rescue* (*Rescue Remedy*) first and throughout the crisis, then go to *Crab Apple*, *Tomato* or *Allemanda* for cleansing. *Hornbeam* strengthens; *Olive* is for the sick and exhausted animal. *Bottlebrush Tree* (Grounding Essence) detoxifies; use *Snapdragon* where the mouth is burned. *Nasturtium* aids the nervous system. See the essences in the "Indigestion" and "Liver Dis-ease" sections.

Gemstones: *Amethyst* and *Kunzite* are calmative; and *Sugulite* balances the aura. All these are detoxifiers, as well as *Coral* and *Bloodstone*. *Malachite* brings things out from within. To aid internal healing after the crisis, use *Celestite*, *Lapis Lazuli*, *Aquamarine* or *Chrysocolla*. *Emerald* is a deep-acting detoxifier in elixir.

Pregnancy

I am a firm believer in spaying and neutering, with breeding reserved for only a few special animals who are sound physically and mentally, and who are in emotional balance. Too many breeders of purebreds ignore all but physical beauty or show standards. The result is a decline in the health and lives of companion purebreds. Breeding for the long, thin collie head has resulted in detached retinas and chorea in a once splendid working animal. Cocker spaniels have become biters and hysterics, dachshunds die of spinal disc dis-ease, and my beloved Siberian Huskies (as well as other large breeds) have hip and nervous problems. Cat breeders promote the same type of defects, with the exaggerated Siamese head resulting in eye-focus abnormalities (squinting) and lowered intelligence. Many puppy and kitty farms produce as many litters as they can without regard for the health of the mother animals or the placement of the babies. There are show kennels that refuse to sell animals as pets and euthanize those who are not of exhibition quality. ("Not exhibition quality" may only mean the wrong coat color.) This kind of breeding is a tragedy, a cruelty and a clear violation of Goddess law. Both of my purebreds came from shelters; they are not exempt from pain.

And what about those loving mutts? Ten million animals were put to death in 1992 by the Humane Societies.[105] There are no homes for these unfortunate animals, and the alternative for them is death by starvation, dis-ease, poisoning or cars. A mixed-breed cat or dog is every bit as wonderful as a purebred animal, and may be genetically hardier. When thousands and thousands of loving animals are dying each week for want of homes, it is just wrong to breed them. Yet it happens, by accident or design, and the mothers and babies need care.

Gestation time for dogs is fifty-nine to sixty-six days (average sixty-three), for cats sixty days plus or minus five (average sixty-three). Birth is near when the mother's body temperature drops below her normal 101.5°, then rises again. The following are tips for making a dog or cat pregnancy easier and more comfortable. Please find good homes for the babies, then spay or neuter your pets.

Nutrition: The pregnant or lactating cat or dog needs the optimal diet, preservative-free prepared food, or the homemade diet with supplements. In general, slightly increase all the supplements in balance. Feed the normal diet for the first half of gestation. Most sources say to double the food ration for the second half, but Wendell Belfield comments that when supplements are adequate less of an increase is needed.[106] Food increases are to be primarily of quality protein, including cottage cheese, eggs, goat's milk, liver and yogurt. Avoid excessive weight gain; it makes for larger babies and more difficult deliveries. As the pregnancy progresses go to smaller, more frequent meals instead of the usual one or two meals per day. Provide increased amounts of pure water. Avoid all chemicals, preservatives and drugs, including worm medicines and toxic flea products.

Naturopathy: If the female chooses to fast herself for a few days at a time, allow it, giving her honey and water until she is ready to resume eating. Be careful not to overfeed. In the last week of pregnancy, give slightly laxative foods like chopped figs, prunes or apricots—but again don't overdo it. At this time also reduce protein, giving goat's milk and oats or barley with less meat. For the last two or three days of the pregnancy, go to a liquid diet of goat's milk and honey, continuing until two days after birthing. Estimated amounts of goat's milk and raw honey for a cat or toy breed dog are about half a teaspoon of honey in a cup of goat's milk twice per day; for large breeds, increase the amounts.[107] Kelp is highly positive to use during the pregnancy. Add cider vinegar in the water bowl. Avoid aloe vera juice during the first month of gestation— it may cause abortion—then use reduced amounts. Liquid chlorophyll is always positive and helps the mother's calcium balance, which is vital. Digestive enzymes and garlic are also highly positive, and use garlic while nursing as an infection preventive for mother and young.

Vitamins and Minerals: The daily supplements are highly important during pregnancy and nursing; increase them all slightly in the last half of the pregnancy. The B and C vitamins are essential for healthy young and problem-free delivery, but do not supplement calcium beyond the daily amounts. Give up to 1,000 mg of vitamin C daily for cats and toy breed dogs, up to 7,500 mg daily for the giant breeds. Vitamin C prevents hip dysplasia in puppies, "fading" puppies and kittens, virtually eliminates morning sickness and septic abortions, and makes delivery and recovery faster and easier, with healthier, sturdier newborns. Give brewer's yeast in increased amounts or a yeast-free B-complex, 15-30 mg per day, with additional vitamin B-9 (folic acid). When given at the time of conception and in the first week of gestation, B-9 prevents spinal cord malformations; all the B-vitamins prevent birth defects. Vitamin E is another essential, give 100 IU daily for cats and small dogs, up to 600 IU daily for giant breeds. Supplement 5-15 mg of zinc daily, as well,[108] and give the usual weekly vitamins A and D. A vegetable-based protein supplement and acidophilus may also be helpful. Start all of the above from before breeding if possible, and continue through pregnancy, birthing and lactation.

Herbs: Raspberry leaf is the traditional birthing herb; given throughout the pregnancy it makes delivery faster and easier, and nursing and recovery problem-free. Use it with chamomile for morning sickness.

(Dogs and cats get this, too.) Slippery elm may be used with the milk and honey (see Naturopathy) as a nutrient. Alfalfa gives full nutrients plus vitamin K, preventing hemorrhaging and speeding clotting in the babies' navels. Nettles are also a good pregnancy tonic. Use shepherd's purse during labor and just after to contract the uterus, bring placentas out more easily, and prevent hemorrhaging; both nettles and shepherd's purse contain vitamin K and iron. Squaw vine and blue cohosh are other birth supporting herbs. Juliette de Bairacli Levy recommends using comfrey, nettles and kelp together throughout the pregnancy.

If the litter has arrived and contractions have stopped, but there still seem to be babies or placentas inside, give a strong dose of raspberry leaf tea, with a spoonful of molasses stirred in every four hours. If this fails, give two tablespoons of pennyroyal infusion with a tablespoon of dissolved epsom salts; this will bring to birth anything remaining in the uterus.[109] (Amounts above are for a medium-sized dog.) It is best to have the mother and litter checked by a veterinarian as soon as possible after the birth. Keep count of the number of placentas brought forth (they should match the number of offspring); watch carefully, as the mothers will eat the afterbirth—and should be permitted to do so.

Homeopathy: During the last three or four weeks of pregnancy, give *Caulophyllum* once a day through the birthing to ease pregnancy and delivery. From the onset of labor until the last infant is born, give *Pulsatilla* every thirty to forty minutes. If the labor is difficult and there is bleeding, swelling or bruising, give *Arnica* every two to four hours for a few days; it may also be used for the last day or two before birthing as a preventive. For deficient milk, give *Urtica*; for hemorrhaging give *Ipecac* (if Arnica fails). To prevent miscarriages early in pregnancy, the remedy is *Viburnum*. A single dose of *Sepia* after birthing quickly returns the uterus to normal.

Cold collapsed infants respond to *Carbo veg*, and *Arnica* helps birthing injury and shock. For weak, sluggish babies difficult to start breathing, use *Helleborus*; where there is fluid and rattling in the chest, give *Antimonium tart*. Give *Hypericum* where limbs have been crushed in the birthing. Dose by crushing the pellet in a few drops of pure water and placing a drop in the cheek pouch with an eyedropper.

Acupuncture/Acupressure: No points are given on the Shin Dog Chart for birthing or pregnancy. On the Cat Chart, point #23 is for delivery of kittens; use it only after labor begins. See a veterinary acupuncturist quickly if there are complications.

Flower Essences: Mother's Essence (*Peach Hibiscus*) supports pregnancy, birthing and lactating. *Cauliflower* aids the birth process and the newborns and use *Squash* to three months. *Nature's Rescue* (*Rescue Remedy*) during birthing is positive for both mother and babies; put some also in the mother's water bowl for a few days after. *Clematis* helps newborns to wake up and breathe; *Walnut* helps the new mother to adjust to the changes in her life. *Crab Apple* or *Tomato* cleanses after birth.

Gemstones: Place a piece of *Malachite* in the nest with the mother during labor, not before—it "brings things out from within." During pregnancy, *Amethyst* and *Chrysocolla* are all-healers; *Emerald* or *Aquamarine* prevents miscarriages. For the young, place a piece of *Rose Quartz* or *Aventurine* in the nest.

Secondary Smoke

Dogs and cats are part of our lives and homes. We provide their environment, food and way of life; they depend upon us totally. It is up to us, therefore, to protect these innocent Be-ings in every way we can. This includes providing safe air for them to breathe and protecting them from the life-shortening effects of living with tobacco smoke. Children in smoking homes suffer from marked increases in respiratory ailments, earaches, allergies, hyperactivity and other dis-eases. Cats and dogs are as sensitive, or more so. All forms of cancer, and dozens of other dis-eases, are caused by nicotine, and the effects on a non-smoking bystander are nearly as severe as on smokers. Eighty-five percent of lung cancers and chronic cardiopulmonary dis-eases are directly related to smoking. If your pet has allergies, asthma, bronchitis, respiratory or breathing problems, heart dis-ease, hyperactivity, liver dis-ease or cancer, the cause may be traceable to living in a smoking home. Animals are dying from smoke at home, and they have nowhere else to go.

Quitting smoking, while not easy, is recommended for both human and pet health. Smoking is as much an addiction as cocaine or crack, and both human and pet go through withdrawal when the human stops. Detoxification after stopping may take as long as two years to complete, as each organ releases toxins at its own pace. Both pet and person may experience stomach upsets and cramping, coughing with phlegm, irritability, anxiety, impatience and depression. These symptoms last for a few weeks, then reappear from time to time for shorter periods less and less often. One cigarette is all it takes for addiction to take over again. Liver cleansing speeds the detoxification process for human and animal; it also helps clear and repair the body. The following remedies help the pet *or* person who must live in a smoking house. For information on quitting smoking, see Diane Stein, *The Natural Remedy Book for Women* (The Crossing Press), p. 304-309. Give yourself and your dog or cat a chance for a healthy life.

Nutrition: Feed the preservative-free or homemade natural diet with supplements—more chemicals are the last thing this animal needs. The supplements are particularly important, as nicotine smoke depletes the body of virtually every vitamin and some minerals. The optimal diet helps to detoxify and protect the body and keeps the immune system strong. A high fiber and high protein diet—with raw meat, veggies and cooked whole grains—is important. Foods that cleanse include raw grated carrots, asparagus, broccoli, brussels sprouts, cabbage, cantaloupe, cauliflower, sweet potato and turnips.[110] The hypoglycemic diet, as for asthma, is positive here.

Naturopathy: Start with a few days' fasting on liquids with enemas of lemon juice, chlorophyll or coffee for quick detoxification; then go to the optimal diet with supplements. If the home can be smoke-free from the start of the fast, so much the better. Keep pure water available at all times, and give herb teas, lemon juice and water, and liquid chlorophyll during the fast. Daily aloe vera juice with liquid chlorophyll helps to clean out the releasing toxins. Kelp is important to provide minerals and detoxify the body. Use apple cider vinegar in the water bowl. Feed raw organic beets or beet juice, starting slowly and increasing gradually to one teaspoon for cats and up to two or three tablespoons for large dogs. Do this once a week at first, then more frequently to prevent too fast a detox for comfort. The cat's or dog's urine will turn red after eating beets, but this is harmless. Garlic aids detoxification and helps support the immune system. Once the pet is eating again, digestive enzymes are important; give raw thymus glandular or combination raw glandular.

Vitamins and Minerals: Feed the recommended daily supplements with additional brewer's yeast or a B-complex tablet, 10-20 mg. Additional vitamins B-9 (folic acid), B-12 (cyanocobalamine), B-1 (thiamine) and lecithin are recommended. Give sodium ascorbate Vitamin C with bioflavonoids, 500-2,000 mg or to bowel tolerance, and give a calcium/magnesium tablet once a day with the C. (These major nutrients are drained from the body by smoke.) For one week give 10,000-25,000 IU of vitamin A and 100-400 IU of vitamin E daily, then go to once a week again, adding 400-800 IU of vitamin D weekly. These, along with vitamin C, are major antioxidants. Give 5-15 mg of zinc daily, plus coenzyme Q10 and/or chromium to balance blood sugar—divide the human dose by body weight. (Zinc is the most important.) Essential fatty acids may help, as will a combination amino acids. For humans add vitamin B-3 and take B-complex in much higher doses.

Herbs: Liver- and blood-cleansing herbs remove toxins from the body. These include alfalfa, dandelion, chamomile, burdock, rosemary, clover, yellow dock and Oregon grape root. Milk thistle (silymarin) is a major liver cleanser and repairer, and helps in breaking addictions. Swedish Bitters is a liver cleanser; mix it with food or honey to make the taste tolerable to pets. Relaxants include chamomile, scullcap or valerian. Black cohosh balances blood pressure, clears the lungs and is calmative. Stevia (one to three drops on food) balances blood sugar. Comfrey, coltsfoot and/or mullein help clear the lungs of toxins. Add a drop of lobelia to other herbs if there is lung congestion. Horsetail grass replaces calcium. The most recommended of these are alfalfa, dandelion and milk thistle used together.

Homeopathy: *Ignatia* is for the cat or dog with nervous symptoms that worsen with exposure to tobacco smoke; the animal is anxious and apprehensive, and has rapid changes of mental and physical condition. There may be a dry, spasmodic cough, and muscle cramps and spasms. *Nux vomica* is for restless irritability and withdrawal symptoms; the animal does not want to be touched. *Chelidonium* is a general liver remedy; *Lobelia* clears congested lungs. A nosode of *Nicotinum* (nicotine) is available from professional homeopaths.

Acupuncture/Acupressure: In humans, the stop-smoking points are on the ears. For pets, do a full body massage, Tellington TTouch session or Reiki session at least once a week. Check the Diagnostic points and work any that the pet reacts to. Also use the Immune Stimulation sequence diagrammed in the "Acupuncture" method chapter. See the section on "Liver Dis-ease" for further points. The respiratory allergy points on the Shin Dog Chart may help; these are #14, #42, #45 and #33.[111] On the Cat Chart, use point #15 for blood cleansing.

Flower Essences: *Crab Apple*, *Allemanda* or *Tomato* essence detoxifies the liver from contaminants. *Dandelion* essence strengthens and regenerates the liver. *Salvia* supports the immune system under stress. *Cerato* is for confidence in the process, for humans and pets. *Hornbeam* strengthens; *Impatiens* is for the irritable, touchy animal; and *Scleranthus* is for the dog or cat with mood swings.

Gemstones: An elixir of *Emerald* helps to detoxify; *Botswanna Agate* or *Smoky Quartz* helps the clearing process. *Amethyst*, *Sugulite*, *Lepidolite* and *Kunzite* stabilize. *Rose Quartz*, *Turquoise* or *Chrysocolla* heals the lungs. *Apatite*, *Citrine*, *Malachite* or *Yellow Topaz* clears the liver. If using *Malachite* or *Chrysocolla* in elixir or water bowl, leave it in the water for no more than half an hour.

Shock

ชิ‐————‐ช

Shock is a veterinary emergency in which quick first aid can make the difference between life and death. A dog or cat can go into shock for a variety of reasons, including trauma or injury, poisoning, hemorrhage, severe infection, burns, heatstroke and dehydration. Being hit by a car is the most common cause in pets. There is also anaphylactic shock, a severe allergic reaction to a drug, chemical or insect bite, and post-operative or anesthesia shock. Inadequate blood circulation is the physiology of the dis-ease, and any condition affecting the heart, blood vessels or blood volume can induce it. The body's response to inadequate blood supply is to shut down. The animal shivers, experiences a drop in body temperature, and is listless, weak and depressed. The pet also has cold feet and legs, pale skin and mucous membranes (look at the gums), and a weak, hard-to-find pulse.

An animal in shock may or may not be conscious. If she is not breathing, give artificial respiration; if there is no heartbeat, give CPR (cardiopulmonary resuscitation, or heart massage). Shutdown of breathing or heartbeat are immediately life threatening. If the pet is unconscious, make sure her mouth and throat are clear and that her tongue is not blocking the air passage. Keep her head lower than her body. If the animal is bleeding, this must next be stopped, with a tourniquet if necessary; then any broken bones can be splinted. Classes in pet emergency first-aid are available from the Red Cross, and are recommended.

If the pet is conscious, let her lie or stand where she wants to—lying down may not be the most comfortable position. It is important to keep yourself and the animal calm, do the necessary first aid, then take the pet to a veterinarian. Wrap cats in a blanket or towel for transport; put larger dogs on something hard and flat, or in a blanket stretcher, then cover with a blanket. Only muzzle dogs if necessary—it impairs breathing. Never muzzle cats.[112]

The following are some holistic first aid tips that help to bring a cat or dog out of shock. Use them as soon as possible. There is no time to waste.

Nutrition: This seems irrelevant in a trauma situation, but in fact it is not. Animals on full nutrition are far less likely to go into shock after injury or trauma than pets not fed on the optimal diet. Give the natural homemade or preservative-free diet with supplements. A pet recovering from trauma also needs all possible nutritional support.

Naturopathy: Do not give solid food to an animal in shock for at least twenty-four hours. Give one teaspoon of raw honey with half a teaspoon of brandy or red wine three times daily. When the animal is completely out of shock, give goat's milk and honey, or honey and water for another day, then go back to the usual diet. Juliette de Bairacli Levy recommends elderberry wine with honey for recovery.[113] You can also add apple cider vinegar to honey and water, and place cider vinegar in the water bowl. Give liquid chlorophyll after the crisis as a restorative, and/or royal jelly or propolis with ginseng.

Vitamins and Minerals: Both Wendell Belfield and Adele Davis report that an animal or human on adequate vitamins C and B-complex is less likely to go into shock after trauma, and that these vitamins are deeply depleted by shock. A pet on a diet too low in protein is more susceptible to shock, while supplemented pets are less likely to go into anesthesia shock during surgeries.[114] Vitamins C and B-complex need to be supplemented in high amounts after trauma, shock or surgery; give a 20-50 mg B-complex supplement, or a lower amount with brewer's yeast (10-20 mg), and vitamin C to bowel tolerance—which may be very high in cases of shock. These vitamins also aid recovery from injuries, hemorrhaging, wounds and broken bones. Vitamins A, D, E and zinc speed healing; a calcium/magnesium tablet reduces pain. Give 10,000-25,000 IU of vitamin A daily for up to a week, then go to weekly supplementing; give 400-800 IU of vitamin D twice a week, going back to once weekly after the crisis. For vitamin E use 100-600 IU daily for a week or two, then decrease. Give 10-25 mg of zinc.

Herbs: A strong whiff of Camphor, Sunbreeze or Tiger Balm may help resuscitate, but it will also antidote homeopathic remedies. Use it once, then go to the homeopathics, coming back to herbs for recovery. After the crisis chamomile tea is a gentle calmative, or give valerian if the animal is upset or in pain. St. John's wort eases body pain and bruising, shepherd's purse or nettles help after blood loss (iron and vitamin K), and comfrey helps heal bruising and speeds the knitting of broken bones. Juliette de Bairacli Levy suggests elderberry tea or lemon balm. A few drops of cayenne tincture placed on the tongue may bring a pet out of shock.

Homeopathy: Make sure that camphor or other strong odors are no longer in the room before using homeopathic remedies. Used immediately and unantidoted, *Aconite* at first onset may bring the animal out of shock immediately with no further danger. Follow it with *Arnica* to limit the effects of injuries, especially after car accidents. Homeopathic *Camphor* is for collapse with diarrhea and extreme coldness. Use *Carbo veg* when breathing is impaired; there is icy coldness, blue tongue and collapse. Use *Cinchona* for fluid loss from vomiting, diarrhea, or for blood loss; the cat or dog is lethargic with weak pulse and sunken eyes. For anaphylactic shock from bee or other insect stings, give *Apis*; and *Veratrum album* is used after surgery for post-operative shock.

Acupuncture/Acupressure: See the Shock and Resuscitation chart in the Acupressure method chapter. The points on the Dog Chart are #1 (GV-26) *Jen chung*, #2 (GV-25) *Pi liang*, #8 (not given) *Erh chien* and #25 (GV-T) *Woei chien*, plus K-1. Use the point between the upper lip and the nose first and immediately. (On the Cat Chart, this is point #8.) Work the point sequence repeatedly until there is response.

Flower Essences: I have used a combination of homeopathic Arnica with *Nature's Rescue* (*Rescue Remedy*) and it revived a shock case immediately. Give Nature's Rescue every few minutes, rubbing it into the gums if the animal is unconscious. Other first aid essences are *Comfrey* and *White Lightnin'*. *Arnica* essence aids trauma and bruising. *St. John's wort* releases pain and fear; *Salvia* restores emotional stability under stress. *Rock Rose* is used for extreme fear, *Star of Bethlehem* for trauma and injury—both are in Nature's Rescue. Give *Penstemon*, *Hornbeam* or *Self-Heal* after the emergency for recovery and strength.

Gemstones: *Amethyst* and *Sugulite* stabilize the physical and unseen bodies during trauma or stress, and *Botswanna Agate* in elixir helps in healing after trauma. *Carnelian Agate* aids cell regrowth after injury. Use *Chrysocolla* or *Lapis Lazuli* as all-healers, or *Aquamarine*, *Angelite* or *Celestite* for soothing after the crisis.

Skin and Coat Ailments

The body's eliminative systems work to release toxins from the pet or human physiology. Sometimes there are just too many toxins for easy removal, or the body's removal systems are inefficient. When too many toxins are processed through the digestive system, intestinal overflow takes them back into the bloodstream. Specialized body cells called mast cells, located just below the skin, react to the blood toxins by secreting histamine. Histamine makes the blood vessels and capillaries more porous, bringing the blood flow into conjuncting tissues. The result is irritation, itching and inflammation. The dog or cat reacts by scratching, chewing and biting the irritated areas, and a skin problem develops. Scratching causes more itching and the problem escalates. The greatest number of mast cells are located around the ears and eyes, on the feet and above the tail base, and on the chest and abdomen. These are the sites of most skin allergies and skin dis-eases.[115]

Skin ailments are the number one condition that a veterinarian treats, and standard veterinary medicine has few answers. Vets see lumps and bumps under the skin, hair loss, parasites and fleas, contact dermatitis from flea collars and other sources, hay fever type allergies around the face, wet and dry rashes, and lick sores. Thyroid deficiencies and estrogen imbalances cause some skin and coat ailments, and too much cortisone and chemicals cause more. The main non-parasite source, however, is food allergies, plus the effects of chemicals and contaminants from pet foods and the environment—effects that most standard veterinarians are only beginning to recognize. Medical/veterinary remedies for the pet without fleas or parasites who still scratches are limited. There are antibiotics, antihistamines and steroids, all of which only suppress symptoms in a temporary way. Once the medication stops, the itching starts all over again and the dog or cat is back for more treatment. The holistic approach goes deeper than the skin, treating the discomfort at its source, the digestive system.

Nutrition: The natural diet, preservative-free or homemade with added supplements, is the key. Those diets were developed by veterinarian Alfred Plechner specially to treat pets with skin conditions and allergies, and they have proven successful. Along with healing skin ailments, these diets have brought increased health, emotional stability, reduced dis-ease (including those deemed chronic and "incurable") and extended pet lifespans. See the method chapter on "Nutrition" early in this book and start the additive-free diet today. Be aware of allergen foods like beef, wheat, corn and tuna; avoid cow's milk products, and be aware that your pet could be allergic to yeast. (Try a yeast-free human B-complex to see if she is.) The change of diet and addition of vitamins and minerals could be all your pet needs to stop scratching.

Naturopathy: Detoxification is central here. Begin with a few days on a liquid fast, giving laxatives, or enemas of lemon juice, or of chlorophyll and acidophilus. Start the pet on daily aloe vera juice with liquid chlorophyll (see the information in the "Naturopathy" chapter). Aloe vera juice alone or with hydrogen peroxide may be used externally. Start the optimal diet coming off the fast, and begin digestive enzymes for at least the first month on the new diet. Give a quarter teaspoon to one teaspoon of enzymes per meal, based on body size, using either those designed for cats or dogs or for humans. The trace mineral powders in the optimal diet are essential for any pet with skin problems, as is kelp, which balances the thyroid. Garlic is a detoxifier and antibiotic especially good for greasy skin. For oily skin also use the lemon rinse after baths described under Fleas. Apple cider vinegar on food or in the water bowl provides potassium. Beet juice or grated carrots cleanse the liver. The dog/cat oils are important for dry skin.

Vitamins and Minerals: The daily supplements with the optimal diet usually do the job. Many skin problems indicate specific deficiencies—especially of vitamins A, E, C or zinc—and animals on oils need more vitamin E. Chronic skin ailments like demodectic mange or seborrhea usually respond to vitamin C; rashes, eczema and hair loss are often due to vitamin E deficiencies; abscesses and sores respond to zinc; and bacterial skin eruptions, scratching and sebaceous cysts require vitamin A.[116] Give 100-400 IU daily of vitamin E, 10,000-25,000 IU of vitamin A, 5-20 mg of zinc, and 500-3,000 mg of vitamin C per day.

Pat Lazarus suggests the following vitamins and amounts for a fifty-pound dog with skin problems: vitamin C 1,000-2,000 mg, vitamin E 400 IU per day, B-complex-50 with B-12, and two tablespoons of cold-pressed vegetable oil (sunflower or sesame) per meal. Additionally, she uses two teaspoons of kelp powder, 30 mg of zinc, 50 mg selenium, and two wheat germ oil capsules per meal,[117] plus one tablespoon per day of bone meal. Vitamin E oil can be used on sores or rashes externally, and/ or vitamin C powder dusted onto irritated skin. If not feeding oils, give essential fatty acids capsules—black currant oil or evening primrose oil, amount determined by body weight.

Herbs: Blackberry tea infusion may be used on the skin for eczema, goldenseal for all skin dis-eases, and witch hazel on bites or itching sores. Comfrey infusion or tincture is an important skin healer. A classic skin remedy is to wash the affected areas with a cooled infusion of blue violet leaf and red clover—this has been effective even for skin cancers, and can also be taken internally. All of the above except witch hazel can be given internally as well. A poultice or compress of very strong green or black commercial tea is positive. For blood cleansing, use burdock with red clover, yarrow, sassafras, Oregon grape root, alfalfa or parsley internally. For eczema give nettles, meadowsweet or elder flowers with an herbal antibiotic (echinacea, Oregon grape root or goldenseal) internally.

Homeopathy: Avoid cortisones and other steroids, as they interfere with homeopathic treatment. *Sulfur* is for chronic skin conditions and dry eczema, and often works when other remedies fail; the pet prefers cool places, dislikes getting wet, has very red body orifices, and dry, hard hair and skin. Chronically thirsty pets who prefer warmth and exhibit dry skin with discharges and burning pain respond to *Arsenicum*; there may also be dry, scaly exzema with itching, inflammation and swelling. When the skin eruptions start as fluid-filled blisters that the animal bites and scratches, the remedy is *Rhus tox. Graphites* is for skin with sticky discharges, *Cantharis* for scaly eruptions with burning and itching, often around the genitals. Use *Merc sol* for wet eczema with pustular eruptions and pimples, much discharge and yellowish brown crusts.

The dog or cat is weakened by exertion and is worse at night. For skin conditions with intolerable itching, try *Mezereum*.

Dry, scaly skin with dandruff responds to *Arsenicum*, or use *Sulfur* for red skin. *Petroleum* is the remedy for cracks in the skin, especially between the toes, that bleed easily. *Cortisone* may be used in homeopathic preparation (not the drug) for stubborn skin inflammations. For cats with miliary eczema and alopecia (baldness), a dis-ease that appears after neutering, *Staphisagria* is the first remedy to try—particularly for the animal who is angry about the surgery; the cat shows scabby bumps, often on the neck or along the backbone, but they can appear all over. If these do not heal the skin, try homeopathic hormone replacement—potentized *Ovarinum* and *Folliculinum* in females, or *Testosterone* in males.

Cell salts may also be used, the following are in 6X potency and should be given twice a day for a few weeks. (They work long-term, but I still prefer full-potency remedies.) Alternate *Ferrum phos* with *Natrum phos* if the pet is irritable and upset. For a nervous animal with greasy hair, odor and itching, try *Kali phos*. For the animal with greasy, oily skin that is irritated and itchy, try *Natrum mur* and check the pet for thyroid imbalance. *Silica* is for the cat or dog with pimples, pus-like discharges, eruptions around the nails, or bumps under the skin. The animal is oversensitive and irritable, and the problems may have begun after vaccination. If a pet has hair loss and poor nutritional background, try *Calc phos* and use the optimal diet.[118]

Acupuncture/Acupressure: Klide and Kung describe a seven-year-old Kerry Blue Terrier with pustular dermatitis, skin thickening and hair loss lasting over a year's time. The dog had been treated by standard veterinary methods with no improvement. Acupuncture (points not given) resulted in "remarkable changes in skin within four treatments."[119] The Shin Dog Chart lists no specific points for skin and coat dis-eases. The Cat Chart gives two points, #5 for dermatitis, itching and constipation, #15 for blood cleansing.

Flower Essences: Give yellow and purple *Allemanda* together for cleansing and hair loss. *Bottlebrush Tree* cleanses the intestines and *Red Ixora* the blood. *Yellow Hibiscus* counteracts the chemicals and toxins in pet foods. *Tomato* is for throwing off toxins, and *Crab Apple* is for general cleansing and detoxifying.

Gemstones: *Bloodstone, Malachite* or *Emerald* in elixir detoxifies. The light blue stones (*Celestite, Aquamarine, Turquoise, Chrysocolla*) soothe, and pink and rose stones (*Rose Quartz, Kunzite, Pink Tourmaline, Lepidolite*) are for the skin. *Amethyst* is a calmative. Natural *Citrine* clears toxins from the digestive system.

Spaying and Neutering

In 1992 the Humane Societies put to death ten million dogs and cats; for all the shelters in the United States, the number reached thirty-seven million. These are horrifying, heartbreaking figures, and responsible pet owners have no business contributing to such suffering. There is no excuse for not having your pet spayed or neutered, simple surgeries performed by all veterinarians with few complications. Where cost is a factor, there are spay and neuter clinics in most cities, and most animal shelters offer low cost—sometimes free—services.

If you want an additional pet, look to shelters instead of breeding. Lots of purebred animals turn up at shelters, too, and the fact that a pet is purebred is no reason to refuse spaying or neutering. There are too many puppies, kittens and older pets in the shelters, needing homes.

A spayed or neutered pet is happier. She does not have the drive to breed, but may still enjoy sexual play. With males there is less roaming and fighting, and no spraying in the house; a neutered male cat or dog makes a gentler, less aggressive pet. Male dogs are still protective of their guardians. Females show no changes whatever, other than they don't become pregnant or go into heat and attract packs of male dogs. Neutered or spayed pets gain weight and get soft only when guardians overfeed and underexercise them. They do not die of uterine, breast or testicular cancer as intact animals do; they do not develop uterine infections, or die giving birth or during often violent mating rituals. The surgery does not change the animal's personality in any way.

There are varied opinions as to when to do the procedure. Most experts suggest waiting until about six months old, either before or right after the first heat for females. For males, waiting until puberty is considered best, although some sources suggest neutering young before the sex urges develop. (Some shelters and vets are experimenting with very early spay/neuters, doing the surgery on even very young puppies, eight weeks old, before adoption.) In male cats, the time of maturity is when the animal's urine suddenly becomes very strong-smelling; do it soon, before he begins to spray.

The following information is to support your dog or cat through the surgery and recovery process. Please have your pet spayed or neutered.

Nutrition: Giving your puppy or kitten the preservative-free or natural homemade diet with supplements is the best way to maintain full health and to offer a rapid recovery after surgery. Pets who are regularly fed supplements recover faster and have less trauma, while malnourished ones develop complications and postoperative or anesthetic shock. Feed a diet higher than usual in protein for a few days, or even a week, before the surgery.

Naturopathy: When your pet comes home, a day or two on a liquid diet is positive. Give broth with tamari or soy sauce in it, and lots of garlic; give honey and water or honey, cider vinegar, and water. These rebalance electrolytes and blood sugar. Dissolve the pet's vitamins in the liquids,[120] but do not give whole pills to an animal who is not eating solid food. After the fast, feed a high protein diet again for at least a week or ten days. Once the pet is eating again, give digestive enzymes to aid assimilation of nutrients. Put apple cider vinegar in the water bowl or on food to speed healing, and give bee products and liquid chlorophyll. Unless the pet becomes constipated, withhold aloe vera juice for about a week after surgery. Continue feeding lots of garlic.

Vitamins and Minerals: Vitamins C, A, E and zinc speed healing. For a few days before the surgery increase the pet's daily amounts of these, giving vitamin C to bowel tolerance (500-2,000 mg); vitamin A with D (10,000-25,000 IU of A with 400-800 IU of D) every day for a few days (instead of weekly); vitamin E (100-600 IU) per day; 5-20 mg of zinc; and a B-complex tablet (10-25 mg) with additional B-5 (pantothenic acid) and B-6 (pyridoxine). With the last meal before the pre-surgery fast, give all of these plus a calcium/magnesium tablet. For the first few days after surgery, dissolve the vitamins into liquids; then begin to place them on food. Return to weekly for the vitamins A and D, decrease the vitamin E after a week, decrease the other vitamins after ten days, and go back to the normal supplements. Surgery depletes the B-vitamins and digestive enzymes, so these may need to be supplemented, in increased amounts over a slightly longer period of time; in this case, keep up the vitamin C (to bowel tolerance).[121]

Herbs: If the stitches develop soreness, start the pet on echinacea internally and dab the incision twice daily with a tincture-soaked cotton ball. Once you have started echinacea, keep the animal on it for ten days, even though symptoms will disappear much sooner. Use this also if the animal is tearing at the stitches; keep her from doing so for at least the first week after surgery. If the incision is clean and remains so, or becomes clean and pink after using echinacea, change the external lotion to soothing calendula tincture for rapid healing. (Vitamin E oil can also be used.) Comfrey is an internal and external healer. Chamomile is soothing and calming, and helps to cleanse the liver of all remaining anesthetic. Use it too if there are digestive upsets.

Homeopathy: *Arnica* may be given for a few days before the surgery and a few days after in decreasing frequency to prevent hemorrhaging and bruising, and speed healing. *Hypericum* helps to repair tissue injury after the procedure. If there has been undue fear, stress or shock, give a dose of *Aconite*; usually only one dose is needed, if any at all. The *Calendula* described above is both herbal and a homeopathic remedy. Give one dose of *Staphisagria* if the pet is angry about the surgery.

Acupuncture/Acupressure: Acupuncture has been described as a means of anesthesia for spaying, but needs to be done by a professional. There are no points listed on the Shin Dog Chart or Ottaviano Cat Chart for surgical recovery. Use the Immune Stimulation Chart, working gently, once or for a few days. The animal may not even need this.

Flower Essences: Give *Nature's Rescue (Rescue Remedy)* for a few days before the surgery, or *Arnica, Penstemon, Celery* or *Salvia* essences. *Self-Heal* aids recovery. *Clematis* helps the pet that remains "out of it" from anesthesia. Give *Olive* for exhaustion. If the incision seems to take a long time to heal, give *Agrimony*. Give *Crab Apple, Yellow Hibiscus* (Aura Essence) or *Purple Allemanda* (Aura Cleansing Essence) to clear the anesthetic. If there is gas or vomiting, give *Chamomile* essence (or chamomile tea). Use the pendulum to test for what is needed.

Gemstones: *Lapis Lazuli* is an all-healer, and *Chrysocolla* heals internally and after surgery.

Spinal Problems and Paralysis

Spinal disc problems, spinal cord injuries and arthritis of the spine (spondylosis) are more frequent in dogs than in cats, and most frequent in aging dogs. These and a condition called spinal myelopathy result in any number of pets being euthanized or put through extensive speculative surgeries. The veterinary/medical system has no answers. Dachshunds, beagles, Pekinese, mixed breeds, and any dogs with long, low backs and short legs frequently develop ruptured or herniated discs. Degenerative spinal dis-ease, or spinal myelopathy, seems to occur more often in large breed dogs, especially German shepherds and Dobermans. In cats, there may also be disc problems or spinal arthritis, but less frequently. Cat spinal dis-ease is most often from injuries: If a cat climbs under the hood of a car, she may be caught in the fan blades when the car is started. Cats may also have their tails run over. Spinal cord infections are another common diagnosis.

Disc problems can happen suddenly or slowly. The animal sits hunched up and may be weak or lame, with a wobbly gait and a lack of coordination. There may be limp paralysis in one or more legs, urinary retention, or bladder or bowel incontinence. Where the injury is in the lower vertebrae, the animal's tail may be paralyzed. A dog or cat with neck involvement or a herniated cervical disc may carry her head high and rigid, be unable to lower her head, or hold herself so her neck looks shortened. In spinal myelopathy, there is progressive lack of control over the rear leg muscles; the hind end sways, paws drag, and the animal has poor appetite and evident pain. There may also be fever with spinal myelopathy. Holistic methods offer hope for these animals, particularly when the dis-ease can be treated early. First get a diagnosis, then locate a veterinary acupuncturist, chiropractor or homeopath (or a human practitioner willing to work with animals), and a holistic veterinarian. More information is given below.

Nutrition: Prevention is always better than trying to heal a manifested dis-ease; the optimal diet with supplements keeps the bones, discs and muscles strong. If an animal is injured, the natural diet hastens healing. Vitamin B-12 deficiency is one suspected cause of spinal degeneration. Although most of these conditions are caused by injuries or heredity, never underestimate the value of high nutrition, both in the prevention and resolution of any dis-ease.

Naturopathy: The major healing methods for spinal dis-ease are vitamins and acupuncture, but Juliette de Bairacli Levy also recommends mustard plasters. This is an infusion of mustard seed or powder, one teaspoon per cup of boiled water. Apply hot (but not burning hot) to the animal's hindquarters and other affected areas. Mustard plasters may also be made by placing the hot herb between two pieces of washcloth, then applying. An alternative compress is castor oil, which has been known to work real miracles for humans. (Keep the animal from licking it, however, as it is laxative.) Kelp in the diet and digestive enzymes are important.

Vitamins and Minerals: Says Wendell Belfield, DVM, "Over the years I have handled about thirty cases of spinal degeneration and managed, with vitamin C, to heal about twenty-five of them."[122] This is an astounding statement, given the current veterinary no-hope record for dis-eases of the spine. His protocol starts with about three days of intravenous vitamin C, followed by high amounts of C at home with vitamin-mineral supplements. (With just oral C, the healing happens, but takes longer.) He describes one case of turnaround in two weeks—it may take more. The animal must remain on very high doses of the vitamin, or the symptoms will recur. Supplement with sodium ascorbate C to bowel tolerance; this may require more than six grams per day, and time of response varies. Pat Lazarus also recommends adding vitamin E (400-600 IU), trace minerals and manganese to the above. Give these supplements with the optimal diet. Feed SOD, as well.

Herbs: For dogs with disc dis-ease, Juliette de Bairacli Levy recommends sage infusions and cayenne pepper capsules (averaging two capsules twice a day for a medium-sized dog) to increase circulation.[123] She describes several successes using these plus the mustard treatment above and organic grape juice. Comfrey, St. John's wort or scullcap repair the nervous system and ease pain. Valerian, scullcap or feverfew are pain relievers and relaxants; white willow is an anti-inflammatory that should be used on dogs only. Alfalfa is an important nutrient, and horsetail grass adds minerals.

Homeopathy: Start with *Nux vomica* for pain, tightness and hindquarter symptoms. If the pet's back suddenly goes out, give *Arnica* initially every two hours. If the animal is sensitive to cold and the spine sensitive to touch, try *Hypericum* both internally and as an external compress. (Use the herb tincture.) If the symptoms worsen in damp weather or seem to improve after the dog or cat starts moving, the remedy is *Rhus tox*. If symptoms get worse with movement, use *Bryonia*; the animal has a staggering gait, wants to be alone, and may bite or howl. *Conium maculatum* is for rear end paralysis; there is stiffness, difficult gait, trembling, loss of strength, and weakness, especially in older animals.

For motor paralysis affecting a front or hind limb, try *Lathrys*; there is a rigid, spastic gait, tottering, and the knees may knock together when walking; a limb hanging down may be swollen or look emaciated. *Gelsemium* may be the remedy in mild cases, where the cat or dog is lethargic. *Plumbum* may help in motor paralysis of the lower limbs; there are cramps and twitching, with the animal in evident pain; the paws are cold and symptoms are worse at night and with motion. Light pressure eases pain. *Silica* in 200C potency may help a lean or undernourished pet with hardening of the nerve sheaths. If motor paralysis is persistent despite homeopathy, Dr. Gloria Dodd suggests considering a diagnosis of pesticide poisoning (especially Malathion or methyl carbamate) and/ or Rabies vaccination toxicity as the cause. Try nosodes of these. See the information in the "Vaccination/Vaccinosis" chapter.

For a slipped disc, *Ruta grav* is used for injuries affecting bone and cartilage, and for vertebrae disorders. It can be used along with *Hypericum* as a pain reliever, particularly when the problem is in the lower spine. If the slipped disc resulted from an injury, start with *Arnica* then go to *Symphytum* (comfrey), or alternate the two. *Augustura vera* is used for nerve damage and spinal cord injuries; it may limit nerve damage from a protruding disc, symptoms of which include stiffness of muscles and joints, paralysis, great difficulty in walking, and pain worsening with pressure; there may be twitching or jerking along the back, or the animal bending backwards and displaying hypersensitivity. For disc injuries and protrusions, Gloria Dodd uses *Ruta* and *Hypericum* together in 10M potency, one to three times daily.

Acupuncture/Acupressure: See an experienced acupuncturist here, as this method has developed its reputation around healing spinal injuries and paralysis considered incurable by standard veterinary means. A variety of points on both charts are for paralysis of various areas of the body. For sciatica, posterior paralysis and all nervous system disorders, use points #20 (GV-20B) *Pai hui,* and #21 (BL-31) *Erh yen.* For posterior paralysis and paralysis of the tail, the points are #22 (GV-2) *Wei ken,* # 23 (GV-1.2) *Wei chieh* and #24 (GV-1.1) *Woei kan.* Shoulder, elbow or foreleg paralysis respond to #40-47. Hind limb paralysis, posterior paralysis and sciatica are needled at #54 (GB-30) *Huan tiao* and #58 (GV-34) *Hou san li.*

The Cat Chart lists points #1, #2 and #5 for front leg paralysis; #12, #13 and #14 for cervical (neck) problems; and #16 for thoracic-lumbar pain. For the hind legs, use points #17-20 for lumbo-sacral and hip pain. Hind-leg paralysis responds to #21, #22, #25 and #26. Lumbar pain takes point #24. Use points #21 and #26 for the lower limbs.

Klide and Kung's *Veterinary Acupuncture* describes several pages of spinal and paralysis healings. For disc problems, they suggest locating the abnormal disc and using needles on the points above and below it. For paralysis in dogs caused by age, they suggest the following points: GV-19, GB-34 and GB-37.[124] See a veterinary acupuncturist as early in the course of the dis-ease as possible.

Flower Essences: Use *Nature's Rescue (Rescue Remedy), Rock Rose* for extreme fear, and *Star of Bethlehem* for serious injury. The last two are also in *Nature's Rescue. Grapefruit* essence is for injuries caused by falls. *Comfrey* flower is a nerve regenerator and first aid essence, and *Self-Heal* releases fear and pain. *Scullcap* helps to heal the nervous system. *Penstemon* or *Hornbeam* gives strength under adverse circumstances. Add *Arnica* essence for injury. *Olive* is for the exhausted, ill or traumatized animal; *Borage* and *Cucumber* aid depression, as does *Pandora Vine* (Hope Essence).

Gemstones: *Chrysocolla* or *Lapis Lazuli* is an all-healer. *Amethyst* is a calmative and nervous system regenerator. Pink, blue or purple *Kunzite, Lepidolite, Boji Stone* or *Amethyst* eases pain. Program a clear *Quartz Crystal* or crystal cluster for the animal's healing; focus your intent on the stone, directing it to heal your pet. Find the most willing stone by pendulum testing.

Stress

Today's pets—and people—are under constant physiological and emotional stress. The city cat or dog does not live a normal life. They live a life that their instincts cannot cope with. Pets receive little exercise, are isolated from their normal social groups, are vaccinated with chemicals that confuse the body, and eat what their guardians bring home in a bag rather than fresh-caught prey. If an animal needs an herb for her digestion or healing, that herb is likely not available. There is probably no way to have completely clean food, water and air, no matter how carefully the guardian may try to provide it. Environmental poisoning is inevitable—from automobile exhaust, from food grown or manufactured with toxic chemicals, from water that receives the runoff from industrial wastes and chemical-laden agricultural fields. Living on a polluted, toxic planet, the human and animal body is faced with stresses no organism was ever meant to endure.

Pets are also subject to high emotional stress. Their lives are entwined with people's—something foreign in the wild and foreign to their inborn instincts. Dogs and cats depend totally on a guardian. In this pressured society a guardian may not always be there for them. If their person is impatient, or not home much, or unwilling to play, the animal is all alone. When their person is stressed, pets take it on—they have no idea how their guardian's fear or pain may change or threaten their own lives.

Animals are surrounded by sensory input humans cannot perceive, and these can be overwhelming also. Any change in routine or daily life means stress to a dog or cat, and while dogs may welcome new experiences, cats do not. Immune system dis-eases, unheard of fifty years ago, are taking their toll on pet and human lives; and these dis-eases are primarily stress related. It is estimated that eighty-five percent or more of human illness is caused by stress, and that figure increasingly carries over for pets. The information in this section will help bolster an animal's ability to handle stress and its effects, to detoxify the poisons, and to live a longer life.

Nutrition: Feed the preservative-free or natural homemade diet and don't forget the supplements. Brewer's yeast is highly important, and the trace minerals (calcium/magnesium, chromium) are relaxants. Watch for allergenic foods and remove them from the diet, particularly milk products and beef. Give high quality protein in the diet, including organic liver once a week, dark-green vegetables, whole grains such as oats and barley, and wheat germ. All of the daily supplements are needed.

Naturopathy: Digestive enzymes in the daily diet aid food absorption, and fasting one day per week helps to tone and rest the digestive system. Aloe vera juice with liquid chlorophyll promotes the quick removal of toxins from the body and prevents constipation; chlorophyll is also an energy strengthener. To reduce stress and build the immune system, give raw honey, bee pollen and other bee products, they are also calmative. Garlic is an internal antiseptic and immune builder, and kelp provides iodine and minerals for thyroid balance. Put apple cider vinegar on food or in the water bowl to provide potassium and minerals, as well as for electrolyte balancing. All of these support the body under stress.

Vitamins and Minerals: If not feeding brewer's yeast, give a yeast-free human B-complex tablet of 10-20 mg daily, with 10 mg additional vitamins B-2 (riboflavin), B-6 (pyridoxine) and B-5 (pantothenic acid). Give vitamin C to bowel tolerance or at least 1,000 mg per day—Anitra Frazier suggests 250 mg of sodium ascorbate powder in food three or four times daily for cats, with larger dogs taking much more.[125] These are the most essential vitamins. In addition give 100-600 IU of vitamin E daily for two weeks, then decrease to once or twice a week. Vitamin A (10,000-25,000 IU) may be used daily for a while, then go back to weekly doses of A with 400-800 IU of D, depending on pet size. Where the animal is highly nervous or exposed to chemical contaminants, give a complete calcium/magnesium tablet daily (if not supplementing the trace mineral powders), Vita-Mineral Mix, or Dog/Cat Powder. Zinc 5-10 mg, half a teaspoon to two tablespoons of lecithin in food, raw adrenal and raw thymus glandular, and combination amino acids or liver extract are positive, as are chromium (in the trace minerals powder) and essential fatty acids.

Herbs: Ginseng with royal jelly in very small amounts is a good combination for stabilizing and energizing. Ginseng is an adaptogen herb, aiding the body to tolerate stress. Alfalfa is a calmative and all-nutrient, good with any other herb. Horsetail grass or oatstraw adds calcium and silica. Several herbs are stress reducers, including oatstraw, hawthorn, motherwort, chamomile, rosemary, sage, passionflower, scullcap and valerian. Lemon balm or vervain are mood raisers and relaxants. St. John's wort or valerian root are sedatives. Stevia and liquid chlorophyll balance blood sugar.

Homeopathy: For the stressed pet that is irritable and weak, with constipation and loss of appetite, try *Nux vomica*; alternate with *Carbo veg* for the animal off her feed. *Ignatia* is for the sensitive, nervous pet who is worse in the mornings and in the open air. Give *Pulsatilla* to a light-colored animal; she is clinging and has changeable moods. For the cat or dog who is high-strung and overexcitable and may be destructive when left alone, give *Scutellaria* (scullcap). *Mag carb* is for the animal whose overwrought nervousness has run her down. Give *Strychninum* for nervous exhaustion. *Aconite* is for the frightened animal, *Arsenicum* for the restless one who paces back and forth. Cell salt *Kali phos* may be given twice a day for a few weeks, or combination cell salts *Bioplasma*, or *Calmes Forte*. (These come in 6X or 12X potencies.)

Acupuncture/Acupressure: An all-over body massage done nightly or weekly does wonders for both pet and person. Don't forget the ears. With the massage do a Tellington TTouch session, or some Reiki. Check the Diagnostic points, releasing any that are tender, and work the Immune Stimulation sequence (maps for these are located in the Acupuncture method chapter). On the Shin Dog Chart, point #20 (GV-20B) *Pai hui* is for nervous disorders and #28 (P-1) *Shin yu* relieves mental stress. On the Ottaviano Cat Chart, point #22 is a general tonic.

Flower Essences: Give *Nature's Rescue* (*Rescue Remedy*) as needed, or put it in the water bowl of an animal under stress. *Water Violet* is a good cat remedy. Use *Aspen* for the cat that hides. *Walnut* eases any changes in the home; *Vervain* is for high-strung pets. Give *Chamomile* essence for tension, stress and nervous indigestion, or *Dandelion* as a muscular relaxant. *Bottlebrush* is for exhaustion. Comfort Essences I and II are for stress (*Lisianthus* and *Lagerfield Rose*), as is Transcendence Essence (*Princess Tree*).

Gemstones: Place a large *Amethyst* cluster in the pet's environment, and additional pieces in the water bowl, on her collar and where she sleeps. Make sure these are cleared frequently. Other stress-reducing gemstones include *Rose Quartz*, *Lepidolite*, *Kunzite*, *Black Tourmaline* or *Angelite*.

Urinary Tract Infections and Kidney Dis-ease

Urinary bladder infections, known as cystitis, are the number one killer of cats. In cats the infection is known as FUS (Feline Urologic Syndrome). In dogs, it is both less usual and far less serious. It is caused by magnesium and phosphorus crystals in the urine that irritate the bladder and urethra. The first symptoms are of frequency, running back and forth to the litter box, or in and out of the house. The animal strains and may void a few drops, but it is itching and burning, rather than fullness, that makes her think she needs to go. There may be traces of blood in the urine.

A pet who suddenly starts wetting indoors, or missing the litter box, likely has a urinary-tract infection and should be checked immediately. Untreated, the swelling in the urethra may close the tube that connects the bladder to the outside of the body; the animal strains and is in great distress, but nothing voids. This is an immediate emergency; take her to a veterinarian (or a veterinary emergency center after hours) for catheterization, or death results.

Some pets, usually male cats, exhibit a chronic form of this syndrome. They seem to always either have a urinary infection, or be getting over one. All evidence for the cause of these infections points to dry foods, commercial foods and the kind of alkaline system (acid is normal) that results from poor-quality diet and the availability of food between meals. Urine with normal acidity dissolves the crystals, preventing the dis-ease.

While veterinarians look for bacteria in the urine and feed low ash diets, Dr. Richard Pitcairn believes that these are not significant factors and that the usual recommendation to moisten dry food and add salt to the diet to increase water consumption is ineffective. Says Dr. Pitcairn:

> Almost invariably the first attack follows a history of feeding dry commercial foods for a long period of time. I've found that the condition is very responsive to diet changes and natural therapies, resulting in a stable cure rather than a temporary alleviation. [126]

Nutrition: Feed a diet completely free of additives and preservatives, go to home cooking, or use the canned natural diets. Avoid allergenic foods, particularly beef and tuna for cats. The diet for FUS or kidney dis-ease is a low-protein one, but the protein is high quality; use lamb, rabbit, turkey or chicken, rice, whole grains, squash, carrots, broccoli, other vegetables and egg yolks. [127] Give no organ meats for a month, no yeast, and add a bit of tamari soy sauce to the food. Prepared foods should have a phosphorus content no greater than .5. (Read the company literature.) Feed two meals per day, leaving no food available between feedings.

Naturopathy: During an attack, fast the animal on a high-nutrient broth, adding a few drops of tamari soy sauce. Put lots of garlic in the soup, and begin the vitamin C protocol described below. If the animal is on antibiotics, give a half teaspoon of liquid acidophilus in meals for two weeks; if there is diarrhea, give slippery elm syrup before meals and a quarter teaspoon of apple pectin on the food. [128] After the fast when the animal is on preservative-free food, give digestive enzymes. For pets with kidney dis-ease, add one half to one teaspoon of sesame oil daily, and raw kidney glandulars. Give one-quarter teaspoon of cod liver oil to cats daily, more for larger dogs according to weight. Delete the yeast from the Vita-Mineral Mix or Cat/Dog Powders, as some urinary infections are worsened by it. Feed one raw egg yolk daily during attacks, and three times weekly after. Cider vinegar in the water bowl or on food is positive; it acidifies the system. Honey with barley water soothes, and chopped parsley is diuretic. For older female dogs who dribble, put a teaspoon of wheat germ oil daily into the food.

Vitamins and Minerals: Vitamin C is essential. Anitra Frazier suggests at the first sign of urinary infection, withholding solid food and giving 500 mg vitamin C in a teaspoon of chicken broth, plus 100 IU of vitamin E. During an attack, along with veterinary care give 250 mg of C three or four times daily, 10 mg B-complex twice a day, 100 IU of vitamin E daily for a month (then decrease to 400 IU once a week), plus one-quarter teaspoon of cod liver oil, or 10,000 IU of vitamin A with 400 IU of vitamin D. After attacks, continue vitamin C in broth or food, (500 mg per day divided into two meals), and vitamins E, A and D weekly.[129] Frazier's information on diet, supplements, care and medication is highly recommended.

Richard Pitcairn offers the same protocol for cats and adds the following recommendations for bladder infections, and kidney or bladder stones, in dogs: Give cod liver oil or 5,000 IU of vitamin A daily for cats and small dogs; 5,000-10,000 IU for medium dogs; and 10,000-20,000 IU for large dogs. Use vitamin C twice daily, 500 mg per day for cats and small dogs; 1,000 mg daily for medium-size dogs; and 500 mg three times per day for large dogs. Instead of yeast in the diet, give a 10 mg B-complex tablet for cats and small dogs, and 20 mg for larger ones. Where there are kidney stones in dogs, add 50-300 mg of magnesium, depending on the size. [130]

Wendell Belfield uses vitamin C, 500-8,000 mg per day, to bowel tolerance, to dissolve kidney stones in cats and dogs. For interstitial nephritis and kidney degeneration, use high amounts of C, A and E. For cats with FUS, he uses a catheter douche of twenty-five percent sodium ascorbate C solution, followed by a change in diet with a multiple vitamin-mineral supplement and 1,000-1,250 mg of vitamin C per day spread over two meals. Serious cases of FUS take as long as six months to heal completely and stop returning.[131] The supplements can prevent recurrences, veterinary drugs, catheterizations, surgeries, even death. When attacks are over, the vitamin C must still be continued daily or they will return.

Herbs: At first sign of bladder infection, replace a third of the pet's drinking water with unsweetened (health food store) cranberry juice.

This can stop many urologic infections quickly and completely; like vitamin C it acidifies the urine and makes the bladder and urinary tract inhospitable to infection bacteria. I have seen it work with both people and dogs. Herbs for urinary tract infections include juniper, buchu, couchgrass (crabgrass), cornsilk, parsley, marshmallow (mallow) root, nettles, dandelion, watercress, uva ursi (bearberry) or yarrow. Bearberry, sage and horsetail grass, used together, are highly effective, as is parsley or nettles.

For cats with chronic FUS, give a strong infusion of horsetail grass, two teaspoons of the herb in half a cup of hot water. Give one-quarter teaspoon of the infusion three times a day for a week or more. For animals with kidney or bladder stones use barberry root, making an infusion of one teaspoon of the root in a cup of water; let steep five minutes then strain. Give three times a day—one teaspoon for cats and small dogs, two teaspoons for a medium-small dog, one tablespoon for a medium-sized dog, two tablespoons for a large dog, and three tablespoons for the giant breeds. Dr. Pitcairn suggests sarsaparilla root where there are small stones and gravel in the urine; make as for barberry, but use double the herb amount.[132] Where there is infection rather than mineral crystals in the urine, herbal antibiotics include echinacea, goldenseal and pau d'arco.

Homeopathy: For urinary obstruction and inability to urinate due to stones, try *Thalaspi bursa pastoris* as emergency first aid. Dose every half hour until the animal urinates; if there is no relief within two or three hours, see a veterinarian immediately. Give *Aconite* also, for distress and fear. For urinary infection without blockage give *Cantharis*; there is frequently, little flow with possibly blood in the urine; and high anxiety, even crying. *Urtica urens* is for the dog or cat with urinary infection who seeks warmth and solitude, and is reluctant to move; there may be blood in the urine. *Apis* is for the animal who refuses warmth; the urine is without blood, but highly concentrated and odorous, and passed in small amounts. Give *Rhus tox* for the animal who develops infections from sitting on cold cement and getting chilled; once sick, she prefers warmth and wants to be touched, is restless and moves frequently, and her urine is scanty but dark, and may contain blood. Again, use *Aconite* if the animal is distressed. *Pulsatilla* may be used for affectionate cats or dogs with FUS.

When FUS is chronic, or after the acute and inflammatory stages mentioned above, try *Equisetum* (horsetail grass); the animal urinates frequently (with little straining), especially at night, and is still uncomfortable even after the inflammation clears. *Eupatorium* is for chronic urinary "gravel" and high albumen content. Where the bladder has thickened and urine has sediment and an ammonia smell, the remedy is *Pareira brava.* There is constant urging, much straining, and thick, dark or bloody urine. *Causticum* can follow *Cantharis* when urinary infections recur or become chronic. This especially benefits the older animal.

Veterinarian Gloria Dodd treats feline urologic syndrome as follows:

> I use the combination homeopathics: *Cantharis* 6X (for painful burning sensation), *Belladonna* 6X (antispasmodic to the urethra and bladder sphincter), *Cuprum metallicum* 50M (very strong antispasmodic . . .), *Berberis vulgaris* 6X (because most cases of cystitis are associated with liver and kidney disfunctions) and *Hydrastis* 6X (lymph drainer of all epithelial lined organs). If there is blood I add *Ferrum phos* 6X. For kidney or urinary bladder stone problems I add liver supportive treatments, for the liver pathology is the basic source of the stone formation in the urinary tract. Again the stone formation is due to a liver toxic with drugs, chemicals and vaccination effects.[133]

Kidney problems (chronic nephritis) in older dogs is a cause of many early dog deaths. Use *Mercurius solubilis* (*Merc Sol*) and follow the animal's reactions. If there is blood in the urine, try *Cantharis.*

Acupuncture/Acupressure: Start with the point for mental stress, #28 (P-1) *Shin yu.* For urinary disorders and nephritis, use #17 (GV-4) *Ming men,* and #33 (BL-23) *Shen yu.* Use point #37 (GB-26) *Pung kung yu* for cystitis, urine retention and blood in the urine. The Ottaviano Cat Chart uses points #16 and #26 for urinary and kidney problems, #23 for urinary infections.

Klide and Kung's *Veterinary Acupuncture* describes treatment of a male cat with stones blocking the urinary outlet. He had been catheterized several times in quick succession, with the blockage still recurring. A total of four acupuncture sessions a week apart were used, focusing on BL-38, BL-40 and BL-41. The cat responded immediately to the treatments, requiring no further medication or catheterization after the first session.[134]

Flower Essences: Give *Nature's Rescue* (*Rescue Remedy*) from beginning to end. *Mimulus* is for fears, *Star of Bethlehem* for shock, *Hornbeam* for fatigue and courage, and *Gorse* to aid hopelessness. *Olive* is for the pet who is exhausted, ill and traumatized. *Salvia* is for stability under stress.

Gemstones: Put a piece of *Citrine* in the pet's bed, on her collar, or even in a corner of the litter box. Use a natural citrine if possible and/or make an elixir of it. Other yellow or amber stones that may soothe and help the bladder and kidneys include *Amber Calcite, Amber* or *Yellow Beryl. Jade* is a traditional stone for kidney and bladder healing.

Vaccination/Vaccinosis

By faithfully giving pets their annual vaccinations, guardians believe they are doing their best to help the animals stay healthy. Unfortunately, this is not the case. Evidence is mounting that vaccinations do harm, and often do not give the protection the veterinary system claims. Vaccinations are an increasingly expensive yearly routine designed to line the pockets of veterinarians. Governments have stepped in also, making rabies vaccinations, at least, mandatory in most states—and also requiring the vaccine be given more often than is safe or necessary.

Vaccines are not always effective, and it is not uncommon for animals to develop the dis-eases they have been vaccinated against. A stressed animal, or one who is ill or has a weakened immune system, may not develop the antibodies the vaccines are supposed to produce. The pet develops the dis-ease, and the standard vet makes excuses or gives the dis-ease another name. Too many dogs develop distemper and too many cats develop feline leukemia after vaccination; many die. Both cats and dogs develop varying levels of other illnesses, as well.

Another result of vaccination is that the immune system, weakened and confused by the number of antigens it has been hit with all at once, goes awry, and any number of new dis-eases may result. Says holistic veterinarian John Fudens in the September-October 1992 issue of *Tiger Tribe*:

> Every skin problem you see is due to vaccinations without fail. Later on in life, arthritic situations and degenerative spinal dis-eases are the result of vaccinations. And I am convinced that FUS in cats is also vaccination-related.

> The rabies vaccination in dogs and cats causes so many problems it isn't funny. It causes personality changes, skin changes, damages the thyroid and endocrine systems. It lowers the immune system tremendously, and after that, of course, the animal becomes fair game for just about any dis-ease.[135]

A frequent vaccination reaction is the return of a previously healed dis-ease or skin problem. Another typical vaccinosis symptom is tumors, sometimes appearing rapidly and all at once all over the animal's body. Homeopaths have long been aware of these reactions in animals and humans, and homeopathy is the best way to deal with them.

But few standard veterinarians will make the connection between a dog's or cat's chronic long-term dis-ease and vaccinations. Long-term immune dysfunction (autoimmune) dis-eases include asthma, arthritis, allergic dermatitis, warts, tumors, gum dis-ease, and irritable bowel syndrome.[136] Richard Pitcairn states that in homeopathic healings, the symptoms of vaccinosis often appear and are released, with the animal making rapid healing gains afterwards.[137] Watch for the cat or dog who after vaccination becomes sicker with whatever dis-ease she has, or who gets sick directly after the injections.

Vaccinations are required any time a pet is boarded, and in many states when she is licensed. They offer the only protection available for some very deadly pet dis-eases. Or do they? What are the alternatives, and what can a pet guardian do to protect her dog or cat from vaccinosis? Here are a few suggestions.

1. Only vaccinate healthy animals. If a pet has just been wormed, is pregnant, sick, going into surgery or receiving steroids, wait. If an animal has just recovered from a dis-ease, give her at least sixty days to recover before vaccinating. Include deworming in the list.

2. Do not vaccinate for several dis-eases at once or give rabies with other vaccinations; separating them is more expensive, but makes less problems later.

3. Insist on killed-virus, rather than modified live, vaccines.

4. Never vaccinate for feline leukemia. Too many cats develop the dis-ease from the vaccination that would not have otherwise.[138]

5. Only vaccinate for dis-eases currently prevalent in your area, a few dis-eases, not several. (Horse vaccinations are routinely handled this way.)

6. Repeat vaccinations infrequently. [139]

Dr. Gloria Dodd states that rabies vaccinations are the most destructive, and that indoor cats and dogs have no need for them at all. The vaccine was not meant to be given annually. She relates brain disorders and chronic degenerative dis-eases, including paralysis in German Shepherds, to rabies vaccination. If the vaccine is administered, it must be the killed-virus form.

Dr. Richard Pitcairn gives instructions for vaccinating dogs and cats. For dogs, rabies vaccinations are required by law but should be done only every two years, with the first vaccine not given earlier than four months of age. (From personal experience, I believe four months is still too young and recommend no earlier than six months.) Distemper and hepatitis shots are given at eight and twelve weeks, with a booster in one year. After that, give a distemper vaccination every three years; no further hepatitis shots are needed. Leptospirosis vaccination is not very effective, and only lasts a few months. Parvovirus vaccine should be given under special circumstances, i.e., when the dog will be exposed to other animals who might be ill, as in a boarding kennel. Give two injections, about two weeks apart, before the expected exposure. For cats, Dr. Pitcairn recommends distemper (feline panleukopenia) injections at eight and twelve weeks of age, repeated every five years; no other vaccinations are recommended for cats.[140] The new Lyme Dis-ease vaccine only is needed in tick infested areas; daily removal of ticks will also prevent the dis-ease. (An indoor cat or dog never sees a tick, and has no need for this vaccine.) Give kennel-cough prevention only for dogs who board or could otherwise be exposed. Despite kennel cough vaccination, Copper contracted the dis-ease from a boarding kennel about two months after. The treatment consisted of vaccinating him *again*, and I was told that this was routine.

Limiting conventional vaccinations is the first step in protecting your dog or cat. The second is antidoting the toxic effects of the vaccinations described below under Homeopathy. The third step is alternative vaccinations, using homeopathic nosodes rather than injection vaccines. This usually requires a homeopathic veterinarian, as vaccination nosodes are often available by prescription only, but results in full immunity without vaccinosis effects. Heartworm prevention is available in this form also. The disadvantages are that a) oral vaccination requires repeated doses (at home), b) homeopathic veterinarians are still too few and far between, and c) government licensing agencies and boarding kennels refuse to recognize nosode vaccination. The veterinary/medical system is adamantly opposed to homeopathy which has been its major competitor from the beginning. It also refuses to recognize homeopathic oral vaccination or to give up those increasingly lucrative vaccination fees.

Nutrition: For an animal with any dis-ease, including those induced by vaccinosis, building the immune system is central; this means providing full nutrition. Feed the preservative-free or natural homemade diet with supplements to keep immune function strong. A conventionally vaccinated animal needs this strength to fight off vaccination reactions and to heal any dis-ease. The autoimmune dis-eases also require as few toxins and contaminants in the food and environment as possible. The optimal diet with supplements is designed for full health and strong immunity in any situation.

Naturopathy: For a pet displaying negative reactions to vaccination or any related and later appearing dis-ease, begin with a few days' fasting, plus laxatives or enemas for detoxifying. Give aloe vera juice with liquid chlorophyll as a detoxifier, and use lots of garlic as an immune builder. Apple cider vinegar on food or in the water bowl also strengthens immunity. Feeding raw grated organic beets or beet juice, starting slowly and increasing gradually to amounts from one teaspoon to one tablespoon weekly, helps to detoxify the liver. (The animal's urine turns red from beets, but this is harmless.) Honey and bee products are immune builders, and kelp supports the thyroid. Give raw thymus glandular or combination glandulars to a pet with weakened immunity.

Vitamins and Minerals: Build the immune system by giving the daily supplements. Vitamin C is the primary immune-boosting vitamin; give 500-2,000 mg per day. (An animal who is ill will take much more.) B-complex reduces stress and repairs stress damage; give 10-20 mg in a yeast-free tablet daily unless feeding brewer's yeast. Vitamin E and zinc are immune strengtheners; give 5-10 mg of zinc and 100-600 IU of vitamin E daily. Give at least weekly a vitamin A and D capsule, 10,000-25,000 IU of A with 400-800 IU of vitamin D. Keeping a pet optimally healthy helps to prevent vaccinosis reactions.

Herbs: Use blue-violet leaf and red clover together as a detoxifier for vaccinosis reaction, whether it be tumors or skin problems. The combination known as Essiac, described under "Cancer," is another universal immune balancer for both immune deficiency and autoimmune diseases; it is also a liver and blood cleanser. Other liver-cleansing herbs include milk thistle (recommended), dandelion, yellow dock, Oregon grape root, burdock or goldenseal. Dandelion is the gentlest, and dandelion and burdock are probably the best tasting.

Homeopathy: Here's where the answers and antidotes are. If giving conventional rabies vaccine, use only killed-virus vaccine and antidote it homeopathically by giving the nosode *Lyssin* (killed-virus rabies) immediately; also use lymphatic drainers for the nervous system and brain. (A *Drainer-Detox* Combination is available from Newton Homeopathics and a "Vaccinations" release combination.) For the other dis-eases use homeopathic vaccinations by nosode, as only rabies vaccination is required by law. The antidoting above neutralizes only the toxic effects, not the protection afforded by the vaccines. [141]

Another antidote recipe after conventional vaccination is to give a dose of the nosode/s immediately. The next day give *Thuja* 30C; one week later start a dose of *Sulfur* daily for a week. Some pet homeopaths only list Thuja, giving it after vaccinations if an animal becomes ill. I have also used it for animals developing tumors and skin problems later and found it effective. Give a 30C dose nightly for three nights, then once a week for two more doses. *Silica* is another possibility; look for hard pimple-like lumps under the skin, especially around the collar area, as an indication for this remedy. Alternate with Thuja. Use as much of the full protocol as is available to you, and contact a holistic homeopathic veterinarian for antidote nosodes and the homeopathic oral vaccinations. Don't expect standard veterinarians to be supportive.

Acupuncture/Acupressure: See the Immune Stimulation Chart in the Acupuncture method chapter for raising pet immunity; see also the

Shin Dog Chart and Ottaviano Cat Chart for specific dis-eases and symptoms.

Flower Essences: *Crab Apple, Allemanda* or *Tomato* detoxifies. *Self-Heal* stimulates inner healing forces, *Celery* supports the immune system, and *Salvia* supports emotions under stress. *Nature's Rescue (Rescue Remedy)* is for any physical or emotional stress.

Gemstones: *Lapis Lazuli, Moonstone, Sugulite* or *Rose Quartz* balances immunity. *Lapis* or *Emerald* is a detoxifier used in elixir. Place an *Amethyst* cluster in the pet's environment as a cleanser, immune booster and calmative. *Clear Quartz Crystal* or *Herkimer Diamond* is also a positive in stones or as an elixir.

Viral Dis-eases

These are infectious dis-eases usually vaccinated for, but as described in the last section, sometimes the vaccinations fail to provide immunity. Viruses are contagious to other pets, so if one dog or cat in a household develops them, treat all the others. A cat or dog with a lowered immune system, or under stress, is more likely to develop viral or bacterial dis-eases. The infectious agents are always in the air or environment, but only the weakened animal gets sick from them. Standard veterinary/medical methods have a poor success rate with infectious dis-eases, and the animals who survive often have lifelong nervous-system, heart or liver damage. Forced feeding, use of steroids for fever, and vaccinations of the infectious agent are the treatment methods. By contrast, holistic methods have stronger success with no nervous system or organ aftereffects, even in cases generally assumed fatal. The treatment methods have been discussed earlier.

Symptoms for infectious dis-eases often begin with runny, slightly watery or half-closed eyes; the third eyelid (the haw or nictitating membrane) may be visible in an animal who is becoming ill.[142] There may be coughing or sneezing, runny nose and eyes, phlegm and mucous congestion, appetite loss with depression and listlessness, and—always—a fever, sometimes very high, hot and sudden. The animal may be vomiting and/or have diarrhea, labored breathing, breathing that rattles, dehydration or excessive thirst, foul stool odor, or blood in stool or vomit. Dogs with distemper may develop hardened foot pads. (The dis-ease is also known as "hard-pad dis-ease.") Kennel cough is harsh and hacking. Bloody vomit and diarrhea accompany parvovirus; collapse, convulsions, muscle twitching, paralysis, and even death may follow. Early treatment is critical; begin as soon as you notice the runny eyes, fever, cough or other symptoms.

Nutrition: An animal who has been fed the optimal natural diet with supplements is less likely to develop these dis-eases and far more likely to survive them if she does. See the section on "Immune Building" for achieving and maintaining optimal health for dogs and cats. See also the chapter on "Nutrition."

Naturopathy: At the first sign of fever or congestion withhold solid food and go to the liquid fast—this is the primary treatment for these dis-eases, along with vitamin C (see below). Juliette de Bairacli Levy believes that it is the forced feeding standardly used that causes fatalities and permanent damage in cases of infectious viral dis-eases. Maintain the liquid fast as long as fever continues and until the temperature remains normal (101. 5°F) for a few days, then slowly reintroduce solid food. If the fever returns, resume the fast again. Liquids for the fast include raw honey in water or barley water (the liquid left from cooking the grain), and pure grape or apple juice from a health food store; the average dose of both for a medium-sized dog is two tablespoons three times per day. Fresh water should be available at all times, and there can be honey in the water. Also give several tablespoons of pure water with very diluted lemon juice (a teaspoon of juice to two tablespoons of water).[143] Use fresh juice, not concentrate.

Apple cider vinegar can be substituted for lemon juice, and also added to drinking water. Aloe vera juice soothes the digestive system, and is a liver cleanser and laxative; liquid chlorophyll with it balances blood sugar and strengthens. All bee products are immune-system boosters. Garlic is an important antibiotic and immune strengthener; crush it, and add the juice to liquids during the fast.

Vitamins and Minerals: Vitamin C is the second component of the essential virus protocol. Wendell Belfield prescribes megadoses of vitamin C, administered intravenously, in amounts of half a gram (500 mg) of sodium ascorbate C per pound of animal body weight, twice a day. Vitamin E and selenium are added, as well as zinc, the B-complex, pantothenic acid (B-5) and B-6. The treatment must be done twice daily without missing a single treatment for a period of about five days in cases of canine and feline distemper, influenza, kennel cough and parvovirus in dogs, and upper respiratory dis-eases in cats. Belfield has achieved remission of FIP (feline infectious peritonitis—usually fatal) if treatment is started early enough. Raw thymus extract, along with vitamin C, may help to boost the immune system. Fluids are also given intravenously to prevent dehydration. Vitamin B-12 and amino acids stimulate appetite after the animal is eating again.[144]

If IV injection of vitamins is out of the question, try the following along with veterinary treatment. Give no solid food while fever and vomiting are present. In cats, use a liquid fast with high amounts of powdered vitamin C dissolved in liquids or water. Give 100 mg per hour of vitamin C in this way for kittens, 250 mg per hour for adult cats. For larger dogs, increase the amounts.[145] Add vitamin E, 50-100 IU three times per day, and cod liver oil for vitamin A, one-quarter to one teaspoonful three times per day. When using high doses of vitamins, decrease them gradually after the animal no longer needs them. Continue with smaller amounts of vitamins C and A, calcium/magnesium, selenium, vitamin E, zinc and B-complex. These can also alleviate central nervous system damage. Acupuncture is recommended in cases of nervous system damage from distemper.[146]

Herbs: Use antibiotic herbs during the full treatment, including goldenseal, echinacea or garlic. Clean congested eyes and nose with cotton balls dipped in infusions of rosemary, elder flowers or chickweed. After the fever, break the fast with slippery elm powder added to water or goat's milk, with half a teaspoon of cinnamon to each cup if there is still diarrhea.[147] Dr. Pitcairn uses the above with the honey water fast, and gives the following herb combination for canine and feline distemper: seven parts powdered goldenseal root, two parts powdered licorice root, and one part powdered ginger root. Stir into a little water, or put the dry powder into capsules. Give one-eighth teaspoon for puppies and toy-sized dogs twice per day; one-eighth teaspoon for small dogs three times per day; one-quarter teaspoon twice per day for medium-sized dogs; and one-quarter teaspoon three times per day for large dogs.

For cats, mix a teaspoon each of echinacea and boneset tinctures. Give two drops every half hour until there is improvement, then two drops every two hours until the cat recovers. If the cat is comatose or nearly so, place a drop of camphor-based ointment (Tiger Balm, Sunbreeze) in front of the cat's nose for a few breaths and repeat every fifteen minutes until there is response.[148] These ointments will antidote homeopathic remedies, however, so if using them give them before the homeopathic.

For dogs with kennel cough, give an herbal cough syrup adjusted to the dog's weight, and a strong peppermint infusion with one teaspoon honey per cup of infusion; give one teaspoon to a tablespoon every three hours. Mullein is another herbal alternative, also for respiratory symptoms; again, add honey.[149]

For parvovirus in dogs, Pat Lazarus uses garlic plus liver-building herbs of dandelion, red beet powder and parsley. For respiratory dis-eases in cats and dogs, she recommends an herbal combination of fenugreek and comfrey. Use these along with the vitamin C protocol.[150] Lobelia relieves congestions and phlegm in the lungs, and may be added to other herbs. Use only a few drops, as too much will cause vomiting that brings up the fluid, but it is what is needed to be removed anyway. Use goldenseal for infections with digestive symptoms, echinacea for upper and lower respiratory dis-eases, and garlic for both.

Homeopathy: At first onset, give *Aconite*, which may abort the dis-ease totally. Give a dose every hour for four hours, than discontinue; symptoms will either worsen or disappear. The next step for influenza/distemper type dis-eases is *Gelsemium*. The animal shows apathy, drowsiness and trembling, complete relaxation; there may be respiratory symptoms and sore throat. If neither of these stops the illness, go to *Distemperinum* (distemper nosode), or a nosode of the diagnosed dis-ease, twice a day in 30C until the animal is well.

For a cough where there is difficult, rapid respiration, a full hard pulse and fever, give *Bryonia*. If the animal is hot and feverish, with glaring eyes, restless and in an excited mental state, try *Belladonna*. When there are flu symptoms, fever, loose cough or sneezing, excessive thirst and soreness, the remedy is *Eupatorium perfoliatum*. Homeopathic goldenseal, *Hydrastis canadensis*, can be used in advanced viral dis-ease, where there is yellow mucous discharge from nose or eyes, and depression. For a weak, depressed, cold animal with vomiting and diarrhea, with the condition worsening after the pet drinks water, use *Veratrum album*. Give *Arsenicum* when there is vomiting, diarrhea with bad odor and a blood tinge, restlessness, and when the animal craves frequent small sips of water. For high fever and weak pulse with putrid, bad-smelling discharges, *Pyrogen* may work. The animal is highly restless, delirious—and seriously ill.

Acupuncture/Acupressure: The Shin Dog Chart lists a number of acupuncture points for distemper, pneumonia, bronchitis and other infectious dis-eases. For the initial states of distemper, use point #2 (GV-25) *Pi liang*; other distemper points include #3 (GV-16) *Ta feng men* for distemper and encephalitis, and #12 (GV-12) *Shen chu* for pneumonia, distemper, and bronchitis. The point for colds is #8 (not given) *Erh chien*. For fever or bronchitis, use point #10 (GV-14) *Ta chui*. Cough, pneumonia, and bronchitis respond to #27 (LU-1) *Fei yu*.

On the Cat Chart, point #5 is for coughs, #15 for infections and blood cleansing. Where there has been nervous system damage from distemper, acupuncture treatments with implants at the points can permanently end seizures and twitching. See a veterinary acupuncturist.

Flower Essences: Give *Nature's Rescue* (*Rescue Remedy*). *Mustard*, *Pandora Vine* (Hope Essence) or *Cucumber* eases depression. Cleansing essences include *Crab Apple, Allemanda, Yellow Hibiscus, Sage* and *Tomato*; *Hornbeam, Self-Heal* and *Penstemon* are general strengtheners. *Olive* is for the very ill animal; *Nasturtium* supports the nervous system. For immune system boosting give *Celery*, with *Tomato* for throwing off dis-ease, and *Salvia* to stabilize during stress. During convalescence use *Zucchini*.

Gemstones: For lymphatic drainage use *Azurite, Azurite-Malachite, Blue Sapphire, Kyanite* or *Lapis Lazuli*. *Chrysocolla* heals the lungs and is an all-healer; *Rose Quartz* boosts the thymus and aids depression. Use *Amethyst* with the other stones. *Emerald* is a deep cleanser and detoxifier. When making elixirs of Malachite or Chrysocolla, leave the stone in the water for no more than half an hour.

Warts

Dog groomers learn to clip older dogs by touch, to avoid hitting hair-hidden skin warts with the clippers. Some breeds seem more prone to develop these, particularly elder cocker spaniels and poodles; these breeds develop dozens of them. In young animals, warts often form in the mouth or on the lips; they are small and pink initially, later developing a rough, white cauliflower appearance. Warts may grow on stalks or against the skin, where they can resemble stuck-on pieces of chewing gum. The growths come and go spontaneously, especially in younger animals. They are caused by a virus, and may appear following vaccination. Whereas younger animals' immune systems soon right themselves, and the warts disappear, those on older dogs or cats remain. The warts on older animals may be the cumulative effect of many years of vaccinations. Small, dry knots under the skin, usually appearing around the collar area, also often appear following vaccination, then spontaneously disappear. While cats develop fewer warts than dogs, they are prone to suddenly break out into all-over tumors under the skin. These can be vaccination reactions, too, and the holistic treatment is the same as that for warts.

The veterinary/medical system burns, freezes or surgically removes warts if they appear in an inconvenient place, or if the animal scratches at them. A wart that is scratched, or cut by a grooming clipper, bleeds. This repeated irritation causes infections. For all-over tumors there are no veterinary answers short of euthanasia. (I have seen them disappear with homeopathy, however.) Also see the sections on "Immune Building" and "Vaccination/Vaccinosis." These are autoimmune reactions to vaccinating and are treatable accordingly.

Nutrition: The optimal natural diet with supplements feeds higher nutrition with fewer contaminants and chemicals. It helps to keep the immune system strong and the body at a lower level of toxicity; it also helps to prevent growths and vaccinosis reactions. Feed egg yolks and organic liver weekly, and garlic, onions, barley, broad beans, carrots, asparagus or Japanese daikon daily. Remove any allergen foods from the diet. Be aware of allergenic foods and remove them from the diet. The supplements are important for immune health. Feed only natural dog biscuits and treats; try substituting carrot sticks for rawhide.

Naturopathy: Begin with a few days of fasting with detoxifying laxatives or enemas. Lemon juice, liquid chlorophyll and coffee enemas are good internal cleansers. Acidify the body system by putting apple cider vinegar in the water bowl, or replacing a third of the water with unsweetened cranberry juice. If there are many warts on the body, use orthophosphoric acid in water—dividing the human dose by body weight. Give lots of garlic. Kelp boosts the thyroid; also feed digestive enzymes.

A number of external naturopathic treatments dissolve warts if used consistently over a period of time. These include dabbing with lemon juice twice daily, followed by a chopped raw onion poultice for fifteen minutes. Mix castor oil and baking soda into a paste and leave it on the wart, or apply a used black teabag for fifteen minutes daily. Raw chopped onion can be mixed with salt and used as a poultice, or tape on a raw garlic clove. Leave most of these poultices on continuously. (How to keep the pet from eating these is another story!)

Vitamins and Minerals: The supplements of the optimal diet are important here as a basis for immune health. Deficiencies of vitamin A, C or zinc may also cause warts. Go to bowel tolerance with vitamin C— 500-3,000 mg daily; an animal with immune disruption may take more C than you expect. Give 5-10 mg of zinc daily, and 25,000 IU of vitamin A every other day for a medium-sized dog, with 800 IU of vitamin D once a week. Vitamin A oil from a pierced capsule, or C made into a paste with water, can also be used topically. Feed brewer's yeast and increase the amount by half, or give a yeast-free B-complex tablet of about 25 mg for a medium-sized dog—or 10 mg for a cat, with additional B-6 (pyridoxine). For older pets, also give B-12 (cyanocobalamine). Use vitamin E internally 100-600 IU daily; also use it externally by piercing a capsule and rubbing the oil onto warts. A liver extract or amino acid combination, raw thymus glandular or combination glandulars, and coenzyme Q10 are also helpful.

Herbs: Juliette de Bairacli Levy considers glandular disruption the source of warts and growths, and recommends kelp as highly important. She also feeds dandelion leaves fresh in the diet (or use an infusion or tincture). Externally touch the warts three times daily with the juice from the stems of dandelion or greater celandine, with the skin (moist side) of unripe papaya fruit or pineapple. Protect normal skin and let the juice dry on the wart.[151] Juice or tincture of mullein, plantain, and chickweed; marigold mixed with turpentine; black walnut or apple cider vinegar mixed with cayenne pepper may also be used externally. Cleansing herbs used internally include chaparral, pau d'arco, goldenseal or Oregon grape root. Chamomile is a gentle liver cleanser. Also dab tea tree oil directly on warts.

Homeopathy: See the section on "Vaccination/Vaccinosis," and do the procedure to antidote the negative effects of the yearly vaccinations. This can be the answer both for warts and for subcutaneous (under-the-skin) tumors. Homeopathic *Thuja* is indicated for tumors and for soft warts that bleed, especially warts around the mouth. Give a 30C potency daily and watch for reactions, then dose according to observation. *Silica* may also be the remedy for vaccination-induced tumors, small knots that appear under the skin, and warts that become infected. Use *Causticum* for fleshy warts or warts on stalks, especially those on the face or eyelids. For large, smooth, flat warts try *Ducamara*. Where soft, irritated bleeding warts do not respond to Thuja, try *Nitric Acid. Antimonium crudum* is for horny, hard warts with a smooth surface. Where there are numerous small itchy warts, give *Calc carb* in 200C once a week until gone. The primary remedies are Thuja and Causticum. (Thuja tincture may be dabbed on externally.)

Acupuncture/Acupressure: See the Immune Stimulation Chart in the method chapter and work the sequence twice a week at first, and then increase to daily. This is for warts only; do not use for tumors.

Flower Essences: See the essences for Vaccinosis.

Gemstones: Any of the following used in the aura or as elixirs boosts the immune system: *Jade, Picture Jasper, Blue Quartz, Amethyst, Rose Quartz, Ruby, Sulfur, Blue Tourmaline* or *Pink Tourmaline. Emerald* in elixir is an important detoxifier, as is *Malachite.*

Worms

Intestinal worms are a fact of life for dogs and cats. Puppies and kittens can be born with them even if the mother is not infested: pregnancy activates tissue-encysted round or larval hookworms that are not active in the intestines; these are subsequently transmitted through lactation to the newborns. Babies should be checked for worms and dewormed as early as two or three weeks of age, and again at five or six weeks. A pot-bellied puppy or a kitten with poor coat and listlessness probably has roundworms. A newborn who is under stress, chilled, overfed or kept in close quarters is more susceptible. After six months, most dogs and cats develop immunity to these types of worms, particularly when the animal is kept in good health. Stress or illness can result in infestations, as can emotional upset or immunosuppressant drugs like cortisone. (These also activate tissue-encysted worms, causing them to re-appear in the intestines.)

Tapeworms are the most common infestation in adult dogs and cats. They are transmitted when the animal eats fleas, lice, roaches, raw fish or infected prey like birds, gophers or other rodents. Tapeworms are visible in the stool; they do not encyst in the tissues like round or hook-worms. The heads attach to the inside of the intestinal wall and may not be completely removed with worming; they reappear relatively soon. Roundworms in the stool resemble coiled springs, and may be vomited by a heavily infested puppy. Other types of worms require microscope analysis to detect and identify.

The animal who needs worming appears sick—she experiences weight loss with increased or decreased appetite, anemia, digestive upsets or vomiting, blood or mucous in the stools, tarry stools, and a decline in health. The animal who is toxic and run-down is more likely to develop internal and external parasites. A sick animal is not a good candidate for worming unless worms are the primary problem. Worm only when it has been determined that worms are present; worming is not recommended as a routine procedure. Avoid over-the-counter wormers, which are toxic. Herbals are far safer. See a holistic veterinarian if they fail.

Nutrition: Feed the preservative-free or natural homemade diet with supplements; an optimally healthy cat or dog is less likely to develop parasites of any kind. Use raw foods as much as possible, and give whole cooked grains. To make absolutely sure that raw meat or poultry is free of worm eggs, use a hydrogen peroxide and water-soak if there is any doubt. Mix a tablespoonful of three percent hydrogen peroxide to six ounces of water and pour over the meat or mix with ground meat; let marinate for an hour.[152] It is far less likely that your pet will pick up worms from fresh raw food than from fleas or scavenging. For dogs, be careful of the source of rawhide, as much of it is prepared under unsanitary conditions and carries worm eggs—as well as being preserved with cyanide! Suspect supermarket or otherwise very cheap rawhide.

Naturopathy: Feed the following every day as a preventative, intestinal cleanser and antiseptic: one-half to two cloves of raw grated garlic; one-half to two teaspoons of bran; and grated raw carrots, turnips or beets.[153] Garlic is the primary preventive, good also for heartworm. Keep the colon free of toxins with aloe vera juice and liquid chlorophyll daily, and give apple cider vinegar in the water bowl. Ground pumpkin seeds, sesame seeds, figs and grated coconut in food also help to expel worms; fiber helps to move worms out of the intestines.

Vitamins and Minerals: Feed the supplements with the daily diet. A dog or cat with worms needs a high level of nutrients to replace what may be lost due to parasites. Deficiencies in dietary protein, iron, vitamin A, B-complex (B-1, B-2, biotin and folic acid, in particular) and zinc may cause an animal to become worm infested. Wendell Belfield recommends the supplemented natural diet, which provides the above, with additional vitamin C (500-2,000 mg) and zinc (5-15 mg) daily. Give the weekly vitamin E, and A with D. Belfield also states that pets fed garlic and parsley capsules daily seldom if ever develop intestinal parasites, and that pregnant animals fed garlic do not transmit worms to their young.[154]

Herbs: A number of herbs help to remove intestinal parasites, and a number of prepared herbal products are now available. Male fern, areca nut, wormwood, wormseed or cina, black walnut extract, southernwood and chaparral are all indicated, as is rue. A pet herbal product called Gentle Dragon, safe and effective for kittens and young puppies, is available from the Whole Animal Catalog (3131 Hennepin Ave. S., Minneapolis, MN 55408, (800) 377-6369). The Natural Pet Care Catalog (2713 E. Madison, Seattle, WA 98112, (800) 962-8266) offers Omphalia 11, an anti-parasite powder made with Chinese herbs. Avena Botanicals has a natural tapeworm, roundworm and heartworm preventive, available from Morrill's New Directions (POB 30, Orient, ME 04471, (800) 368-5057). All of these are herbal and effective; check other natural pet catalogs for others.

Juliette de Bairacli Levy offers a somewhat complicated herbal protocol for worming dogs and cats naturally. It is repeated by Dr. Richard Pitcairn and Anitra Frazier. The herbs are garlic, wormwood and rue, placed in capsules for a treatment course of fasts and laxatives that takes about a month. See their books for the information.

Homeopathy: Before worming puppies or kittens, give a dose of *Sulfur* if the coat is dry and unthrifty, or *Calc carb* if the baby is fat and seems top heavy; these strengthen the animal for the process. Then alternate *Chenopodium* and *Cina* 3X twice a day for a week, stop for a week, and repeat. If used continuously in this way, the two remedies will normally keep puppies or kittens free of roundworms. If these fail, give *Natrum phos* two or three times daily if using 6X cell salt potency, or once or twice per week if using it in 30C. If the pet with roundworms strains when eliminating stool and has bad breath, the remedy is *Spigelia* dosed every few days. For irritable, angry pets with intense anal itching, *Cina* (wormseed) is the roundworm remedy, or *Teucrium Marum*. *Abrotanum* (southernwood) is for the pet with roundworms where there is evident weight loss, poor digestion, distended abdomen, constipation alternating with diarrhea, good appetite and undigested food in the stool.

For tapeworms, *Felix mas* (male fern) is used morning and evening over a few weeks, with the higher potencies more effective. The animal responding to this remedy is also constipated. Give *Merc cor* for tapeworms when there are bloody, slimy, foul-odored stools. Give *Granatum* for tapeworm when there is weight loss, good appetite and itchy paws.

Acupuncture/Acupressure: No points are given on the Shin Dog Chart or Ottoviano Cat Chart for aid in eliminating worms.

Flower Essences: *Crab Apple*, *Allemanda* and/or *Tomato* are for cleansing and detoxifying. *Self-Heal* aids a pet in developing immunity and in recovery. Use *Penstemon* with other essences. *Garlic* essence repels fleas and internal parasites.

Gemstones: *Malachite* brings things out from within, or try *Azurite-Malachite*, *Emerald* or *Obsidian* in elixir, or in the aura.

[1] Anitra Frazier with Norma Eckroate, *The New Natural Cat*, pp. 354-358.

[2] Richard Pitcairn, DVM, and Susan Hubble Pitcairn, *Dr. Pitcairn's Complete Guide to Natural Health for Dogs and Cats*, pp. 176-177.

[3] Delbert O. Carlson, DVM, and James M. Giffin, MD, *The Dog Owner's Home Veterinary Handbook*, p. 335; and *The Cat Owner's Home Veterinary Handbook*, p. 359.

[4] Wendell O. Belfield, DVM, and Martin Zucker, *How to Have a Healthier Dog*, pp. 141-149; and *The Very Healthy Cat Book*, pp. 134-146.

[5] Francis Hunter, MRCVS, *Homeopathic First-Aid Treatment for Pets*, p. 86.

[6] James F. Balch, MD, and Phyllis A. Balch, CNC, *Prescription for Nutritional Healing*, p. 78.

[7] Alfred J. Plechner, DVM, and Martin Zucker, *Pet Allergies: Remedies for an Epidemic*, p. 20.

[8] Anitra Frazier with Norma Eckroate, *The New Natural Cat*, p. 277.

[9] Alan M. Klide, VMD, and Shiu K. Kung, Ph.D., *Veterinary Acupuncture*, p. 230.

[10] Dr. Richard Pitcairn, DVM, and Susan Hubble Pitcairn, *Dr. Pitcairn's Complete Guide to Natural Health for Dogs and Cats*, p. 180.

[11] Juliette de Bairacli Levy, *The Complete Herbal Handbook for the Dog and Cat*, p. 150.

[12] James F. Balch, MD, and Phyllis A. Balch, CNC, *Prescription for Nutritional Healing*, p. 91.

[13] Anitra Frazier, "Nurturing Underweight Cats: Part I, The Starving Stray," in *Tiger Tribe Magazine*, March-April, 1993, pp. 6-8.

[14] Richard Pitcairn, DVM, and Susan Hubble Pitcairn, *Dr. Pitcairn's Complete Guide to Natural Health for Dogs and Cats,* pp. 181-183.

[15] Juliette de Bairacli Levy, *The Complete Herbal Handbook for the Dog and Cat*, p. 152.

[16] Alan M. Klide, VMD, and Shiu K. Kung, Ph.D., *Veterinary Acupuncture*, p. 231.

[17] Anitra Frazier with Norma Eckroate, *The New Natural Cat*, p. 350.

[18] James F. Balch, MD, and Phyllis Balch, CNC, *Prescription for Nutritional Healing*, p. 98.

[19] *Ibid.*

[20] Alan M. Klide, VMD, and Shiu K. Kung, Ph.D., *Veterinary Acupuncture*, pp. 239-240.

[21] Anitra Frazier with Norma Eckroate, *The New Natural Cat*, p. 351.

[22] Delbert G. Carlson, DVM, and James M. Giffin, MD, *Dog Owner's Home Veterinary Handbook*, p. 6; and *Cat Owner's Home Veterinary Handbook*, p. 26.

[23] Juliette de Bairacli Levy, *The Complete Herbal Handbook for the Dog and Cat*, p. 246.

[24] Anitra Frazier with Norma Eckroate, *The New Natural Cat*, p. 362.

[25] Richard Pitcairn, DVM, and Susan Hubble Pitcairn, *Dr. Pitcairn's Complete Guide to Natural Health for Dogs and Cats,* pp. 192-193.

[26] Pat Lazarus, *Keep Your Pet Healthy the Natural Way*, pp. 159-166.

[27] Morton Walker, DPM, "Venus Flytrap—Cancer and AIDS Fighter of the Future," in *Natural Health Magazine*, September/October, 1992, pp. 44-46; and "Letters," *Natural Health Magazine*, May/June, 1993, p. 6.

[28] Richard Pitcairn, DVM, and Susan Hubble Pitcairn, *Dr. Pitcairn's Complete Guide to Natural Health for Dogs and Cats,* pp. 191-193.

[29] Diane Stein, *The Natural Remedy Book for Women* (Freedom, CA: The Crossing Press, 1992), pp. 146-147.

[30] Richard Pitcairn, DVM, and Susan Hubble Pitcairn, *Dr. Pitcairn's Complete Guide to Natural Health for Dogs and Cats,* p. 213.

[31]Juliette de Bairacli Levy, *The Complete Herbal Handbook for the Dog and Cat*, pp. 165-166.

[32]Anitra Frazier with Norma Eckroate, *The New Natural Cat*, p. 296.

[33]Anitra Frazier, *The New Natural Cat*, p. 256.

[34]D.C. Jarvis, *Folk Medicine*, p. 111.

[35]Wendell O. Belfield, DVM, and Martin Zucker, *How to Have a Healthier Dog*, p. 251.

[36]Juliette de Bairacli Levy, *The Complete Herbal Handbook for the Dog and Cat*, pp. 167-168.

[37]*Ibid.*, pp. 168-169.

[38]Richard Pitcairn, DVM, and Susan Hubble Pitcairn, *Dr. Pitcairn's Complete Guide to Natural Health for Dogs and Cats,* pp. 198-200.

[39]Anitra Frazier with Norma Eckroate, *The New Natural Cat*, p. 304.

[40]Richard Pitcairn, DVM, and Susan Hubble Pitcairn, *Dr. Pitcairn's Complete Guide to Natural Health for Dogs and Cats,* pp. 200-201.

[41]Juliette de Bairacli Levy, *The Complete Herbal Handbook for the Dog and Cat*, pp. 169-170.

[42]Anitra Frazier with Norma Eckroate, *The New Natural Cat*, pp. 296-297.

[43]Joan Harper, *The Healthy Cat and Dog Cookbook*, p. 100.

[44]Juliette de Bairacli Levy, *The Complete Herbal Handbook for the Dog and Cat*, p. 153.

[45]*Ibid.*, p. 84.

[46]Wendell O. Belfield, DVM, and Martin Zucker, *How to Have a Healthier Dog*, pp. 113-115.

[47]Pat McKay, *Reigning Cats and Dogs*, pp. 107-108.

[48]Richard Pitcairn, DVM, and Susan Hubble Pitcairn, *Dr. Pitcairn's Complete Guide to Natural Health for Dogs and Cats,* p. 210; and Anitra Frazier with Norma Eckroate, *The New Natural Cat*, pp. 311-312.

[49]Alfred Plechner, DVM, and Martin Zucker, *Pet Allergies: Remedies for an Epidemic*, pp. 34-35.

[50]James F. Balch, MD, and Phyllis Balch, CNC, *Prescription for Nutritional Healing*, pp. 169-170.

[51]Wendell O. Belfield, DVM, and Martin Zucker, *How to Have a Healthier Dog*, p. 178.

[52]Wendell O. Belfield, DVM, and Martin Zucker, *The Very Healthy Cat Book*, pp. 126-127.

[53]Richard Pitcairn, DVM, and Susan Hubble Pitcairn, *Dr. Pitcairn's Complete Guide to Natural Health for Dogs and Cats,* pp. 212-213; and George Macleod, MRCVS, DVSM, *Dogs: Homeopathic Remedies*, pp. 44-45.

[54]Alan M. Klide, VMD, and Shiu K. Kung, Ph.D., *Veterinary Acupuncture*, pp. 240-243.

[55]Delbert G. Carlson, DVM, and James M. Giffin, MD, *Cat Owner's Home Veterinary Handbook*, pp. 74-76.

[56]Anitra Frazier with Norma Eckroate, *The New Natural Cat*, pp. 326-331.

[57]*Ibid*, pp. 329-330.

[58]Juliette de Bairacli Levy, *Cats Naturally: Natural Rearing for Healthier Cats* (London and Boston: Faber and Faber, Ltd., 1991), pp. 95-96.

[59]Wendell O. Belfield, DVM, and Martin Zucker, *The Very Healthy Cat Book*, pp. 163-176.

[60]Anitra Frazier with Norma Eckroate, *The New Natural Cat*, p. 330.

[61]Gloria Dodd, DVM, in Diane Stein, *Natural Healing for Dogs and Cats*, p. 95.

[62]Pat McKay, *Reigning Cats and Dogs*, pp. 17-18, 49.

[63]*Ibid.*, pp. 107-113.

[64]Susan R. Griffin, *Win the Flea War Naturally . . . Without Toxins*, pp. 8-9.

[65]Wendell O. Belfield, DVM, and Martin Zucker, *How to Have a Healthier Dog*, pp. 172-174; and Alfred Plechner, *Pet Allergies: Remedies for an Epidemic*, pp. 18-23.

[66]Alfred Plechner, DVM, and Martin Zucker, *Pet Allergies: Remedies for an Epidemic*, pp. 11 and 19.

[67]Anitra Frazier with Norma Eckroate, *The New Natural Cat*, pp. 343-345.

[68]*Ibid.*, pp. 256, 344.

[69]Grace McHattie, *Your Cat Naturally*, p. 87.

[70]Anitra Frazier with Norma Eckroate, *The New Natural Cat*, p. 345.

[71]Richard Pitcairn, DVM, and Susan Hubble Pitcairn, *Dr. Pitcairn's Complete Guide to Natural Health for Dogs and Cats*, p. 216.

[72]Anitra Frazier with Norma Eckroate, *The New Natural Cat*, p. 289.

[73]Pat Lazarus, *Keep Your Pet Healthy the Natural Way*, pp. 145-155.

[74]Juliette de Bairacli Levy, *The Complete Herbal Handbook for the Dog and Cat*, p. 199.

[75]James F. Balch, MD, and Phyllis Balch, CNC, *Prescription for Nutritional Healing*, p. 210; Wendell O. Belfield, DVM, and Martin Zucker, *The Very Healthy Cat Book*, pp. 124-126; and Alfred Plechner, DVM, and Martin Zucker, *Pet Allergies: Remedies for an Epidemic*, pp. 33-34.

[76]Richard Pitcairn, DVM, and Susan Hubble Pitcairn, *Dr. Pitcairn's Complete Guide to Natural Health for Dogs and Cats*, p. 184.

[77]Juliette de Bairacli Levy, *The Complete Herbal Handbook for the Dog and Cat*, p. 204.

[78]Richard Pitcairn, DVM, and Susan Hubble Pitcairn, *Dr. Pitcairn's Complete Guide to Natural Health for Dogs and Cats*, pp. 184-186.

[79]Francis Hunter, MRCVS, *Homeopathic First-Aid Treatment for Pets*, pp. 73-74.

[80]Alan M. Klide, VMD, and Shiu K. Kung, Ph.D., *Veterinary Acupuncture*, p. 239.

[81]Richard Pitcairn, DVM, and Susan Hubble Pitcairn, *Dr. Pitcairn's Complete Guide to Natural Health for Dogs and Cats*, p. 187.

[82]Joan Harper, *The Healthy Cat and Dog Cookbook*, p. 86.

[83]D.C. Jarvis, *Folk Medicine*, p. 107.

[84]James F. Balch, MD, and Phyllis Balch, CNC, *Prescription for Nutritional Healing*, p. 104

[85]Pat McKay, *Reigning Cats and Dogs*, pp. 107-108.

[86]*Ibid.*, p. 31.

[87]Pat Lazarus, *Keep Your Pet Healthy the Natural Way*, p. 102.

[88]Diane Stein, *The Natural Remedy Book for Women*, pp. 241-242; and James F. Balch, MD, and Phyllis Balch, CNC, *Prescription for Nutritional Healing*, pp. 139-141.

[89]Anitra Frazier with Norma Eckroate, *The New Natural Cat*, p. 377.

[90]Richard Pitcairn, DVM, and Susan Hubble Pitcairn, *Dr. Pitcairn's Complete Guide to Natural Health for Dogs and Cats*, pp. 224-225.

[91]Juliette de Bairacli Levy, *Cats Naturally*, p. 104; and *The Complete Herbal Handbook for the Dog and Cat*, pp. 205-206.

[92]Anitra Frazier with Norma Eckroate, *The New Natural Cat*, p. 378.

[93]Richard Pitcairn, DVM, and Susan Hubble Pitcairn, *Dr. Pitcairn's Complete Guide to Natural Health for Dogs and Cats*, pp. 235-237; Anitra Frazier with Norma Eckroate, *The New Natural Cat*, pp. 378-381 and 405-408. Juliette de Bairacli Levy uses the same recipes.

[94]Adele Davis, *Let's Get Well*, p. 136.

[95]Juliette de Bairacli Levy, *The Complete Herbal Handbook for the Dog and Cat*, pp. 214-218, 247, 248.

[96]Anitra Frazier with Norma Eckroate, *The New Natural Cat*, pp. 381, 409.

[97]Richard Pitcairn, DVM, and Susan Hubble Pitcairn, *Dr. Pitcairn's Complete Guide to Natural Health for Dogs and Cats*, p. 253; and Anitra Frazier with Norma Eckroate, *The New Natural Cat*, pp. 387-391.

[98]Juliette de Bairacli Levy, *The Complete Herbal Handbook for the Dog and Cat*, p. 222.

[99]Anitra Frazier with Norma Eckroate, *The New Natural Cat*, p. 201.

[100]Adele Davis, *Let's Get Well*, p. 265.

[101]James F. Balch, MD, and Phyllis Balch, CNC, *Prescription for Nutritional Healing*, p. 330.

[102]Delbert G. Carlson, DVM, and James M. Giffin, MD, *Cat Owner's Home Veterinary Handbook*, pp. 36-44; *Dog Owner's Home Veterinary Handbook*, pp. 14-22.

[103]James F. Balch, MD, and Phyllis Balch, CNC, *Prescription for Nutritional Healing*, p. 94.

[104]Juliette de Bairacli Levy, *The Complete Herbal Handbook for the Dog and Cat*, pp. 238-242.

[105]Figure given to me by The Humane Society of the United States, Tallahassee, Florida branch, June 25, 1993, by phone.

[106]Wendell O. Belfield, DVM, and Martin Zucker, *How to Have a Healthier Dog*, p. 101.

[107]Juliette de Bairacli Levy, *The Complete Herbal Handbook for the Dog and Cat*, pp. 59-62.

[108]Wendell O. Belfield, DVM, and Martin Zucker, *How to Have a Healthier Dog*, pp. 100-110; and *The Very Healthy Cat Book*, pp. 91-98.

[109]Juliette de Bairacli Levy, *The Complete Herbal Handbook for the Dog and Cat*, p. 66.

[110]James F. Balch, MD, and Phyllis Balch, CNC, *Prescription for Nutritional Healing*, pp. 291-92. Most of this section is from Diane Stein, *The Natural Remedy Book for Women*, pp. 304-309.

[111]Alan M. Klide, VMD, and Shiu K. Kung, Ph.D., *Veterinary Acupuncture*, p. 231.

[112]Delbert G. Carlson, DVM, and James M. Giffin, MD, *Dog Owner's Home Veterinary Handbook*, p. 25; and *Cat Owner's Home Veterinary Handbook*, p. 46.

[113]Juliette de Bairacli Levy, *The Complete Herbal Handbook for the Dog and Cat*, p. 249.

[114]Wendell O. Belfield, DVM, and Martin Zucker, *How to Have a Healthier Dog*, p. 227; and Adele Davis, *Let's Get Well*, pp. 267-268.

[115]Alfred Plechner, DVM, and Martin Zucker, *Pet Allergies: Remedies for an Epidemic*, pp. 26-27.

[116]Wendell O. Belfield, DVM, and Martin Zucker, *The Very Healthy Cat Book*, pp. 199-211.

[117]Pat Lazarus, *Keep Your Pet Healthy the Natural Way*, pp. 95-97.

[118]Richard Pitcairn, DVM, and Susan Hubble Pitcairn, *Dr. Pitcairn's Complete Guide to Natural Health for Dogs and Cats,* pp. 238-240.

[119]Alan M. Klide, VMD, and Shiu K. Kung, Ph.D., *Veterinary Acupuncture*, p. 247.

[120]Adele Davis, *Let's Get Well*, pp. 265-268.

[121]*Ibid.*

[122]Wendell O. Belfield, DVM, and Martin Zucker, *How to Have a Healthier Dog*, p. 219.

[123]Juliette de Bairacli Levy, *The Complete Herbal Handbook for the Dog and Cat*, p. 224.

[124]Alan M. Klide, VMD, and Shiu K. Kung, Ph.D., *Veterinary Acupuncture*, pp. 230-231.

[125]Anitra Frazier with Norma Eckroate, *The New Natural Cat*, p. 240.

[126]Richard Pitcairn, DVM, and Susan Hubble Pitcairn, *Dr. Pitcairn's Complete Guide to Natural Health for Dogs and Cats*, p. 187.

[127]Pat Lazarus, *Keep Your Pet Healthy the Natural Way*, pp. 132-136.

[128]Anitra Frazier with Norma Eckroate, *The New Natural Cat*, pp. 335-336.

[129]*Ibid.*, pp. 331-336.

[130]Richard Pitcairn, DVM, and Susan Hubble Pitcairn, *Dr. Pitcairn's Complete Guide to Natural Health for Dogs and Cats*, pp. 186-190.

[131]Wendell O. Belfield, DVM, and Martin Zucker, *How to Have a Healthier Dog*, pp. 199-203; and *The Very Healthy Cat Book*, pp. 195-198.

[132]Richard Pitcairn, DVM, and Susan Hubble Pitcairn, *Dr. Pitcairn's Complete Guide to Natural Health for Dogs and Cats*, pp. 186-190.

[133]Diane Stein, *Natural Healing for Dogs and Cats*, pp. 98-99.

[134]Alan M. Klide, VMD, and Shiu K. Kung, Ph.D., *Veterinary Acupuncture*, p. 247.

[135]Luke Granfield, "Vaccinosis," in *Tiger Tribe Magazine*, September-October, 1992, p. 23.

[136]Anitra Frazier with Norma Eckroate, *The New Natural Cat*, pp. 265-266.

[137]Richard Pitcairn, DVM, and Susan Hubble Pitcairn, *Dr. Pitcairn's Complete Guide to Natural Health for Dogs and Cats*, p. 251.

[138]Luke Granfield, "Vaccinosis," p. 25.

[139]Richard Pitcairn, DVM, and Susan Hubble Pitcairn, *Dr. Pitcairn's Complete Guide to Natural Health for Dogs and Cats*, p. 251.

[140]*Ibid.*, pp. 250-252.

[141]Dr. Gloria Dodd, in Diane Stein, *Natural Healing for Dogs and Cats*, p. 90.

[142]Laura Sykes, "Eyes Are Windows to the Soul," in *Tiger Tribe Magazine*, November-December, 1992, pp. 11-13.

[143]Juliette de Bairacli Levy, *The Complete Herbal Handbook for the Dog and Cat*, pp. 173-175.

[144]Wendell O. Belfield, DVM, and Martin Zucker, *How to Have a Healthier Dog*, pp. 237-243; and *The Very Healthy Cat Book*, pp. 184-185.

[145]Richard Pitcairn, DVM, and Susan Hubble Pitcairn, *Dr. Pitcairn's Complete Guide to Natural Health for Dogs and Cats*, p. 206.

[146]Pat Lazarus, *Keep Your Pet Healthy the Natural Way*, p. 112.

[147]Juliette de Bairacli Levy, *The Complete Herbal Handbook for the Dog and Cat*, pp. 173-175.

[148]Richard Pitcairn, DVM, and Susan Hubble Pitcairn, *Dr. Pitcairn's Complete Guide to Natural Health for Dogs and Cats*, pp. 203-207.

[149]*Ibid.*, pp. 247-248.

[150]Pat Lazarus, *Keep Your Pet Healthy the Natural Way*, pp. 114-118.

[151]Juliette de Bairacli Levy, *The Complete Herbal Handbook for the Dog and Cat*, p. 271.

[152]Pat McKay, *Reigning Cats and Dogs*, pp. 17-18.

[153]Richard Pitcairn, DVM, and Susan Hubble Pitcairn, *Dr. Pitcairn's Complete Guide to Natural Health for Dogs and Cats,* p. 255.

[154]Wendell O. Belfield, DVM, and Martin Zucker, *How to Have a Healthier Dog,* pp. 122-124; and *The Very Healthy Cat Book*, pp. 218-219. Also, Adele Davis, *Let's Get Well*, p. 156.

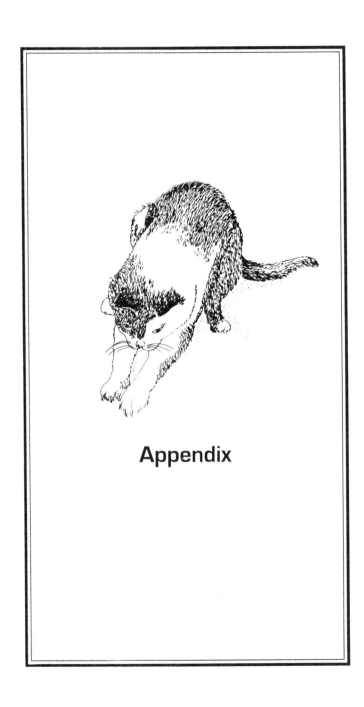

Appendix

Crystal Work with Animals

by Marion Webb-DeSisto, Lic. Crystal Healer

Crystals and animals can form a perfect partnership. They often work together more harmoniously and with greater success than crystals and humans. I believe this is because the essence/beingness of crystals and animals is very similar, having remained much closer to the Goddess/ Great Spirit/Source than that of souls who are incarnating within human form. In many ways we have become disconnected from our point-of-origin, whereas they have maintained firm links with it.

If, like me, you are an avid collector of crystals and stones and you display some of them on windowsills or shelves near doors and windows, you may have noticed that birds often come around as if picking up on some invisible signal. Over the years many stray dogs and cats have also arrived on my doorstep and, again, I'm convinced this is due mainly to the essence vibrations sent out by my crystal collection. Each animal recognized an energy pattern with which it had resonance.

Several months ago I had an amusing incident occur when I was sitting in a bus station, waiting for a bus which would take me to the middle of England to do some crystal healing work. My overnight bag was on the floor at my feet and, apart from clothing, etc., it also contained a number of my favorite crystals and stones. Suddenly, from nowhere it seemed, there were about 25 to 30 pigeons and sparrows converging on me. They hopped and walked around my feet, all seeming to be looking right at me, expectantly. Since neither I nor anyone within my immediate vicinity was eating food, the scene quickly began to look most odd and I became aware of many curious and suspicious stares from the surrounding people. The birds stayed with me for quite some time, keeping close to my feet and my bag and not attempting to wander off to other awaiting passengers. Eventually, my bus arrived and I went outside to board it, not, thank goodness, followed by my feathered friends!

And so, having recognized this mutual bond, this interaction which takes place between crystals and animals, it naturally follows that crystals and stones can be used to help our pets enjoy a healthier and better balanced existence. Some excellent methods of how to achieve this have been given earlier in this book. Before writing further information, however, I would like to take a moment to address some very basic needs of crystals.

No matter in what way we choose to work with crystals, we must primarily have the conviction and understanding that the world of minerals is a form of existence which radiated out from the Goddess, even as we are. When seeking the help of crystals and stones, there must first be love and respect for them. They are our distant cousins, and deserve nothing less than what our all-loving parent eternally gives to us.

They are extremely empathetic to the vibrations of all things which surround them. Therefore, the first and most loving thing we can do for them is to cleanse them of any negativity which they may have absorbed at some time. Many different methods of cleansing can be found in books about crystals, but I prefer visualization techniques which involve draining the negativity from the crystal/stone and asking that it be transmuted to the Light in order to reach its highest form. Before beginning this exercise, I ground and center myself and ask for help from only the highest angelic realms. This ensures protection for both me and the crystal. I then ask the crystal to self-heal not only itself, but all of its original structural parts, no matter where they may exist upon/within this planet and others, this star system and others, this galaxy and others, and this universe and any others. Next I mentally imprint upon the crystal or stone, with its permission, a healing symbol which has been given to me by my Spirit Guides and I dedicate it to the Highest Good. This can be done in the form of a prayer, a verbal ritual, or in whatever way feels right for you. Following this, I ask the crystal to tune itself to whatever specific work I will be doing. I never "program" my mineral friends; they have the right to free will just as we do. (To date, no crystal nor stone has ever refused my requests.) Finally, I thank it in advance for the help it will be giving me. I always remember to thank it and cleanse it at the completion of its work, as well. Before my crystals begin a "resting" phase between work, I ask them to tune themselves to continual self-healing.

Within the following suggestions of crystal work with animals, I have not usually specified which particular type of crystal or stone to use. This is because I am convinced that they are much more able to know what is correct for each animal and each situation. Go with what feels right and, of course, what is practical and available to you. If you open up and listen to them, they will "tell" you what you need to know. If, however, you don't feel you are getting the message, then try dowsing with a pendulum over a group of crystals and stones, asking to be shown which is best for _____ (specify the work). This is always an accurate determination method.

Crystals can be tuned to purify your pet's drinking water and to imbue this liquid with the properties for promoting health and well-being. Once you have tuned the crystal, hold it, point facing downwards, a few inches above the water, asking it to project this healing and purifying energy into the liquid. Repeat this procedure with each refill of water.

This pre-tuned crystal can also be used in the same manner to send its energy into a bowl of food, whether canned, kibbled or table scraps. Or place a similarly tuned crystal inside a bag of kibbled food, to remain there until the bag is empty. Be careful that the crystal doesn't fall into the bowl along with the food. Your pet might ingest it if it is very small!

Leave a tuned crystal in your pet's bed. (You may have to hide it under the cushion; animals like to play with crystals.) You can tune it to work on all kinds of things, whatever is helpful to your pet and you, i.e., getting rid of fleas, healing a health problem, stopping a puppy wetting in the night, enhancing obedience training, helping a new kitten or puppy to accept the separation from its mother, assisting your canine or feline friend to pass over into the spirit world without pain when its days of mortal existence are coming to an end, etc. Be creative and resourceful. Only use crystal help in a positive way and always qualify your request with the words, ". . . if it is appropriate and right for _____ (your pet's name) at this time." This will make sure you are not going against your dog's or cat's free will.

If your pet spends time outside in your yard, tune several crystals to the task of being your pet's guardians, asking them to ensure that she doesn't leave the yard and subsequently come to harm. Place the crystals in the corners of your yard or equidistant from one another along the boundaries of your land and bury them a few inches below the surface of the ground. You may wish to mark their location in some manner in the event that you need to retrieve them at some time in the future. If this method of protection isn't suitable for you, then take a photograph of your pet while she is outside and place a guardian crystal on the developed print. Keep the crystal and the photo in a special or sacred place such as an altar. With either of these suggestions, try reinforcing the protection by stating, "Should _____ (your pet's name) get loose, then please protect her from . . . ." (qualify the type of harm which might happen, i.e., cars, poisoning, becoming lost, being stolen, getting into fights with other animals, etc.). Whether your pet lives indoors or outside it will also need protection at the spirit level, so asking a crystal to tune itself to help in this way is very beneficial. Again, placing the crystal on a photograph of her will ensure twenty-four-hour protection.

Crystals can be placed in litter trays, having been tuned to help eliminate odors. They can be asked to help deter your cat from scratching the furniture or your puppy from chewing on everything in sight. They will even encourage your dog to shed her hairs outside instead of indoors. You only have to ask. All forms of illness, skin problems, etc. can be treated solely with crystals, or you can request that the crystals work in partnership with conventional or alternative medicine. If your pet loses a limb, an appropriately tuned crystal will ease this trauma, giving the animal a sense of the missing limb. Should she develop cataracts, try placing crystals around your home and asking them to become her eyes so that she doesn't fall or bump into things. Visualize this working like radar or sonic waves when you are tuning these crystals. All forms of crystal healing/adjustment/therapy work best when the tuned "helper" stays within the aura of its patient. Because an animal's auric body is far more extensive than that of a human, the desired results can be fully achieved.

If you are attempting or are well able to communicate with your pet, try tuning a crystal to enhance this process. You will be surprised at the increase in awareness and understanding for both of you.

Crystal healing using layouts and gridworks can be given to animals. However, unless your pet is asleep or quite ill, it probably won't lie still long enough for you to achieve anything. I personally believe this form of healing should not be taken lightly, whether it is for animals or humans. It should only be attempted after you have been working quite extensively with crystals and are knowledgeable in sacred geometry and healing work. You can, however, make your pet "feel good" by combing its aura, even if it is 100% healthy. Using a small crystal cluster (I would recommend Amethyst) and holding it a few inches away from the animal's body, start gently combing from slightly above the head downwards towards the feet and along the body to just beyond the top of the tail. Do not at any time comb in an upward motion. If you are not familiar with auric work, first try closing your eyes, relaxing, and then slowly moving your hands towards your pet's body. At some point you should begin to feel a sensation in your palms and/or fingertips; it may come as a warm or tingling feeling. Once you have identified this, you can open your eyes and begin to move your hands along the body contours, noting the differences between one area and another. Always keep your hands a little distance away from the body and use gentle, slow movements, never sudden or jerky ones. Some people do not "feel" auras, but can "hear" or "see" them. Whatever works for you is fine; there is no right or wrong method. The strengths and weaknesses of the inner senses are as individualistic as those of the five physical senses. As with other crystal work, remember to cleanse, dedicate, tune and thank the cluster.

If your dog or cat is sick and is lying still, you may be able to build a healing/protective pyramid around her which will promote the return of good health. Using four small to medium-sized clusters—these can be Clear Quartz, Smoky Quartz, Amethyst, Citrine, or whatever feels right to you—begin by placing one cluster a few inches beyond the tail end of your pet and another a few inches beyond her head. Check that these clusters are level with each other by drawing an imaginary line from the one at the head, down along your pet's back to the one beyond the tail. Next place the other two clusters on either side of the animal, one at an appropriate distance from the midpoint of the back and the other similarly from the underbelly. You will know the exact distance to place them away from the body when you realize that these four clusters are the base points of your pyramid, and each needs to be equidistant from the other. These clusters do not have to be all the same type of Quartz and, if you have less than four, you can substitute with any object which has a religious/spiritual meaning for you, i.e., a rosary, a religious picture, a Goddess symbol or statue, a totem animal or fetish, a talisman or amulet, etc. Do try, however, to have clusters at the head and tail of your pet. Now stand close to her and begin to construct the other dimensions of your pyramid by holding your hands, palms downwards and arms spread out, over the head and tail clusters. Please stand to do this; don't kneel or sit, otherwise your pyramid will be too confining. After a few moments you should feel a warmth or tingling sensation within your palms. When you do, move your hands slowly upwards, palms facing inwards, to a central point above your pet's body. Visualize or sense a large crystal forming the point of your pyramid and allow your palms to make contact with it. After you have done this exercise a few times, you will be able to "see" and/or "feel" this crystal; mine is a beautiful clear Celestite point. Bring your hands back down to their original position over the head and tail clusters and then repeat these upward and downward movements twice more. As you are doing this, know that you are building the boundaries of your pyramid; "feel" these two edges of your creation. Next move to a position where you can repeat this process over the other two base points of your pyramid. When you have completed the third downward movement, begin to move around the outside of your construction, running your hands up and down the four sides to check for holes and to seal the edges. You will be able to "feel" the pyramid in some way. Do not worry if, while constructing it, you appear to be moving in and out of its boundaries. You are its creator and will not disturb its form until you make an intentional decision to do so.

When everything is built to your satisfaction, either sit, kneel, or stand close to one side of your pyramid and place your palms on that side. Relax and begin to imagine/sense yourself opening up to become a channel through which the radiant, loving, healing energy, of which we are all a part, can pass. Feel it moving down through your crown to your heart, where it builds and intensifies until it radiates out along your arms and into your hands. Visualize it streaming from your palms and fingertips, penetrating the side of your pyramid and filling the whole interior with its loving, healing, and protecting essence. If it helps your visualization, "see" it as golden or pure white, as green or blue, and hold the conviction that it is restoring wellness to your pet. Keep channeling this energy from outside yourself. Try not to break the link, otherwise you will be projecting your own healing energy into the pyramid. This will quickly deplete you of your life force for a while.

You will readily gain a sense of when to stop channeling. As this occurs, remember to send a large "Thank you" on behalf of your pet and yourself. Remove the crystal clusters, remembering to thank and cleanse them. Then dispel the energy field of the pyramid by sweeping it away with your hands or any object you feel is appropriate. I use a very large white feather which was given to me when I visited the Seven Sacred Realms and experienced the power of the medicine wheel on a shamanistic journey that I took last year. As you sweep this energy away, mentally send it to the Light so that it can be used for the Highest Good.

You can also begin to discover how well your pet's physical, emotional, mental, and spiritual bodies are by dowsing her chakras. These energy centers have been referred to earlier in this book and also in *Natural Healing For Dogs And Cats* by Diane Stein. You should never dowse with a crystal pendulum directly over the animal's chakras unless you have an understanding of their energy flow, but you can use another method which is equally as accurate. Using your receptive hand (usually your left if you are right-handed) for sensing, and holding the pendulum, swinging freely and away from your pet's body, with your right hand, begin by requesting help from only the highest angelic realms. Ask to be shown each chakra's energy flow on the inward breath (energy intake) and, starting with the crown chakra, place your receptive hand a few inches above this energy point. The pendulum should quickly respond by swinging in a clockwise circular motion. Move your hand down over the main chakras all the way to the root one and the pendulum will swing alternately in one circular direction and then the other. Begin again at the root chakra, asking to be shown the energy flow on the outward breath (energy output) and, starting counterclockwise, the pendulum will swing, alternating its direction for each chakra. You may also want to be shown the energy flow, inward and outward, of your pet's minor chakras. Any up-and-down or side-to-side movement, instead of circular, means the chakra's energy flow is not correct. Very wide circles may indicate that the chakra is open too wide, and little or no movement usually means the chakra is blocked. If there is no movement, move your receptive hand a little and, if the pendulum begins to move properly, the chakra is fine, it just means that your hand was directly over the central point of energy flow, the "eye" where there is no movement. Sometimes you will see the pendulum swing diagonally in one direction and then it will change to the opposite diagonal direction. This is known as a "star" and means the chakra is undergoing change and, therefore, should not receive any healing/adjustment. It is important to remember that the energy flow of chakras is constantly changing. You could repeat this exercise a few hour later and see totally different responses from the pendulum. If, however, over a period of days or weeks you observe the same problems, you may wish to seek the help of an experienced crystal healer, Reiki master, or spiritual healer for your pet.

Whether you try auric combing, pyramid building or chakra dowsing, it is essential to ground and center both yourself and your pet before, during, and at the end of the treatment. There are books available which will give you specific exercises for ensuring these things. What you are basically doing is maintaining the connection with the Earth Mother so that you and/or your pet don't go flying off into other dimensions (this is grounding); also you are keeping an acute sense of where you and your pet are in relationship to the physical compass points as well as the vaster, more complex directions of the universe and other levels of existence (this is centering).

It is equally important to protect yourself and your pet when pursuing any form of metaphysical work. Again, much information on this can be found in books. For the novice I would say, "Keep it simple!" Say a prayer, visualize you and your pet totally surrounded/enveloped in the pure, white Light, or hold a protective amulet. Even though these suggestions are not complex and involved, they will be very powerful for you as long as you have faith and conviction in whichever one you choose. As mentioned before, asking for help from the highest angelic realms and remembering to give thanks afterwards will also keep away anything which is not of the Light. Finally, when doing any type of crystal work with animals, never forget to respect their free will; only ask for what is appropriate and in keeping with each animal's right to choose.

These then are a few ways in which crystals can be of help to animals. If you take the time to listen to crystals, they will give you many more. So be attentive to them and become their friend. Both your life and that of your pet(s) will take on a fuller and richer meaning. Enjoy working with our crystal cousins, have fun, and always experiment in a positive manner.

Love and Light
Marion Webb-De Sisto
(June 19, 1993—New Moon in Gemini)

Referrals

Holistic Veterinary Associations

American Holistic Veterinary Medical Association
2214 Old Emmorton Rd.
Bel Air, MD 21014
(410) 569-0795
(Referrals)

International Veterinary Acupuncture Society
2140 Conestoga Rd.
Chester Springs, PA 19425
(215) 827-7245
(Referrals)

National Center for Homeopathy
801 N. Fairfax #306
Alexandria, VA 22314
(703) 548-7790
(Referrals, Booklists)

Toxicology Hotline for Animals
University of Illinois College of Veterinary Medicine
2001 S. Lincoln Ave.
Urbana, Illinois 61801
1-800-548-2423   ($30 charge on credit card)
1-900-680-0000   ($20 first five minutes, then $2.95 per minute
(Poison Center)   on phone bill)

American Veterinary Chiropractic Association
POB 249
Port Byron, IL 61275
(309) 523-3995
(Referrals)

California Holistic Veterinary Medical Association
c/o Beth Wildermann, DVM
17333 Bear Creek Rd.
Boulder Creek, CA 95006

Holistic Veterinarians

Many of these holistic practitioners are also available for phone consultation work. Contact them for prices and requirements.

California
Sheldon Altman, DVM
2723 W. Olive Ave.
Burbank, CA 91505
(818) 845-7246
Holistic Animal Clinic
John Craige, VMD
John Ottaviano, OMD
N. Hollywood, CA
(818) 769-5800
Nancy Scanlon, DVM
La Habra, CA
(213) 691-7751

Connecticut
Stephen Tobin, DVM
Meriden, CT 06450
(203) 238-9863

Florida
Jan Bellows, DVM
9111 Taft St.
Pembroke Pines, FL 33024
(305) 432-1111
John H. Fudens, DVM
Affinity Holistic Veterinary Clinic
29296 US 19 N., Suite 104
Clearwater, FL 34621
(813) 787-6010
David Goodman, DVM
8335 W. Atlantic Blvd.
Coral Springs, FL 33071
John C. Haromy, DVM
3631 Hwy 60 E.
Lake Wales, FL 33853
(813) 676-5922
Anne Lampru, DVM
3816 W. Humphrey
Tampa, FL 33614
(813) 933-6609
H.S. Stoneman, DVM
10 Fort Royal Isle
Fort Lauderdale, FL 33308
(305) 564-1388
Russell Swift, DVM
3511 W. Commercial Blvd, Suite 227
Fort Lauderdale, FL 33309
(305) 739-4416
Leslie S. Wilner, DVM
6487 Taft St.
Hollywood, FL 33024

Hawaii
William F. Falconer, DVM
Kula, Maui, HI
(808) 878-2488

Indiana
Carolyn S. Blakey, DVM
Westdale Animal Clinic
1821 W. Main St.
Richmond, IN 47374
(317) 966-0015

Maryland
Christina B. Chambreau, DVM
908 Cold Bottom Rd.
Sparks, MD 21152
(301) 771-4968
Wendy Thacher, DVM
7764 Chatfield Lane
Ellicott City, MD 21043
(410) 379-0671

Massachusetts
Roger L. DeHaan, DVM
531 Amesbury Rd.
Haverhill, MA
(508) 521-1899

Nevada
Joanne Stefanatos, DVM
1325 Vegas Valley Dr.
Las Vegas, NV 89109
(702) 735-7184

New Jersey
Charles T. Schenck
Edgebrook Veterinary Hospital
777 Helmetta Blvd.
E. Brunswick, NJ 08816
(908) 257-8882

North Carolina
Donald K. Hamilton, DVM
Charles E. Loops, DVM
Asheville, NC 28806
(704) 254-5778

Pennsylvania
Deva K. Khalsa, VMA
Animal Healing Center, Inc.
1724 Yardley-Langhorne Rd.
Yardley, PA 19067
(215) 493-0621

South Carolina
Jeanne R. Demyan, DVM, CVA
All About Pets, Inc. Animal Hospital
409 Old Buncombe Rd.
Travelers Rest, SC 29690
(803) 834-7334

West Virginia
Jane Laura Doyle, DVM
(304) 258-5819

Veterinary Chiropractors

Marshall Harris
1884 Como Avenue
St. Paul, MN 55108
(612) 943-2899

Daniel Kamen
Petipulation
3421 N. Arlington Hts. Road
Arlington Hts, IL 60004
(708) 394-3530

Bernard Presser
7036 E. Colfax Avenue
Denver, CO 80220
(303) 355-4686

Dick Plummer
Springfield Chiropractive
1111 Springfield Road
Inman, SC 29349
(803) 578-1181

Sharon Willoughby, DVM
Options for Animals
POB 249
Port Byron, IL 61275
(309) 523-3995

Veterinary Homeopaths

The following list was provided by the National Center for Homeopathy.

California
John B. Limehouse, DVM
10742 Riverside Dr.
N. Hollywood, CA 91602
(818) 761-0787

Connecticut
Stephen Tobin, DVM
26 Pleasant St.
Meriden, CT 06450
(203) 238-9863

Florida
John H. Fudens, DVM
Affinity Holistic Clinic
29296 US 19 N.
Clearwater, FL 34621
(813) 787-6010

Georgia
Michelle Tilgham, DMV
5398 E. Mountain St.
Stone Mountain, GA 30083
(404) 498-5956

Maryland
Christina B. Chambreau, DVM
908 Cold Bottom Rd.
Sparks, MD 21152
(301) 771-4968

Monique Maniet, DVM
7330 Carroll Ave.
Takoma Park, MD 20912
(301) 270-4700

Wendy Thacher, DVM
7764 Chatfield Lane
Ellicott City, MD 21043
(410) 379-0671

Carvel G. Tiekert, DVM
2214 Old Emmorton Rd.
Bel Air, MD 21014
(410) 569-7777

Massachusetts
Jeffrey Levy, DVM
71 Ashfield Rd.
Williamsburg, MA 01096
(413) 268-3000

Robert G. Sidorsky, DVM
Rt 2
Shelburne Falls, MA 01370
(413) 625-9517

Michigan
Lynne M. Friday, DVM
5346 Main St.
Lexington, MI 48450
(313) 359-8828

Nevada
Joanne Stefanatos, DVM
1325 Vegas Valley Dr.
Las Vegas, NV 89109
(702) 735-7184

Wendy Thacher, DVM
7764 Chatfield Lane
Ellicott City, MD 21043
(410) 379-0671

New York
Iris Ramirez-Prestas, DVM
Candor Animal Care
90 Main St. Box 5
Candor, NY 13743
(607) 659-4220

North Carolina
Donald K. Hamilton, DVM
485 Old County Home Rd.
Asheville, NC 28806
(704) 254-4224

Charles E. Loops, DVM
140 Mallard Court
Chapel Hill, NC 27514
(919) 932-1343

Ohio
Donn Griffith, DVM
3859 W. Dublin-Granville Rd.
Dublin, OH 43017
(614) 889-2556

Pennsylvania
Deva Kaur Khalsa, VMD
1724 Yardley-Langhorne Rd.
Yardley, PA 19067
(215) 943-0621

C. Edgar Sheaffer, DVM
11 Flowers Dr.
Mechanicsburg, PA 17055
(717) 838-4879
(717) 795-9799

South Carolina
Jeanne R. Demyan, DVM, CVA
Travelers Rest Animal Hospital
409 Buncombe Rd.
Travelers Rest, SC 29690
(803) 834-7334

Vermont
George Ganzberg, VMD
RR1 Box 373 White Creek Rd.
N. Bennington, VT 05257
(802) 442-8714

Virginia
Eric P. Hartmann, DVM
McLean Animal Hospital
1330 Old Chain Bridge Rd.
McLean, VA 22101
(703) 356-5000

Wisconsin
Marta W. Engel, DVM
RR1 Box 1198
Soldiers Grove, WI 54655
(608) 734-3711

Veterinary Acupuncturists

The following is a list of certified Veterinary Acupuncturists. For more information or other referrals, contact:

The International Veterinary Acupuncture Society
c/o Meredith L. Snader, VMD
2140 Conestoga Road
Chester Springs, PA 19425
(215) 827-7245

This list is reproduced by permission of the IVAS.

Alabama
Eugene E. Saffen, DVM
2490 Hiway 45
Eight Mile, AL 36612
(205) 457-1247

Arkansas
Jeanne Olson, DVM
1684 Palomino Drive
North Pole, AK 99705

Bill D. Presley, DVM
Box 1184
Mountain Home, AR 72653
(501) 492-5775

Arizona
James C. Armer Jr., DVM
HC 66 Box 2118
Cornville, AZ 86325
(602) 634-7538

Vicki Baumler, DVM
3828 East Talowa Street
Phoenix, AZ 85044
(602) 496-9332

Candy D. Burton, DVM
Sahuaro Vista Veterinary Clinic
333 West Cool Drive
Tucson, AZ 85704
(602) 297-3313

Patricia P. Freerick, DVM
6202 West Ina Road
Tucson, AZ 85742
(603) 744-3552

Lea Harvey, DVM
1830 East Cortez Drive
Gilbert, AZ 85234
(602) 892-4130

Judith Stolz, DVM
2682 North El Dorado Drive
Chandler, AZ 85224
(602) 992-4560

California
Kris Ahlberg, DVM
P.O. Box 862
Solvang, CA 93464
(805) 688-9245
Fax no.: 1-805-344-2216
(do voice call first)

Sheldon Altman, DVM
2723 West Olive Avenue
Burbank, CA 91505
(818) 845-7246

John P. Araujo, DVM
105 North Lima Street
Sierra Madre, CA 91024
(818) 355-2924

Leslie B. Berryman, DVM
4535 Longs Trail
Vacaville, CA 95688
(707) 447-8559

Constance J. Bridgeforth, DVM
8041 Ney Avenue
Oakland, CA 94605
(510) 845-3633

John W. Byrd, DVM
31441 Avenida De La Vista
San Juan Capistrano, CA 92675
(714) 661-8522

Lauren Al Cauer, DMV
2801 Oceanside Boulevard
Oceanside, CA 92054
(619) 757-2442

J. Lauren DeRock, DVM
3898 Stagecoach Road
P.O. Box 312
Copperopolis, CA 95228
(408) 778-1186

Hannah M. Good, DVM
2943 South Citrus Street
West Covina, CA 91791
(408) 633-2013

Jack H. Gregg, DVM
79705 Bermuda Dunes Drive
Bermuda Dunes, CA 92201
(213) 691-7751

Jack H. Gregg, Jr., DVM
P.O. Box 2513
La Habra, CA 90631
(213) 691-7751

Raphael H. Jimenez, DVM
P.O. Box 432651
San Diego, CA 92143-2651
Work No.: 91-661-21127 (Mexico)
Fax No.: 91-661-20750

William E. Hiatt, DVM
2506 Lincoln Boulevard
Venice, CA 90291
(213) 306-8707

Ed Hill, DVM
9818 Mission Blvd.
Riverside, CA 92509

Ann-si Li, DVM
Campanile Veterinary Clinic
5666 Telegraph Avenue
Oakland, CA 94609
(510) 652-1003

Douglas Lemire, VMD
Montecito Animal Hospital
1252 Coast Village Circle
Santa Barbara, CA 93106
(310) 275-7138

John B. Limehouse, DVM
L'house Vet. Clinic of Holistic Med.
10742 Riverside Drive
North Hollywood, CA 91602
(818) 761-0787
Fax no.: (818) 761-0719

Don E. Lundholm, DVM
10130 Adams Avenue
Huntington Beach, CA 92646
(714) 964-1605

Almeda L. Lynn, DVM
3220 Alpine Boulevard
Alpine, CA 92001
(619) 445-5683

Kevin James May, DVM
560 North Johnson
El Cajon, CA 92020
(619) 444-9491

Walter A. McCall, DVM
2160 South Winchester Boulevard
Campbell, CA 95008
(408) 378-5190
Fax no.: 1-408-379-2504

Ken S. Ninomiya, DVM
3624 Via Pacifica Walk
Oxnard, CA 93035
(805) 984-6293

Henry Pasternak, DVM
Highland Veterinary Hospital
526 Palisades Drive
Pacific Palisades, CA 90272
(213) 454-2917

Kerry J. Ridgeway, DVM
4120 Meadowbrook Road
Garden Valley, CA 95633
(916) 333-1539
Fax no.: 1-916-333-2134

Nancy Scanlan, DVM
Gregg Animal Hospital
P.O. Box 2513
La Habra, CA 90631
(310) 691-7751

Cheryl Schwartz, DVM
East-West Animal Care Center
1201 East 12th Street
Oakland, CA 94606
(510) 534-3924

Marshall E. Scott, DVM
2955 Van Buren Boulevard H-8
Riverside, CA 92503
(714) 359-0363

Larry Paul Siegler, DVM
57 Indian Rock Court
San Anselmo, CA 94960
(415) 388-4300

Robert Smatt, DVM
5621 Balboa Avenue
San Diego, CA 92111-2705
(619) 278-1575

Priscilla A. Taylor-Limehouse, DVM
L'house Vet. Clinic of Holistic Med.
10742 Riverside Drive
North Hollywood, CA 91602
(818) 761-0787
Fax no.: 818-761-0719

Greg Ugarte, DVM
13040 McKinley Avenue
Chino, CA 91710
(714) 628-1137

Patricia Ungar, DVM
Kensington Veterinary Hospital
3817 Adams Avenue
San Diego, CA 92116
(619) 584-8418

Thomas Van Cise, DVM
1560 Hamner Avenue
Norco, CA 91760
(714) 737-1242

Mark H. Wright, DVM
7340 Firestone Boulevard #117
Downey, CA 90241
(310) 928-2234

Colorado
David H. Jagger, MRCVS
5139 Sugarloaf Road
Boulder, CO 80302-9217
(303) 449-7936

Janice Pacinelli, DVM
5015 Raleigh
Denver, CO 80212
(303) 458-5428

James E. Watson, DVM
7007 E. Peakview Place
Englewood, CO 80111
(303) 770-6545

Connecticut
Dr. Med. Vet. Daniela D. Leu
853 Orange Street
New Haven, CT 06511
(203) 785-3247

Allys Maybank, VMD
43 Quarry Road
Granby, CT 06035
(203) 653-2257

Richard D. Mitchell, DVM
Fairfield Equine Associates, P.C.
755 Main Street
Monroe, CT 06468
(203) 261-7724

Nancy P. Sawyer, DVM
60 Cedar Gate Road
Darien, CT 06820

Allen M. Schoen, DVM, MS
R.R. #2
Sunset Terrace
Sherman, CT 06784
(203) 354-2287

Carolyn M. Weinberg, DVM
Fairfield Equine Associates
755 Main Street
Monroe, CT 06468
(203) 261-7724

Neil C. Wolff, DVM
Blue Cross Animal Hospital
530 East Putnam Avenue
Greenwich, CT 06830
(203) 869-7755

Delaware
Greig A. Howie, DVM
Dover Animal Hospital
1151 South Governor's Avenue
Dover, DE 19901
(302) 674-1515

Lorraine S. Parris, DVM
1211 Newport Gap Pike
Wilmington, DE 19804
(302) 998-8851

Florida
LaVonne Congdon, DVM
2924 Woodrich Drive #B
Tallahassee, FL 32301

Robin Cannizaro, DVM
326 49th Ave. N.
St. Petersburg, FL 33703
(813) 528-0298

Joseph Demers, DVM
4982 South US Highway 1
Palm Bay, FL 32905
(407) 725-6444

Lynn Duffy, DVM
6341 Biggs Street
Englewood, FL 34224
(813) 474-1165

Deborah A. Ford, DVM
700 North East 10th Avenue
Pompano Beach, FL 33060
(305) 782-1224

Jeffrey A. Goldberg, DVM, MS
Rt #2 Box 664
Newberry, FL 32669
(904) 372-6603

John C. Haromy, DVM
Haromy Animal Clinic
3631 Highway 60 East
Lake Wales, FL 33853
(813) 676-5922

Anne Lampru, DVM
3816 West Humphrey Street
Tampa, FL 33614
(813) 933-6609

Deborah L. Marshall, DVM
2611 Anderson Road, #1
Coral Gables, FL 33134
(305) 446-8575

Jack L. Musgrave, DVM, MS
Suncoast Mobile Veterinary Clinic
5732 Rowan Road
New Port Richey, FL 34653
(813) 848-8030

Richard Panzer, DVM, MS
313 N.W. 15th Avenue
Gainesville, FL 32601
(904) 392-8260

Nancy J. Saxe, DVM
3530 Lantana Road
Lantana, FL 33462
(407) 439-0694

Alyce M. Sims, DVM
Riverside Animal Clinic
2641 Park Street
Jacksonville, FL 32204
(904) 353-7308

Lyndall Soule, DVM
P.O. Box 941
Roseland, FL 32957
(407) 984-1952

Pamela J. Wood, DVM
5142 Glencove Lane
West Palm Beach, FL 33415-7468
(407) 433-2244

Georgia
Howard, Rand, DVM
2000 Bill Burdock Road
Marietta, GA 30062
(404) 973-4133

M. Spencer Newman, DVM
Lenox Animal Hospital and Bird Clinic
2425 Colonial Drive North-East
Atlanta, GA 30319
(404) 237-0316

Michelle Tilghman, DVM
Loving Touch Animal Center
5398 East Mountain Street
Stone Mountain, GA 30083
(404) 498-5956

Hawaii
Ihor John Basko, DVM
POB 798
Hanalei, HI 96714-0798
(808) 828-1330
(808) 822-9207

William P. Falconer, DVM
POB 156
Kula, Maui, HI 96790
(808) 871-5656

Idaho
Ronald L. Hamm, DVM
2337 Lago Liberty Rd.
Grace, ID 83241
(208) 427-6233

Illinois
Mary Baukert, DVM
2460 Fir
Glenview, IL 60025
(708) 729-7997

Charles E. Lindley, DVM
206 West Illinois Street
Oblong, IL 62449
(618) 592-3222

Ellen M. Paul, DVM
2603 Southwood Drive
Champaign, IL 61821
(217) 344-1017

Gregory A. Petkus, DVM
1161 South Batavia Avenue
Batavia, IL 60510
(312) 879-0190

Judith Rae Swanson, DVM
1465 West Catalpa, Apt. #1E
Chicago, IL 60640
(312) 561-4526

Indiana
Carolyn S. Blakey, DVM
Westside Animal Clinic
1821 West Main Street
Richmond, IN 47374
(317) 966-0015

Terry Durkes, DVM
Western Avenue Animal Hospital
909 North Western Avenue
Marion, IN 46952

Edwin H. Page, DVM
2209 Huron Road
West Lafayette, IN 47906
(317) 494-8548

Andrew A. Pickering, DVM
Wabash Valley Animal Hospital
3004 South 7th Street
Terre Haute, IN 47802
(812) 232-5414

Bruce Sickels, DVM
Countryside Veterinary Clinic
R.R. #4 Box 263
Union City, IN 47390
(317) 964-7119

Iowa
Mary A. Anson, DVM
Box 333
Brighton, IA 52540
(319) 694-2815

Janis D. Potter Bell, DVM
617 N. 1st Street
Green, IA 50636

Camme H. Cottom, DVM
RR #6 Box 173
Bloomfield, IA 52537

Richard J. Holliday, DVM
203 2nd Street NE
Waukon, IA 52172
(319) 568-3401

Charles L. McDaniel, DVM
RR 2 Box 31
Radcliffe, IA 50230
(515) 899-2257

Roger P. Reppert, DVM
303 Main
Ireton, IA 51027
(712) 278-2577

Robert A. Telleen, DVM
1128 McDuffie Drive
Box 48
Jefferson, IA 50129
(515) 386-3600

Gary D. Van Engelenburg, DVM
109 W. 1st Street
Sumner, IA 50674
(319) 578-3216

Kansas
Jeffrey F. Van Petten, DVM
Rt 1 Box 98
Meriden, KS 66512
(913) 484-3358

Kentucky
John R. Baker, DVM
P.O. Box 322
Burlington, KY 41005

Betty Ann Boswell, DVM
Belknap Office Building
1810 Sils Avenue
Louisville, KY 40205

Alan R. Dorton, DVM
Woodford Veterinary Clinic
P.O. Box 108
Versailles, KY 40383
(606) 873-7361

Roger A. Magnusson, DVM
4233 Greenhaven Lane
Goshen, KY 40026
(502) 228-8493

Howard Rennecker, DVM
3375-D Tates Creek
Lexington, KY 40502
(606) 266-3215

Sabra St. Germain, DVM
Ambulatory Veterinary Services
1220 Versailles Road
Lexington, KY 40383-1491
(606) 254-4525

Earl Sutherland, DVM
P.O. Box 12009
Lexington, KY 40579-2009
(606) 281-9112

Walter W. Zent, DVM
4430 Newtown Pike
Lexington, KY 40511
(606) 255-5103

Louisiana
David M. Lowdermilk, DVM
2512 Brown Circle
Bossier City, LA 71111
(318) 742-9997

Janet W. Olcott, DVM
4574 Highway 24
Gray, LA 70359
(504) 868-1230

Maine
David A. Jefferson, DVM
23 Googin Street
Lewiston, ME 04240
(207) 782-8318

Maryland
Donald J. Carren, DVM
725 Whitehall Plains Rd.
Annapolis, MD 21501-6141
(301) 757-2555

Monique Mainet, DVM
Takoma Park Animal Clinic
7330 Carroll Avenue
Takoma Park, MD 20912
(301) 270-4700

Deborah M. McMichael, DVM
Little Seneca Animal Hospital, Inc.
13009 Wisteria Drive
Germantown, MD 20874
(301) 972-1691

John W. Stott, DVM
POB 70
Lothian, MD 20711
(301) 627-8668

Carvel Tiekert, DVM
2214 Old Emmorton Road
Bel Air, MD 21014
(410) 569-7777

Mark D. Wysocki, DVM
1309 Stockett Square
Belcamp, MD 21017-1101
(410) 569-7774

Massachusetts
Bud Allen, DVM
Family Veterinarian
P.O. Box 478
Haydenville, MA 01039

Sarah L. Cochran, DVM
Mass Equine Clinic
75 Locust Street
Uxbridge, MA 01569
(508) 278-6511

Liza M. Hoberg, DVM
6 Linnaean Street
Cambridge, MA 02138

Allys Maybank, VMD
7 Russell Road
Westfield, MA 01085
(415) 362-1551

Mary P. Patterson, DVM
Combined Veterinary Services
249 High Street
Ipswich, MA 01738-1242
(608) 887-5877

Richard P. Rodger, DVM
5 Waterville Street
North Grafton, MA 01536
(508) 839-2293

Daryl Smiley, DVM
95 Townsend Street
Pepperell, MA 01263-1203

Michigan
Harold D. Sheridan, DVM
16025 68th Street
Coopersville, MI 49404

John M. Simon, DVM
Woodise Animal Clinic
410 North Woodward
Royal Oak, MI 48067
(313) 851-0272

Michael H. Stajich, DVM
4618 Packard
Ann Arbor, MI 48104

Russel W. Wagner, DVM
7045 Traverse Avenue
Benzonia, MI 49616
(616) 882-9906

Minnesota
Daniel P. Hartsell, DVM
RR #7 Box 12
Alexandria, MN 56308

Mississippi
A.P. Carney, DVM, Dipl. ABVP
POB 3728
Meridian, MS 39305
(601) 693-7333

Missouri
Sherri Russell, DVM
2402 E. McCarty
Jefferson City, MO 65101
(314) 635-0435

Montana
Roderk S. Meier, BS, DVM
POB 117
Sweetgrass, MT 59484-0117

Nebraska
Bernard Fletcher, DVM
P.O. Box 159
Arlington, NE 68002-0159
(402) 359-4333

Joseph E. Landholm, DVM
1345 Crestdale Road
Lincoln, NE 68510-4972
(402) 483-4862

Carl G. Martin, DVM
Box 702
Valley, NE 68064
(402) 359-4233

Diane E. Simmons, E Ed, B Sc, DVM
3414 Horning Road
Plattsmouth, NE 68048
(402) 593-6556

Nevada
Joanne Stefanatos, DVM
1325 Vegas Valley Drive
Las Vegas, NV 98109
(702) 735-7184

New Hampshire
Gretchen E. Ham, DVM
82 Franklin Street Apts. #1
Derry, NH 03038-1949
(603) 329-6689

New Jersey
Jo Anne Greenberg, VMD
Emerson Animal Hospital
371 Kinderkamack Road
Emerson, NJ 07630
(201) 262-2950

James D. Kenney, DVM
P.O. Box 512
Colts Neck, NJ 07722-0512
(908) 462-9403

Charles A. Moore, DVM
P.O. Box 6099
Freehold, NJ 07728-6099
(908) 446-4151

Gloria B. Weintraub, VMD
190 Route 70
Countryside Animal Hospital
Medford, NJ 08055
(609) 953-3502

New Mexico
B. Dee Blanco, DVM
POB 5865
Santa Fe, NM 87502
(505) 983-2022

New York
Stephen O. Abel
Oneida Animal Hospital
101 Genesee Street
Oneida, NY 13421
(315) 363-1992

Donald J. Baker, DVM
P.O. Box 328
Floral Park, NY 11002-0328

Bruce C. Campbell, DVM, CVA
5383 Thomas Road
Canandaigua, NY 14425
(716) 394-2288

Richard W. Fredericks, DVM
North Shore Veterinary Hospital
835 Fort Salonga Road
Northport, NY 11768
(516) 757-0522

Robert F. Hirt, DVM
154 Orchard Park Road
West Seneca, NY 14224
(716) 824-4108

Richard J. Joseph, DVM
The Animal Medical Center
510 East 62nd Street
New York City, NY 10021
(212) 838-8100

D. Evan Kanouse, DVM
Brookfarm Veterinary Center
Rt. 3 - Box 234
Patterson, NY 12563
(914) 878-4833

William S. Kelley, DVM
Baldwinsville Animal Hospital
2372 West Genesee Road
Baldwinsville, NY 13027
(315) 635-5921

Cynthia Jean Lankenau, DVM
6713 Luther Street
Niagara Falls, NY 14304
(716) 735-7400
(716) 735-3204

Robert C. O'Keefe, DVM
P.O. Box 532
Norwich, NY 13815
(607) 334-4335

Howard W. Rothstein, DVM
Saugerties Animal Hosptial
163 Ulster Avenue
Saugerties, NY 12477
(914) 246-6150

Ronald A. Scharf, DVM
71 Ryckman Avenue
Albany, NY 12208
(518) 459-3396

Linda A. Schneider, DVM
246 Hidden Brook Trail
Victor, NY 14564
(716) 924-7861

Martin Stampler, DVM
1230 East 9th Street
Brooklyn, NY 11230
(718) 434-1919

Michele Ann Yasson, DVM
P.O. Box 291
Rosendale, NY 12472-0291
(914) 658-9720

North Carolina
Donald K. Hamilton, DVM
485 Old County Home Road
Asheville, NC 28806
(704) 254-4224

John H. Koontz, DVM
4306 Roxboro Road
Durham, NC 27704
(919) 471-1579

William M. Martin, DVM
Fletcher Animal Hospital
6795 Hendersonville Road
Fletcher, NC 28760
(704) 684-4244

Patricia McKee Pagel, MS, DVM
78 Green Tree Trail
Chapel Hill, NC 27516

Betsy J. Pethick, DVM
Quail Corners Animal Hospital
1613 Millbrook Road
Raleigh, NC 27609
(919) 876-0739

Ohio
Marvin J. Cain, DVM
7474 Greenfarms Drive
Cincinnati, OH 45224-1210
(513) 522-3883

Paul E. Clemens, DVM
17800 Munn Road
Chagrin Falls, OH 44023
(216) 548-1311

Gail E. Counts-Jock, DVM, MS
101 Pierly Road
Portsmouth, OH 45662
(614) 353-5758

Jon H. Ellis, DVM
1920 U.S. 68 North
Xenia, OH 45385
(513) 372-9976

Chris Gilbert, DVM
7630 State Route 118
Greenville, OH 45331-9359
(513) 548-0968

Donn W. Griffith, DVM
3859 West Dublin-Granville Road
Dublin, OH 43017
(614) 889-2556

R.L. Jeffries, DVM
1796 White Road
Grove City, OH 43123
(614) 875-4253

Lewis L. Israel, DVM
521 Oakwood
Bryan, OH 43506
(419) 636-1038

Brad D. Luckenbill, DVM
2522 Conwood Drive
Beavercreek, OH 45434-6911
(513) 426-6521

Ronald L. McNutt, DVM
1796 White Road
Grove City, OH 43123
(614) 875-4253

Robert Montgomery, DVM
1396 East High Avenue
New Philadelphia, OH 44663
(216) 339-2363

George D. Norris, DVM
Animal Hospital of Worthington
5756 North High Street
Worthington, OH 43085
(614) 885-0333

Donald J. Peteya, DVM
124 Miller Road
Avon Lake, OH 44012
(216) 935-5297

Kriston N. Sherman, DVM
5260 Catains Court
Columbus, OH 43220-2404
(614) 459-6985

Charles A. St. Jean, DVM
1739 Street - Rt. 61
Sunbury, OH 43074

Cletus N. Vonderwell, DVM
840 West Ohio Street
Delphos, OH 45835
(419) 583-3829

Oklahoma
Kim Edwards-Mitchell, DVM
P.O. Box 658
Bristow, OK 74010
(918) 367-3152

Darrel R. Kramer, DVM
Prairie Hills Veterinary Services
4224 Ryan Drive N.E.
Piedmont, OK 73078
(405) 373-4255

Howard L. Mitchell, DVM
P.O. Box 658
Bristow, OK 74010
(918) 367-3152

Rebecca C. Jestes, DVM
All Pets Veterinary Hospital
619 East Redbud
Stillwater, OK 74076
(405) 624-8622

F. Gary McNeill, DVM
9308 North Rockwell
Oklahoma City, OK 73132
(405) 728-7387

William H. Mitchell, DVM
P.O. Box 658
Bristow, OK 74010
(918) 367-2257

Oregon
Robert H. Anderson, DVM
Polk Veterinary Clinic
1590 East Ellendale Street
Dallas, OR 97338
(503) 623-8316

Lynda A. Clark, DVM
11611 S.E. Market Street
Portland, OR 97216

Daniel P. Clifton, DVM
Barbur Blvd. Veterinary Hospital
10629 South West Barbur Boulevard
Portland, OR 97219
(503) 246-4226

Gary J. Dilon, DVM
7518 South East Hogan Road
Gresham, OR 97080
(503) 666-8387

Laird M. Goodman, DVM
Murrayhill Veterinary Hospital
14831 S.W. Teal Boulevard
Beaverton, OR 97007
(503) 627-0300

Michael Partington, DVM
17061 South Burk Road
P.O. Box 283
Beavercreek, OR 97004-0283
(503) 632-7050

April J. Plummer, DVM
24241 Anderson Road
Clatskanie, OR 97016
(503) 556-3084

Royce N. Snook, DVM
13180 North Rim Road
Crooked River Ranch, OR 97760
(503) 356-3339

Pennsylvania
John Harthorn, DVM
R.R. # 1
Box 151
Avella, PA 15312
(412) 345-3350

Deva Kaur-Khalsa, DVM
Edgewood Village Veterinary Clinic
1724 Yardley-Langhorne Road
Yardley, PA 19067
(215) 493-0621

Alan M. Klide, VMD
VHUP - Anesthesia
3850 Spruce Street
Philadelphia, PA 19104-6010
(215) 898-5902

Marjorie M. Lewter, DVM
RR #2 - Box 155F
Ulster, PA 18850

Louise I. Morin, VMD
Delaware Valley Animal Hospital, PC
266 Lincoln Highway
Fairless Hills, PA 19030

Meredith L. Snader, VMD
2140 Conestoga Road
Chester Springs, PA 19425
(215) 827-7245

Judith M. Shoemaker, DVM
498 East State Road
West Grove, PA 19390
(215) 869-3346

Michael S. Tierney, VMD
Keystone Vet. Hosp. & Eq. Ctr.
428 Brownsburg Road—
RD #2 - Upper X
Newtown, PA 18940
(215) 598-3951

Patricia A. Whittaker, MS, VMD
370 Tree Lane
Aspers, PA 17304
(717) 677-9543

Jeanne F. Wordley, VMD
402 West 3rd Street
Media, PA 19063-2601
(215) 566-9019

Theodore Yuhas, VMD
501 South 2nd Street
Philadelphia, PA 19147
(215) 627-5955

South Carolina
Jeanne R. Demyan, DVM
Traveler's Rest Animal Hospital
409 Old Buncombe Road
Traveler's Rest, SC 29690
(803) 834-7334

Stan Gorlitsky, DVM
Low Country Animal Medical
  Center
25 Short's Landing Road
Lady's Island, SC 29902
(803) 524-0198

Ronnie Hu Fulmer, DVM
2301 North Lyttleton Street
Camden, SC 29020
(803) 432-3061

Tennessee
Pamela J. Chandler, DVM
2252 Mangum
Memphis, TN 38134

Texas
Nancy A. Bozeman, DVM
P.O. Box 151223
Arlington, TX 76015
(817) 429-5588

Paul R. Bruton, DVM
1125 Cable Creek
Grapevine, TX 76051
(817) 481-1382

Elaine Caplan, DVM
P.O. Box 164304
Austin, TX 78716
(512) 328-2289

Norman C. Ralston, DVM
12500 Lake June Road
Balch Springs, TX 75180
(214) 286-6407

Brian A. Reeves, DVM, BS
Reeves Small Animal Clinic
2711 University Boulevard
Tyler, TX 75701-7465
(214) 566-2212

Larry D. Shaw, DVM
12500 Melville Drive - #309A
Montgomery, TX 77356-5405
(713) 367-6283

Cory E. Stiles, DVM
9521 East Westheimer
Houston, TX 77063

Jake R. Wells, DVM
818 Austin Street
San Antonio, TX 78208
(5120 225-6531

Utah
Eric D. Foster, DVM
2361 East 3300 South
Salt Lake City, UT 84109
(801) 487-7791

Kimberly Henneman, DVM
Aequus Veterinary Service
6337 South Highland Drive #334
Salt Lake City, UT 84121
(801) 265-1459

Vermont
Mark A. Basol, DVM
34 Main Street
Vergennes, VT 05491
(802) 877-3371

Jackquelin Bird, DVM
Vergennes Animals Clinic
34 Main Street
Vergennes, VT 05491
(802) 877-3371

Virginia
Harold P. Alterman, VMD
3509 Sterling Avenue
Alexandria, VA 22304
(703) 866-4100

Scott W. Anderson, DVM
400 College Avenue
Ashland, VA 23005
(804) 798-3281

Stephen G. Dill, DVM
R.R. 2 Box 156
Barboursville, VA 22923-9602
(804) 985-4795

Joyce C. Harman, DVM, MRCVS
P.O. Box 193
Orlean, VA 22128
(703) 364-4077

Jordan Kocen, DVM, MS
Parkway Veterinary Clinic
5749 Burke Centre Parkway
Burke, VA 22015
(703) 323-9020

Janet I. McKim, DVM
Middleburg Animal Hospital
P.O. Box 368
Middleburg, VA 22117
(703) 687-6144

William H. McCormick, VMD
Middleburg Equine Clinic, Inc.
P.O. Box 1100
Middleburg, VA 22117
(703) 687-5249

Anita B. Walton, DVM
Locust Grove Vet. Care
137 Larkspur
P.O. Box 488
Locust Grove, VA 22508-0488
(703) 972-3869

Fayette Witherell, DVM
P.O. Box 477
Fodderstack Road
Flint Hill, VA 22627
(703) 675-3772

Washington
Bruce R. Bierbaum, DVM
Issaquah Veterinary Hospital
795 First N.W.
Issaqua, WA 98027
(206) 392-6211

Michael H. Cable, DVM
Big Valley Equine Services, P.S., Inc.
25297 Big Valley Road N.E.
Poulsbo, WA 98370
(206) 779-5557

Nell Carolyn Coffman, DVM
27401 99th Avenue S.W.
Vashon Island, WA 98070
(206) 463-3607

Beverly J. Hall, DVM
16418 7th Place West
Lynnwood, WA 98037
(206) 743-5802

Kate Schottman, DVM
9514 8th Avenue N.W. Apt. #305
Seattle, WA 98117
(206) 392-7387

Katherine C. Waters, DVM
2110 N.W. Couch Street
Camas, WA 98607
(206) 834-2356

West Virginia
Jane L. Doyle, DVM, CVA
POB 560
Berkeley Springs, WV 25411-0568
(304) 258-5819

Wisconsin
Maria Glinski, DVM
1405 West Silver Spring Drive
Glendale, WI 53209
(414) 228-7655

Mike D. Kohn, DVM
1014 Williamson
Madison, WI 53703
(608) 255-8608

Mark Mattison, DVM
N3662 Scenic Drive
La Crosse, WI 54601
(608) 812-3466

Thomas W. Myers, DVM
St. Anna Veterinary Clinic, S.C.
W2132 Hwy Q
Elkhart Lake, WI 53020
(414) 898-4227

Deborah Schroeder, DVM
1314 Jennifer Street
Madison, WI 53703
(608) 255-2977

John M. Turnbull, DVM
1514 Hoffman Place
Onalaska, WI 54650

Wyoming
Virgil Humphreys, DVM
Tri-County Veterinary Service
2409 Big Horn Ave - Mounted Rte.
Worland, WY 82401
(307) 347-3842

Animal Communicators and Psychics

Psychics
Laurel Steinhice
6712 Currywood Dr.
Nashville, TN 37205
(615) 356-4280

Marion Webb-DeSisto (Former)
38 Covington Gardens
Armoury Rd.
London, SE8 4LA
England

Animal Communicators
Kate Brower Solisti
Santa Fe, NM
(505) 984-8876

Morgana Davies
243 Knight St.
Providence, RI 02909
(401) 273-1176

Sue Goodrich
Escondido, CA
(619) 480-2474

Anastacia Gourley
POB 514
Everett, MA 01054
(413) 548-9806

Carol Gurney
3715 N. Cornell Rd.
Agoura, CA 91301
(818) 597-1154

Samantha Khury
1251 10th St.
Manhattan Beach, CA 90266
(310) 374-6812

Betty Lewis
Amherst, NH
(603) 673-3263

Penelope Smith
Pegasus Publications
POB 1060
Point Reyes, CA 94956
(415) 663-1247

Marion Webb-DeSisto
c/o 24 Roberta Lane
Lowell, MA 01852

Other Practitioners

Analytical Research Labs
8650 N. 22nd Ave.
Phoenix, AZ 85021
(800) 528-4067
(Heavy Metal Analysis,
Mineral Analysis)

Critter Oil
SuDi Company
POB 12767
St. Petersburg, FL 33733
(813) 327-2356

Gloria Dodd, DVM
Everglo Ranch
POB 1242
Gualala, CA 95445
(Audio-Cassettes $8.95 + $1 postage)
Note: *Dr. Dodd is no longer in practice
and can't offer consultations or advice.*

Essiac
Dr. Gary Glum
Silent Walker Publishing Co.
POB 29856
Los Angeles, CA 90009
(310) 271-9931

Edgar Fischer, Manager
Carnivora-Forschungs-GmbH
Postfach 8
Lobensteiner Strasse 3
D-8646, Nordhalben,
Germany
Phone 011-49-9267-1642
FAX 011-49-9267-1040
Carnivora Manufacturer

Dr. Helmut Keller, MD
The Chronic Disease Control
  and Treatment Center
Am Reuthlein 2
D-8675, Bad Steben
Germany
Phone 011-49-9288-7815
Carnivora Cancer Treatment

Barbara Meyers
Holistic Animal Consulting Center
29 Lyman Ave.
Staten Island, NY 10305
(718) 720-5548
Grief counseling, Bach Flower Remedies

Mary Ryan
Certified Bach Counselor
Lantana, FL 33462
(407) 588-5382

Mary Ann Simonds
Wisdom Stone Farms
17101 NE 40th Ave.
Vancouver, WA 98686
(206) 573-1958
Natural Healing, Consulting

Linda Tellington-Jones
POB 3793
Santa Fe, NM 87501-0793
(800) 854-TEAM
Tellington TTouch

Linda S. Yborra, MA
(215) 353-0120
Allergies, Health, and Behavior
  Problems

Resources

Flower Essences

Bach Centre
Mount Vernon
Stowell, Eallingford
Oxon, OX10 OPZ
England

Essential Essences by
   Diane Stein
POB 1436
Olney, MD 20830-1436
(301) 570-1990

Flower Essence Society
POB 1769
Nevada City, CA 95959
(916) 265-0258
(800) 548-0075

Greenhope Farms Flower Essences
POB 125
Meriden, NH 03770
(603) 469-3662

Kathleen Harms
3914 Leona St.
Tampa, FL 33629
(813) 837-6212

Ozark Flower Essences
HC 73 Box 160
Drury, MO 65638
(417) 469-2616
(417) 679-3391

Perelandra Center for Nature Research
POB 3603
Warrenton, VA 22186
(703) 937-2153 (24-hour Machine)

Mary Ryan
Certified Bach Counsellor
Lantana, FL 33462
(407) 588-5382

Traditional Flower Remedies of Dr.
   Edward Bach
Ellon USA, Inc.
644 Merrick Rd.
Lynbrook, NY 11563-2332
(516) 593-2206

Gemstones

Heaven and Earth
POB 224
Marshfield, VT 05658
(800) 942-9423
(Gemstones, Gem Jewelry)

Treasures Metaphysical Bookshop
4353 W. Kennedy Blvd.
Tampa, FL 33609-2126
(813) 287-BOOK

Wegner Crystal Warehouse
4013 West Magnolia Blvd.
Burbank, CA 91505
(818) 841-5050
(Walk-in Sales Only)

Wegner Quartz Crystal Mines
POB 205
Mount Ida, AR 71957
(501) 867-2309

Herbs

Amrita Herbal Products
Rt 1 Box 737
Floyd, VA 24091
(703) 745-3474

Coyote Moon Herbs
POB 312
Gainesville, FL 32602
(904) 377-0765

Eclectic Institute Inc.
11231 SE Market St.
Portland, OR 97216
(800) 332-4372
(503) 256-4330

Frontier Cooperative Herbs
POB 299
Norway, CA 52318
(800) 365-4372

Great American Bulk Foods
4121 16th St. N.
St. Petersburg, FL 33707
(813) 521-4372

Herbal Research Foundation
POB 120006
Austin, TX 78711

Iris Herbal Products
POB 160
San Cristobal, NM 87564
(505) 586-1802

ITM Herb Products
2017 SE Hawthorne
Portland, OR 97214
(800) 544-7504
(503) 233-4907
(Chinese Herbs, Juliette de Bairacli Levy's
Anti-Parasite Worming Powder)

Homeopathy

Beckett's Apothecary
1004 Chester Pike
Sharon Hill, PA 19079
(800) 727-8188
(Remedies, Mail Order)

Boericke and Tafel
1011 Arch St.
Philadelphia, PA 19107
(800) 272-2820
(Remedies, Excellent "Family Guide,"
Mail Order)

BRI
POB 290866
Davie, FL 33329-0866
(800) 733-4874
(Homeopathy for Pets Video)

Dolisos America, Inc.
3014 Rigel Ave.
Las Vegas, NV 89102
(800) 365-4767
(Free Catalog)

Dr. Goodpet Laboratories
POB 4489
Inglewood, CA 90309
(800) 222-9932
(213) 672-3269
(Combination Line for Pets, Vitamins,
Catalog)

Hanson Homeopathic Herbal Medicine
4540 Southside Blvd. #5
Jacksonville, FL 32216-5458
(904) 641-6301
(Largest Homeopathic Supplier in the
South)

HoBoN
POB 8243
Naples, FL 33941
(813) 643-4636
(800) 521-7722
(Combinations for Pets and People—
Recommended)
(Sells only to Practitioners)

Homeopathic Education Services
2124 Kettredge St.
Berkeley, CA 94704
(800) 359-9051 (orders only)
(510) 649-0294 (information)
(Books, Tapes and More)

Homeopathic Information Resources,
Ltd.
Oneida River Park Dr.
Clay, NY 13041
(800) 289-4447
(Remedy Kits, Books, Tapes)

National Center for Homeopathy
801 N. Fairfax St. Suite 306
Alexandria, VA 22314
(703) 548-7790
(Referrals, Books)

Newton Laboratories
612 Upland Trail
Conyers, GA 30207
(800) 448-7256
(Single Remedies, Kits, Combination
Line for Pets)

Standard Homeopathic Services
210 W. 131st St.
Box 61067
Los Angeles, CA 90061
(800) 624-9659
(Remedies, Books, Kits)

Washington Homeopathic Products
449114 Del Ray Avenue
Bethesda, MD 20814
(800) 336-1695
(Remedies)

Natural Pet Foods

All the Best
8047 Lake City Way
Seattle, WA 98115
(800) 962-8266

Cornucopia Products
Veterinary Nutritional Associates
229 Wall St.
Huntington, NY 11743
(516) 427-7479
(Non-allergic pet foods)

Lick Your Chops, Inc.
50 Water St.
South Norwalk, CT 06854
(203) 854-5001

Natural Balance Pet Foods
(213) 221-3207

Natural Life Pet Products
12975 16th Ave. N. Suite 100
Minneapolis, MN 55441-4531
(800) 367-2391

Nature's Recipe
341 Bonnie Circle
Corona, CA 91720
(800) 843-4008
(714) 278-4280

Nutro Products, Inc.
445 Wilson Way
City of Industry, CA 91744
(818) 968-0532
(Some foods use Ethoxyquin)

PetGuard, Inc.
POB 728
Orange Park, FL 32073
(800) 874-3221
(904) 264-8500

Precise
POB 630009
Nacogdoches, TX 75963
(800) 446-7148

Sensible Choice
Royal Canine USA, Inc.
1600 Heritage Landing, Suite 112
St. Charles, MO 63303-8484
(800) 592-6687

Solid Gold
1483 N. Coyamaca
El Cajon, CA 92020
(619) 465-9507

Wow-Bow Distributers
309 Burr Rd.
Northport, NY 11731
(516) 499-8572

Wysong
1880 N. Eastman Rd.
Midland, MI 48640
(800) 748-0188

Pet Products and Catalogs

Cartilade
Ocean Health Products
POB 860
Putney, VT 05346
(802) 463-1343
(800) 477-5108
(Shark Cartilage—
Capsules $35.20/100
Powder $174.40/pound)

Companion Pet
5345 Bridge Rd.
POB 135
McNaughton, WI 54543
(800) 442-7387
(Catalog—General)

Critter Oil
The SuDi Company
POB 12767
St. Petersburg, FL 33733
(813) 327-2356

Drs. Foster and Smith
2253 Air Park Rd.
POB 100
Rhinelander, WI 54501-0100
(800) 826-7206

Eco Safe Products
POB 1177
St. Augustine, FL 32085
(800) 274-7387
(Herbal Products, Flea Products)

Felix
3623 Fremont Ave. N.
Seattle, WA 98103
(800) 24-FELIX
(Catalog for Cats)

Halo, Purely For Pets
3438 E. Lake Road, Suite 14
Palm Harbor, FL 34685
(813) 787-4256
(Anitra's Vita-Mineral Mix,
Herbal Flea Products, Ear Wash,
Vitamins)

Institute for Traditional Medicine
2017 SE Hawthorne
Portland, OR 97214
(800) 544-7504
(Chinese Herbs, Juliette de Bairacli
Levy's Anti-Parasite Powder)

Morrill's New Directions
POB 30
Orient, ME 04471
(800) 368-5057 (USA)
(800) 649-0744 (MA)
(Holistic Pet Catalog)

Sharks Don't Get Cancer
by Dr. William Lane
(802) 463-9404
(Mail Order, Book on Shark Cartilage)

R.C. Steele
Wholesale Kennel Supplies
1989 Transit Way
Box 910
Brockport, NY 14420-0910
(800) 872-3773
(Catalog—General)

Swanson Health Products
Pox 2803
Fargo, ND 58108
(800) 437-4148
(Shark Cartilage—Capsules $36.00/100)

The Home Pet Shop
POB 2010
Hazleton, PA 18201-0676
(800) 274-5828
(Catalog—General)

The Whole Animal Catalog
3131 Hennepin Ave. S.
Minneapolis, MN 55408
(800) 377-6369
(Catalog—Pet Enzymes, Gentle Dragon)

Very Healthy Enterprises
POB 4728
Englewood, CA 90309
(310) 672-3269
(Catalog—Hol. Rem., Homeo., Enzymes)

VM Nu-ri Inc.
1012 Hort Dr.
POB 286
Lake Geneva, WI 53147
(Orthophosphoric Acid)

Wow-Bow Distributors
309 Burr Rd.
E. Northport, NY 11731
(516) 499-8572
(800) 326-0230
(Hol. Pet Catalog—Essiac, Enz., Vit.)

Bibliography

Altman, Sheldon, DVM. *An Introduction to Veterinary Acupuncture.* Monterey Park, CA: Chan's Corporation, 1981.

American Red Cross. *First Aid and CPR For Your Dog and Cat.* Tampa, FL: American Red Cross Tampa Bay Suncoast Chapter, 1993.

Bach, Ellon, USA, Inc. "Animals and the Bach Flower Remedies." Lynbrook, NY: Ellon Bach USA, Inc., 1990.

Balch, James F., M.D., and Phyllis Balch, CNC. *Prescription for Nutritional Healing.* Garden City Park, NY: Avery Publishing Group, 1990.

Belfield, Wendell O., DVM, and Martin Zucker. *The Very Healthy Cat Book: A Vitamin and Mineral Program for Optimal Feline Health.* New York, NY: McGraw-Hill Book Co., 1983.

Belfield, Wendell O., DVM, and Martin Zucker. *How to Have a Healthier Dog: The Benefits of Vitamins and Minerals for Your Dog's Life Cycles.* New York, NY: New American Library, 1981.

Boericke and Tafel. *The Family Guide to Self-Medication—Homeopathic.* Philadephia, PA: Boericke and Tafel, Inc., 1988.

Carlson, Delbert G., DVM, and James M. Giffin, MD. *Cat Owner's Home Veterinary Handbook.* New York, NY: Howell Book House, 1990.

Carlson, Delbert G., DVM, and James M. Giffin, MD. *Dog Owner's Home Veterinary Handbook.* New York, NY: Howell Book House, 1983.

Cummings, Steven, FNP, and Dana Ullman, MPH. *Everybody's Guide to Homeopathic Medicines.* Los Angeles, CA: J.P. Tarcher, Inc., 1984.

Davis, Adele. *Let's Get Well.* New York, NY: New American Library, 1965.

de Bairacli Levy, Juliette. *The Complete Herbal Handbook for the Dog and Cat.* London and Boston: Faber and Faber Ltd., 1991.

Fireman, Judy. *Cat Catalog: The Ultimate Cat Book.* New York, NY: Workman Publishing Co., 1976.

Fox, Michael W., DVM. *The Healing Touch: The Proven Massage Program for Cats and Dogs.* New York, NY: Newmarket Press, 1981.

Frazier, Anitra. "Nurturing Underweight Cats: Part II, The Anorexic." In *Tiger Tribe Magazine*, March-April, 1993, pp. 6-8.

Frazier, Anitra. "Nurturing Underweight Cats: Part I, The Starving Stray." In *Tiger Tribe Magazine*, January-February, 1993, pp. 6-7.

Granfield, Luke. "Vaccinosis," in *Tiger Tribe Magazine*, September-October, 1992, p.23.

Griffin, Susan R. *Win the Flea War Naturally . . . Without Toxins.* St. Petersburg, FL: The SuDi Company, 1990.

Harper, Joan. *The Healthy Cat and Dog Cookbook.* Richland Center, WI: Pet Press, 1988.

Hunter, Francis, MRCVS. *Homeopathic First-Aid Treatment for Pets.* Great Britain: Thorsen's Publishers, Ltd., 1984.

Jarvis, D.C., MD. *Folk Medicine: A New England Almanac of Natural Health Care from a Noted Vermont Doctor.* New York: Fawcett-Crest Books, 1958.

Klide, Alan M., VMD, and Shiu K. Kung, Ph.D. *Veterinary Acupuncture.* Philadelphia, PA, University of Pennsylvania Press, 1977.

Lazarus, Pat. *Keep Your Pet Healthy the Natural Way.* New Canaan, CT: Keats Publishing Co., 1983.

McHattie, Grace. *Your Cat Naturally.* New York: Carroll and Graf Publishers, 1992.

McKay, Pat. *Reigning Cats and Dogs.*

Pitcairn, Richard, DVM, and Susan Hubble Pitcairn. *Dr. Pitcairn's Complete Guide to Natural Health for Dogs and Cats.* Emmaus, PA: Rodale Press, 1982.

Plechner, Alfred J., DVM, and Martin Zucker, *Pet Allergies: Remedies for an Epidemic.* Inglewood, CA: Very Healthy Enterprises, 1986.

Stein, Diane. *The Natural Remedy Book for Women.* Freedom, CA: The Crossing Press, 1992.

Tellington-Jones, Linda with Sybil Taylor. *The Tellington TTouch: A Breakthrough Technique to Train and Care For Your Favorite Animal.* New York, NY: Viking Press, 1992.

Tenney, Louise, MH. *Health Handbook: A Guide to Family Health.* Provo, UT: Woodland Books, 1987.

Trattler, Dr. Ross. *Better Health Through Natural Healing.* New York, NY: McGraw Hill Book Co., 1985.

Walker, Morton, DPM. "Venus Flytrap—Cancer and AIDS Fighter of the Future?" In *Natural Health Magazine*, September-October 1992, pp. 44-46.

INDEX